Voices of the Turtledoves

Pennsylvania German History and Culture Series,
Number 3

Publications of the Pennsylvania German Society,
Volume 36 (2002)

Arbeiten zur Geschichte des Pietismus
Sonderband
Im Auftrag der Historischen Kommission zur Erforschung des Pietismus
Herausgegeben von Martin Brecht, Christian Bunners und Hans-Jürgen Schrader

Editor
Simon J. Bronner
The Pennsylvania State University, Harrisburg

Editorial Board
C. Richard Beam, Millersville University
Donald F. Durnbaugh, Juniata College
Aaron S. Fogleman, Northern Illinois University
Mark Häberlein, University of Freiburg, Germany
Donald B. Kraybill, Messiah College
Kenneth McLaughlin, University of Waterloo, Canada
A. Gregg Roeber, The Pennsylvania State University, University Park
John D. Roth, Goshen College
Hans Schneider, Philipps University, Marburg, Germany
Denise A. Seachrist, Kent State University, Trumbull
Richard E. Wentz, Arizona State University
Marianne S. Wokeck, Indiana University–Purdue University, Indianapolis
Don Yoder, University of Pennsylvania

Voices of the Turtledoves

The Sacred World of Ephrata

JEFF BACH

THE PENNSYLVANIA STATE UNIVERSITY PRESS
UNIVERSITY PARK, PENNSYLVANIA

PUBLISHED IN GERMANY BY VANDENHOECK & RUPRECHT
GÖTTINGEN, GERMANY

Library of Congress Cataloging-in-Publication Data

Bach, Jeff, 1958–
Voices of the turtledoves : the sacred world of Ephrata / Jeff Bach
p. cm. — (Pennsylvania German History and culture series ; no. 3)
Includes bibliographical references and index.
ISBN 0-271-02250-7 (cloth : alk. paper)
1. Ephrata Cloister.
2. Mysticism—Pennsylvania—History.
I. Title.
II. Publications of the Pennsylvania German Society (2002).
Pennsylvania German history and culture series ; no. 3.

BX7817 .P4 B33 2003
286'.3'097481—dc21
2002153329

Copyright © 2003 The Pennsylvania German Society
All rights reserved
Printed in the United States of America
Published by The Pennsylvania State University Press,
University Park, PA 16802-1003

It is the policy of The Pennsylvania State University Press to use
acid-free paper. Publications on uncoated stock satisfy
the minimum requirements of American National Standard
for Information Sciences—Permanence of Paper for
Printed Library Materials, ANSI Z39.48–1992.

Vandenhoeck & Ruprecht ISBN 3-525-55827-9

Bibliography information published by
Die Deutsche Bibliothek in Germany.
Die Deutsche Bibliothek lists this publication
in the Deutsche Nationalbibliografie; detailed bibliographic
data is available on the Internet at http://dng.ddb.de.

To the WOMAN IN THE WILDERNESS

CONTENTS

List of Illustrations ix
Acknowledgments xi
List of Abbreviations xv
Prelude 1

Introduction 3

1 The Religious Thought of Ephrata
  Conrad Beissel 25

2 The Religious Thought of Ephrata
  Other Writers 49

3 "Holy Church Practices"
  Ritual at Ephrata 69

4 Manly Virgins and Virginal Men
  Gender at Ephrata 97

5 "God's Holy Point of Rest"
  Ephrata's Mystical Language in Space and Time 115

6 Roses in the Wilderness
  Ephrata's Manuscript Art 141

7 "Heavenly Magic"
  Hidden Knowledge at Ephrata 171

Epilogue 193

Bibliographical Essay 197
Notes 219
Index 271

ILLUSTRATIONS

1. Conrad Beissel's Europe   15
2. Lancaster County (modern boundaries)   20
3. Locations of German Sabbatarian congregations, eighteenth century   22
4. Monastic habits worn at Ephrata   91
5. Vignette in "Der Christen ABC"   119
6. Sachse's view of Mount Zion   120
7. Hibshman's survey of Ephrata   122
8. Peniel (Saal) and Saron   124
9. Figures from Welling's *Opus Mago-Cabbalisticum et Theosophicum*   125
10. Ceiling beams in Peniel   126
11. Hexagram on floor plan of Peniel (Saal)   128
12. Unrestored cell in Saron   131
13. Restored cell in Saron   132
14. Bethania   134
15. Partial site map of Ephrata   136–137
16. Letter V in "Der Christen ABC"   144
17. Tailpiece in Christoph Schütz's *Güldene Rose*   145
18. Rose design   147
19. Lily in "Der Christen ABC"   148
20. Ephrata sunflower   150
21. Ephrata pilgrim   151
22. Cross and doves within heart   152
23. Tulip design   154
24. Pomegranate or poppy   155
25. Thistle or carnation   156
26. Ephrata *Fraktur* labyrinth   158
27. Sample alphabet   161
28. Sisters in habits   165
29. Grape arbor   168

ACKNOWLEDGMENTS

A book such as this is ultimately the fruit of many gifts beyond my own labor, for which I am grateful. Most of all I thank my wife, Ann, and our daughters, Elizabeth and Rebecca, for their love and forbearing patience more often than I should have asked.

My gratitude goes to Donald F. Durnbaugh for planting the seed of interest in Ephrata. He and Hedwig T. Durnbaugh have offered many helpful suggestions and comments throughout my years of working on this project. Ted Campbell and David Steinmetz guided me in the maze of doctoral studies at Duke University. Helpful questions and comments from Thomas Robisheaux, Bradley Longfield, Stanley Hauerwas, Russell Ritchey, and Susan Keefe have been invaluable. J. Samuel Hammond in the Rare Book, Manuscript, and Special Collections Library of Duke University gave invaluable assistance with some of the Jantz Collection of Baroque Literature.

For a decade various staff members at the Ephrata Cloister have helped me generously, and only constraints of space are responsible for my failure to thank each of them by name. I owe considerable debts of gratitude to Nadine Steinmetz and Clarence Spohn for helping me with source material and pointing out many details to consider along the way. They gave me priceless assistance during a summer as Scholar in Residence at Ephrata in 1995, for which I also thank the Pennsylvania Historical and Museum Commission. During that summer and since then, Stephen Warfel, Senior Curator of Archaeology for the State Museum of Pennsylvania, has continued to teach me through his observations and careful questions. Since then, Michael Ripton and Michael Showalter have been just as generous in helping me with source material, pointing out things I have missed and raising questions. These and many other staff and volunteer workers at the Ephrata Cloister have helped me and welcomed me during work time there. Craig A. Benner of Ephrata deserves special thanks for help with photographic images for this

ACKNOWLEDGMENTS

book. For generous hospitality during research trips to Ephrata and to our family during the Scholar in Residence stay I owe Robert and Carolyn Wenger more gratitude than I can pay. Their generosity and friendship have helped this project all along the way.

Several people have given help with important primary source material. Jonathan Stayer at the Pennsylvania State Archives offered longsuffering assistance with music manuscripts, Ephrata imprints, and research questions. His generous help with the actual materials of the Sachse Collection on loan to the Pennsylvania State Archives from the Seventh-Day Baptist Historical Society was invaluable. The staff of the Free Library of Philadelphia also helped me with important manuscript sources, as did staff at the Historical Society of Pennsylvania, both in Philadelphia. I must still thank Helen Manelli and Jana Faust, former librarians at Bethany Theological Seminary when it was located in Oak Brook, Illinois, who allowed me to use Gichtel's works at the time they were trying to pack Bethany's Cassel Collection for the move to Richmond, Indiana. Both were generous under very trying circumstances. Donald F. Durnbaugh has provided hospitality and help with manuscript and printed sources at Juniata College. Amos Hoover welcomed me to his Muddy Creek Farm Library, where I was able to work with Brother Philemon's manuscript of excerpts from Madame Guyon's writings. Erika D. Passantino called my attention to an important letter by Peter Miller in the archives of the Franckesche Stiftungen in Halle, Germany.

Lucy E. Carroll and L. Allen Viehmeyer have offered me many helpful comments from their own fruitful labors to identify Ephrata hymn authors, understand their tunes, and make sense of the complex family of printed hymnals and manuscript music books from colonial Ephrata. I would be lost without their help. Don Yoder has offered valuable comments from his long scholarly career and his knowledge of Pennsylvania German *Fraktur.*

This project has brought me the acquaintance of some German colleagues whom I would be thankful to count as friends. Hans Schneider at Philipps Universität in Marburg has directed me to source material and secondary literature, and offered encouragement and hospitality. The Reverend Marcus Meier has offered good advice, research suggestions, and good conversation, in addition to serving as a book supplier. Similarly, the Reverend Peter Vogt has shared insights and questions in stimulating conversations about Pietism. More recently, Konstanze Grutschnig-Kieser has made me aware of connections between Ephrata and other German Radical Pietists and pointed me toward helpful secondary literature. Hermann Ehmer, of the Landeskirchliches Archiv in Stuttgart, has helped with research suggestions and directed me to important articles. I am grateful for the help and kindness of them all.

ACKNOWLEDGMENTS

Trish Sadd and Zachary Noffsinger Erbaugh, employees at different times of Bethany Theological Seminary, have given priceless assistance with computer technology through the years. They saved me more than once from the *turba tremenda* of the computer. I thank Simon Bronner, Peter Potter, Cherene Holland, and Tim Holsopple at Penn State University Press and Barbara Salazar, copyeditor, for their help throughout the publication process.

To many others who have helped along the way I extend gratitude as well. I thank Marie Kachel Bucher, the last living member of the German Seventh-Day Baptist congregation at Ephrata, for encouragement through the years. While many have helped, final responsibility for errors in this book goes to me, and gratitude for all the assistance to make it possible goes to them.

ABBREVIATIONS

This list shows abbreviated references of frequently cited works. All first citations of other works are given in full only the first time they appear. The works of Jacob Boehme, keyed to the 1730 edition, are cited by volume number. In this practice I have followed Andrew Weeks's model in his biography of Boehme. When more than one work appeared in a given volume, a brief title is given. Johann Georg Gichtel's writings, all of which are letters, are also cited by volume number.

BLT	*Brethren Life and Thought.*
Brother Kenan's Notebook	[Brother Kenan, or Jacob Funk], Untitled, unpaginated manuscript, Sachse Collection, Seventh-Day Baptist Historical Society, on loan to Pennsylvania State Archives, Harrisburg.
CE	Lamech and Agrippa [Peter Miller], *Chronicon Ephratense* (Ephrata: [Typis Societatis], 1786).
Contemporaries	Felix Reichmann and Eugene E. Doll, trans. and eds., *Ephrata as Seen by Contemporaries,* Pennsylvania German Folklore Society, vol. 17 (Allentown: Schlechter's, 1953).
DE, Pars I	Friedsam Gottrecht [Conrad Beissel], *Deliciae Ephratenses, Pars I . . . Geistliche Reden* (Ephrata: Typis Societatis, 1773).
Dissertation	[Conrad Beissel], *A Dissertation on Man's Fall* [trans. Peter Miller] (Ephrata: [Typis Societatis], 1765).

ABBREVIATIONS

Ephrata	James E. Ernst, *Ephrata: A History,* Pennsylvania German Folklore Society, vol. 25 (Allentown: Schlechter's, 1953).
Ephrata Cloisters	Eugene E. Doll and Anneliese Funke, *The Ephrata Cloisters: An Annotated Bibliography* (Philadelphia: Carl Schurz Memorial Foundation, 1944).
Ephrata Commune	E. G. Alderfer, *The Ephrata Commune: An Early American Counterculture* (Pittsburgh: University of Pittsburgh Press, 1985).
FLP	Free Library of Philadelphia.
FLP B. Ms. 22	[Conrad Beissel], "Conrad Beissel Letterbook," paginated manuscript, Borneman Collection, B. Ms. 22, Free Library of Philadelphia.
GdP	Martin Brecht, Klaus Deppermann, Ulrich Gäbler, and Hartmut Lehmann, eds., *Geschichte des Pietismus,* 3 vols. (Göttingen: Vandenhoeck & Ruprecht, 1993–2000). Each volume, cited here by number, has a separate title.
German Sectarians	Julius F. Sachse, *The German Sectarians of Pennsylvania: A Critical and Legendary History of the Ephrata Cloister and the Dunkers,* 2 vols. (Philadelphia: for the author by P. C. Stockhausen, 1899–1900; rpt. New York: AMS Press, 1970–71).
Historical Archaeology	Stephen G. Warfel, *Historical Archaeology at Ephrata Cloister* (Harrisburg: Pennsylvania Historical and Museum Commission, 1995–). Series published annually. Year of publication is given in parentheses; each issue covers the previous year's investigations.
HSP	The Historical Society of Pennsylvania, Philadelphia.

ABBREVIATIONS

HSP Ac. 1926	"Register vor den Bruder und Schwestern die in und ausser Efrathaer (Gemeinschaft) gestorben sind," variously paginated manuscript, Cassel Collection, Ac. 1926, Historical Society of Pennsylvania, Philadelphia.
JHSCV	*Journal of the Historical Society of the Cocalico Valley.*
Klostergeschichte	Oswald Seidensticker, *Ephrata, eine amerikanische Klostergeschichte* (Cincinnati: Mecklenborg & Rosenthal, 1883).
LC	Library of Congress, Washington, D.C.
LuW	Ezechiel Sangmeister, *Leben und Wandel des in GOTT ruhenten Ezechiel Sangmeisters; Weiland Einwohner von Ephrata,* 4 vols. (Ephrata: Joseph Bauman, 1825–27); trans. Barbara Schindler in *Journal of the Historical Society of the Cocalico Valley* 4–10 (1979–85).
MHT	Peter C. Erb, ed., *Johann Conrad Beissel and the Ephrata Community: Mystical and Historical Texts,* Studies in American Religion, vol. 14. (Lewiston, N.Y.: Edwin Mellen Press, 1985).
MKZ	[Johannes Hildebrand et al.], *Mistisches und Kirchliches Zeuchnüß Der Brüderschaft in Zion, Von den wichtigsten Puncten des Christenthums* (Germantown: C. Saur, 1743).
PMHB	*Pennsylvania Magazine of History and Biography.*
PSA	Pennsylvania State Archives, Harrisburg.
PuN	*Pietismus und Neuzeit.*
"Rose"	"Die Rose oder der angenehmen Blumen zu Saron geistlichen ehe verlöbnüs mit ihren himmlischen Bräutigam. Ephrata den 13: des 5: Mon 1745." Variously paginated manuscript, Cassel Collection, Ac. 1925, Historical Society of Pennsylvania, Philadelphia.

ABBREVIATIONS

SS   Jacob Boehme, *Sämtliche Schriften*, ed. Will-Erich Peuckert and August Faust (Stuttgart: Frommans Verlag, 1955–61), 11 vols., facs. rpt. of *Theosophia Revelata. Das ist: Alle Göttliche Schriften des Gottseligen und Hocherleuchteten Deutschen Theosophi Jacob Böhmens*, ed. Johann Georg Gichtel and Johann Wilhelm Ueberfeld (Amsterdam, 1730).

vol. 1. *Aurora, oder Morgenröthe im Aufgang.*
vol. 2. *Beschreibung der drey Principien Göttliches Wesens.*
vol. 3. *De tribus principia, oder Vom dreyfachen Leben des Menschen. Viertzig Fragen von der Seelen.*
vol. 4. *De incarnatione verbi, oder Von der Menschwerdung Jesu Christi. Von sechs theosophischen Puncten. Sex puncta mystica, oder Kurtze Erklärung von sechs mystischen Puncten. Der Weg zu Christo.*
vol. 5. *Schutz-Schriften wieder Balthasar Tilken. Bedencken über Esaiä Stiefels Büchlein. Schutz-Rede wieder Gregorium Richter. Unterricht von den letzten Zeiten.*
vol. 6. *De signatura rerum, oder, Von der Geburt und Bezeichnung aller Wesen. Von der Gnadenwahl. De testamenta Christi, oder von Christi Testamenten.*
vol. 7. *Mysterium Magnum* (vol. 1).
vol. 8. *Mysterium Magnum* (vol. 2).
vol. 9. *Betrachtung Göttlicher Offenbarung. Tafeln. Clavis. Theosophische Sendbriefe.*
vol. 10. *Historischer Bericht von dem Leben und Schriften, Jacob Böhmens. Das Leben Jacob Böhmes*, by Will-Erich Peuckert.
vol. 11. *Register über alle theosophischen Schriften Jacob Böhmens.*

ABBREVIATIONS

TP Johann Georg Gichtel, *Theosophia Practica,* 3d enlarged and expanded ed., 7 vols. (Leyden, 1722).

ZS Irenici Theodicäi [Conrad Beissel], *Zionitischen Stiffts I. Theil Oder eine Wohlrichende Narde* (Ephrata: Drucks der Brüderschaft, 1745).

PRELUDE

Koch-Halekung, as Germans heard and wrote it, was a term meaning "den of serpents." The Lenne Lenape people (Delaware Indians) gave this name to a level area near a tight bend in a creek in a forested region the English called Penn's Woods, or Pennsylvania. The creek came to be known by the English corruption of this place name, Cocalico. Snakes reportedly infested the place.[1]

Archaeological evidence shows that indigenous peoples came to Koch-Halekung for centuries before recorded time, leaving stone points and tools as evidence of their hunting activities. Long after these early peoples, as Europeans pushed native peoples of the Delaware Valley farther westward, a small group of German immigrants occupied this former hunting ground. Here they built a settlement and named it Ephrata.

INTRODUCTION

Georg Conrad Beissel (1691–1768),[1] founder of the Ephrata community, wrote to a friend in Heidelberg in the mid-eighteenth century, "I wish in all my expressions to be understood magically and mystically."[2] A German immigrant, Henry Ezechiel Sangmeister (1724–86), had arrived at Ephrata a few years earlier, in the spring of 1748. Later antagonistic to Beissel, Sangmeister recounted, "I committed myself to his [Beissel's] prayers at all times, but he used a style of language that I could not understand."[3] By 1762, Peter Miller (1710–96), heir apparent to leadership at Ephrata, wrote in a hymnal preface that there was at Ephrata "a language among the people of God" that few speak anymore, and "those who speak it are hard to understand."[4]

On first encountering Ephrata's writings, readers often puzzle over the mix of erotic and religious metaphors abounding in the community's voluminous devotional literature, letters, hymns, and poetic texts. This book investigates the eighteenth-century Sabbatarian monastic community at Ephrata through their religious language and its European sources as the primary, but not sole, avenue of interpretation. This book proposes that Conrad Beissel and others at Ephrata used familiar elements from German Radical Pietism to create a language and ritual practices to convey a mystical awareness of God. The concept of a mystical awareness of God comes from Bernard McGinn's definition of mysticism as an anticipation and awareness of God's immediate presence among those seeking it. Part of the purpose for what may be called Ephrata's mystical language was to draw adherents into a linguistic labyrinth of delight mingled with penitence. Beissel's labyrinth invited followers to "lose" earthly attachments in order to find God in what Beissel promoted as a foretaste of paradise. While not all at Ephrata shared Beissel's views, nor did all find God or paradise at Ephrata, Beissel's language so shaped the ways in which many conducted their lives there that his mystical language is a key to interpreting Ephrata. Many people at Ephrata sought to be united with Christ in mystical union, like the turtledoves frequently found in pairs in Ephrata's art. The writers gave voice to Ephrata's language for the quest of each soul to be joined to Christ, like a pair of turtledoves.

The Ephrata community, or Ephrata Cloister, was called by its own members *der Lager der Einsamen,* or Camp of the Solitaries. German-speaking contemporaries often called them *Beisselianer* (Beisselites) or *Siebentäger* (Sabbatarians). Their internal history, *Chronicon Ephratense,* published in 1786, is an important, but not always reliable, source of information about them. The *Chronicon* was edited by Peter Miller under the pseudonym Agrippa, and published in 1786, but was based on a manuscript chronicle reportedly kept by Jacob Gaas, or Brother Lamech, who died in 1764. An English translation by J. Max Hark, published in 1889, has made the chronicle more accessible.[5] The name Ephrata first appeared in print in 1736, in a hymnal for the community.[6] Beissel reportedly bestowed the name around this time. Ephrata was a Protestant Sabbatarian community of Christian mystical devotion and practice. With celibate orders for women and men and a congregation of married families, known collectively as the "householders," the community flourished from about 1730 to about 1770. The community began as Beissel became leader of a Brethren, or Dunker [*Neu-Täufer*] congregation in Pennsylvania in 1724, then formally separated from them by rebaptizing some of his followers in 1728. In 1732 he withdrew to the banks of Cocalico Creek. Members soon followed, and there they built up a religious community that peaked at about three to five hundred members and associates around mid-century. In addition to building large monastic houses and

INTRODUCTION

chapels, the community developed an important milling center and established a printing press by 1745. They created the first examples in Pennsylvania of the manuscript art known as *Fraktur* and printed the largest book produced in colonial America. Beissel wrote the first treatise on music composition produced in the colonies.

Because of these significant achievements in colonial America, the Ephrata community has invited various interpretations. The relatively few who have written about Ephrata have often defined the community either in light of mysticism or as a sectarian group. The portrait of Ephrata provided here, drawn from all major printed writings by its members as well as from manuscripts, music books, and architectural works, focuses on the unique religious language and ritual of this distinctive community, virtually unknown beyond the circle of regional interest.

THE PROBLEM OF EPHRATA

Mysticism is a compelling approach to the study of Ephrata for several reasons. Ephrata writers themselves identified their writings as "mystical," such as Beissel's *Mystische und sehr geheyme Sprueche* (1730), the *Mistisches und Kirchliches Zeuchnüß* (1743), and Sangmeister's *Mystische Theologie* (1819–20). Those who deeply influenced Conrad Beissel, such as Jacob Boehme[7] and Johann Georg Gichtel,[8] who published Boehme's complete works, have been described as mystics.

A working definition of the mystical element of Christianity, offered by Bernard McGinn, is that part of its belief and practices that concerns the preparation for, the consciousness of, and the reaction to what can be described as the immediate or direct presence of God. Many writers emphasize religious experience and union with God as the defining characteristics of mysticism. Acknowledging the importance of the particular religions in which one discusses mysticism, Bernard McGinn is one scholar who has allowed the possibility of comparative studies of mystical elements among religions.[9]

"Mysticism" as a noun appeared in Christianity only in the seventeenth century, in French as *la mystique,* as Michel de Certeau has shown.[10] Without defining mysticism as such, Certeau examined it through literary criticism. He called it a discipline, "mystics," in which received language was used in a new way. Certeau saw the new discipline emerging as the received tradition of perceived religious and political unity, cosmological and religious order, fractured in the early modern era.

According to Certeau, "mystics" as a discipline "had to determine its procedure and define its object" as it charted a new verbal topography and new procedures. While practitioners could counsel how to journey in the mystical way, they could not define the journey's object: the Divine Other. Certeau believed that this impossibility doomed the discipline to die "of the question from which it was formed." The mystic discipline disappeared at the close of the seventeenth century as the Enlightenment ushered in a new assurance of knowledge emptied of God. As Certeau admits, however, the "ghost" of mystical discourse persisted in places where the Enlightenment's triumph was delayed. Ephrata was such a place.[11]

The contributions that McGinn and Certeau make to defining mysticism advance the examination of Ephrata beyond two earlier efforts by John Jacoby and F. Ernest Stoeffler. The earlier work, Jacoby's *Two Mystic Communities in America,* is a vague comparison of Ephrata with Oneida.[12] Stoeffler's *Mysticism in the German Devotional Literature of Colonial Pennsylvania* sets Ephrata in context with other religious groups and publications in colonial Pennsylvania. A pioneering effort, Stoeffler's work defined mysticism as "the total complex of efforts which man has made and is making towards the immediate apprehension of the divine, and whatever may be the results of this experience in daily life." Stoeffler, however, applied this definition almost totally to mystical experience.[13] A few samples illustrate the importance of mystical expressions as characteristic of Ephrata's literature. Beissel wrote, "God is an incomprehensible Nothing, and I am an incomprehensible 'I.'" Those seeking God will suffer "until all Being is dissolved into Being Nothing, and all Something is dissolved into Nothing." Beissel explained, "So we live in his [God's] holy Being: his life is our life, and we have become in him, that we are what we are."[14] A devotion written probably by Sister Bernice (Maria Heidt) counseled any seeking sister to direct herself singly and solely to Christ. "First then can complete union happen with her holy husband, Jesus, her heavenly bridegroom."[15] These examples, and others to follow, show that Ephrata authors created a mystical literature, and that inquiring about mysticism at Ephrata can bear fruit in efforts to interpret the community and its literature.

While the study of mysticism offers a fitting interpretive tool for Ephrata, its members' efforts to form a distinct community invite attention to the sociological dimension of relationships with their neighbors. Ernst Troeltsch's typology of church, sect, and mystics, while formative for the study of small, distinct religious groups, has limitations.[16] Ephrata fits many of his characteristics of a "sectarian" group. Yet their use of the vocabulary of mysticism suggests that Ephrata is a hybrid in Troeltsch's typology. Bryan Wilson has tried to sharpen the sociological typology of sectarian groups, but Ephrata's literature, ritual, and material culture are too complex to fit neatly within his precise categories.[17]

Nevertheless, Ephrata writers used the dichotomy of sect and church. They turned "sect" in its pejorative sense on its head by applying it against the Christian traditions established on the European continent. The community's confession of faith stated: "There is a difference between the Church and a sect. A sect gives birth to itself from the will of a man and in general is conducted under the same man, and is ruled with human understanding. The Church may be compared to a woman; submission is characteristic of woman, just as ruling is characteristic of a man."[18]

One obvious problem with defining a "sect" is the power behind those doing the defining. Those who control the definition control the placement of dissenters. The Ephrata community clearly conceived of themselves as "Church." But their concept of "Church" differed radically from the religious bodies that upheld European Christendom. Ephrata considered the two major Protestant traditions to be sects, founded by two men, Martin Luther and John Calvin. Beissel also considered Roman Catholicism a sect dominated by male will.[19] Thus Ephrata construed the meaning of "sect" in ways different from the dominant Christian traditions of Europe, even as those traditions saw groups like Ephrata as sects.

Bryan Wilson also holds that all sects presuppose varying responses to a world that is seen as evil. Here he sets the sect not against a dominant church but against the world, another common dichotomy in studies of sectarian movements. Conrad Beissel saw the world as divided between two opposing races (*Geschlechte*): "the children of God and the children of the course of this world [*Kinder dieses Weltlaufs*]."[20] Attending to Ephrata's relationship with the people around them adds a helpful comparative dimension to an interpretation of Beissel's group. In this book, references to Ephrata as a sectarian group means a small group with a fairly specific identity, at times cohesive, at times contentious, in distinction to yet never isolated from the people surrounding them.

This work focuses on the religious language of Conrad Beissel and colonial Ephrata as one manifestation of Christian mysticism and on the European sources of Beissel's thought. At times the tools of theology, at times insights from literary theory help to focus on the way Ephrata's authors operated with their unique language and set of rituals in their search for the presence of God. Sociological considerations of the construction of a small group, or sect, in distinction to dominant religious bodies and the wider culture, also help here to put Ephrata in profile. The methodology of this work also draws on interdisciplinary insights from the study of gender and in limited ways from the study of architecture and folk art. No single methodology can say everything about Ephrata; neither can this book. For present purposes, this book examines colonial Ephrata as a community of mystical Christianity, whose unique language for the search for the immediate presence of God influenced choices about how its members organized their lives, their space, and their time.

HISTORICAL OVERVIEW

Georg Conrad Beissel was born March 1, 1691 in Eberbach, in the Electoral Palatinate, the tenth child of a baker, Matthias Beusel (also spelled Beisel), who died before Conrad's birth. Matthias received the privilege of town baker for three-year terms in 1683, 1686, and 1689. In 1683 the family rented living quarters in the "town bakehouse behind the church." Matthias died September 19, 1690.[21] Conrad's mother, Anna Köbler Beusel, died May 28, 1699, when he was eight. Bedfast, five days before her death she received four gulden from church alms because "the poverty of this widow and her children is so great."[22] Orphanhood and poverty are repeated themes in Beissel's later writing.[23]

Upon the death of Matthias Beusel, his older brother, Johannes Beusel (1627–1710), intervened on behalf of the family. Johannes was a mayor (*Schultheis*) and Reformed schoolmaster in the nearby town of Strümpfelbrunn.[24] Johannes Beusel appealed to the Eberbach town council to permit his son Justus to succeed Matthias Beusel as the town baker so that Matthias's widow and children could continue to live in their quarters. The council appointed Justus, replacing the interim town baker, and Matthias's family apparently stayed on in their home.[25] The aged uncle Johannes Beusel may have influenced Conrad's understanding of the Reformed faith.

Eberbach, on the Neckar, was part of the Holy Roman Empire of the German Nation, comprising more than 250 provinces and territories. Southwestern Germany had not recovered from the sufferings of the Thirty Years' War (1618–48), which had effectively paralyzed population growth, economic development, and social mobility for decades.[26] Germany lacked the stimulation that enabled many other European nations to recover from the war. Germany had no ties to territories that could provide natural resources or serve as export markets. Foreign investors shied away from Germany. Multiple coinage, customs barriers, and a lack of an effective communication network hindered Germany's economic recovery.[27]

Agriculture suffered in Germany during these years of hardship. Generally grain prices fell during most of the seventeenth century into the second quarter of the eighteenth. Slow population growth in Germany tended to keep demand for agricultural products low, while the calamities of war and bad harvests reduced supplies. In the second half of the eighteenth century, population grew, keeping pace with gains made in the amount of cultivated land and yields. Thus the nutritional level of the general population remained poor and even deteriorated in the second half of the eighteenth century.

When Beissel was born, the Electoral Palatinate suffered further from the depredations of the Nine Years' War (or War of the Grand Alliance), 1688–97. The war began after Louis XIV made a dynastic claim to the Electoral Palatinate. Eventually German princes, the Dutch, the Austrian Habsburgs, and finally the English and the Spanish joined in the Grand Alliance to confine Louis. Both France and the Grand Alliance hired as many as thirty thousand Swiss soldiers, who ended up fighting each other on different sides of the war.

Louis XIV torched the Palatinate during his retreat across it in 1688. In 1693 the French burned Heidelberg and bombarded its castle. The winters of 1693–95 were particularly cold, reducing the food supply. When the Peace of Rijswijk (1697) ended the war, political boundaries were left about where they had been in 1679. Louis abandoned his claim to the Palatinate but kept an eye out for the successor to Spain's childless Habsburg king, Charles II.

When Charles II died in 1700, Louis supported the monarch's last will, which favored Louis's grandson Philip of Anjou as successor to the Spanish throne. Louis moved troops into the Spanish Netherlands in 1701, precipitating the War of the Spanish Succession. The Dutch, English, Austrians, and Prussians forged a new alliance against the Sun King. Once again the Palatinate straddled Louis's warpath. In 1703, first French, then English troops afflicted the Palatinate. In 1707 the French pillaged the Palatinate, Württemberg, and Baden again. Treaties in 1713–14 ended the war.[28]

As war tore the Electoral Palatinate repeatedly during these years, Conrad Beissel grew into early adulthood. Although Ephrata's internal history, the *Chronicon Ephratense*, suggests that Conrad "led a sorry life" after his mother's death, Beissel himself wrote of a "godly youth" during which he strove for "utmost purity." Elsewhere, however, he described himself as a "berry fallen from the vine of Sodom."[29] Even if he were interested in religion at an early age, Beissel was surely also vulnerable to the temptations of youth.

Beissel was reportedly apprenticed as a youth to a baker, and supposedly he also learned to fiddle. The Ephrata chronicle recounts time spent as a journeyman in Strasbourg and in Mannheim. Beissel reportedly worked in Mannheim for a baker named Kantebecker. When Beissel spurned the romantic advances of his master's wife, the young man was sent away.[30] The *Chronicon*'s suggestion that Beissel lived in Strasbourg and Mannheim after his conversion is probably out of sequence.[31] Sometime before 1715, Beissel landed in Heidelberg as a journeyman for a baker named Prior. Beissel thanked him thirty-eight years later for his efforts when Beissel left the city under difficult conditions, perhaps even expulsion.[32]

The vast majority of Germans at this time were rural and poor, with varying social patterns according to town and territory. At the bottom of the social scale were cottagers and day workers, who subsisted from day to day. The economic hardships of the eighteenth century swelled the ranks of these poor. Just above them were the peasants, with varying amounts of land. Those who could not subsist from their land often adopted a secondary occupation, such as some kind of artisan work.[33] The merchants who sold their wares often instigated this cottage work, also known as the putting-out system.[34] A whole family might share aspects of the supplemental work, which was often spinning and weaving. These rural artisans were outside guild membership and regulations. Because they were always vulnerable to market fluctuations, an economic crisis might force them to move. This combination of artisan work and some agricultural work was not uncommon in southwestern Germany in the early eighteenth century.

In the cities, guilds controlled much of the lives of artisans who attained the rank of master of a trade. These households made up the urban lower class (*Kleinbürgertum*). To these households also belonged journeymen and apprentices. Guilds rigidly controlled admission of new members and competed for political influence. This system maintained social stratification and economic stagnation in German cities throughout much of the eighteenth century, postponing the arrival of industrialization.[35] These conditions shaped Conrad Beissel's childhood and early adulthood.

Beissel experienced a religious conversion in a Pietist group in Heidelberg in 1715, according to his letters and the *Chronicon*.[36] Pietism was a renewal movement within Protestantism in the seventeenth and eighteenth centuries, in its German manifestation typically credited to Philipp Jakob Spener, who introduced small-group meetings, *collegia pietatis*, for edification in his Frankfurt congregation in 1670. Small-group meetings had already been used in the Dutch Reformed renewal movement known as the *nadere reformatie*, or further (or second) reformation. The *nadere reformatie*, like German Pietism in general, sought a completion of the Reformation in moral improvement and devotion to match the sixteenth-century reform of doctrine. A German Reformed pastor, Theodor Undereyck, had introduced the use of small groups in Mühlheim in 1665, unbeknownst to Spener.[37] To the use of small groups Spener added a renewed eschatology, "the hope of better times to come" (*die Hoffnung künftigen besseren Zeiten*).[38] Johannes Wallmann has named the small groups and eschatology as the defining marks of Lutheran Pietism. Pietism was characterized by a strong interest in ethical behavior and reliance on the Bible. Some Pietist authors stressed an affective response to one's awareness of justification by faith. August Hermann Francke, who established the education and charity center at Halle, popularized the idea that the struggle of repentance (*Bußkampf*) was necessary before one could break through to an awareness of forgiveness.[39]

A more mystically inclined member of Spener's Frankfurt congregation, Johann Jakob Schütz, embraced a more radical eschatological hope and more separatist outlook. He eventually led a dissatisfied group out of Spener's congregation; they became known as the Saalhof circle.[40] This was the beginning of Radical Pietism, a strongly separatist wing of the Pietist movement.[41] During the 1690s, many Radical Pietists sharpened their eschatology to the point of expecting Christ's return in the new century. Many of these separatists doubted that any faithful church could exist, and consequently some pursued their faith outside of the churches of Christendom.[42] Small Pietist groups, whether in or outside the church, met for mutual encouragement with no clergy present. Their efforts for renewal and their private meetings were sometimes perceived as a threat to the established church system, and some rulers suppressed them.

Pietism was part of a stream of religious renewal in Europe, responding to the doctrinal precision of Protestant Orthodoxy and the triumph of the Catholic reclamation in Europe, or Counter-Reformation. Ted Campbell has called this stream of religious renewal in Catholicism and Protestantism a "religion of the heart," emphasizing experiential faith and affective response to it, as well as ethical improvement and outreach in mission and charity. This renewal in the seventeenth and eighteenth centuries spawned Pietism in the Reformed tradition in the Netherlands and in the Lutheran faith in German lands, Denmark, and Sweden, and contributed to the Evangelical Awakening in Great Britain, with leaders such as George Whitefield and the Wesleys. In Catholicism this "religion of the heart" found expression in Jansenism, Quietism, and renewed devotion to the Sacred Heart of Jesus.[43]

This religious renewal flowed through the Baroque era, with its emphasis on emotional response in art, architecture, and music.

By the beginning of the eighteenth century, Radical Pietism spread to the Palatinate. In June 1701 in Lambsheim, near Mannheim, a day laborer named Matthias Baumann (d. 1727) experienced religious visions over a five-day period. Baumann believed God commissioned him to preach repentance before the impending final judgment.[44] He stopped attending the Reformed Church and worshiped with local Mennonites. After arrests in 1702 and 1706, Baumann emigrated to Pennsylvania and founded a small group, the *Neu-geboren* (the Newborn) in the Oley Valley, in present-day Berks County. Baumann reportedly visited Conrad Beissel some years later in the Conestoga region, preaching sinless perfection. While Baumann expounded, Beissel told him to smell his own excrement and see if that pertained to perfection.

Pietist activity in the Palatinate quickly heated up as itinerant laymen came preaching repentance. The separatist Johann Georg Rosenbach preached in 1703 to about one hundred at a home in Heidelberg, and then in Mannheim.[45] In 1706 the itinerant Radical Pietist Hochmann von Hochenau made a circuit in the Palatinate, probably at the invitation of Alexander Mack. The son of a wealthy miller and member of the Schriesheim town council, Mack had already sold his interest in the family mill to his brother that year. Their father died that summer.[46] When a Schriesheim official broke up Hochmann's preaching service there in August 1706, the group scattered. Eleven of Hochmann's followers went to Zuzenhausen, near Heidelberg, where they stayed with Hans Bechtold, a Mennonite, who also claimed to be a Pietist.[47] Hochmann surfaced in Mannheim in September and was arrested there. The punishment of forced labor on the city fortifications turned into open-air preaching services that aroused sympathy among Mannheim citizens. Meanwhile, Mack moved his family to Schwarzenau, a tiny village in Wittgenstein, where the ruling family, known for Pietist sympathies, welcomed religious dissenters. Hochmann had already preached the return of Christ in the spring of 1700 in Berleburg, the seat of government for Wittgenstein.

Pietist activity continued in and around Heidelberg. On May 1, 1708, a group of men were arrested in Schriesheim for holding unsupervised religious meetings. One of them was Alexander Mack's father-in-law, Johann Valentin Kling, an elder in the Reformed parish and member of the town council.[48] Another person in the group, Esbert Bender, was a wool spinner originally from Herborn, recently a resident of Heidelberg. Bender later joined the *Neu-Täufer,* then later moved to Ephrata.[49] During questioning Kling named among the friends of his group one Johann Adam Haller, former clerk of the

INTRODUCTION

Reichskammer. Another friend was a baker from Frankenthal named Schatz, who with his wife and her brother had fled the Palatinate after being arrested for holding devotional meetings.[50]

Jacob Schatz, a native and master baker of Frankenthal, had experienced "awakening" as a result of Hochmann's preaching in 1707. Schatz later recounted that "the pastors and guild leaders all together wanted to persecute" those awakened by Hochmann. In 1708 Schatz and three others moved to Düdelsheim, in the Marienborn region of Isenburg.[51] Isenburg was also a Reformed territory, its ruling family related by marriage to the ruling family in Wittgenstein and somewhat hospitable to religious dissenters. Jacob Schatz and his wife later gave Conrad Beissel lodging.

Some of Kling's group were arrested again in 1709, this time with two brothers, Johann Georg and Nicholaus Diehl. They named among their friends a certain Johann Adam Haller, a student, and Anna Maria Pastoir, wife of the Heidelberg professor Philipp Ludwig Pastoir, although she had not attended their meetings.[52] The *Chronicon* later named a Haller, the brothers Diehl, and Mrs. Pastoir as members of the group in which Beissel experienced conversion in 1715. Julius Sachse claimed without documentation that Beissel's Heidelberg Pietist circle was a Rosicrucian chapter.[53] The unlikeliness of this claim will become clear in Chapter 7.

Beissel's Heidelberg friends probably knew the thought and perhaps the writings of Jacob Boehme, the German visionary and spiritualist. The Haller in their circle may be the Haller with whom Johann Georg Gichtel corresponded; at least Ephrata's chronicle identifies him as such. Gichtel published Boehme's full corpus of writings in Amsterdam and popularized Boehme to Radical Pietists in Germany and to the Philadelphian Society. The Philadelphian Society grew out of a network of readers of Boehme in England, under the leadership of Jane Leade. The German branch of the Philadelphian Society similarly grew from among Boehme's readership. Johann Wilhelm Petersen and his wife, Eleanora von Merlau Petersen, a member of the Saalhof separatists in Frankfurt, were leaders of the Philadelphian group in Germany. Publications by Leade and her associates John Pordage and Thomas Bromley were quickly translated into German and printed on the continent. The two branches carried on a lively correspondence.[54] Gichtel was one of many important links between them. It is probable that Beissel's Pietist circle in Heidelberg knew Boehme's thought and had some correspondence with other Boehmists.

While working as a baker with Prior in Heidelberg, Beissel allegedly plunged into "mathematics,"[55] which may have included the numerology important in his 1728 book, *Mystyrion Anomias*. Numerology figured in the works of Radical Pietists such as Johann Jacob Zimmermann (1634–94) and Christian cabbalists such as Christian Knorr von Rosenroth (1636–89). Both men influenced Johannes Kelpius (1670–1708), who led a group of hermits to Germantown, Pennsylvania, in 1694. Later Beissel claimed that he immigrated to Pennsylvania partly to join the Kelpius community. In addition, the former Reformed minister and professor Heinrich Horch sought to use numerology to interpret symbolic numbers in the Bible and predict Christ's return.[56]

In Heidelberg, Beissel encountered legal trouble for his religious activity. Conflict within the bakers' guild may have contributed to his troubles, perhaps leading to arrest. His final sermon in *Geistliche Reden* claimed explicitly that he was expelled from the Palatinate. His letters indicate that he must have left Heidelberg around 1718. Beissel remembered the Palatinate with both love and loathing. He referred to his departure as his "orphanhood," his loss of his fatherland compounding the bitter grief of losing his parents. Yet he also prophesied its utter destruction for rejecting him.[57]

Beissel fled from Heidelberg to Düdelsheim in the Marienborn area of Isenburg (Figure 1) and found refuge with Jacob Schatz, the baker originally from Frankenthal. By the time Beissel arrived, Schatz had associated with the Community of True Inspiration and hosted meetings in his home. The Inspirationists had arisen in 1714 and were formally organized in 1715 over a controversy about false versus true inspiration. Influenced by the French Prophets, the Inspirationists believed that the Holy Spirit gave them direct revelations. One of their number, the famous physician Dr. Johann Samuel Carl, reportedly treated Beissel in Marienborn during a severe illness. Beissel visited their services, but he was moved from the adult gatherings to the children's meetings when two young women became disturbed by his presence. He withdrew from the Inspirationists and reportedly lived for a time with Georg Stieffel. Here Beissel worked as a wool spinner and received charity from a nobleman, Junkerroth.[58]

Some writers have mistakenly followed Julius Sachse's claim that Beissel went to Schwarzenau and may have met Alexander Mack. This is unlikely, because the account of Mack's meeting with Beissel in 1730 in Pennsylvania indicates that Mack did not recognize Beissel.[59] They almost surely would have met had Beissel lived in Schwarzenau before Mack left there in 1719. Also, Beissel would not have met the *Neu-Täufer* in Marienborn. The entire Dunker group there was expelled in 1715 for baptizing adults. Beissel arrived

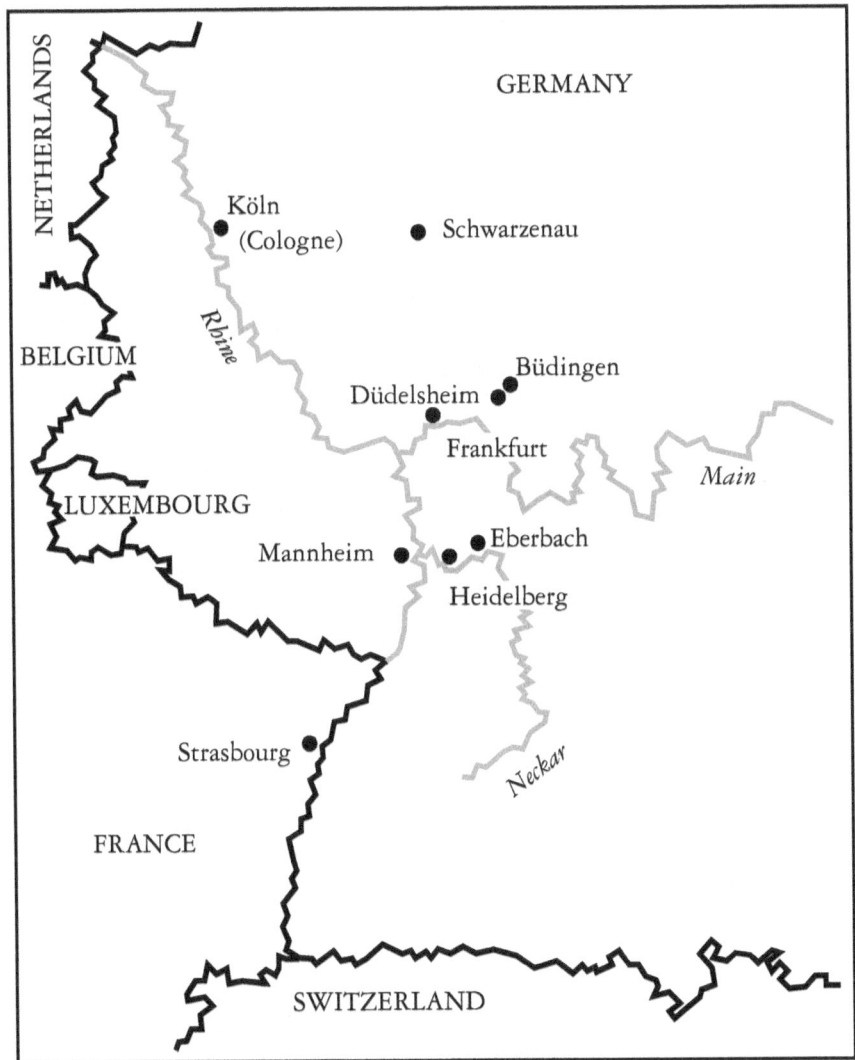

Fig. 1 Conrad Beissel's Europe.

in Düdelsheim a few years later. While he probably did not know the *Neu-Täufer* personally in Europe, he surely knew about them.

Beissel's reasons for emigrating to America in 1720 are still not completely known. He may have sought simply to escape his abject poverty, or perhaps to join a group of hermits led by Johannes Kelpius, as the *Chronicon* reported. The same volume claimed that two of Beissel's friends, Georg Stieffel and Jacob Stuntz, persuaded him to emigrate with them.[60] The chronicle also claimed that some tried to dissuade Beissel from emigrating. Dr. Samuel Carl allegedly encouraged Beissel to stay and maintain important friendships, but Beissel persisted.

Political events in the Palatinate may have convinced him that confessional chaos was about to break out again. Prince Elector Carl Philip succeeded his childless brother, Johann Wilhelm, in 1716, continuing the Roman Catholic Pfalz-Neuburg family line. Carl Philip recalled the Heidelberg Catechism because of its condemnation of the mass. In 1719 he claimed the Holy Spirit Church of Heidelberg for his court church, despite the settlement of 1648 allowing Reformed and Catholics to share it. The prince elector ordered the removal of an interior wall dividing the worship space and sent the Reformed congregation elsewhere. Protestant rulers reacted so strongly that, as Reginald Ward has noted, for a moment in 1719 many Protestants thought they perched on the brink of another disastrous religious war.[61] This situation may have contributed to Beissel's decision to leave Europe permanently.

Conrad Beissel reportedly sailed with four friends: Georg Stieffel, Jacob Stuntz, Simon König, and Hennrich von Bebern. Stuntz reportedly paid Beissel's passage. Beissel arrived in Boston in October 1720, on the ship *Elizabeth and Hannah,* and then traveled to Philadelphia. The hermit community of Johannes Kelpius (1673–ca. 1708) near Germantown had disbanded, but Beissel imbibed the views of a few surviving members, such as Conrad Matthäi. Meanwhile Beissel apprenticed himself for a year to a weaver, Peter Becker (1687–1758), in Germantown. Becker was a native of Düdelsheim, where Beissel had lived with Jacob Schatz. Becker was baptized by the *Neu-Täufer* in 1714. Upon their expulsion in 1715, he went with many others to Krefeld. After conflicts within the congregation there, a group emigrated to Pennsylvania in 1719, with Becker as a leader.[62] However, they did not resume worship together in Pennsylvania until 1723.

Beissel and his friends followed a stream of immigrants from southwest Germany and Switzerland that began in 1683 and swelled dramatically in the decades after his arrival in Pennsylvania. Aaron Fogelman has identified three phases of German immigration to the colonies, based primarily on motivation for leaving. From 1683 to 1709, primarily religious repression drove a few hundred to emigrate. Between 1709 and 1714, the British crown actively recruited German and Swiss immigrants to help produce naval stores. Poor harvests after the harsh winter of 1709 in the Palatinate heightened the lure of the new land. Religious issues remained a factor for a minority of the few thousand emigrants in this period. The third period, 1717–75, saw by far the largest outpouring of Germans and Swiss. A few still fled religious hardship, but the overwhelming majority of the some 80,000 in this third wave sought better economic conditions. Pennsylvania, with its religious toleration, drew the majority of Germanic immigrants, although a large concentration settled in New York's Hudson Valley.[63] Beissel arrived in 1720, when Pennsylvania's non-native population numbered perhaps 100,000, about a third of them of Germanic origin. By 1730, about 4,000 African slaves were held in Pennsylvania.[64]

While the large majority of the Germanic immigrants in Pennsylvania belonged to Lutheran or Reformed churches, a small but significant minority adhered to one of about a dozen dissenting sectarian groups. The first German settlers, a group of Mennonites turned Quakers, mostly from Krefeld, had established Germantown, just outside of Philadelphia, in 1683. The Kelpius group arrived in 1694 and set up a short-lived separatist community on Wissahickon Creek.[65] More Mennonites arrived, followed by Dunkers in 1719, then Schwenckfelders in 1734 and Moravians in 1741. Other small groups were also represented, such as the Inspirationists, the New Born of Oley, and a group in Conestoga known as New-Mooners. When Beissel came to Pennsylvania, a few hundred Mennonites and maybe fewer than fifty Dunkers represented the sectarian people.[66] Other separatists found in Pennsylvania freedom to abstain from joining any religious organization. A severe shortage of clergy helped the dissenters' situation: only four ministers were available to serve twenty-six German Reformed congregations and three Lutheran clergymen for twenty-seven congregations in 1740.[67]

Beissel's decision to leave Germany reflected the mixture of motives that drove many people to emigrate after 1717. Some had experienced difficulties over religion. Many had chafed under the limitations of economic stagnation and social rigidity in Germany. Some immigrants, including many at Ephrata, had been displaced at least once before they moved to Pennsylvania. Beissel, like some Radical Pietists, was a poor artisan who probably had to apprentice himself for survival upon his arrival. In place of the uncertainties of both Europe and the frontier, the Ephrata community eventually offered to newly arriving immigrants food, assistance with shelter, and social fellowship in a language of the old country. The motifs of homelessness, orphanhood, and pilgrimage permeate Ephrata's spirituality. Beissel often called himself one "who possesses nothing" and "on pilgrimage to silent eternity." These phrases reflect the social conditions that he and some followers experienced.[68]

After one year with Becker, Beissel moved to Conestoga. This region, drained by Conestoga Creek, was sparsely settled by Swiss and German

Mennonites and other Protestants.[69] Beissel lived somewhat as a hermit, at first sharing a household on Mill Creek (Mühlbach) with Jacob Stuntz.[70] Later Stieffel joined them, as did a young man from Holland, Isaac von Bebern, probably related to the Hennrich von Bebern who emigrated with Beissel, Stuntz, and Stieffel.

In Conestoga, Beissel encountered small religious groups, some familiar, some perhaps new. Bebern, related to a Mennonite-Quaker family among the first settlers in Germantown, took Beissel in 1722 to Bohemia Manor, the fading remnant of a community of followers of Jean de Labadie in northern Maryland. Bebern had relatives there.[71] Upon their return, Michael Wohlfahrt (1687–1741), a wandering Radical Pietist originally from Memel, on the Baltic (now Klaipeda, Lithuania), visited them. Thus began a relationship that later would bring Wohlfahrt back as a leader in Beissel's congregation.

The household on Mill Creek broke up in 1723 after Michael Wohlfahrt left for the Carolinas. Stuntz sold the cabin to recoup Conrad's transatlantic fare. Alone again, Beissel moved about a mile away to a place known as Swede's Spring. Soon Wohlfahrt rejoined him. Years later, in a letter to a friend in Mannheim, Beissel remembered thinking that in this period of relative solitude he had triumphed "in the quiet of the spirit, separate from all men, to serve my God in his holy temple."[72]

In the autumns of 1722 and 1723 the *Neu-Täufer,* or Dunkers, renewed their fellowship through visitations led by Peter Becker. The *Chronicon* credited Beissel for this "awakening."[73] On Christmas Day, 1723, Peter Becker baptized eight people in Wissahickon Creek in Germantown and led a love feast that evening. Evangelizing and worship continued in 1724 in the backcountry. In November they organized what became the Coventry congregation near present-day Pottstown. On November 12, 1724, Becker preached in Conestoga. Five persons requested baptism. A sixth came forward as Becker administered the rite, and Beissel stepped up as the seventh and last candidate.[74]

Thus at the age of thirty-three Conrad Beissel received baptism among the *Neu-Täufer.* He brought with him the Radical Pietist longing for spiritual love among believers. He had drunk from springs of Boehmist thought in Heidelberg, mingled with Inspirationists, the loosely knit Philadelphians, the Dunker preacher Becker, adherents of Kelpius, the fading Labadists, and the Mennonites. Yet he also held the separatist distrust in organized religious groups. Many groups influenced Beissel, but he never embraced any fully. This unresolved tension ran through Beissel's career and the Ephrata community.

INTRODUCTION

The new little congregation at Conestoga chose him as their leader. Apparently Beissel already enjoyed positive regard in the area. Even a detractor such as Ezechiel Sangmeister reported years later that Conrad Beissel was greatly loved and admired among the sectarian people in Conestoga between 1721 and 1724.[75] Beissel's reputation was in part that of a prayerful, loving man. The congregation's choice of Beissel was not unlikely.

Soon after his baptism, Beissel began to honor Saturday, the seventh day, as a personal observance of the Sabbath. He also taught that celibacy is superior to marriage. He did not require the congregation to observe the seventh day, and continued to lead worship on Sunday. The seventh-day Sabbath and celibacy, plus probably his charismatic personality, brought him into conflict with the rest of the Dunkers. Beissel's supporters closed ranks around him. In 1725 he moved into a cabin built for him on the farm of Rudolf Nägele, formerly the Mennonite pastor in the Conestoga region, whom Beissel baptized. Other congregation members followed suit, and a nascent community began.

In December 1728 Beissel led six members to reenact the baptism he had received from the Brethren four years earlier, in order to "give it back" to them. Jan Meyle, whom Becker had immersed at the first Brethren baptism in 1723, assisted Beissel. The rebaptisms in 1728 formally marked the rupture that had begun in 1725.[76] Beissel evangelized and the congregation grew. Apparently a couple named Permersdorff created some internal dissent around 1728–30.[77]

Beissel published a booklet on the Sabbath in 1728 and another against marriage two years later. In 1730 he also published a collection of maxims and poetry and a small hymnal of mostly original texts, thus launching a career as a prolific poet. In 1732 he abruptly surrendered leadership of the congregation and moved again to solitude, this time on the banks of Cocalico Creek, a few miles away. He actually joined Emmanuel Eckerlin, who with his brothers had joined Beissel's congregation earlier. Emmanuel had built a squatter's cabin on the Cocalico. Soon members followed Beissel and a settlement grew. They earned fame for their charity. Celibates lived in hermit cabins, and married couples with children, or householders, settled among them.

A boom of communal building began in 1735, when members built the first monastic house, called Kedar. At this time he organized the sisters into the Order of Spiritual Virgins. The celibate men were organized into the Zionitic Brotherhood around 1738, when their house, Zion, was built. They raised dormitories and chapels at the rate of almost one a year from 1735 until 1746, when Bethania and its chapel were completed. In 1740 Beissel ordered celibates still in hermit cabins to enter monastic houses;[78] not all complied.

In 1735 Beissel and Wohlfahrt evangelized in the Tulpehocken region. They won the Reformed minister, Peter Miller, who had been educated at Heidelberg, and Conrad Weiser, the Indian interpreter, among others. Beissel won converts from the Germantown Dunkers in 1738, including two sons of Alexander Mack.[79] He also gathered members among Welsh and English Sabbatarians. Members settled around Ephrata, creating outposts named Zoar, Massah, Hebron, and Kadesh. Zoar is today's Reamstown (Figure 2).

Beissel chose Israel Eckerlin (Brother Onesimus) as prior when Wohlfahrt (Brother Agonius) died in 1741. Probably with the help of his older brother, Samuel Eckerlin (Brother Jephune), Israel led an economic expansion by buying and building mills on the creek. They developed a lively trade with

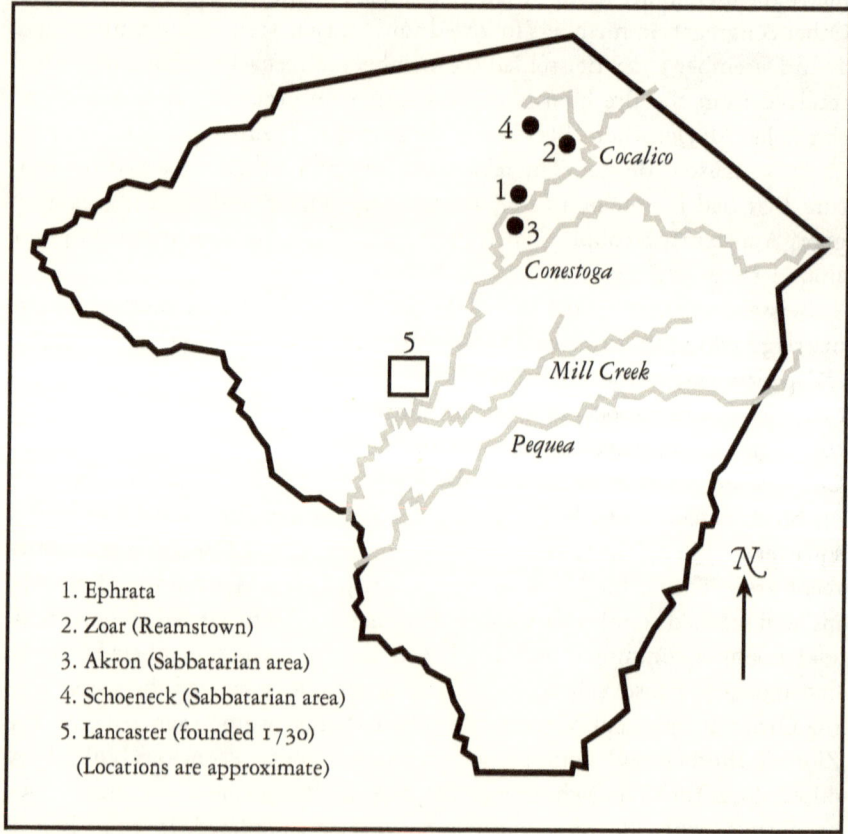

Fig. 2 Lancaster County (modern boundaries).

INTRODUCTION

Philadelphia, and Ephrata became an important milling center on the Pennsylvania frontier.[80]

Around 1740, the celibate brothers requested that Beissel be called "Father" along with his self-chosen spiritual name, Friedsam Gottrecht, meaning "Peaceable, Right with God." The title of "Father" would replace the title of "Brother," used by all the celibate men. Some members, such as Johannes Hildebrand, resisted calling Beissel "Father."[81]

The years between 1740 and 1745 brought other conflicts. A householder, Ludwig Blum, and the sisters introduced choral singing and composition around 1740. Beissel took over the choir, however, and Blum left. In 1742 Beissel scuttled the community's participation in the ecumenical synods led by Count Nicolaus Ludwig von Zinzendorf. Tensions with Israel Eckerlin over leadership and the expanding economy led Beissel to expel him in 1745.

Beissel's Ephrata peaked between 1745 and 1755 with perhaps three hundred or more residents, including celibates and families. The communal economy crested just before Beissel expelled Israel Eckerlin. His expulsion may have preserved the unique religious life for the short term. Beissel reorganized the celibate orders in 1745, naming the sisters the Roses of Saron and the men the Brotherhood of Bethania. Ephrata's unique material culture reached its zenith during these years. The scribes created some of their best manuscript art after 1745. The composition of hymn texts and tunes flourished, as did Beissel's devotional writing. The community established its printing press in 1745, second only to Christopher Saur's for German printing in colonial Pennsylvania.

Some turns of events presaged future decline. New converts arrived from Gimbsheim between 1749 and 1751, including several Beissel relatives. However, many of them moved on to York County, where a congregation formed on the Bermudian. A youth revival in 1748 fizzled. Several sisters died young in 1747–48.[82] The Seven Years' War (1756–63) put Ephrata in harm's way and helped to slow immigration.

During and after the war, Beissel wrote and cycled in and out of illness. He was reportedly severely ill around 1741 and was ill again in 1762.[83] Yet on three occasions around 1764 he traveled the hundred miles to the Antietam Valley, near present-day Waynesboro, to visit a new congregation, eventually Snow Hill. Ephrata residents scattered as far away as South Carolina (Figure 3), although their settlements were not intentional extensions of the community.

Beissel fought his last battles with familiars. In 1764 a small party of disgruntled former residents returned from Virginia, led by Ezechiel Sangmeister and Samuel Eckerlin. Because Samuel was the last living signatory who

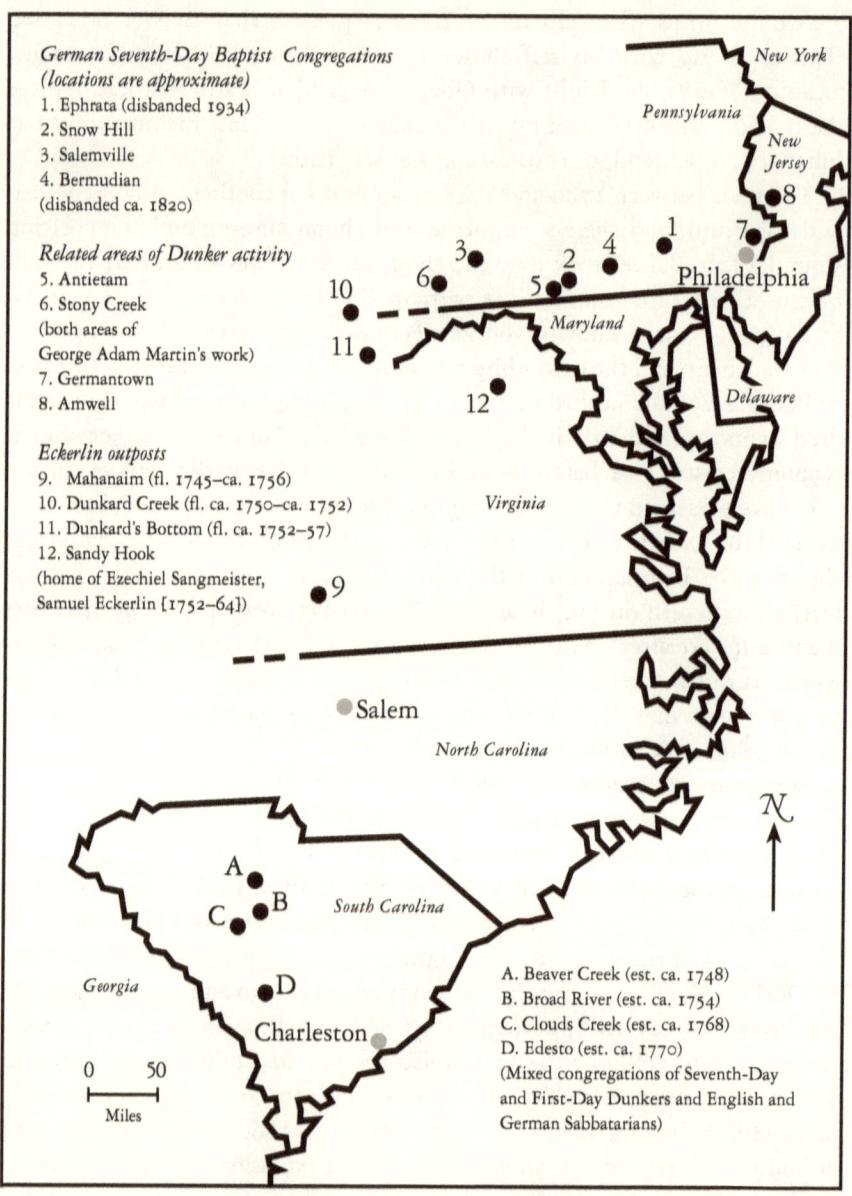

Fig. 3 Locations of German Sabbatarian congregations in the eighteenth century.

still acknowledged his part in a joint deed to community land, his party was entitled to live on the property. A protracted legal battle finally reached the Pennsylvania Assembly, despite supposed scruples against using courts of law. At the same time, the prioress, Mother Maria Eicher, reportedly attempted to separate the sisters completely from their affiliation with the celibate brothers. Beissel deposed her around 1764, although she remained as a sister in Saron.[84] Beissel failed to secure a dismissal of Eckerlin's land claim, and he could not bring Sangmeister's faction into conformity with community life.[85] Finally, after Beissel's death in 1768, all parties reached an agreement in 1770, allowing vowed celibates to retain the property and allowing Eckerlin and Sangmeister's faction lodging and some food.

Sangmeister's autobiography portrayed Beissel's last years as rancorous and indulgent in food, drink, and sexual affairs.[86] Beissel may have drunk liquor, perhaps even to inebriation, for the pain in his aging body. If Beissel was sexually involved with any women, it had to be well before his final years. Remembered as a "living skeleton til his death,"[87] Beissel could hardly have had the stamina in his seventies for the lasciviousness that Sangmeister portrayed.

Beissel died an old man on July 6, 1768, attended by the aging celibates. Although Peter Miller led the declining band of celibates and Georg Adam Martin held forth at Antietam, Beissel's death greatly dimmed the already declining fires of piety at Ephrata.[88] Certainly a product of the Old World, Conrad Beissel and his associates formed a community shaped by religious views that were rooted in that world yet were impossible to realize there. Threaded through a complex network of religious connections, their religious world was strung taut by difficult social conditions that spanned Europe, England, and North America. Beissel and the Ephrata settlers could make concrete this religious vision, with its flaws, only in the toleration and economic opportunities of William Penn's colony.

Conrad Beissel preached God's impending destruction of European Christendom, calling believers to prepare in lives of self-denial for the coming paradise of eternity. He embodied both fiery and prayerful charisma that rarely became routine to his listeners. Beissel promised and lived a rigorous training of body and soul in anticipation of eternity. Ephrata delivered a somewhat better here-and-now by sharing economic resources and labor, providing housing, and removing celibate women from the dangers of childbirth. Those who fled to Beissel at the supposed evening of the cosmos prepared for God's unmediated presence in what they hoped was the dawn of the eternal Sabbath. Few, if any, could know that the hardships of the Old World would yield in Pennsylvania not to an angelic paradise but to a new colony of prosperity and toleration. Precisely that toleration allowed them to give visible form and expression to their Christian faith and practices, originally honed on the margins of Protestant dissent in Europe. They embodied this faith in one of the most singular constructions of gender identity in the American colonies.

THE RELIGIOUS THOUGHT OF EPHRATA

Conrad Beissel

Conrad Beissel's collaborator Michael Wohlfahrt once reportedly told Benjamin Franklin that the Ephrata Sabbatarians "fear that if we should once print our confession of faith, we should feel ourselves as if bound and confined by it, and perhaps be unwilling to receive further improvement." As late as 1790, Peter Miller (1709–96) wrote, "We have no creeds, our standard is the New Testament."[1] Wohlfahrt explained well why the Ephrata community and the Schwarzenau *Neu-Täufer* (Dunkers) hesitated to write a definitive confession of faith.

The Ephrata community nevertheless wrote some statements of faith, such as the *Mistisches und Kirchliches Zeuchnüß der Brüderschaft in Zion* (Mystic and churchly testimony of the brotherhood in Zion) in 1743. Beissel's *Dissertation on Man's Fall,* first published in 1765 in an English translation by Peter Miller, summarized many of his major beliefs.[2]

Johannes Hildebrand (1679–1765) wrote significant treatises. Ezechiel Sangmeister (1723–84), a disgruntled critic of Beissel, nevertheless shared many of his core beliefs and expressed them in an autobiography and a volume on mystical theology. Mindful of Wohlfahrt's cautions not to impose more order on Ephrata's writings than the authors themselves would, let us examine some of Beissel's central beliefs.

SOURCES OF BEISSEL'S THOUGHT

Conrad Beissel drew on a variety of religious sources. His major source was Jacob Boehme's thought, particularly as Johann Georg Gichtel interpreted it. Beissel considered direct religious experience to be as authoritative as Scripture. At times he appealed to the authority of the earliest centuries of Christianity, although he gave it less weight than personal experience. The ritual practice of the Dunkers, too, helped to shape Beissel's religious views.

Gichtel's influence on Beissel was clear to the Moravian leader August Gottlieb Spangenberg, who wrote in 1737 that Ephrata was Gichtelian.[3] Later Sangmeister noted that Gichtel's writings were authoritative and accessible at Ephrata.[4] Mainly through Gichtel, the Philadelphian Society network in England and Germany,[5] and the work of Gottfried Arnold, the history professor and Pietist, Beissel absorbed and adapted Boehme.[6]

Two major hermeneutical presuppositions determined Beissel's use of Scripture. First, from Heinrich Horch's *Mystische und Profetische Bibel,* or Marburg Bible (1712), Beissel adopted allegorical and typological interpretation. While Beissel never credited Horch directly, Peter Miller's preface to *Deliciae Ephratenses, Pars I* (1773) named Horch explicitly.[7] Beissel's second presupposition, derived from Inspirationist influence, was his confidence in the direct religious experience of revelation.

Horch chose the biblical books of Song of Solomon and Revelation as the interpretive keys for finding a "hidden" or mystical meaning of the whole Bible. He also used typology for an eschatalogical, or prophetic, interpretation of Scripture and events of his time. Horch divided the Song of Solomon into an allegorical chronology of Christianity. After an initial purity as the bride of Christ under persecution (Song of Sol. 1:5–3:6), the Church was under the Christian emperors (3:7–5:1), then under Antichrist, presumably Roman Catholicism, up to Horch's present (5:2–16). Finally (6:1–8:14) the "newly kindled fire in Philadelphia" (*das in Filadelphia* [sic] *neu angezündete feuer*) will prepare the Church for marriage to Christ, "the heavenly Solomon" (*den himmlischen Salomon*).[8]

Horch correlated his outline with another chronology that he based on the seven letters of Revelation. The letter to Ephesus, for example, represented the first Christians. Smyrna represented myrrh, standing for the persecuted churches, an incense to God (parallel to Song of Sol. 3:6). The sixth letter to "Filadelfia" represented a brotherly love when the faithful would be of one heart and one soul. Finally, when "Filadelfia's love unfortunately cools off," a brief, lukewarm seventh era would ensue, followed by Christ's glorious reign.[9]

Horch viewed earliest Christianity as a movement of initial pure love for Christ and fellow Christians. Thus he shared the portrayal of the first Christians in the historian Gottfried Arnold's *Wahre Abbildung der Ersten Christen* (1696). Like most in the Philadelphian movement, Horch anticipated a rekindling of the initial pure love at the end time, just before Christ's return. He believed that the Philadelphian era was his own time, to be followed soon by a brief seventh era (the Laodicean period) and then the coming of Christ. To the language of bridal mysticism and the soul's espousal to Christ Horch added the heightened eschatology of Radical Pietism.

Experiential inspiration shaped Beissel's use of Scripture and preaching. The visiting Swedish provost Israel Acrelius described Beissel's bodily gestures while preaching in 1753. Beissel "threw his head up and down, his eyes hither and thither; pulled at his mouth, his nose, his neck."[10] These movements resemble the gyrations of Inspirationists as Eberhard Ludwig Gruber described them in 1716: "shaking of the head, drooping of the mouth, twitching of the shoulders, wobbling of the knees, and trembling of the legs."[11]

Acrelius noted that the Ephrata brethren "indeed read the Scriptures, but believe themselves to be possessed of an 'inward light,' which transcends the outward." The Sabbatarians believed that their public speaking came "from the immediate light and impulse of the Spirit,"[12] whereas the Dunkers, as Spangenberg observed, "consider the Scriptures to be an outward witness that one ought to hold just as the Scriptures say."[13] Beissel, in contrast, read Scripture through what he believed was his immediate, inward experience of the Holy Spirit.

Beissel found a third significant authority for his views, though somewhat less weighty, in Christian antiquity, particularly as described by Gottfried Arnold, the historian and friend of Radical Pietists. As Jürgen Büchsel has shown, Arnold portrayed the first Christians as models of rebirth, spirituality, and ethical conduct.[14] Arnold employed his account of ancient Christianity to criticize the church system of his time. Beissel endorsed this critique. Gradually Beissel instituted some of the ascetic practices of Arnold's portrayal, as Peter Erb has noted.[15] Still, Beissel turned not to the first century after Christ but primarily to the first state of the androgynous Adam in paradise, as Boehme portrayed it. Beissel preached that this paradise was at hand, for Christ would soon return.

The *Neu-Täufer* of Schwarzenau provided another important influence on Beissel, primarily through their ritual practice, much of which Ephrata adopted. Whether this Dunker influence was Radical Pietist or Anabaptist was a question pursued in the last half of the twentieth century. C. David Ensign proposed that Boehmist thought is the defining characteristic of Radical Pietism, and he argued for a close similarity between the Dunkers and Ephrata. The Dunkers' relation to Ephrata, he suggested, might resemble that of the "Roman Catholic faithful and a religious order."[16]

Ensign's thesis grew out of a debate that characterized much of Brethren historiography in the second half of the twentieth century. Brethren scholars such as Floyd Mallott, William Willoughby, Ensign, Durnbaugh, Vernard Eller, Dale Brown, and more recently Dale Stoffer and Carl Bowman have asked whether Dunkers origins were primarily Pietist or Anabaptist. This debate, more pronounced between about 1960 and 1970, responded in part to Robert Friedmann's work on Mennonite piety, which set the Anabaptist movement in opposition to Pietism.[17]

Ensign argued that the Dunkers were primarily Radical Pietists in origin. He cited their endorsement of celibacy, though they did not require it, and their use of the ban as traits that Radical Pietism shared with Ephrata. While the Dunkers admired celibacy, however, they believed that God "instituted marriage in paradise."[18] They did not hold Gichtel's view, derived from Boehme, of an androgynous Adam, whose sexual desire led to the fall into sin. Virtually *no* Radical Pietists practiced the ban, contrary to Ensign's thesis.[19] The impulse for congregational discipline came to Ephrata and the Dunkers from both Reformed Pietism and the Anabaptist tradition.

Portraying Anabaptism and Pietism as polar opposites is less helpful for understanding Dunker origins or Beissel's community for at least two reasons. First, neither Pietism nor Anabaptism existed as pure types. German Pietism contained radical and separatist tendencies from its beginnings in 1670, as Johannes Wallmann showed in demonstrating the influence of Johann Jakob Schütz in Frankfurt. Schütz seems to have known little of Boehme, but he was interested in chiliasm, in Tauler's sermons, and in cabbala.[20] Surviving Anabaptist groups also manifested diversity, ranging from the tolerant and prosperous Dutch Mennonites to the Amish rigorists after 1693, with other groups in between in Switzerland, Alsace, and the Palatinate.[21]

Second, the influences between the surviving Anabaptist traditions and Pietism in the seventeenth and eighteenth centuries may be more porous than Robert Friedmann admitted. He proposed that Pietism eviscerated the strong biblical discipleship of sixteenth-century Anabaptism. He defined Anabaptism as a movement of uncompromising discipleship, expressed in fellowship, love, and readiness to "suffer in conflict with the evil world order." Friedmann defined Pietism as "a quiet conventicle-Christianity," concerned primarily with an "inner experience of salvation" and "not at all" with "a radical world transformation."[22] Friedmann overlooked such Anabaptist spiritualists as Hans Denck and David Joris, the latter of whom took up more room than any other Anabaptist in Gottfried Arnold's account of Christian history, *Unparteyische Kirchen- und Ketzer-Historie.*[23] Also Friedmann underestimated Pietism's ethics and outreach, embodied in the charity and mission at Halle. Any polar opposition of Pietism to Anabaptism oversimplifies both movements, which have common emphases in some manifestations.[24]

Ephrata illustrates the complex relationships between Pietist and Anabaptist groups in the early eighteenth century. Many Mennonites found their way to Ephrata, such as Rudolf Nägele, an early Mennonite minister in Conestoga, and families such as Graff (Groff), Funk, Guth (Good), and Wenger.[25] The Ephrata Press reprinted important Mennonite works, among them *Güldene Aepffel in Silbern Schalen* (1745), *Ernsthafte Christenpflicht* (1745, 1770), and Thieleman van Braght's *Martyrer-Spiegel* (1748). Friedmann judged the *Martyrer-Spiegel* to be "authentically Anabaptist,"[26] yet Pietist Ephrata produced its first translation into German. While Ephrata may have acted only as printers contracted by the Mennonites, the financial loss on the *Martyrs' Mirror* suggests a motivation other than profit.[27]

On a foundation of Boehmist thought transmitted through Gichtel and the Philadelphian Society, Conrad Beissel constructed his religious thought with Scripture read through the hermeneutics of Horch and of direct religious experience. Beissel fashioned the outward practice of his community from the ritual life of the Dunkers, sometimes drawing on the model of ancient Christianity. He created a unique synthesis of religious thought and practice from the Old World embodied in a singular religious community in the New World.

BEISSEL'S THOUGHT: EARLY WRITINGS

Beissel's earliest known writing that can be dated with some confidence is a letter written probably in 1725, if the *Chronicon* is reliable. The letter condemned two of his acquaintances, A. W. and D. C. of Oley (probably Georg Adam Weidner and David Caufmann or Kaufmann)[28] for circumcising each other. The letter reveals that many major elements of Beissel's thought were in place within a year of his baptism in 1724.

The impetus for the circumcision probably came from Philadelphian literature, contrary to Julius Sachse's theory that proselytizing Jewish traders instigated the event.[29] Thomas Bromley, an English Philadelphian, wrote in his booklet titled *The Law of Circumcision* that circumcision symbolized a celibate life devoted to God. "We must deny the relationship of man to woman," Bromley counseled. A Snow Hill copybook with excerpts from books received from Ephrata contains a long portion from the German translation of this work.[30]

Bromley probably developed his conviction in part from Jacob Boehme's comments that male circumcision was commanded in order to show that "the animal mixing of man and wife is disgusting before God's holiness."[31] Gichtel shared this view, endorsing celibacy.[32] Beissel wrote later that God commanded circumcision of the male organ "to show that before God's holy eyes it is disgusting."[33] While Beissel endorsed celibacy, he condemned circumcision, arguing that grace and promise in the new covenant supersede the old covenant of the law, of which circumcision was a sign.

Beissel's speculative Boehmist thought emerged in the letter as he traced the promise of grace through "the seed of woman" (*Weibes-Samen*) from Eve to Sarah to Mary. According to Beissel, Sarah's pregnancy "without the doings of a man" (*ohne Zuthun des Mannes*) prefigured the virginal conception and birth of Jesus, the truly "virginal man" (*jungfräulicher Mann*). Beissel also alluded to the so-called Priesthood of Melchizedek by writing that the reborn enter into "the inward Holy of Holies" and offer prayers "like a holy incense [*Rauchwerk*]." These words followed Gichtel closely.[34]

In this letter Beissel signaled his efforts to create a mystical language for the presence of God. The redeemed, he wrote, learn "to speak a new language and serve God unceasingly in his holy temple."[35] For Beissel, the special awareness of God's presence was analogous to God's presence at the ancient Jerusalem temple. Awareness or experience of this special presence of God requires a special language. Thus in what may be one of Beissel's early letters in Pennsylvania, central themes of his later thought, such as the Sabbath, celibacy, the creation of a special language for God's presence, and unique constructions of female and male gender, are already present.

Beissel's first known publication, *Mystyrion Anomias,* defended the Sabbath, one of his earliest distinctive teachings. No copy of the 1728 German version is known, but an English translation from the next year survives.[36] Oswald Seidensticker, Julius Sachse, and the historians who depended on Sachse have unconvincingly attributed Beissel's Sabbatarianism to a legalistic, "Judaizing" observance of the Old Testament.[37]

Beissel's Sabbatarian convictions grew from Radical Pietist thought, with some help from English Sabbatarians. The *Chronicon* noted the influence of English Seventh-Day Baptists on Beissel.[38] Some of the English Sabbatarians were Keithian Baptists. This group, originating in the 1690s from the erstwhile Quaker, George Keith (ca. 1638–1716), adopted the seventh-day Sabbath and immersion baptism around the turn of the eighteenth century. Able Noble, formerly a Quaker, and Thomas Rutter, whom Bernard Köster (formerly of the Kelpius community) baptized, became early English Sabbatarian Baptist leaders. Three congregations were founded near Philadelphia: Newtown about 1700, Pennepek about 1701, and East Nantmeal (French Creek) in 1722.[39] Köster's involvement reveals interaction among German Radical Pietists, English Baptists, and dissenting Quakers.

George Keith's earlier contacts mark a trail to Radical Pietism. An associate of George Fox, he also befriended the Quaker Benjamin Furley and pursued an interest in the Christian cabbala of Christian Knorr von Rosenroth and Francis van Helmont.[40] Bernard Köster's association with the Keithian circle also brought in some Radical Pietist thought. Köster's guide, Johannes Kelpius, had corresponded with Stephen Momfort (or Mumford), a Sabbatarian Baptist who emigrated from England to Rhode Island and in 1671 organized the first known Seventh-Day Baptist congregation in America.[41] Since Beissel understood no English, the German Radical Pietist links were important transmitters of this English Sabbatarian influence.[42]

The thought of the Philadelphian movement prepared a way for Sabbatarianism. Jacob Boehme had set his theosophy in systems of sevens. He described seven "source spirits" (*Quell-Geister*) or qualities of God. The seventh and highest quality, "corpus," contains within itself all the others in a state of completion.[43] He described the Godhead as seven concentric circles.[44] Boehme tied this vision to the six days of creation and "the Sabbath or day of rest." It is "divine sound in power, or the realm of joy."[45] Yet Boehme did not observe the seventh day or advocate the practice.

Thomas Bromley, the English Philadelphian, used Boehme's theosophy to chart the soul's progress toward the presence of God in *The Way to the Sabbath of Rest* (1690). In the seventh and final stage, the "will is wrought up into a constant union with Christ." Raised above the material, the soul will be "more reduced to a passive silent waiting for the opening of the eternal temple."[46] Bromley did not observe the seventh day, nor was his book explicitly chiliastic. For Bromley, the Sabbath symbolized a mystical state of union with God in Christ.

The Germantown hermit Johannes Kelpius merged Sabbatarian metaphors with chiliastic eschatology from German Philadelphians such as Johann Wilhelm Petersen and his wife, Eleanora von Merlau Petersen.[47] They helped to spread the apocalyptic hopes of the English Philadelphian Society in the 1690s. In 1699 Kelpius advised Stephen Momfort to watch for signs of the "restitution of all things and glorious Sabbath, or the continual days of rest."[48] From the remnants of the Kelpius community, such as Conrad Matthäi, Beissel absorbed Sabbatarian metaphors and chiliastic thought from German and English Philadelphians. All of these influences fitted well with Beissel's Reformed background. Reformed Pietism stressed Sabbath observance on Sundays. The earlier Dutch movement, the *nadere reformatie*, and German Reformed ministers influenced by it, such as Samuel Nethenus, emphasized keeping Sunday as the Sabbath as a sign of piety.[49]

Beissel's *Mystyrion Anomias* combined a Calvinist emphasis on the Sabbath as the Law of God with the eschatology of German Philadelphians. The title, alluding to the "mystery of lawlessness" (II Thess. 2:3–10), heralds the chiliastic tone. The seventh day is "a type of Eternal Rest," prefiguring the coming millennium. Christians who do not observe the seventh day belong to the whore of Revelation,[50] a Radical Pietist metaphor for Europe's established churches.

Beissel worked out a numerology for his chiliasm. The number 6 represents churches enslaved to six days of work, meaning that they permit work on the Sabbath. Because three such established traditions, Catholic, Reformed, and Lutheran, observed the first day, they formed three 6's, or the number of the beast in Revelation: 666. Believers should leave "Babel," the Antichrist traditions, in the "evening of the sixth age," before the impending dawn of God's eternal Sabbath.

Beissel argued that the Sabbath was a free gift of God's grace. Keeping the seventh day enacts one's love for God.[51] With this latter argument Beissel adopted part of the Dunkers' rhetoric for immersion baptism out of obedience moved by love.[52] Here he added a pietistic modification to his more Calvinist claim that the Law commanded the Sabbath. In *Mystyrion Anomias* Beissel mentioned his Boehmist anthropology, referring to the "Virginal Man Adam," who had "pure, godly, and heavenly Wisdom as his Companion" in paradise. "Wisdom" refers to the divine Sophia, the female aspect of God, central to Boehme's theology. As Adam had been wed to Sophia, so Christ would wed the pure Church at the final, great Sabbath. The literal Sabbath each week is a joyous "Preludium" to that final rest.[53]

This first treatise briefly raised many aspects of Beissel's thoughts. With vestiges of a Calvinist theology of grace and Sabbath, Beissel embraced Radical Pietist chiliasm critical of the established churches. Beissel barely hinted at his Boehmist anthropology, but it is present. He called seekers to leave the established churches rather than try to improve them. "Antichrist doth not belong in the Seventh Time or Number, but must be destroyed."[54] This critique worked even in tolerant Pennsylvania, where Sunday laws led authorities to imprison a few of Beissel's group briefly for working on Sundays.[55]

Beissel's second early distinctive teaching was celibacy, derived more explicitly than Sabbatarianism from Radical Pietism. Gichtel loathed sexual intercourse, which he called "carnal whoring, also in the marital state," a "horror to God."[56] The early Dunkers valued celibacy, although they also accepted marriage. The early Inspirationists seem to have had reservations about marriage. While Beissel had contact with both these groups, he adopted Gichtel's stronger views.

Although no copies of Beissel's treatise *Die Ehe, das Zuchthaus fleischlicher Menschen* (1729) are known, the 1743 confession of faith, *Mistisches und KirchlichesZeuchnüß der Bruderschaft in Zion*, suggests some of the thought of the 1729 booklet. According to the *Mistisches und Kirchliches Zeuchnüß*, marriage was introduced as a "disciplinary ordinance for fallen people."[57] No one should remain in only one "school" (*Schule*) for a lifetime. Thus marriage "must be dissolved" for those who could advance to celibacy.

In addition to original hymns in Beissel's hymnal, *Göttliche Liebes- und Lobes-Gethöne*, Ben Franklin's press issued his *Mystische und sehr geheyme Sprueche* (Mystical and very secret sayings), both in 1730. In the latter work, Beissel demonstrated that he was creating mystical literature, speaking with a "new tongue," writing a language for the presence of God.

The meanings of the mystical sayings are often hidden. What may appear to be advice about marriage, family, and agriculture take on completely different meanings for initiates in Boehme's view of an androgynous God and Gichtel's teachings of celibate love for Sophia, the divine female. The sayings about marriage may best illustrate Beissel's early efforts to create a mystical language.

56. No single man shall see the face of God, for he lives for himself and brings forth no fruit. But whoever is in holy matrimony lives not for himself, for he seeks to please his wife, because in her he is fruitful. [Kein einzeler wird das angesicht Gottes schauen, dann er lebet ihm selber, und bringet keine frucht. Wer aber in der heiligen Ehe stehet, der lebet ihm selber nicht, dann er suchet seinem weibe zu gefallen, dieweil er in ihr fruchtbar ist.]

54. A man will much rather commit adultery with another's wife than to content himself with that wife which God has given him. [Der mensch bricht viel lieber die Ehe mit eines andern weib, als dasz er sich vergnügen läset, an dem weibe, dasz ihm Gott zugesellet.]

62. Forsake not the wife of your youth and be careful with all diligence, lest your heart fall to a foreign woman. [Verlasz nicht das weib deiner Jugend, und hüte dich mit allem fleisz, dasz dein Hertz keinem fremden weibe zufalle.][58]

At first these maxims appear to confirm traditional Christian teachings about marriage, fidelity, and childbirth. But in light of saying 53, "Wisdom is a beautiful thing, yet she has not many lovers, for she is chaste" (Die weiszheit ist ein schön ding, doch findet sie nicht viel liebhaber, dann sie ist keusch), completely different meanings emerge. The sayings do not advocate marriage at all; they advocate celibacy. Boehme, Arnold, and Gichtel had all written that only virgins can be betrothed to Sophia. Beissel followed Gichtel's extension of the marriage metaphor, instructing celibates to produce spiritual children, or new converts, with Sophia. Adulterers are those who forsake celibacy and Sophia for a human wife, as Adam did.

Most of the mystical sayings, like much of Beissel's subsequent writings, had a hidden sense that split the meanings of the words in two. Sachse missed the point by calling the maxims "simply moral proverbs, orthodox in the fullest sense." Walter Klein did little better, stating that Beissel's "effusions are estimable, but soporific." At least Klein recognized that they represent a "useful digest of Beissel's spirituality."[59]

A possible companion to the proverbs, the "Mystisches und sehr Geistreiches ABC" (Mystic and very spiritual ABC), was a rhymed acrostic that appeared at the end of the 1732 hymnal, *Vorspiel der Neuen Welt*.[60] The ABC served as a primer for those seeking God. "Be earnestly diligent to want nothing and to know nothing, so God will be everything to you, that you can be at rest," counseled Beissel. He paraphrased the words of the fourteenth-century mystic Johannes Tauler: "Immerse yourself in your not knowing and not wanting to know. Remain much more in silence and rest without illumination and feeling."[61]

Two sayings warned against judging the affairs of others.[62] Here Beissel embraced the individualism of Radical Pietism, in contrast to the disciplined ecclesiology of the Dunkers he had left. The Dunkers rejected what they called the "false freedom" of not offering or receiving correction. Here the Anabaptist ecclesiology and practice of the ban[63] led even further than such seventeenth-century Reformed Pietists as Samuel Nethenus and Theodor Undereyck, who advocated church discipline. Ephrata gradually abandoned the ban. By 1792, one of Beissel's successors, Georg Adam Martin, denounced the ban as pharisaical in a lengthy section of his *Christliche Bibliothek*.[64]

Conrad Beissel's early writings, while not systematic, reveal themes derived primarily from Jacob Boehme and Gichtel's transmission of them, especially through German and English branches of the Philadelphian Society. These themes included concepts of God with a female aspect, Divine Sophia, and the original human as created androgynous. Both undergirded his advocacy of celibacy. Beissel built his Sabbatarian views on radical chiliasm reinforced by Boehme's cycles of sevens. The maxims and ABC spun threads for weaving his mystical language for God's presence, in which silent eternity swallows up all words.[65]

BEISSEL'S THOUGHT: MATURE AND LATER WRITINGS

Between 1732 and 1742 the Ephrata community apparently published little other than a large hymnal, *Zionitischer WeyrauchsHügel*.[66] However, Beissel continued writing letters and poetry. A new flurry of publication after 1742 makes that year one plausible date for dividing the early from the maturing publications of the community. Further impetus to define their faith came from the troubled participation of the Ephrata Brethren in Count Zinzendorf's Pennsylvania synods in 1742. Ephrata also had acquired at least one press by 1745, which made publishing easier.[67] However, the theosophical epistles published in 1745 and the spiritual speeches published in 1773 included pieces written throughout Beissel's career. Thus it is difficult to determine which works published later reflect his later thought.

The first of Beissel's mature publications, aside from hymn texts, appeared in 1745. A volume of theosophical epistles, it appeared in two formats. The first, titled *Zionitischen Stiffts, I. Theil,* had a preface by Israel Eckerlin. The second version, without that preface, was released after Eckerlin's expulsion as *Urständliche und Erfahrungsvolle Hohe Zeugnüsse Wie man zum Geistlichen Leben Und dessen Vollkommenheit gelangen möge.* A recently discovered copy, now at the Ephrata Cloister, contains both prefaces and title pages.[68] With a new title page and six more letters, the work was reissued in 1773 as *Deliciae Ephratenses, Pars II.*

Beissel's other major mature published work was a volume of speeches, or *Geistliche Reden* (spiritual speeches, or sermons). Printed after his death as the first of the two volumes of *Deliciae Ephratenses* in 1773, the sermons, like the epistles, were not systematic. The preface indicated that they were not so much sermons as essays or devotions. In addition, Beissel wrote more letters and mystical sayings.[69]

The printed letters were preceded by thirty-eight *Gemütsbewegungen,* or meditations. Like the epistles, they mixed autobiography with religious teaching.[70] Of the letters, the first thirty-three were addressed to friends in Europe. Epistles 34–67 (34–73 in the longer variant) he wrote to female and male members in the Ephrata community. Some letters evidence conflict; others record Beissel's prophecies or speculations.[71]

Of the pieces in *Geistliche Reden,* the most significant are the first composition (which is not the first sermon) and the last sermon. The first is Beissel's *Dissertation on Man's Fall,* also known as the *Wunderschrift.* This work comes closest to presenting his religious views somewhat systematically. Its importance is clear in the fact that it was printed at least three times at Ephrata. The final sermon is a lengthy allegory, partly autobiographical, about the Church and the virginal life. These works are steeped in Boehme's and Gichtel's drama of sin and redemption framed in gender conflict.

Beissel often cast the mystical journey in apophatic language, or the *via negativa.*[72] A seeker prepares for the immediate presence of God through the denial and loss of self. Beissel wrote: "God is an incomprehensible Nothing, and I am an incomprehensible 'I,' and we will have to suffer . . . until all 'I'-ness and all Being is dissolved into Being Nothing, and all Something into the Nothing . . . where all 'I'-ness and all duplicity, where all self-ness ceases."[73]

In another meditation he described how this dissolution leads to union with God. "So we live in His holy Being: His life is our life, and we have become in Him that [which] we are, and what we are. His life is transformed in us, and [it] has transformed our nothingness and dissolved the bonds of futility. . . . He has become We, and we in our 'We'-ness have become nothing."[74] This language echoes some of Boehme's most mystical passages. In *De signatura rerum,* Boehme described at length how at the crucifixion Jesus took on humanity's sin and opened paradise for people. Boehme wrote: "So my inward person has died with Him in Christ's death. . . . Paradise will be in me. All that God the Father has and is will appear in me."[75] Gichtel echoed Boehme's thought: "When divine light broke through in my will [*Gemüt*], it showed me Jesus, and taught me to hold to Jesus, so my 'I'-ness and knowing had to be put to death."[76] Beissel drew from both to shape his language for the presence of God.

Two earlier writers, John Jacoby and F. Ernest Stoeffler, commented on apophatic mysticism at Ephrata. Jacoby noted self-renunciation as of "first in importance" in Beissel's approach to being joined to God. Stoeffler saw self-renunciation and withdrawal as the two most prominent emphases of Ephrata mysticism. Stoeffler characterized their self-denial as avoiding all "enjoyments and physical pleasures," especially "gratification of the sex impulse." In comments based primarily on the *Dissertation,* Stoeffler's emphasis on withdrawal at Ephrata ignored the group's active charity to the indigent, which Beissel taught and the cloister often offered.[77]

Beissel also cast the mystical journey in cataphatic language,[78] or the *via positiva,* in which the soul gains union to Christ, or Sophia, much as in a marriage. Heinrich Horch, Gottfried Arnold, and others at the turn of the eighteenth century had helped to make this spiritual metaphor more popular again among Protestants.[79] Beissel developed the bridal imagery extensively in the *Dissertation* and the last sermon of the *Geistliche Reden.*

Beissel's use of the metaphor of marriage to Christ or Sophia goes further than Stoeffler's observation that "love for Christ" was "the most outstanding" emphasis in Ephrata's mysticism. Beissel saw this love as so consuming that one would forsake human marriage in exchange for total surrender to God. Stoeffler acknowledged that Ephrata "made it their chief care in this life to be one with Christ in the perfection of love."[80] Both Jacoby and Stoeffler, however, believed that Beissel overly stressed the relationship with Christ to the point of abhorring sex. Indeed, Jacoby's criticism of Ephrata's celibacy overshadowed all his analysis.

Beissel's *Dissertation on Man's Fall* summarized his major beliefs in an account of the spiritual journey. It was first published in 1765, in an English translation by Peter Miller. The first German edition, with annotations by Peter Miller, was published in 1773 as the first essay in *Deliciae Ephratenses, Pars I.* The preface to a German edition published in 1789 stated that the work had appeared in 1760.[81] The *Chronicon,* however, claimed that during intense inspiration and illness around 1741 Beissel wrote a *Wunderschrifft*, which the *Chronicon* identified as the *Dissertation*. Sachse claimed to have seen a manuscript copy of the original and to possess a copy of the first edition, which he dated 1745. Since this copy lacks a title page, the date of the first publication remains open. Nevertheless, a German version of the *Dissertation* surely existed before the version of 1765.

Appearing at first to be a psychosexual hodgepodge, upon closer examination the *Dissertation* actually possesses a kind of internal order. Beissel framed the work with a prologue and conclusion based on his personal religious experience, typical of Pietist literature.[82] The introduction reveals his inner struggles as he learned the secret of the cross and of the fall of the first human.[83] The conclusion ends with his desire to be united to Sophia, the female aspect of God.

Seven identifiable theological topics appear in the *Dissertation*'s body: (1) Lucifer's rebellion (the archetypal sin) and the doctrine of God; (2) creation and sin (the two falls); (3) ministry and authority; (4) soteriology; (5) Christology/Sophiology; (6) ecclesiology; and (7) restoration (eschatology), dealing first with restoration generally, then with the order of restoration.[84]

The *Dissertation* opened with the question of theodicy, inquiring "where the power of evil originated." Beissel lamented that the "very desire to do good caused the evil in me to be so active."[85] Boehme's influence is evident, for theodicy plays an important role in his works.[86] Beissel's answer began with the fall of the first human. Beissel, like Gichtel, blamed the fall on Adam's observation of animals and his desire to be sexually differentiated like them, leading to "adultery" with Sophia, Adam's intended spouse. This desire, according to Beissel, mirrored Lucifer's primal rebellion, which had separated divine gender characteristics in God.[87]

The second topic of the *Dissertation* further develops Beissel's concept of Adam's two falls into sin. Beissel held Boehme's and Gichtel's view that the first human was androgynous, as God was. Physiologically Adam bore the divine image in that he lacked genitals and intestines. Adam absorbed nourishment "magically" from paradisial fruit and had the potential to reproduce without sex.[88]

Boehme had not identified two distinct falls. In *Der Weg zu Christo*, however, he implied at least two components to Adam's fall.[89] Boehme held that Adam fell into sin when his "Imagination" turned away from desiring God, without identifying which desires turned Adam away.[90] Gichtel claimed that the first part of the fall occurred as Adam named the animals and "saw the tinctures [i.e., genders] separated" (*die Tincturen geschieden*). When Adam realized that he lacked a gender-differentiated mate, his "imagination" desired a mate. He fell asleep, and Sophia, the divine female characteristic, "went into her ether and Eve was revealed."[91]

Beissel wrote that as Adam saw the differentiated animals, he committed adultery against the heavenly Sophia by desiring a physical mate. Then Adam's "heavenly femaleness withdrew from him," and he "fell down and died." For Beissel, this was not a literal death but the sleep during which God created Eve. This was the first fall. God now placed even more weight on the commandment not to eat the fruit of the tree of the knowledge of good and evil. Here Beissel drew from his Reformed background. Through the strictness of the Law, sin would be revealed through the transgression itself.[92] The sin Beissel worried about was not Calvin's satanic pride but the sexual desire for a mate against which Gichtel warned.[93]

According to Beissel, the second fall occurred when Eve "meddled with the serpent" and was "poisoned more by the serpent's magic than its words."[94] Disobeying God's command not to eat the forbidden fruit gave them a false wisdom, resulting in sexual desire. The first couple lost the fading vestiges of androgyny. With Boehme, Beissel rejected Calvin's doctrine of predestination.[95] Beissel wrote that God gave all people free will, which is not the "cause of our damnation" [*Ursach unserer Verdammnus*] but a sign of God's love and mercy. Yet Beissel acknowledged that people with free will do not "reach for the better" (*greifen wir nicht nach dem Bessern*).[96]

Beissel did not reject completely a concept of original sin, as Peter Erb and others have pointed out.[97] Beissel did not accept the Mennonite and Dunker view that infants are covered by the grace of Christ until they reach the age to confess sin and faith.[98] By Beissel's time, the Swiss Anabaptists had accepted Dutch Mennonite statements on this point.[99] Beissel claimed that although infants "have not sinned, they are not therefore innocent, for there is in them an evil manner." He concluded not that they were automatically damned but that "through a kind of purgatory they must be separated from original evil." The Mennonites and Dunkers accused him of spreading heresy.[100] Yet even with this theology, Beissel did not draw the conclusion that infant baptism is necessary.

The fourth theme in Beissel's *Dissertation*, soteriology, appears in gendered terms. (The third theme, ministry and authority, will be discussed below.) Under the fourth topic, Beissel asked how can the "God-troubled femaleness come again to her true husband, so that he does not dominate her in grimness?" Jesus Christ is the one virginal man (*jungfräulicher Mann*), possessing "heavenly femaleness" (*himmlische Weiblichkeit*), who remained obedient unto death and a faithful "husband" (*Mann*) to Sophia, thus atoning for Adam's rebellious male self-will.[101]

"Christ," wrote Beissel, "is now the reconciliation between fire and light, and has made again one out of both."[102] These terms reflect Boehmist concepts. Fire is wrath, the "principle" of God the Father. Light warms but does not burn. It is the "principle" of the Son, who embodies the love and mercy of God. Fire and light illustrate how God's wrath and mercy can be reconciled in one God. Beissel, like Boehme, locates this reconciliation in Jesus Christ.

The center of Beissel's thought consists of a twofold rebirth to reverse Adam's twofold fall into sin. This concept appears in many of his letters as well as the *Dissertation*. The concern for rebirth reflects Pietism's adaptation of the central Protestant concern for justification by faith alone. Israel Acrelius, the Swedish Lutheran minister, rightly noted that at Ephrata, justification by faith was not forensic, or *non imputata,* the classic Protestant understanding of justification.[103] For Beissel, the Law's condemnation leads sinners to experiential rebirth, not imputed righteousness.

Spiritual rebirth, for Beissel, takes place through two conversions. Neither Boehme nor Gichtel had a concept of two distinct conversions. For Beissel, "awakening" to one's sinfulness leads to a first conversion. One turns to rules, hoping to overcome sinfulness through outer works of morality. But the first conversion aims only at "innocence and purity of body," falling short of total spiritual renovation.[104] In the first conversion, one stands before the first death, or natural death, which is less painful than the second death. One hopes to be rewarded for good works. Since the first conversion cannot remove sin in its "innermost root," however, the believer "must be condemned to death as an evildoer." The "will must begin to sink down into its own Nothing and doubt its good works."[105]

The second death is the "secret and mystic death" (*geheimen und mystischen Tode*), in which "life and salvation in its innermost root, with power within, is revealed." The mystic death is more painful, because there is no hope of reward. Works are inadequate because through the Law "our best works are made as sin," so that humans will fully deny self. Then "grace shows itself when the person is killed through the Law." This death leads to "new life in God through His Spirit," marked by repentance and amendment of living.[106] Baptism by immersion in water confirms this "new covenant of grace" (*neuer Bund der Gnaden*), whose promises "rest on the death of Jesus Christ." Believers must be "brought through baptism into conformity with his death," which promises resurrection.[107]

While Beissel used Calvinist language about sin, law, and death, he fused it with mystical language of death and rebirth through grace, to be followed by a moral and penitent life. For Beissel, rebirth was not a reward for the sheer effort of repentance, as his detractors often maintained. Stoeffler too hastily claimed that "love was substituted for the concept of saving faith" at Ephrata.[108] Rather, Beissel's dismissal of good works led to a spiritual, mystical identification with Christ's death and resurrection, apprehended through faith, that enabled a life of repentance founded on grace.

The fifth theme in the *Dissertation,* Christology, Beissel had already broached. Under this heading Beissel described spiritual rebirth through mystic death in a different way. For birth into new spiritual life, the mystic death becomes a mystic impregnation (*Schwängerung*). He wrote that "everything that is brought into dying through death on the cross, all of that will be delivered to the eternal Spirit, or to the heavenly Motherhood, for glorious flourishing in the womb."[109] This passage expresses one of Beissel's conceptualizations of the Trinity, in which "God is our father, Christ is our brother, and the Holy Spirit is our mother."[110] In this view, which is not Beissel's only Trinitarian formula, the Spirit acts with Sophia, "the eternal mother, or heavenly femaleness," to give spiritual birth to believers.[111]

The third theme in Beissel's *Dissertation* is ministry and authority. Beissel criticized "unreborn" ecclesiastical and secular authorities who lacked the "word of heavenly impregnation" (*das Wort in der himmlischen Besamung*), which the apostles had internally. Without rebirth, a leader is only "a steward over the animal characteristic" (*Verwalter über die thierische Eigenschafft*). A "servant of the new covenant" (*Diener des neuen Bundes*) must be spiritually reborn.[112]

In the *Dissertation* Beissel barely mentioned the "congregation or community [*Gemeinde*] of the Christian Church," his sixth topic. The Church consists of those who die with Christ on the cross and have been "delivered into the womb of the eternal Mother."[113] The Church was perhaps the most conflicted topic of Beissel's theology, reflecting both his separatism and his affiliation with religious groups. Brief examples from some of his other writings will help illumine his concept of Church.

In early treatises Beissel contrasted the "true Church" or "children of God" with the "false church," the whore of Revelation. Small and persecuted, the "true Church" speaks "with new tongues" about the presence of God.[114] Despair that a "true Church" could never be attained led many Radical Pietists to separate from the institutional churches. Yet many, like Kelpius and Hochmann von Hochenau,[115] also sought out the loving fellowship of the "philadelphian" church, a noninstitutional fellowship of mutual love. This tension is clear in Beissel's cycles of living alternately in solitude and as director of a visible community.[116]

The true Church, according to Beissel, is marked by at least two signs: prophecy and suffering. Beissel claimed that the outpouring of "the spirit of prophecy" (*Geist der Weissagung*) inaugurated the Church at Ephrata.[117] The "Babel church," or established churches of Europe, lost the "Holy Spirit, which unifies all language."[118] But at Ephrata, at the end of time, the "prophetic Spirit" was gathering the true Church, which "speaks the one mother language."[119] Ephrata's unique language, according to Beissel, came directly from the Spirit.

As for the second identifying mark of the Church, even the name Ephrata signified suffering to Beissel. In place of Beissel's planned solitude, "Ephrata built itself up in pure suffering and distress." According to the *Chronicon*, the name came from his allegorical reading of the death of Rachel in childbirth on her way to Ephrath(a), or Bethlehem (Gen. 35:16–20).[120] Rachel represented Beissel's beloved solitude. When his followers arrived, the solitude evaporated, and the community brought more struggle. He often quoted a passage that Gichtel paraphrased, "We must pass through many tribulations into the Kingdom of God" (Acts 14:22).[121] This suffering as a mark of the Church stands in paradox with the "sweet love" of Christ/Sophia, which is like a noble pearl. While suffering "tastes bitter to our nature" and brings us to Christ's cross, this is God's great sweetness.[122] When Ephrata's believers focused excessively on their penitential lives, self-pity at times replaced their joy in Christ's presence, as Stoeffler noted. This joy faded somewhat in Beissel's later writings.[123]

Beissel, like Gichtel, believed that his followers, the so-called priests of Melchizedek, could effect forgiveness for others through prayer.[124] Consequently Beissel sometimes exaggerated the merits of his ministry as he aged. Although capable of humility, Beissel also indulged at times in self-aggrandizement, prompting accusations of messianic pretensions, as Christopher Saur charged in 1739.[125] When Beissel lost sight of Christ the High Priest, he could be quite egotistical. When his followers sought balance in their spiritual lives, they embodied a community of prayerful ministry to the needy.

In later years, the atoning power of the Priesthood of Melchizedek apparently contributed to a belief by some at Ephrata that God would not even see any sinful acts they might commit.[126] Sangmeister accused Beissel of preaching that "God neither knew or saw" the community's evil.[127] Beissel never wrote such a claim explicitly, but his exaggerations in regard to the Priesthood of Melchizedek could lead to such a conclusion.

Restoration, the seventh and final topic of the *Dissertation,* was a belief popular among Radical Pietists. Johann Wilhelm and Eleanora von Merlau Petersen claimed to have discovered independently the doctrine of a universal restoration in 1694, although Merlau inclined toward this view before her marriage in 1680. Jane Leade, the Philadelphian Society leader, wrote in 1694 that she received a vision about this belief in 1693. The Petersens had read Leade's book.[128] According to the doctrine of universal restoration, after a long period of purification after death, the souls of sinners will be restored by God's love to fellowship in the presence of God. Leade proposed that even the devil would be restored to God. Hochmann defended universal restoration in his 1702 confession of faith. Alexander Mack included it in his *Rechte und Ordnungen,*[129] although it is not clear that the Dunkers were unanimous in this belief. Christoph Schütz (1693–1750), another Radical Pietist in Germany, defended universal restoration as a coming golden time, but denied restoration of the devil.[130]

In the *Dissertation,* the final restoration would end male domination, purging creation of violence and power. All of creation would then be restored to eternal androgyny.[131] Yet in one letter Beissel wrote that godless people would be cast out "to the devil" and be "tortured for eternity and eternity, in an indissoluble bond of pain."[132] However, little else by Beissel supports this passage. In general he believed in universal restoration.

Beissel's *Dissertation* did not present all of his religious thought. It does reveal the Boehmist foundation for his beliefs about God, creation, sin and salvation, Christ and Sophia, proper rule in the Church, and restoration. In the *Dissertation* the intensities of some of his earlier writings have shifted, especially regarding conversion and eschatology. These shifts do not signal that he abandoned the earlier views. The last of his *Geistliche Reden* shows continuity in the themes of his early and mature ministry, even if modes of expression changed. Throughout, Beissel used heavily allegorical language that sometimes hid as much as it revealed.

The most remarkable of the sixty-seven *Geistliche Reden* is the last. It is titled "Very Secret Riddle Hidden from the World Concerning the Eternal Mother's Church Time and State: and What it will be, When the Same Is Revealed after Her Long Widowhood."[133] By placing it last in the printed sermons, Miller set it as a conclusion to the framework that began with the text of the *Dissertation.* These two works reveal much of the core of Beissel's views and his use of language for seeking the presence of God.

The last sermon begins in the first person. Praising God for refining him until he was without will, a young man rejoices as his presumably elderly widowed mother arranges his wedding to a noble virgin. The mother disciplines and cares for him. The hidden virgin has courted no others.[134] Both the mother and the virgin represent the divine Sophia as well as the Church. The widowed mother also recalls Beissel's own mother.

The young man seeks an "unspoiled virgin" with whom to have unblemished children "like the dew of the red dawn," like angels. He has saved his virginity until his wedding day. The youth's chastity earned the virgin's affection.[135] This is surely a rare literary instance of a man's boasting about preserving his virginity. Whether it pertained to Beissel factually is an open question, although he claimed as much.

Upon finding "coarse threads" (*groben Faden*) in his linen wedding garment, the young man appeals to the mother, who reworks it. Suddenly the narrative shifts from first to third person. The young man is now an unruly child who takes the clothes to a tailor for alteration. Unable to manage the child, the mother first tries patience. Then she offers a breast to the child, who only beats the air. She puts the boy off her lap, disciplines him with a rod, and casts him out. The narrator comments that "the expulsion of the child from this land created a great stir."[136] Here the first mother may imply Sophia's discipline[137] while also alluding autobiographically to Beissel's expulsion (or departure) from the Palatinate.

An old widow in an old castle hears the child's cry and invites him by letter to live with her. She reveals that she was rejected by her husband long ago. Here the widow is similar to Sophia as a widow, who was rejected by Adam. The old widow informs the boy that the first mother who rejected him was not "the true wife of the husband, but a mean-spirited one," whom the husband took because he rejected "the true wife"—that is, the second widow.[138]

The old widow secretly spreads a table with wine and bread in the youth's room. Still in love with the virgin, he is "not yet old enough to have a wedding."[139] Nevertheless, a wedding festival begins, and he dances with the bride.

Suddenly an angry alarm is raised. Enemies "from Amon and Moab," from "Edom," with "the Egyptians and the Moors," come to trample the bride and the widow's children, because it is the last night before the glorious wedding day. The enemies may represent civil and ecclesiastical authorities, or members of the various religious traditions in Europe warring against dissenters. Suddenly an "eternal king" intervenes, and the old mother's appearance changes to blinding glory. Watchers announce the approaching bridegroom's procession. Many people fall asleep, saying that only commoners will attend the wedding. Meanwhile, a different bridegroom, not the youth, arrives. The groom enters the palace silently and the door is shut.[140]

The wedding is supposed to last one long week, more than seven days. At first, guests eat only common fare. At midweek the old mother sends a maid to bring a golden goblet of the best wine from a small cask. All of the guests get giddily drunk and prophesy. Some bystanders insult them, but an angel dazes the grumblers. The second old widow can be both Sophia and the hidden Church for which Beissel longed. Her wine bestows the gift of prophecy, which for Beissel was a mark of the true Church. In a different letter Beissel wrote that the outpouring of the Holy Spirit makes "us so drunk and mindless that we may be led into the bridal chamber" of union with Sophia.[141] The drunkenness and prophecy probably represent Beissel's belief that the Spirit visited Ephrata uniquely.

On the last day of the wedding, the youth prepares for marriage. The virgin begins to direct music, and the guests sing. On this evening a "virginal host as though in concert" (or in prelude, *im Vorspiel*) gather, dancing and making bridal wreaths for one another.[142] The virginal choir may represent Ephrata members living in celibacy while awaiting Christ's return.

The youth's wedding does not take place and the text suddenly breaks out of allegory. Although some might have thought that the "eternal Sabbath" had arrived, it was not to be. This was not the wedding banquet of the Lamb but the wedding of the mother to the right husband. Beissel may have implied that the community at Ephrata was not, after all, the eschatalogical community. Rather, they had merely found the right leader (meaning Beissel) to prepare them for the Lamb's wedding. Beissel could also mean that Sophia had found in him the right husband, or leader, for her offspring. Ephrata was "a fore-Sabbath" but not yet the final wedding.[143]

Beissel then narrates an apocalyptic vision of the virginal host in God's final victory. Jesus has sanctified them in their virginity. They have not a fire of wrath but a "virginal fire" that is won "through the sweating of blood and afterward the Cross." This victory conquers "the dragon" and all who whored with it. Then the earth will be set on fire and pass away.[144]

At last the narrator sees the "promised virgin." A voice tells him to practice "annihilation of my [Beissel's] self [*Verwerden meiner selbst*], that I may learn the holy sinking down into the self, and in consequence, become virginal myself."[145] Then the promised virgin would "encompass me with a paradisial little flame of light, completely transform me in her, and make me female, and at the same time incorporate me in her upper choir of virgins, who together make up the bride of the Lamb. As soon as the number is full, a wedding will indeed be held."[146] At this final wedding, "the Lord our God will be only One," and will rule. The oneness of God refers also to a final unification of the genders, divided since Lucifer's fall. In this final union, anticipated in the mystical life on earth, Beissel concludes, "Now my wedding is also held. Amen. Hallelujah."[147]

The final sermon ends the volume much as it began, with mystical discourse centered on a spiritual union for Beissel to the divine female through self-denial. The sermon grandly recapitulates Beissel's lifelong distinctive teachings of the seventh-day Sabbath (i.e., the end of the weeklong wedding), celibacy, prophecy, and radical eschatology. The sermon expresses some images from his own hard life as an orphan and refugee. Typical of Gichtel's ambiguous metaphors, the widows, virgins, and brides in the allegory overlap, portraying Sophia, the Church, the bride of Christ, and Beissel's mother and homeland.

The sermon may appear to parallel Johann Valentin Andreae's *Chymische Hochzeit Christiani Rosenkreutz* (The chemical wedding of Christian Rosenkreutz). Both allegories are about a weeklong wedding at a castle, with a mysterious virgin figure. However, striking differences separate the allegories. Beissel's narrator's white garment lacks the distinctive insignia (four red roses) of Christian Rosenkreutz's. Beissel's allegory lacks secret vaults, inscriptions, and coffins with corpses. In Beissel's allegory, mothers, widows, and virgins marry, but no king or queen appears as host, as in the Rosenkreutz tale. Beissel devotes no special day to alchemy. His sermon involves mostly commoners rather than the noble and wise elite of the Rosenkreutz allegory. Beissel's tale ends with an apocalyptic vision and personal mystical union with God within the virginal Church. The *Chymische Hochzeit* ends with Rosenkreutz's induction into the "Knights of the Golden Stone."[148] The significant differences between the *Chymische Hochzeit* and Beissel's sermon outweigh the likenesses. The dissimilarities argue against any theory that Beissel was writing an explicitly Rosicrucian allegory.

Conrad Beissel's theology, built from Gichtel's transmission of Boehme and the German and English Philadelphians, expresses both an individual and a communal quest for redemption from a twofold primal sin rooted in sexual desire. His mystical language led pilgrims to a twofold conversion, consummated in a "mystic death," the end of all one's good efforts. The mystic death was synonymous with the mystic impregnation, a rebirth into a priestly, celibate life of penance, prayer, and service. This mystic death and rebirth were the gifts of God's sheer grace, not a reward for heroic asceticism.

RELIGIOUS THOUGHT: CONRAD BEISSEL

Beissel's mystical language guided seekers in further purgation and illumination empowered by grace after rebirth, anticipating union with God and the union of genders through Christ/Sophia in the eternal Sabbath. This theological centerpiece, which Beissel uniquely synthesized from a variety of sources, was shared and at times contested at Ephrata.

THE RELIGIOUS THOUGHT OF EPHRATA

Other Writers

Other writers at Ephrata shared many of Beissel's religious views, even if they disliked Beissel. Two of them, Johannes Hildebrand and Ezechiel Sangmeister, often criticized Beissel but shared much of his theology and commitment to the Sabbath and celibacy.[1] An exploration of their writings reveals that many of Ephrata's distinctive beliefs were broadly shared in the community, and were not the results of one domineering leader.

JOHANNES HILDEBRAND

Johannes Hildebrand's (1679–1765) immigration date remains uncertain. He bought land at Germantown, where he was a tawer [*Weisgerber*]. According to Ezechiel Sangmeister, Hildebrand had been married fifty-four years when he died. Hildebrand and his wife had five daughters and five sons.[2]

Sangmeister claimed that Hildebrand had been "awakened" thirty years at the time of his death in 1765. This reference could not have been to Hildebrand's first religious activity, since Sangmeister reported Hildebrand's association with the Dunkers in Germantown when the Conestoga congregation was organized, in 1724. The *Chronicon* described Hildebrand as "one of the first awakened in Germany," at the beginning of the eighteenth century.[3] Sangmeister reported that Hildebrand moved to the Conestoga area in the summer of 1726 to associate with Beissel's congregation, leaving the Dunkers because they had "only an empty shape and form." He sold his farm in Germantown to Anna Eckerlin, the widow of Michael Eckerlin and mother of the young men who would lead a division at Ephrata twenty years later.[4] By 1727 Hildebrand had come into conflict with Beissel. In 1728 Hildebrand joined the Dunkers at Conestoga, who did not follow Beissel, and was reportedly made a minister.[5] Around 1736 he moved back to Germantown, leaving the Conestoga farm to his children.[6] His daughter Margaretha[7] married Johann Valentin Mack in Germantown, presumably by 1732, when their daughter was born. Hildebrand returned to Ephrata around 1738 with the Macks and some others from Germantown.[8]

A "great lover of the mystical writings" with "deep insight into the writings of Jacob Boehme,"[9] Hildebrand probably was among the abler students of Boehme at Ephrata. In 1743 he wrote some polemical pieces against the Moravians that also expounded his theology. They included a Boehmist account of spiritual rebirth, *Schrifftmässiges Zeuchnüß von dem Himmlischen und Jungfräulichen Gebährungs-Werck* (Written testimony concerning the heavenly and virginal birthing work) and a piece on conversion and sanctification, *Wohlgegründetes Bedencken der Christlichen Gemeine in und bey Ephrata von dem Weg der Heiligung* (Well-grounded consideration of the Christian Church in and by Ephrata concerning the way of sanctification). He also wrote a longer work on spiritual rebirth that was reprinted in Württemberg, *Eine Ruffende Wächterstimme* (A calling voice of the watcher). He wrote a treatise on comets and later published a critique of congregational life.[10] The *Schrifftmässiges Zeuchnüß* shows strong similarities to Ephrata's confession of faith, the *Mistisches und Kirchliches Zeuchnüß der Brüderschaft in Zion* (Mystic and churchly testimony of the Brotherhood in Zion) (1743).

Although the title indicates its origins in the Zionitic Brotherhood, the *Mistisches und Kirchliches Zeuchnüß* gives the best single summary of Ephrata's beliefs and practices. It reflects much of Beissel's thought, ending with a lengthy verbatim quotation from his first theosophical epistle. Sachse and many subsequent historians mistakenly contended that the Zionitic

Brotherhood was a clandestine order based on "the Egyptian cult of mystic Freemasonry."[11] On the contrary, the *Zeuchnüß* has strong parallels to writings by Beissel, confirming that the document reliably presents the community's beliefs.

The *Mistisches und Kirchliches Zeuchnüß* also bears similarities to Hildebrand's *Schrifftmässiges Zeuchnüß*, suggesting that he had a strong hand in writing the confession. Prefatory comments in Hildebrand's treatise on sanctification strengthen this possibility. He noted that the Zionitic Brotherhood had composed their confession of faith and that others at Ephrata had written against the Moravians, but all the works were set aside and not published. Then friends of Hildebrand requested to see Ephrata's answers to Moravian accusations. Hildebrand wrote, "The brothers handed their writing over to me" and "did not let it go to print," referring to the *Mistisches und Kirchliches Zeuchnüß*. Hildebrand reported that the brotherhood did not oppose his sending the work to press.[12] Thus he was probably the final editor and contributing author of the *Mistisches und Kirchliches Zeuchnüß*. The similarities to Beissel's thought show fundamental agreements between him and Hildebrand.

The *Chronicon* reports several polemical works written against the Moravians contemporaneous with the *Mistisches und Kirchliches Zeuchnüß*. Beissel ordered "a brother" to write against their "undisciplined life and carnal quest for conversion."[13] This was probably the little tract *Unpartheyisches Bedencken Ueber das Bekehrungs-Werck der Herrenhutischen Gemeine in Pennsylvanien* (Nonpartisan reflections on the conversion work of the Moravian Church in Pennsylvania). It is bound and consecutively paginated with the *Mistisches und Kirchliches Zeuchnüß*. The specific reference to conversion in the tract's title suggests that this is the work to which the *Chronicon* refers.

Sachse, however, inserted into his citation of the *Chronicon* passage the name of Jaebez, or Peter Miller, as the author of the pamphlet, which Sachse assumed was the *Mistisches und Kirchliches Zeuchnüß*. He believed that the pamphlet's "style and temperate argument" verified Miller's authorship. Furthermore, Sachse mentioned the series of publications related to Hildebrand without discussing their contents. Seidensticker did not identify an author for the *Mistisches und Kirchliches Zeuchnüß*, but he left open the implication of Miller's authorship by referring to the pamphlet and to the unknown scope of Miller's work at Ephrata. These interpolations lack documentation and are unconvincing.[14]

The *Chronicon* also reported that the prior, Israel Eckerlin, wrote a supplement to the anti-Moravian polemic on conversion, *Unpartheyisches Bedencken*, "which was not less biting."[15] Eckerlin's piece is probably the tract appended to *Unpartheyisches Bedencken,* titled *Ein Kurtzer Bericht von den Ursachen, warum die Gemeinschafft in Ephrata sich mit dem Graffen Zinzendorf und seinen Leuten eingelassen* (A short report of the causes, why the community in Ephrata involved themselves with Count Zinzendorf and his people). *Ein Kurtzer Bericht* indicates that the author regretted an initial openness to the Moravians. This matches the *Chronicon*'s description of the work and Eckerlin's initial contacts with Zinzendorf. The work is consecutively paginated with the *Mistisches und Kirchliches Zeuchnüß* and *Unpartheyisches Bedencken*. Surviving copies have all three works bound together, even though different authors wrote them. Hildebrand, however, seems to have given final shape to the brothers' confession of faith.

The *Mistisches und Kirchliches Zeuchnüß* presents Ephrata's beliefs under seven numbered headings plus a final unnumbered one: (1) "God and the Fall of the Human"; (2) "The Spread of the Human Family and the Church of the Old Covenant"; (3) "Christ Jesus, the Mediator of the New Covenant"; (4) "The Christian Church"; (5) "The Twofold Estates in the Church"; (6) "The Church's Rule"; (7) "Submission and School Discipline"; and the final article, "The First Awakening of Repentance and Faith, etc. and the Judgment of God Concerning Fallen Humanity."[16]

In the *Mistisches und Kirchliches Zeuchnüß,* the first article on the doctrine of God opens with lines from Tauler: "Gott ist ein einiges Ein, ein unbegreifliches Nichts, ein unumfaßliches und unsichtbares Wesen."[17] This passage mirrors Beissel's nineteenth meditation in the theosophical epistles, where he wrote that "God is an incomprehensible Nothing."

The first article also reflects Gichtel's adaptation of Boehme's creation story. Adam was created so that "Wisdom as his maiden was betrothed to him." As a result of Lucifer's poisoning of creation, through Adam's "too strong Imagination, his eye became impure. Then the Virgin Sophia left him because her chaste marriage bed was soiled." Because "the Fall had to be revealed in Adam's essence and root," God "let a tree of temptation grow the fragile fruit of Good and Evil."[18] The second fall occurred when Adam and Eve ate this fruit. This first article repeats Beissel's more detailed view of the two falls in the *Dissertation on Man's Fall.*

The second article of the *Mistisches und Kirchliches Zeuchnüß* explains the Sabbath and the further sins of humanity, leading to the priesthood of Aaron and "the church of the Old Covenant." God added the seventh day and "blessed it in a special way" because of the "wheel of the six days" resulting from human sins. The Sabbath is "a high precious gift of grace from God" (*ein hochtheures Gnaden-Geschenck Gottes*). It will last "until the anxious birth of the six days' work of the children of God is dissolved and is transformed into the same Sabbath."[19] This article summarizes the brief description of the Sabbath in Boehme's *Magnum Mysterium*,[20] and agrees with part of Beissel's explanation of the Sabbath in *Mystyrion Anomias*. Beissel's eschatological view of the Sabbath is present but somewhat less pronounced in the *Mistisches und Kirchliches Zeuchnüß*. Beissel's defense of the Sabbath in *Mystyrion Anomias*, based partly on the Mosaic law, is absent here, showing Ephrata's continued drift away from Beissel's early Calvinism.

The second article notes that God instituted the priesthood of Aaron because in Adam's fall "the grim fire torture was ignited." The fire of God's wrath required appeasement until Christ would come as reconciler, embodying the "love of the Father." According to Gichtel, the Aaronic priesthood was founded and kindled "with the wrath fire," unlike the Priesthood of Melchizedek, which was founded "with the love fire."[21] Drawing on Gichtel's thought, the *Mistisches und Kirchliches Zeuchnüß* states that the Aaronic priesthood arrogates power to forgive sins through animal sacrifices. In contrast, Christ instituted the Priesthood of Melchizedek by offering himself as a sacrifice.

God required animals to be sacrificed because Adam fell into sin by speculating on their divided genders,[22] a point that the *Mistisches und Kirchliches Zeuchnüß* explained in more detail than Beissel's *Dissertation*. As spiritual priests of Melchizedek, some Ephrata celibates abstained for a time from meat and from using animal labor.[23] They believed that since God ended animal sacrifice with Christ's death, spiritually reborn Christians should not kill animals or work them. How extensively the celibates observed a vegetarian diet remains uncertain. Their reluctance to kill animals ran parallel to their pacifism, which they held at least until the Revolutionary War.[24]

In addition to milder views about animal labor and general pacifism, Ephrata rejected slavery, as did the Dunkers and Mennonites. Ephrata printed in 1763 the first German translation of the Quaker Anthony Benezet's critique of slavery. However, Jacob Kimmel (1757–1814) held in slavery an African-American woman between 1787 and 1789. This is the only known instance of slaveholding at Ephrata, and occurred twenty years after Beissel died.[25]

The third article in the *Mistisches und Kirchliches Zeuchnüß*, on Christology, notes that believers must have experiential, not just intellectual, faith in Christ. "If Christ is to be resurrected according to the inward understanding of the spirit in us, so he must first be crucified to us according to the knowledge of the letter."[26]

Calling this the "high holy secret of our restoration" (*hoch-heiliges Geheimnuss unserer Wiederbringung*), the author counsels a personal identification with

Christ in death and resurrection and an experiential rebirth. This view is nearly identical with that of Hildebrand's treatise *Wohlgegründetes Bedencken*. In that work Hildebrand contended that one must "die daily, that is, one repents daily and is made perfect in Christ."[27] The Christology and soteriology of both the *Mistisches und Kirchliches Zeuchnüß* and Hildebrand's *Wohlgegründetes Bedencken* direct believers to a mystical, spiritual identification with Christ's death and resurrection.

The third article also confesses Christ as "Son of the living God," the "express image of his being," who "put on our humanity over his heavenly humanity." Jesus overcame the powers of darkness in Gethsemane, "completed his holy sacrifice on the cross," and went "below with the power of reconciliation which he won to preach to spirits in prison." Finally "resurrected from the dead," he "ascended into heaven and dissolved the church of the Old Covenant."[28] He founded the "church of the New Covenant" (*Kirche des neuen Bundes*) with the patriarchs, whereupon followed "the outpouring of the Holy Spirit" (*die Ausgiessung des H.[eiligen] Geistes erfolget*).

Using Boehmist language, the author notes that "the divine birthing work (*das Göttliche Gebährungs-Werck*)" was now possible, because "now Adam's cleft [or tear, *Riß*] was healed, and Wisdom entered again into the open side of her virginal husband, Jesus."[29] This passage repeats nearly verbatim a passage about the crucifixion in Hildebrand's *Schrifftmässiges Zeuchnüß*. It also echoes Beissel's soteriology in his *Dissertation* and in some of his letters. However, the *Mistisches und Kirchliches Zeuchnüß* lacks the more detailed speculation on Christ's androgyny found in Beissel's *Dissertation*. This Christology imported heterodox concepts from Boehme that churchly Pietism, Protestant Orthodoxy, and contemporary Dutch and Swiss Anabaptists would not have accepted.

Ecclesiology occupies the fourth through sixth articles of the *Mistisches und Kirchliches Zeuchnüß*, far more space than Beissel's *Dissertation* gave to the Church. The fourth article distinguishes between sect and true Church. A sect derives from the will of a man and is ruled by the man and human understanding. The Church, by contrast, "may be compared to a woman [*Weib*]," and "submitting is characteristic" of a woman, just as "ruling is with a man [*Mann*]."[30] While Beissel was often autocratic, he claimed to possess a divinely restored female characteristic, and thus to be healed of a dominating nature.

The fourth article extends to the Church the image of Sophia's union with Christ through his wounded side. The wound that united Christ and Sophia, however, persisted in a tear in the attempted union of the characters of Sophia and the Church. This teaching corresponds to many examples in Beissel's writings of the bride who enters Christ's side, such as the 1725 letter and *Mystyrion Anomias* (1728). Adam's lost virgin, Sophia, prefigures the bride married to the Lamb in Revelation, the Church. The last of Beissel's printed sermons used this allegory extensively to refer to both the "heavenly femaleness" (*himmlische Weiblichkeit*) and the "Mother Church" (*Mutter Kirche*), among other things.[31] These concepts demonstrate a close agreement between the *Mistisches und Kirchliches Zeuchnüß* and Beissel.

According to the *Mistisches und Kirchliches Zeuchnüß*, the "Church is a virginal wife" joined to her "husband," Christ, through his open side. In him she "is fruitful, that she can give birth to her children."[32] With notable reserve, the *Mistisches und Kirchliches Zeuchnüß* claims that "in so far as we have been brought into this holy discipline and confines, to that extent we confess ourselves to be members" of the Church.[33] Suffering is a mark of the true Church, as it is for Beissel.

The fourth article describes the birth of spiritual children, or "paradisial birthing work" (*Paradisisches Gebährungs-Werck*). Wisdom needs no "driving male will for impregnation [*Besamung*]," but possesses both "male fire and seed within herself." When the male will is curbed, men "will participate in the mystic impregnation, in which our man's will, having sunk under itself, becomes female."[34] These phrases echo Beissel's *Dissertation* and a later letter to Peter Becker in 1756. To Becker he wrote that Sophia has in herself "the fire of the holy seed for heavenly fruitfulness" (*das Feuer des heiligen Samens zur himmlischen Fruchtbarkeit*). Male believers must present to her "a pure Matrix" (*eine reine Matrix*) and bring the fiery male will "into a sinking, and in a certain manner, become female."[35]

When the rebirth restores femaleness to men, they no longer need Eve's femaleness, that is, a wife. A reborn male has "enough on his own land for fruit and farming." This agricultural metaphor refers to the ministry of the gender-balanced reborn to beget spiritual children by winning converts. It echoes some of the agricultural aphorisms in Beissel's *Mystische und sehr Geheyme Sprueche* (1730).[36] Ephrata's theology extended the individual's spiritual rebirth to a church of the reborn. Individually and corporately the reborn are wed to Christ/Sophia.

The fifth article discusses ecclesiology by identifying two separate estates (*Stände*)[37] within the Church: the house estate (*Haus-Stand*) and the solitary estate (*Stand der Einsamen*). The house or household estate consists of married couples and their children. The solitary estate consists of those who are "not strangled by the yoke of the world"—by spouses, children, and possessions.

The two estates mixed together during the Old Covenant (Old Testament), but in the Christian Church they should be clearly separated. God's economy in the Church separates not female and male but married and celibate. This teaching is striking when we remember that the work was published in the same year that several householder couples were separating and moving into Hebron as celibates. The original dividing wall in the middle of the building symbolized spatially the separation of spouses. This distinction between celibate and married members was already expressed spatially by 1741. In July 1740 Beissel had turned the meetinghouse at Kedar over to the sisters and ordered the householders to worship in Zion's meetinghouse with the celibate brothers. In the summer of 1740 he ordered the destruction of the meetinghouse at Kedar and the construction of a new meetinghouse for householders only. The new meetinghouse was completed in 1741 and named Peniel (today's Saal). With the loss of Kedar's meetinghouse, all of the celibates worshiped together in the brothers' meetinghouse on Mount Zion, while householders worshiped in Peniel. This arrangement lasted from 1741 until 1745, when Beissel reorganized the celibate orders.[38]

Marriage in the house estate is "a disciplinary ordinance for fallen people." It is one of the "schools" (*Schulen*) that discipline people spiritually until they are capable of the superior celibate life. This article defends divorce as a Christian option, but with the goal of taking up a celibate, ascetic life. For "godly married people" to progress in their calling, "this estate [of marriage] must [again] be dissolved."[39] This account of marriage as a "disciplinary school" probably reflects some of Beissel's thought in the now lost book *Die Ehe das Zuchthaus fleischlicher Menschen*.[40] Legal divorce was rare in the eighteenth century, and the *Mistisches und Kirchliches Zeuchnüß* did not advocate arbitrary divorce or serial marriage. Of course, some solitaries may have found the celibate life a welcome way out of marriages they had come to regret.

The sixth article, about church governance, featured the Priesthood of Melchizedek, in contrast to the Priesthood of Aaron, introduced in the second article. The "priestly order of Melchizedek of the Church of the New Covenant under the leadership of the great high priest Jesus Christ"[41] is no priesthood of all believers but God's elite, equipped for their ministry through suffering. The Priesthood of Melchizedek is open to both women and men. These priests lay their souls before others as an anathema. Then such a priest becomes "a cause of salvation" (*Ursache des Heils*) for them, because priests of Melchizedek have the power to intercede with Christ for forgiveness of others' sins.

Although Boehme referred to Christ as a high priest like Melchizedek, Gichtel claimed that the Priesthood of Melchizedek could not be found in Boehme's writings. Gichtel claimed rather that God's Spirit revealed it to him. According to Gichtel, a priest of Melchizedek must be conformed to Christ and "bear the sins of the world, and without ceasing, by offering his soul for all people, reconcile and transmute the wrath of God." While he believed that Christ did this work in the believer,[42] Gichtel frequently overemphasized the human role, compromising the uniqueness of Christ's redemptive work. At Ephrata the celibates' Priesthood of Melchizedek became a spiritual elite in contrast to the householders. Related to ministry, the sixth article names "Church practices" (*Bräuche*), which include baptism, "breaking bread" (*Brodbrechen,* meaning the love feast and Eucharist). and washing of feet (discussed in Chapter 3).

Under the seventh article, "Submission and School Discipline," the author stated that the Church considers subjection to God as the highest matter. Subjection can break "an entire monarchy, together with so many powers and authorities," and brings freedom. Humility wins greatness, as Christ demonstrated by washing the disciples' feet. Christ's "kingdom will not fall, because it consists of deepest lowliness."[43]

The final, unnumbered article, headed "The First Awakening of Repentance and Faith," rehearses teachings on justification and rebirth based largely on Beissel's first theosophical epistle, which presents his concept of two conversions and the mystic death. Only after one is condemned to death under the Law is faith born.[44] This lengthy quotation ends the document in Beissel's words verbatim.

With the article on repentance and faith, the *Mistisches und Kirchliches Zeuchnüß* brings together the metaphors of mystic death, spiritual marriage of the soul with God, and spiritual rebirth through mystic impregnation. These three central concepts express the core mystical elements of Ephrata's religious thought. These three moved Ephrata beyond churchly Pietism's concept of rebirth to create a unique language to express the immediate presence of God.

In 1743 Johannes Hildebrand published the *Schrifftmässiges Zeuchnüß von dem Himmlischen und Jungfräulichen Gebährungs-Werck.* The full title indicates that the author wrote it against the Moravians' view of marriage. Hildebrand claimed that a divine illumination for the treatise came as Beissel spoke during the burial of Margareta Thoma, who died February 1, 1743 (1742 old style).[45] Hildebrand's real inspiration, however, was Jacob Boehme's *De incarnatione verbi* (1620).

Hildebrand's revelation concerned the "wonderful mystery" of why Christ's side had to be opened with a spear at his death. It models the way believers should offer themselves in daily sacrifice unto "total mortification of their old animal nature."[46] Thus the death of Christ is both redemptive for believers and an experience with which they identify by faith for rebirth and sanctification. Christ's crucifixion and resurrection as means to rebirth form the center of Boehme's *De incarnatione verbi*. Ten chapters in the second of the three parts of this work are devoted to the need for seekers to participate in an experiential identification with Christ's death in order to experience rebirth.

Hildebrand opened by referring to Boehme's account of an androgynous Adam created from divine essence.[47] Then Hildebrand followed Gichtel's interpretation of the fall of Adam, who gazed and marveled at "the two sorts of divided gender characteristics" of the animals and desired a mate of his own.[48] Adam then fell asleep. God took from Adam's side a rib, the "strong magical female power in Adam," his "virginal matrix," his "rose garden and femaleness" (*Weiblichkeit*).[49] Before this sleep, Adam could have reproduced spiritual children with Sophia, but without sexual activity. When Eve was created, she and Adam still could have reproduced without intercourse. The "Heavenly Virgin," or Sophia, was within both, only "divided in two images."[50] Hildebrand concentrated less on Adam's loss of Sophia as spouse than on the loss of Adam's virginal womb.

Adam and Eve succumbed to the temptation of eating the forbidden fruit of the tree of knowledge of good and evil. Beissel's *Dissertation* focused on the command and their transgression, while Hildebrand recounted the results in Boehme's language.[51] Hildebrand wrote that a "harsh [*streng*] impression" hardened their paradisial bodies to bone and flesh, adding a "stinking food sack" (stomach) and "reproductive members." According to Hildebrand, the location of human reproductive organs at the lower part of the body, "according to the manner of the animals," showed that the organs are a "disgust before God's holiness." This teaching repeated Gichtel's denigrating observation that the reproductive organs lie "at the hind part of animals" to show that God "has no pleasure in these animal members."[52]

Hildebrand stated that Adam's lost spiritual womb was restored in the second Adam, Jesus Christ. When Christ died on the cross and a soldier opened his side with a spear, a "heavenly virginal womb was built for him" during the sleep of death.[53] While Boehme's *De incarnatione verbi* tended to emphasize how the piercing quenched God's wrath over the broken androgyny, Hildebrand stressed how the piercing reunited the genders, creating a virginal womb for spiritual birthing. Like the fourth article in the *Mistisches und Kirchliches Zeuchnüß,* Hildebrand noted that human reproduction reached its end at Christ's death, and "conception and birth in the spirit in virginal power was replaced." Now a "spiritual virginal humanity could be born out of the heart of Jesus Christ burning in love."[54] Boehme stressed Sophia's role in moving one to repent. Beissel and Hildebrand stressed Sophia's union with Christ to restore gender balance and a virginal womb to give spiritual rebirth, so that people might then live in celibacy. Hildebrand also abstrusely contrasted the single heart of Jesus as the place of rebirth to the kidneys, which he described as "the second heart." The kidneys are divided, "one in a male and the other in a female characteristic."[55]

For Hildebrand, the heart of Jesus is a womb. Christ's "heart of love stands wide open in his opened side." Christ "wants to take us into himself and give birth to us anew according to the image of God."[56] Hildebrand exclaimed that the "true nourishment for people must be sucked out of the breast of Jesus, from His heartfelt love."[57]

While the Moravians shared with Ephrata a devotion to the wound in Christ's side, Hildebrand accused the Moravians of merely accepting Christ's merit and not "undertaking the self-chosen process of suffering" in self-denying repentance.[58] For their part, the Moravians feared that Ephrata's emphasis on repentance and self-denial smacked of righteousness through works. Thus the Moravians and Ephrata shared a beloved metaphor for spiritual rebirth from the wound in Jesus' side but drew opposite conclusions about the beliefs and behavior associated with it. These differences resulted in sometimes virulent mutual denunciations.[59]

Hildebrand concurred with much of Beissel's thought about the androgynous creation, a twofold fall, and rebirth. In the *Schrifftmässiges Zeuchnüß* Hildebrand attacked Moravian views of marriage ordained in paradise and infant baptism by adopting Gichtel's and Beissel's view that sexuality resulted from sin. While Beissel framed his views in the *Dissertation* by the question of theodicy, Hildebrand framed his treatise by Christology and anthropology. Hildebrand's enduring concern with the "virginal womb" is more focused than Beissel's.[60] Twin themes of rebirth through a spiritual rather than carnal reunion of genders and the resulting ascetic life dominate Hildebrand's *Schrifftmässiges Zeuchnüß* and Beissel's *Dissertation.* In addition, the similarities between the *Schrifftmässiges Zeuchnüß* and the *Mistisches und Kirchliches Zeuchnüß* suggest that Hildebrand played a major role in the latter work. Both show that Johannes Hildebrand, despite disagreements with Beissel's leadership, was a major organizer and defender of Ephrata's religious views. He agreed with much of the core of Beissel's theology.

Hildebrand passed over eschatology in the *Schrifftmässiges Zeuchnüß*. In 1746, however, he wrote a defense of the prophetic significance of the comet of 1742, and in a letter in 1759 he endorsed a manuscript by Valentin Mack predicting the destruction of Antichrist in 1777.[61] Like Beissel, Hildebrand believed that the last days before Christ's return were at hand.

Hildebrand's views on the Church reflected the conflicted views within the Ephrata community, as his own ties fluctuated through the years. In 1754 he published a short critique of organized churches, *Ein Gespräch zwischen einem Jüngling und einem Alten von dem Nutzen in Gottseeligen Gemeinschafften* (A conversation between a youth and an older person about the usefulness of godly fellowships). This work expressed the Radical Pietist tension between a gathered community of believers and the individual's private fellowship with Christ.

Spiritual rebirth for Hildebrand begins when the soul "becomes pregnant from the divine seed" of God's Word. Then God and the Spirit of Christ reveal "the new humanity in your soul."[62] These lines repeat the *Schrifftmässiges Zeuchnüß* and Ephrata's confession of faith. Even if other members of the congregation (*Gemeine*) have the Spirit, however, they "communicate nothing of it" to a seeker.[63] The community (*Gemeinschafft*) "consists of outwardly visible, bodily members," but the Spirit of God and Christ dwells invisibly "in each true member of the congregation secretly in the hidden ground of the soul."[64]

According to Hildebrand, a church community's discipline may help purify the soul early in the spiritual journey, but eventually a believer no longer needs a congregation's counsel. Hildebrand cared only for the reborn soul, not a church of the reborn, as the Dunkers and Mennnonites sought. He granted that such souls experience a close fellowship, but it has no visible form. "The pure love of God" is "a bond that inseparably binds the soul with the entire Church from Abel onward," such as "no outward form, ceremony or writing can bind so firmly."[65] By this time Hildebrand had fully accepted Radical Pietism's concept of an invisible church consisting of individuals who share love, but who share no outward organization or practices. He ended the treatise by criticizing the efficacy of prayers for the dead, probably aimed at Beissel's concept of the Melchizedekian priesthood.

Hildebrand remained in the Ephrata community until his death in 1765. He helped to define and defend Ephrata's beliefs, drawing on Boehme and Gichtel. Although Beissel reportedly tried to have some of Hildebrand's writings destroyed, they appear to be second only to Beissel's in articulating Ephrata's faith.

RELIGIOUS THOUGHT: OTHER WRITERS

EZECHIEL SANGMEISTER

Georg Heinrich Sangmeister also contributed to Ephrata's mystical literature, although he criticized Beissel severely. Sangmeister took the spiritual name Ezechiel at Ephrata and adopted it legally at his naturalization in 1765.[66] Born in Beddingen (now a part of the town of Salzgitter), Germany, to a schoolmaster's family, Sangmeister traveled as a journeyman joiner at age sixteen to Württemberg. Eventually he emigrated with his master to Pennsylvania in 1742. During the four years he worked to pay his passage, he met Anton Hellenthal (Höllenthal), who introduced him to Wilhelm (or Wilhelmus) Jung. A shoemaker in Philadelphia, Jung helped to direct potential converts to Ephrata. Sangmeister and Hellenthal gave up plans to return to Germany and went to Ephrata in March 1748.[67] Dissatisfied with Beissel and the Ephrata community, they left in 1752 for Virginia, where they befriended Samuel Eckerlin. A small Ephrata-like community gathered around Sangmeister in the Shenandoah Valley, but the indigenous peoples were hostile, and in 1764 most of the group returned to Ephrata.

Sangmeister began writing an autobiography in 1754. From 1825 to 1827, Joseph Bauman published four parts of it, recounting the years 1748–69, plus Ezechiel's annotations of an excerpt from a manuscript of the *Chronicon Ephratense*. Sangmeister's *Leben und Wandel* denounced what he saw as Beissel's and the community's hypocrisy. He accused them of numerous sexual affairs and financial chicanery, and laced his book with references to dreams, magic, and ghosts. In fairness to Sangmeister, he criticized his closest friends equally harshly.

Felix Reichmann disputed the authenticity of Sangmeister's diary, claiming that Bauman published a "compilation" under Brother Ezechiel's name.[68] Klaus Wust has convincingly demonstrated that Sangmeister described events and people during his sojourn in Virginia (1752–64) that only an eyewitness could have known.[69] Sangmeister is a valuable witness to Ephrata's life and spirituality.

Sangmeister's two known published works, *Leben und Wandel* and *Mystische Theologie*, give insights and some contrasts to Ephrata's religious views and life.[70] Although highly critical of Beissel and the community's rituals, Sangmeister agreed with most of Beissel's teachings, and he prized "the holy Boehme." Unlike Beissel, Sangmeister absorbed elements of Quietism from "the mystical authors," such as Madame Guyon and Miguel Molinos, whose *Spiritual Guide* he found more valuable than a "hat full of gold."[71] Brother Ezechiel claimed to have special, direct experiences of the presence of God.[72]

In sum, Sangmeister represents a variant within, not a break from, Ephrata's mystical language.

Sangmeister's career illustrates how influences from Quietism, spread through Radical Pietism by writers such as Gottfried Arnold and Pierre Poiret, both shaped and troubled Ephrata.[73] Sangmeister befriended Stephan Koch (Brother Agabus) and Johann Rissmann (or Reissmann), known as Brother Philemon at Ephrata.[74] Koch advised Brother Ezechiel to use Beissel's writings in moderation and recommended unnamed "mystical writings." Koch once told Sangmeister not to put worship and love feasts in any "more important place than sweeping," which chafed even Brother Ezechiel. Yet Koch also counseled Sangmeister to return to the cloister from Virginia.[75] Brother Philemon filled a copybook with handwritten excerpts from Madame Guyon's letters taken from a 1730 German edition.[76] Several excerpts counsel a silent, inner spiritual life to find God's presence. Koch and Rissmann added encouragement to Sangmeister's embrace of quietist aloofness.

Sangmeister's career illustrates the fault line of conflicted ecclesiology running through Ephrata. The line marks the tension in Radical Pietism between a gathered community and an individual quest for God. Encouraged by the more quietist piety of Koch, whom Sangmeister called his "leader," Brother Ezechiel favored a more eremitic life distanced from ritual and community. Yet he maintained a household fellowship of the like-minded. Although baptized by Beissel, Brother Ezechiel criticized the Sabbatarians for rebaptizing some members multiple times, making the rite a "laughingstock." In Virginia he refused to baptize a convert, sending him to Ephrata instead.[77] At first Brother Ezechiel participated in love feasts at Ephrata, but gradually he absented himself from them, criticizing what he believed to be their hypocrisy. In some respects, Sangmeister's activities mirrored Beissel's earlier life as a separatist hermit before his baptism.

A personal, interior experience of God's presence superseded Sangmeister's relationship with the community. He wrote later that in Philadelphia he was already "drawn in a soft, loving" manner and "communed with my inner self" in a totally internal prayer "without words and without decisions and thought. Essentially it was the presence of God in my soul."[78] Although Sangmeister's language is reminiscent of some of Beissel's, his emphasis on no words, decisions, or thoughts in prayer reflect more of Quietism. He focused on a mystical awareness of God's presence in the individual "inner self," without ritual or spoken word.

Joseph Bauman published Brother Ezechiel's *Mystische Theologie,* a work in three parts, from 1819 to 1820, although Sangmeister wrote it mostly between 1774 and 1778.⁷⁹ The first part warns seekers against six erroneous ways to find God and describes a reliable seventh way. In the second part, Sangmeister warns that the American war for independence is a sign of God's impending judgment. The third part schematizes history into seven epochs corresponding to the seven days of creation in Genesis, and offers spiritual counsel.

In the first part of the *Mystische Theologie,* Brother Ezechiel counseled seekers that "they will find the Lord in the ground of the heart" and warned against seven kinds of errors in seeking God.⁸⁰ The first erring group separates from the world but ignores inward, disciplining grace. The second group sets out to "storm against Babel," but retracts their judgments.⁸¹ The third sort tries to convert others by their own will, rather than God's. The fourth group loves to read books. Even though Sangmeister considered the "writings of the saints as a great gift from God," they are good only if they "drive the person inward."⁸² Souls of the fifth sort "run from one group to another," claiming that their own group is right. The sixth group separates from all sects, but resists any "discipline in love" for their own improvement. They "also discipline no one in love."⁸³ He may be referring to the Eckerlin brothers.

The "true children of God," the seventh sort of seekers, pass through much misery and "are found by God in the arid wilderness." They find God in themselves and live hidden among the "quiet in the land."⁸⁴ They also exhort, discipline, and remind. Brother Ezechiel surely numbered himself in this group. He found in the mystics the models for finding God's presence inwardly and individually, apart from others.

Sangmeister dated the second part of *Mystische Theologie* in 1778, in the opening years of the Revolutionary War. He attempted an exposition of Matthew 24 but abandoned it midway through the second part of the chapter.⁸⁵ The result was a rambling, confused warning of God's judgment.

In the third part of the *Mystische Theologie,* Sangmeister traced the six days of creation as six epochs leading to a seventh age of Sabbath rest. The format was familiar, as already evidenced in Horch's *Profetische und Mistische Bibel,* Bromley's *Way to the Sabbath of Rest,* and Beissel's *Mystyrion Anomias.*

Sangmeister's first epoch extends from creation to Noah and the Flood. The second epoch continues to the death of Jacob.⁸⁶ Sangmeister used the third day, whose epoch includes Moses and Joshua, to reflect on Adam's sin. God's creation of vegetation with seed in itself (Gen. 1:12) meant for Sangmeister that vegetation contains "both tinctures, male and female," for propagation. In other words, he believed that plants reproduced without cross-fertilization. Thus a vegetarian diet would best aid in progress toward paradisial androgyny.[87] Brother Ezechiel echoed the views of Boehme, Gichtel, and Beissel that circumcision indicates God's displeasure with reproduction. Sangmeister grounded the practices of celibacy and a vegetarian diet in a Boehmist view of the creation story, including an androgynous first human.

The midpoint of Sangmeister's fourth epoch was the birth of Jesus, parallel to the creation of the sun on the fourth day. Sangmeister included a prayer, reminiscent of Tauler, for the mystic birth of Christ in the believer. "O my Jesus," wrote Brother Ezechiel, "give birth to yourself anew in us."[88] In Sangmeister's fifth epoch, the fish and birds represent martyrs and hermits, respectively, who are distinct from Babel, the fallen churches.

The sixth epoch is the lowest, because of the creation of animals, and the noblest, because God created humans in the divine image. The creation of animals and Adam on the same day represented God's foreknowledge "that humans would fall to animal life."[89] Yet even in the sixth epoch, God still has a chosen few, the *"Mysticorum"* (mystics). God "gives birth" to the mystics "according to his image." A mystic has two types of soul in one person: the martyr and the solitary. Through the martyr's soul, "in their bodily lives, nature is crucified through daily death." The solitaries "have been born of God." Mystics also have "male and female [characteristics] in one person" and give birth to spiritual sons and daughters.[90] Here he shared Beissel's and Hildebrand's views on the androgyny of the spiritually reborn and their giving spiritual birth to new converts.

In the seventh epoch, God's work ends in "a blessed time of rest and a thousand-year Sabbath for an image of eternal rest." The final restoration (*Wiederbringung*) begins, when "all that was lost in Adam will be born anew again."[91] Here Sangmeister agreed with Ephrata's Sabbatarian schema of universal restoration.

In the remaining pages of the *Mystische Theologie,* Sangmeister rehearsed in somewhat confused, simplified form the androgynous creation story and Adam's two falls found in Beissel's, Gichtel's, and Hildebrand's thought. Adam had both genders in order to "give birth in a magical way." Humans can recover the reunited genders only through the love of Jesus, which "softens the masculine fire" and "makes it sink" much more than "all womanliness could from the outside." Not sexual intercourse but God's love tames the fires of the male will.[92]

While naming the animals, Adam desired to have both "heavenly Sophia and a woman" (*himmlische Sophia und ein Weib*). When he fell into a deep sleep, God took a rib and formed the woman. Then came "the second test" (*die zweyte Probe*), when God forbade them to eat the fruit of the tree of knowledge of good and evil. This was "the beginning of the Law" (*Anfang des Gesetzes*). The heavenly Virgin faded away and the human couple transgressed the commandment.[93]

Sangmeister's main differences from Beissel derive from Brother Ezechiel's stronger leanings toward Quietism. He preferred "prayer without words" and disdained rituals, singing, and calligraphy as spiritual disciplines.[94] Brother Ezechiel more readily sought the birth of Christ within the soul without outward means. For Sangmeister, a community had little, if any, significant role in spiritual rebirth.

Like Beissel in his later years, Brother Ezechiel tended to overdramatize his own sufferings, perhaps to verify in his own mind his status as a martyr. Although Sangmeister never suffered persecution in Europe, he surpassed Beissel in pervasive self-pity. He rarely found the moments of joy or triumph that mark some of Beissel's poetry, especially before 1745.

Sangmeister and Beissel had much in common. Both wrote what they identified as mystical literature. Brother Ezechiel observed the Sabbath, grounding his practice in eschatological Boehmist thought, although it differed from Beissel's in some details. Sangmeister based his practice of celibacy on a view of an originally androgynous human and twofold fall into sin, derived from Gichtel. Sangmeister approved of Beissel's concept of two conversions.[95] Brother Ezechiel believed in a future universal restoration and claimed to receive dreams from God.

Sangmeister shared Beissel's preference for fasting and a spare, vegetarian diet. At times he observed night prayer vigils alone or with his own household. He wore the monastic habit of Ephrata as late as 1769. Later, however, he moderated his ascetic regimen.[96] Although he criticized a sectarian community, Brother Ezechiel shared house fellowship with Anton Hellenthal, two Kelp (Kölb) brothers, and their sister, Catharina. Through the Kelps, Sangmeister's faction outlived Beissl's vowed celibate orders, as Clarence Spohn has pointed out. The Kelps died between 1815 and 1818, a few years after the death of Ephrata's last vowed nun, Sister Melania, in 1813.[97] Thus celibacy at Ephrata formally ended in the eremitic separatism in which Beissel began.

Jacob Duché, son of the mayor of Philadelphia, described Brother Ezechiel's household in 1771 as consisting of "four or five brethren," who separated themselves from the rest because of "some difference with respect to their forms of discipline and worship" but claimed a right to their share of the communal food. Eschewing the habit, the dissenters wore "shorter coats with leathern girdles, large white hats instead of hoods," and beards.[98] No doubt Samuel Eckerlin's legal claim to Ephrata land helped to maintain the little band's roost on Mount Zion.[99] Resolution of the disputed claim in 1770 may have freed Sangmeister's faction to abandon the monastic robe, since they no longer needed to conform to ensure their food supply.

Ezechiel Sangmeister's writings and piety represent far more continuity with Beissel than a break from him. Sangmeister departed from Beissel less over the mystical quest for the immediate presence of God than over the social expression of that quest.

CONCLUSION

From Gichtel's and Boehme's views of God and humanity, Conrad Beissel and many of his associates developed a mystical language for the presence of God. Lucifer's rebellion disturbed the divine androgyny of God. Adam's lust divided the human unity of gender. Human sin, not divine providence, led to sexual differentiation and intercourse. Using Boehmist material imported into the biblical story, Beissel and Ephrata upset traditional Protestant assumptions about the singular fabric of marriage, family, church membership, and territorial citizenship.

Hildebrand, Sangmeister, and others accepted Beissel's interpretation of the drama of redemption with female and male agency to restore the broken androgyny through the offspring of a woman, but not a man. Jesus Christ, androgynous and born of the Virgin Mary, atoned for male wrath on the cross and reunited with Sophia so that together they became the agents of spiritual rebirth. Redemption, in Ephrata's thought, was a participative, contemporaneous process, not solely a historic event in the past.

Similarly, Hildebrand and Sangmeister shared much of Beissel's mystical language and his departure from Protestant understandings of justification by faith alone. All three taught a rebirth through two conversions and a mystic death, which they identified with Christ's death. Only then could seekers be spiritually reborn and consecrated to the spiritual Priesthood of Melchizedek, to worship and intercede for others in prayerful lives of celibacy.

Whether to undertake the quest individually as solitaries or corporately in monastic orders remained an unresolved question for Beissel and more so for Sangmeister. The dichotomy of a collective of hermits and a community of shared monastic life persisted in unstable tension until the last celibates died in the early nineteenth century.

With their mystical language, the Ephrata brethren fished for new members and fended off external attacks and internal dissent. When external or internal foes pressed too hard, some at Ephrata settled on Beissel as the embodiment of God's extraordinary presence. Then the mystical language propped up Beissel's autocratic ways and enabled him to take the place of the authorities they rejected.

Ephrata invited the disaffected to lose themselves in a mystical language and be found by God, experiencing rebirth and the beginnings of paradisial life. In excess, the metaphors meant to dissolve ungodly appetites actually reinforced them. When grounded in the work of Christ and Sophia, the metaphors helped sustain a community of prayer and charity. In successes and failings, Ephrata's singular language created a unique community of faith and practice in the holy experiment of Pennsylvania.

3

"HOLY CHURCH PRACTICES"

Ritual at Ephrata

The Ephrata community developed a variety of ritual practices to enact their mystical language for the search for and awareness of God's presence. Ephrata adapted much of their ritual practice from the Dunkers. While a distinction between beliefs and practices is necessarily somewhat arbitrary, it allows for a close exploration of the practices and interpretations of both groups' rituals.

Often eschewing the term "sacrament," Ephrata's confession of faith (*Mistisches und Kirchliches Zeuchnüß*) named rituals such as baptism, foot washing, and the Lord's Supper as "holy church practices" (*H[eiligen] Kirchen Gebräuchen*).[1] Although Peter Miller sometimes used the term "sacrament," especially for the Lord's Supper, the term "practices" (*Bräuche*) better fits Ephrata's rituals. Beissel and the Sabbatarians developed a system of ritual that differed from the two Protestant sacraments of baptism and Eucharist[2] and from the seven sacraments of Roman Catholicism.

Church practices, for the purposes of this chapter, are special or symbolic actions, often with material objects, that helped constitute and draw individual members and the group as a whole to awareness of the presence of God. These practices are symbolic in the sense in which Miri Rubin defined symbols: "historically created vehicles of reasoning, perception, feeling and understanding." Such symbols carry power to communicate knowledge, evoke emotions, and prompt moods.[3] At Ephrata the community employed these symbolic behaviors to create a rich fabric of practice to reinforce Beissel's teachings. Ephrata developed a wide repertoire of rituals central to their life, with both shared and contested interpretations, creating a unique local culture concerned with the nearness and transcendence of God. Not all of the practices described in this chapter held equal importance. Tonsure, for example, was not as important as baptism. Some rituals were practiced temporarily; others persisted through the colonial period. Ephrata writers barely explained some practices, such as tonsure, while lavishing attention on others, such as baptism. Certainly not all members shared uniform interpretations of the church practices. Some interpretations varied over time. In Ephrata's literature and reports about them, however, some practices and interpretations recur with sufficient frequency to suggest a degree of consensus on observance and some meanings. Remembering the cautions given here and that Ephrata authors never attempted a systematic explanation of their practices, let us explore some of their religious rituals as enactments of their mystical language for the presence of God.

BAPTISM

The Radical Pietism of the Philadelphian movement and Inspirationists influenced Beissel first. These groups rejected the necessity of water baptism. More than eight years after his conversion among Radical Pietists, Beissel received baptism among the Schwarzenau Brethren in Pennsylvania. Because Ephrata began as a Dunker congregation, the Sabbatarians drew many practices from the Dunkers after separating from them, at times adopting unique interpretations of those practices. Practices common to both Ephrata and the Brethren include believers' baptism by threefold immersion; the love feast, which includes foot washing, a common love meal, including the bread and cup of the Eucharist; anointing for healing; laying on of hands in consecration; and the holy kiss.[4]

Baptism earned the Schwarzenau Brethren their name in Europe: the *Neu-Täufer*, or New Anabaptists, to distinguish them from the "old" Anabaptists, the Mennonites, who baptized by pouring (affusion). Baptism by immersion prompted the nickname *Tunker,* or Dunker in English,[5] or Dumplers or Tumblers, the latter two corrupted from the Dutch *dompelaar,* meaning one who dunks.[6] In order to understand baptism at Ephrata, one must consider the Brethren practice and meanings of baptism, which Beissel received in 1724.

Emerging from Radical Pietism, those who joined in the first immersion baptisms of the Brethren in 1708 in Schwarzenau originally shared the separatists' rejection of infant baptism. They found no accounts of infant baptism during Christian antiquity in Gottfried Arnold's histories or in the New Testament. The Radical Pietist E. C. Hochmann von Hochenau preached that no water baptism was necessary, only baptism by the Holy Spirit.[7] Arnold's histories provided testimony for believers' baptism.

Those who eventually became Brethren felt stirrings as early as 1703 and 1706 to receive immersion baptism.[8] "Two foreign brothers" who visited Schwarzenau sometime between 1706 and 1708 apparently preached the necessity of baptism by immersion, and the eight who launched the *Neu-Täufer* movement decided to adopt the practice. The identity of these foreigners is unclear, but the Dutch Collegiants' practice of immersion baptism and later contacts between Brethren and Collegiants suggest that the foreign brothers may have been Collegiants.[9] As a renewal movement arising from the Remonstrants, the Collegiants did not view baptism as a ritual of entry into an organized church, since they despaired of creating any church except a "general church of Christ." Collegiants baptized with one forward immersion those who confessed faith that Jesus Christ brings salvation and that the Bible is the true word of God. Because the Collegiants prized toleration above all, baptism represented an act of individual piety rather than a rite of a church.[10]

The Schwarzenau Brethren, however, appealed to Jesus' baptism as an example to be followed. The Brethren believed they were practicing baptism in an apostolic manner. The act symbolized repentance of sin and trust in Christ's gracious forgiveness. For them baptism marked entrance into the visible Church, which would submit to Christ in obedience as a response in faith. Mutual discipline within the Church represented the continuing commitment to the Church begun at baptism. Church discipline, characteristic of Swiss and Dutch Anabaptists and significant in Reformed Pietism, marked the Brethren's sharp break from the Radical Pietists, who sought to tolerate everything in the name of love.[11]

Two Brethren tracts from Europe devote nearly half of their length to believers' baptism by immersion. According to the early Brethren, Christ commanded and ordained immersion baptism upon the confession of faith by believers who repent of sin and acknowledge Christ as the unique source of God's forgiveness through his death and resurrection. Baptism is also a sign of spiritual rebirth. While obedience to baptism is necessary, "salvation is not dependent upon the water, but only upon the faith which must be proved by love and obedience."[12]

In a treatise, *Rights and Ordinances* (1715), Alexander Mack, Sr., explained that no one enters "the Lord's church without first being baptized in water upon confession of faith in Jesus." Those who enter baptism in obedience are born of "true faith and love of God" and attain cleansing, which "frees them from future punishment" for sin.[13] Baptism consists of three immersions, one in each name of the Trinity. With water baptism comes the baptism of the Holy Spirit, which the Brethren enacted by the officiant's laying of hands on the baptizand in the water and praying for the Spirit to baptize.

Christoph (or Christopher) Wiegner, a Moravian of Schwenkfelder descent, described a Brethren baptism he attended in Pennsylvania in 1734:

> When they reached the water's edge, they sang the hymn "Christ our Savior Speaks to Me." After this, one of their teachers went into the water and the one to be baptized kneeled before him in the water. He then asked him once more: 1. if he believed Jesus Christ was the Son of God; 2. if he rejected totally the devil, the world, sin, and all hypocritical worship; 3. if he would remain faithful to Jesus' teaching to his death. Each time at the naming of the Father, the Son and the Holy Ghost, three times, his hands upon his head, he was immersed forward into the water. After this he prayed over the baptizand in the water. The baptizand then prayed, also in the water. When he arose from the water, he was greeted with the kiss of peace. The one who had baptized then gave a short address to those who had come. Thereafter they held a lovefeast, a footwashing, and broke bread with one another.[14]

The Schwarzenau Brethren did not fix a liturgy for baptism in Europe or colonial America. The act that Wiegner witnessed closely resembled a Brethren baptism described in 1711 in Germany.[15] Conrad Beissel's baptism in 1724 was probably much like the ones described in these accounts.

Peter Miller described how Ephrata members received baptism to the Swedish minister Israel Acrelius in 1753. When the candidates come to the water, the "minister there puts to them the necessary questions." After answering, the candidate "falls down upon his knees in the water" and covers mouth and nose with his hands. The officiant "then lays his right hand crosswise over the other's hands" and, "holding his left hand behind his [the candidate's] neck," then "plunges the person under the water."[16] Miller argued that immersion was the necessary mode of baptism. Although Miller's account is short and came two decades after the founding of Ephrata, it probably describes a typical baptism among Beissel's Sabbatarians.

The *Chronicon* emphasized Beissel's superiority to the Brethren at his baptism.[17] While Seidensticker, Sachse, and Beissel's biographer Walter Klein stressed this part of the *Chronicon*, they overlooked Beissel's letters, which reveal that he had many more beliefs about baptism. Others repeated this oversight.[18] The *Chronicon* itself noted that Beissel viewed the act as a transplantation into Christ's death, renouncing even the self. Beissel also wished to be baptized in order to become a child of the new covenant.[19] Beissel's correspondence refers repeatedly to baptism as total denial of self, identification with the death of Christ, and a sign of the new covenant of grace. His theology of baptism was much fuller than what historians have extracted from the *Chronicon*.

In a letter in 1725, Beissel wrote that the source of salvation is the "innocent spilled blood of the little Lamb." This salvation "is presented [*vorgestellt*] to us in the covenant of grace through the water of baptism."[20] This belief suggests vestiges of Reformed Pietism, which brought the federal theology of Johannes Coccejus to Germany, especially through Reformed pastors such as Theodor Undereyck and Heinrich Horch.[21]

In addition to Reformed sources, Beissel drew on Jacob Boehme, who had linked baptism to covenant. He wrote that the sacraments of baptism and Eucharist are "testaments" of Christ. They are actions that serve as "seals" to ratify the "eternal covenant of God" through Christ.[22] Reflecting his Lutheran background, Boehme maintained that faith and God's Word must be joined to the water for baptism to be sacramental.

In the 1725 letter, Beissel criticized "despisers of outward baptism,"[23] signaling a shift from his earlier indifference to church rituals. He passed over the Calvinist association of circumcision and infant baptism as parallel signs of God's covenant. Instead, Beissel tied circumcision to celibacy, following Gichtel. Boehme had linked circumcision to renunciation of lust,[24] yet he also defended infant baptism, arguing that circumcision prefigured infant baptism. Beissel retained some influences of both Reformed Pietism and Boehmist thought in his concept of covenant, yet he broke with them both by insisting on believers' baptism by immersion, as did the Dunkers.

Beissel scattered his views on baptism in his letters. No later than 1735, he wrote that baptism enacts a believer's identification with the death and resurrection of Jesus Christ. Beissel probably held this view earlier. The "promises of the new covenant rest on the death of Jesus Christ." Through "baptism we are planted with him in the same death." Believers are "buried in the same death," in which "occurs the promise of a new resurrection with a new body of power." One is "brought through the baptism of Jesus Christ into conformity with his death," which does away with the sinful body.[25] In 1738 Beissel stressed the believer's confession of sin and of faith at baptism, claiming that "to baptize someone who cannot give his word to it" is "against the new covenant." He denounced parents who live in "pride, envy, strife, whoredom, deceit and lies," yet bring infants to baptism.[26]

Here Beissel broke decisively from Boehme's views of baptism. While Boehme denounced immorality on the part of the infant's parents, he believed that "both parents and congregants, as well as the believing baptizer and godparents, work with their faith in the child's 'characteristic' [*Eigenschaft*], and present it [i.e., the child] with their faith into the covenant of Christ."[27] In other words, the faith of parents, godparents, and congregation could attach to the child, bringing it into covenant with God.

Beissel wrote that purification from sin comes by "faith in Jesus Christ, which is ratified [*bestätigt*] through the new covenant of grace in the water of baptism, where we attain the forgiveness of sins through faith in Jesus Christ."[28] Beissel then linked baptism to his mystical understanding of rebirth, in which "the will must sink down into its own nothing." A "different light" then illumines seekers, bringing them to "the Lamb" and to "baptism in water in which the covenant of grace is opened through the word of the Father." Grounding redemption in the crucifixion and resurrection of Jesus Christ, Beissel continued that "in the water of baptism, which equally contains in itself the covenant of grace in new resurrection power, we renounce all life and pleasure of life."[29] Beissel then named the personal identification with the dying and resurrection of Christ as the "secret and mystic death" (*geheimen und mystischen Tod*).[30] Here Beissel combined Reformed theology's concept of the covenant of grace with a mystical identification with Christ's death in self-renunciation, attaching both concepts to baptism. The "mystic death" is no forensic imputation of Christ's justification. Self-renunciation leads to an ascetic life moving toward sanctification.

Beissel gave a special interpretation to the Trinitarian baptismal practice. Believers are "immersed three times in the water, in the name of the Father, the Son and the Holy Spirit in order to show that the outward person according to all three parts must descend and be judged."[31] At each believer's baptism God's word is "a magic and essential speaking into the whole person, in spirit, soul and body."[32] This passage echoes Boehme's description of baptism as God's covenant applied to the human spirit, soul, and body.[33] Beissel conceded that not all who are outwardly baptized are necessarily children of God. He claimed only to "show the covenant, namely how it is ratified with such powerful and important witnesses" (i.e., baptism).[34]

Inspired by Gichtel and others, Beissel developed an additional element for baptism, namely, betrothal to the divine virgin Sophia.[35] In his *Dissertation on Man's Fall,* Beissel referred to Jesus' immersion in the divine female waters to quench the "fire source" (*Feuer-Quell*) of male wrath, perhaps alluding to baptism. In baptism, not in sexual intercourse, the two genders are brought into androgynous temperament by Christ.[36]

Beissel wrote that "Christ Jesus, the knight," helps believers to attain the bride, "to whom [we] are betrothed in the water of holy baptism through the death of Adam on the cross."[37] This phrase exemplifies Beissel's mystical language of suffering with its overload of meanings. Obviously the biblical Adam of Genesis did not die on a cross; Jesus did. Through allegory, Beissel condensed the stories of the paradisial Adam of Boehme into the fallen Adam of Genesis 2, the "second Adam," Jesus, who died on the cross (Rom. 5), and the "Adam" of each sinner's rebellious humanity, which must be "put to death" if one is to share in the resurrection of Christ. This compact phrase illustrates supremely how Beissel understood the Boehmist creation story, Christ's redemptive death, and each seeker's mystic identification with Christ's death and celibate betrothal to Sophia. All of these meanings weigh down his words for the mystical life.

In an undated letter Peter Miller referred to baptism as a betrothal to Christ and separation from the world. "Baptism is both the letter of divorce that we give to the spirit of this world and also the betrothal [*Ehe-Verlöbnuß*] that we institute with Christ, our heavenly bridegroom."[38]

From the influence of Reformed Pietism, Beissel expanded the significance of the covenant of grace in baptism, so that justification no longer consisted of only an objective grace imputing righteousness. Drawing from Radical Pietism, Beissel portrayed baptism as a personal identification with Christ's death and resurrection, which radicalized the covenantal theology of Reformed Pietism. From Gichtel's transmission of Boehme, Beissel interpreted the sacraments as "testaments" of Christ, sealing the covenant. Gichtel's sexualized anthropology and account of androgynous Adam's sin were wedded to Beissel's understandings of baptism. Thus baptism could symbolize the quenching of sexual desire in water, a betrothal to the divine Sophia, and watery birth from her femaleness. Immersion baptism and Beissel's interpretations of rebirth reinforced each other. Similarly, baptism was more fitting for the mature, who, unlike infants, were aware of sexual identity and urges.

Beissel shared the Schwarzenau Brethren's interpretation of baptism as the portrayal of the forgiveness of sins through Christ's death and a spiritual rebirth by faith. Both the Dunkers and Beissel accepted the Mennonite view that baptism inaugurated a life of discipleship that could well lead to suffering. But Beissel emphasized a mystical aspect to suffering discipleship. Baptism allows a subjective identification with the dying and rising of Jesus Christ. Thus Beissel taught that baptism led to discipleship in an ascetic life. Some Mennonite and Dunker expressions about baptism lent themselves to this interpretation, but neither group drew the conclusion of regulated ascetic living. Because believers should identify perpetually with the death and resurrection of Christ, Beissel could accept and encourage repeated rebaptisms of those who had already received the rite.[39] Because the Dunkers saw baptism as entrance into the Church, they did not repeat baptism of a believer already baptized.

Officiating at baptism sometimes served as a sign of Beissel's authority over the community of celibates. After the Eckerlins departed, for example, most of the celibates received baptism again. Beissel permitted only a few to officiate at baptisms among the Sabbatarians.[40]

One of Ephrata's innovations was baptism on behalf of the dead, a practice virtually unique to them and the Mormons in the history of Christianity. Only a passing note in the *Chronicon* mentioned the practice.[41] According to the chronicle, Emmanuel Eckerlin and Alexander Mack, Jr., asked Beissel in 1738 to baptize Eckerlin on behalf of his mother and Mack for his father. In part, this account served Ephrata's polemical interests by associating Dunker baptism with the dead, which the spiritually vital at Ephrata might correct. The *Chronicon* alluded to the obscure passage in 1 Corinthians 15:29 about baptism for the dead but offered no explanation of the text. No other Ephrata literature known so far mentions the practice. The chronicle reported that some householders still submitted to the practice as late as 1786. Ephrata may have been the source for Mormon baptism for the dead. The Whitmer family from the Ephrata area settled near Joseph Smith's boyhood home and some joined his movement.[42]

LOVE FEAST

The Ephrata community also retained the Eucharistic ritual of the Schwarzenau Brethren known as the love feast, altering some of its practice and interpretation. It consisted of foot washing, a love meal together, and then the Eucharist proper, the bread and cup. The Schwarzenau Brethren developed the ritual by harmonizing New Testament accounts of the Last Supper, never separating the bread and cup from the other parts of the love feast. They found support in Gottfried Arnold's description of the early Christians' observation of the Eucharist or "Lord's Supper [*Abendmahl*] mostly in remembrance of love and faithfulness of their redeemer," doing so "always at their love meals [*liebes mahlen*], and never otherwise."[43]

In addition to the Schwarzenau Brethren, the Community of True Inspiration briefly experimented with observing love feasts between 1714 and 1716.[44] They held only five, probably borrowed from the pattern of the Brethren, including a meal, foot washing, and the Eucharist. Beissel probably met the Inspirationists after they abandoned the practice, but its memory would have been fresh.

With the love feast the Schwarzenau Brethren reversed the trend of Protestant reformers to reduce the number of sacraments and their liturgical elements. Contrary to Albrecht Ritschl's thesis that Pietism betrayed the Protestant Reformation by fleeing the world for a private, ascetic piety akin to medieval Catholic monasticism,[45] the Dunkers believed that they were reclaiming practices of ancient Christianity. The Dunkers, who sought to do "only what Scripture clearly commands," adopted ritual practices that Protestantism, a movement that claimed scriptural authority, had reduced.

Alexander Mack, Sr., presented the Dunker understanding of the Lord's Supper in *Rights and Ordinances* (1715). Claiming to argue primarily from Scripture, Mack maintained that the Lord's Supper should include a real meal (1 Cor. 11:20), which must be held in the evening (*Abendmahl*), as Gottfried Arnold had described.[46] At the Lord's Supper, Mack wrote, believers should "wash one another's feet" as Jesus commanded (John 13:14). They also "broke the bread of communion, drank the chalice of communion, proclaimed the death and suffering of Jesus, praised and glorified his great love for them." They would also admonish one another to follow "all his commandments," to resist sins, and to "love one another truly." Thus they anticipated "the Great Supper" with Christ "at the close of the world,"[47] or the wedding banquet of the Lamb of God at the last judgment (Rev. 19). The Dunkers stressed that only baptized believers partake of the love feast, using the ban to exclude known sinners from the celebration.[48] This practice reflects the influence of some Mennonite literature. An equally likely source of influence is Reformed Pietism, through Undereyck, Horch, and Samuel Nethenus, all of whom strongly emphasized discipline at the Lord's table.[49]

The Schwarzenau Brethren and the Ephrata community probably adopted foot washing from Mennonite influence. Many in the Dutch Mennonite tradition had practiced foot washing, although it was probably never universal among them, and perhaps was not done at every Lord's Supper observance. Some passages in Menno Simons's writings suggest that some Dutch Mennonites may have practiced foot washing also as a hospitality ritual.[50] The Mennonites' Dordrecht Confession of 1632 prescribed foot washing as symbolic of renewed cleansing from sin and of humility.[51] During the seventeenth century, however, as many Dutch Mennonites rose in wealth and status, the practice died out rapidly.[52]

In the Amish division among the Swiss Anabaptists in 1693, Jacob Ammann's opponents accused him of an innovation in requiring foot washing at the Lord's Supper.[53] Swiss Anabaptists who fled to the Alsace and Palatinate during the seventeenth century had subscribed to the Dordrecht Confession in a document known as the Ohnenheim Attestation in 1660.[54] Jacob Ammann's insistence on foot washing reveals at least a limited accommodation by Swiss Anabaptists to Dutch Mennonite practice. The Swiss Anabaptists apparently did not practice foot washing before Ammann's schism. At the beginning of the eighteenth century, Ammann's group was the only Anabaptist group that regularly observed foot washing with the Lord's Supper. The Anabaptist friends of the Dunkers, then, probably included some Amish.

Ephrata's confession of faith, the *Mistisches und Kirchliches Zeuchnüß*, includes foot washing along with "bread breaking," or the Lord's Supper, among the church practices. Foot washing, baptism, and the Lord's Supper are like a seal on God's covenant of grace.[55] The confession's article on subjugation and "school discipline" interpreted foot washing as a sign of Jesus' great humility, which disciples should practice. Foot washing is rarely mentioned in Ephrata writings, although the interpretations of cleansing and humility, held by the Mennonites and Dunkers, may be analogous. Ephrata also used foot washing as a ritual of greeting and hospitality. The *Chronicon* reported two instances when a pair of celibate brothers washed the feet of newly arrived visitors, one washing the guests' feet and the other drying them.[56]

A detailed description by an American visitor at a love feast at Ephrata in 1769 provides perhaps the earliest known written report of this ritual among the branches of the Schwarzenau Brethren. Charles Mifflin, a Philadelphia Quaker, went to Ephrata in 1769 (about a year after Beissel's death) to learn German in an effort to improve his business contacts.[57] While there, he was invited to attend a love feast held for celibate sisters and brothers in the home of a married couple. Mifflin described his experience in a letter to his father. Mifflin's editings appear in brackets.

Last seventh Day one of the married Brothers made a Supper & invited [His] all the [Brothers and sisters] the convent to it & I went amongst the rest, accordingly [at 4 oclock] we marched off in Procession, the Brothers first & the Sisters after them, when we came into the House the Brothers kiss'd the Man & the Sisters the Woman after this ceremony we seated our selves, (then they began to preach) several of them) which the Man & Woman of the House [being present] hearkened to, then they arose & left us but returned again presently with two Tubs of Water which had almost set me to laughing however I held it in as well as I could to see what was to be done with the[m] water now they all fell to stripping off their shoes & stockings & the man [of the house] washed the Brethern's Feet [& his] Wife the Sisters, then in comes [another Brother] a man with an apron & wipes the Brothers Feet, & a Sister also does the same Office to the [Nuns] others. I should have undergone the Ceremony but my Feet were not so clean as I could [should] have desir'd them.

This being over and the Tubs removed they fell to preaching & from [after] that to Singing until the Candles were [lit] brought in [which put an End to it] directly after [then] [Martin?] comes in with a great Basket full of [little] wooden Plates, [which are like the] which being distributed among us was followed by [two or three Loaves of Bread cut in slices] [illegible words] boil'd meat beef & Soup which was serv'd up in earthen Pans, & they were so placed that four of us could eat out of two [of the] Pans, & between [every] two pans was four slices of Bread. And [now being thus prepared] we all drew our Weapons & fell too heartily, but I was disapointed [*sic*] about our drink which was nothing but Pure Water.

When [we were] done with the Victual, the husband who was our waiting man remov'd them, then came the Sacrament, or bread breaking as they call it which being over they fell to Singing & then took their leave [at about seven oclock] by kissing as before. [The Man of the House]

Given from my Cell at Ephratah this 29 day of the 11 month 1769[58]

The practice of one person washing the feet of the entire group and a second person drying them represents a manner of foot washing known among the Brethren as the "double mode."[59] Mifflin's is the earliest known description of the practice.

Visitors in the following decade reported that the celibates ate mutton during the love meal.[60] Certainly the love meals augmented and contrasted with the fasting and meager, mostly vegetarian diet of the celibates, especially as they lived in Ephrata's early decades. The love meals may have portrayed to members the abundance of the Lamb's kingdom to come.

Mifflin's account offers no details about the "bread breaking," or Eucharist, but Peter Miller explained the ritual in 1753 to Israel Acrelius. According to Miller, Beissel administered the elements of bread and a drink from a common cup from an altar, or "small, high table," which Acrelius saw in the meetinghouses at Bethania and Saron (today's Saal). The bread was probably narrow strips of unleavened bread, such as Ephrata and other branches of the Brethren still use at Communion. According to Miller, communicants filed up to receive what he called "the sacrament in bread and wine" from Beissel.[61] Ephrata writers called the bread breaking (Eucharist) variously a sacrament and a practice.

Beissel's distribution of the elements apparently departed from Dunker practice. The *Chronicon* recounted a conflict that emerged over Beissel's manner of officiating when he visited at the emerging daughter congregation at Antietam, from which today's Snow Hill German Seventh-Day Baptist congregation developed. Beissel insisted on distributing the elements to each communicant, as he did at Ephrata.[62] This practice differed from the manner of the Dunkers, who were numerous in the area. According to Dunker practice, after a prayer of thanksgiving for the bread, one communicant breaks a piece from a long, narrow strip of unleavened bread and gives it to the member sitting adjacent, who in turn breaks a piece for the next communicant, and so on until all have received bread. Then all eat together. Usually the leading pastor initiates the distribution to the first recipient, but all participate in distribution. Likewise, after a prayer of thanksgiving, members pass a common cup around the table, each taking a drink as it passes.[63]

During his visit to Antietam, Beissel wished to administer the elements in his own manner. According to the *Chroncion,* he took offense at the Dunker's "Corinthian manner" because "they held that everything must be equal" and they wanted to have "no privilege or person of majesty [*gemajestätete Person*] among them."[64] Such egalitarianism offended Beissel, as it would have other Protestant ministers of the time. While the Dunkers enacted a priesthood of all believers by having all members participate in distributing the elements to one another, Beissel considered himself a superior minister and administered the elements himself. He rarely permitted anyone else to baptize or administer the Communion portion of the love feast.[65]

Ephrata writings reflect little of the interpretations of the Eucharist within the love feast, especially in comparison with the attention given to baptism. Peter Miller commented on the "mystery of the bread breaking" in an undated letter to a Lutheran man. For Miller, the meaning of breaking bread among a group of believers is that "through this [act they] become one body."[66] Ephrata's confession of faith described the bread breaking as a seal of God's covenant. According to the confession, "On this [practice] God must have laid down his presence in a special manner." Lest anyone consider this emphasis excessive, the author darkly reminded the faithful that even though "the ark of the covenant was an outward thing," yet thousands of "people fell and died" because of it.[67] From such words one may conclude that Ephrata saw the love feast as a ritual to promote a special awareness of God's presence.

The Ephrata community held love feasts often and sometimes for special occasions. As early as 1730 an Inspirationist in Germantown, Johann Adam Gruber, wrote to Germany that the Sabbatarians had frequent "bread breaking." The love feasts often lasted long hours, sometimes until midnight or later.[68] One of the few Inspirationist love feasts in Europe had lasted sixteen hours![69] When Ezechiel Sangmeister first came to Ephrata in 1748, they held love feasts two and three times a week. From 1748 to 1752, the year he left Ephrata, he counted a total of sixty-four special love feasts, or an average of sixteen a year. Apparently various sectors of the community held additional love feasts.

Sangmeister called the love feasts "quarrel feasts" because Beissel scolded the congregation for their sins. The love feasts of the Dunkers and the Sabbatarians included preliminary preaching for self-examination and repentance to prepare for Communion. While Beissel may have preached excessively or excoriated members for petty offenses, he and the Dunkers attempted to follow the instructions of I Corinthians 11 in urging participants to examine themselves. Sangmeister's critique suggests that not all members found the ritual equally meaningful.[70]

The Ephrata community held love feasts for special occasions. Sometimes a family might have a love feast and invite only certain members of the church. The community held love feasts to consecrate new buildings. The ritual also marked the death of an important member or anniversary of a death. Sangmeister recounted that the community held a love feast upon Michael Wohlfahrt's death in 1741, and annually on the anniversary, even when Sangmeister lived at Ephrata, between 1748 and 1752.[71] Ephrata may have wished to imitate the ancient Christian practice of commemorating saints' deaths.

Sometimes one of the celibate orders held its own love feast. When the sisters held one, Beissel was the only male present. On these occasions various sisters "officiated in all things"[72] except the distribution of the elements, which was always Beissel's prerogative. These occasions when women assisted with the Communion ritual were probably unique in all of colonial America.

The routinization of the love feast at Ephrata, fixing which acts constituted it and validating Beissel's distribution of elements, contributed to what Victor Turner called "normative communitas," reinforcing social identity and control. At the same time, the varying occasions, the varying groups that might call a love feast, and the variations in the length of the ritual and its speech acts contributed to what Turner called "spontaneous communitas" (or "existential communitas"), reinforcing a creative and spontaneous sense of direct and immediate relationship and social identity.[73] These celebrations invoked a common identity, a community quite different from others among colonial commoners, yet probably never free of contention over interpretation. The love feast connected special events and the memory of some of the dead to a ritualized awareness of the presence of God. The love feast pointed toward and at times enacted the presence of God, at least for some members.

ANOINTING

A much less attested practice for Ephrata and the Dunkers during the colonial period is anointing with oil for healing. The practice derives from the biblical injunction in James 5 to anoint and pray for the sick. No descriptions from colonial times of how the Ephrata Sabbatarians or the Dunkers performed the ritual are known. The *Chronicon* noted that as Brother Agonius lay dying, he requested anointing, "according to the custom [*Gebrauch*] of the first Christians." Beissel officiated, and Samuel Eckerlin, whose later business interests included an apothecary shop, provided oil.[74] Although the pattern of practice at colonial Ephrata is unknown, apparently anointing for healing did not preclude care by a physician, such as could be found at the time. Brother Gideon (Christian Eckstein) practiced as a physician among the Sabbatarians.

THE HOLY KISS

The holy kiss came from the Radical Pietist legacy. Gottfried Arnold recounted that the early Christians expressed mutual love with "the kiss of love and peace," with which they often "witnessed to their union." Arnold stressed the kiss and the terms "sister" and "brother" as marks of love among early Chrisitans.[75]

Some circles of Radical Pietists actually practiced the holy kiss. Catharina Elisabeth Wetzel's fellowship earned a scandalous reputation in 1699 in Laubach when their kissing seemed to pass the boundary of holiness into eroticism.[76] Strong sisterly and brotherly love was supposed to characterize the "Philadelphian Church" of the Radical Pietists and the Philadelphian Society. The Schwarzenau Brethren in Europe exchanged the holy kiss among themselves as a greeting, to welcome new members at baptism, and at the love feast. The Schwarzenau Brethren observed this act because it was biblical and was a practice from Christian antiquity. The Ephrata brethren probably retained the holy kiss for the same reasons.

Because both the Brethren and the Ephrata Sabbatarians withheld the holy kiss from a baptized member who was under the ban, the holy kiss identified membership and status boundaries.[77] When used as a greeting, the kiss helped to show who belonged; withholding the kiss identified those who violated of the group's identity. Additionally, the holy kiss distinguished the group from other church groups around them. For the Radical Pietists and related groups that practiced it, the holy kiss supposedly marked a mutual love that they alleged was lacking in the established churches.

No descriptions of how the Sabbatarians actually practiced the kiss are known. Typically the holy kiss included a handshake. The Old German Baptist Brethren continue today the nineteenth-century practice of offering a light kiss upon the lips, brother to brother or sister to sister, but never across the gender line.[78] This may have been the practice in the eighteenth century at Ephrata[79] and among Dunkers. It is probable that at Ephrata no one exchanged kisses across the gender line. This restraint would mark the kiss as one of affection between siblings rather than an erotic kiss. While some might question whether the kiss expressed homoeroticism, the consistent model of spiritual betrothal between Sophia and men and between Christ and women at Ephrata indicates a heterosexual orientation in their understanding of erotic or romantic love.

LAYING ON OF HANDS

The Ephrata Sabbatarians, like the Schwarzenau Brethren, practiced an imposition of hands by the minister at a new member's baptism and in prayer for healing with anointing, as well as for consecrating leaders. The *Chronicon* described at least two occasions when Beissel laid hands on men chosen to be subordinate leaders, consecrating them with prayer before the gathered congregation.[80] This ritual for consecrating leaders runs throughout the history of Christianity back to the New Testament.

At Ephrata, Beissel considered himself the foremost among the spiritual Priesthood of Melchizedek, constituted by the celibates. Hardly the egalitarian priesthood of all believers of Spener or even the Dunkers, the Priesthood of Melchizedek consisted of spiritual athletes. Celibacy supposedly aided the life of prayer required of such priests. Hochmann von Hochenau had "ordained" people in the Priesthood of Melchizedek spontaneously with the imposition of hands in the weeks before Easter 1700 in Berleburg. Gichtel expounded on the spiritual Priesthood of Melchizedek among his associates, the Angel Brothers (*Engel Brüder*),[81] celibate men who cultivated a devotional life and acts of charity. Gichtel's loosely associated group was a prototype for the celibate orders at Ephrata.

Beissel developed a hierarchy of ministry, justified in part by the elite order of the Priesthood of Melchizedek as a cadre superior to other members of the community, with Beissel on top. His early title of *Vorsteher* (which Hark translated as "superintendent") probably comes from the Inspirationists. Their confession of faith in 1716 included a prophecy inaugurating the office of *Vorsteher,* the one to whom God would give the gift of prophecy and of discernment of true from false prophecy.[82]

Beissel also accepted the title of "Father," apparently at the instigation of Israel Eckerlin and the Zionitic Brotherhood in late 1738 or early 1739.[83] Walter Klein alluded to possible Catholic influence, but neither Ernst nor Alderfer interpreted "Father" in that way.[84] Roman Catholicism may well have been one influence; Radical Pietism's Priesthood of Melchizedek may also have contributed to this practice. According to Gichtel, the ministry of such priests included not only prayers of intercession, even reconciliation of others with God, but also begetting spiritual offspring with Sophia or Christ.[85] Beissel's claim to lead many members to conversion, which many of them confirmed, garnered him the title of "Father."

Beissel led best when dependable assistants helped him. Michael Wohlfahrt (or Brother Agonius) served as the most important male assistant until his death in 1741. One couple whom Wohlfahrt converted, Michael and Maria Catherine Müller, called him their "church father."[86] However, Beissel certainly governed as the primary "father." As Brother Agonius weakened during his final years, Beissel tried out various candidates to lead the Zionitic Brotherhood, and finally consecrated Israel Eckerlin as the prior (*Abt*) in 1740.[87] After the expulsion of Eckerlin in 1745, various brothers headed the order for short periods until Peter Miller emerged as Beissel's most trusted assistant.[88] In earlier years, Beissel had attempted to place various subordinates as leaders of outlying congregations, such as Emmanuel Eckerlin at Amwell, New Jersey. None succeeded. A group of members from each of these daughter congregations typically moved to Ephrata, precipitating the collapse of the congregations they left. Beissel's charisma and his difficulty in sharing power contributed to this pattern. Only Georg Adam Martin successfully led a lasting congregation approved by Beissel, Antietam/Snow Hill. Even after Martin moved on to Somerset County, Snow Hill flourished, thanks to capable local leaders. After Peter Miller succeeded Beissel at Ephrata, the center of energy shifted to Snow Hill.[89]

In addition to the office of prior, Beissel instituted the office of prioress to supervise the celibate sisters. He picked Maria Eicher over her older sister, Anna. While the date of her installation is uncertain, it must be earlier than 1741, when Beissel addressed her as the *Abtissin* in a letter.[90] The chronicle of the sisterhood, "Die Rose," gave no date for Maria's installation, but claimed that as "spiritual mother" she collaborated in designing the sisters' habit with Beissel and Martin Bremer, who died in 1738.[91] Maria received the titles Mother and *Vorsteherin*,[92] clearly more equal to Beissel's position as Father and *Vorsteher* than to the priors. "Die Rose" credited her with helping to set the daily schedule and rules of conduct for the sisters. During her rule, at least two women, Sisters Marcella (Maria Christina Saur) and Eugenia, assisted as subprioresses. After Mother Maria was deposed, around 1764, Sister Jael (Barbara Meyer) succeeded her.[93] The sisterhood was reorganized in 1745 as the Roses of Saron and structured into seven classes; it is unclear whether they were hierarchical.[94]

Despite egalitarian thoughts among some Radical Pietists, ministry at Ephrata developed in a hierarchical pattern under the authority of Beissel, assisted by the prioress and prior. Ministry in the Ephrata fellowship was concentrated geographically at Ephrata around Beissel's personality and control, as his assistants often competed for a share of power.

MONASTIC LIFE: DEVOTIONAL AND ASCETIC PRACTICES

Tonsure

In 1740 Conrad Beissel introduced the practice of tonsure, shearing a round disk (*Platte*) in the hair. According to Ezechiel Sangmeister, Alexander Mack,

Jr. (Brother Timotheus), and Christian Eicher (Brother Eleasar) complained to Beissel that they still lacked something spiritually. In addition to rebaptizing them, Beissel then introduced tonsure. It reportedly symbolized the celibates' vow of perpetual chastity. The *Chronicon* described the first ceremony. Beissel ordered Israel Eckerlin (Brother Onesimus), prior of the celibate men, to kneel and take the "vows of eternal chastity" (*Gelübde zur ewigen Keuschheit*). Then Beissel sheared a disk in his hair. Then Brother Onesimus rose and cut a tonsure in the hair of Beissel and "the other brother." Beissel appointed a date when the entire celibate brotherhood would receive the tonsure after a public reading of the vows. The same day Beissel proceeded to Kedar's *Bäthaus*, where he cut the hair of the sisters short and tonsured their heads upon the reading of their vows. The celibates reportedly instituted a quarterly renewal of the tonsure to mark their vows of chastity. In 1745, according to Sangmeister, Beissel and Israel Eckerlin greatly elaborated the ritual.[95] By then the tonsured brother or sister received a holy kiss from the celebrant and from two other brothers or sisters. How long or how regularly the celibates observed this practice is unknown.

The description of tonsure suffered varying elaborations by later historians. Seidensticker mocked the ceremony but read the *Chronicon* correctly.[96] Sachse repeated Hark's translated account, emphasizing the Roman Catholic affinities. Ernst greatly embellished the account, repeating the confusions of Hark's translation errors. Ernst suggested that Ephrata abandoned tonsure when the Eckerlins left in 1745. During the reform rituals after their departure, however, Beissel rebaptized and cut the hair of the celibates, simply omitting the tonsure on that occasion. When the celibates actually abandoned tonsure is unknown. Alderfer created further error by mistakenly crediting Israel Eckerlin with instituting tonsure.[97] According to the *Chronicon*, Israel Eckerlin was the first to receive tonsure, not the one who instituted it.

Tonsure aroused controversy among members. Some objected that Scripture forbade the faithful to shave the head, and that Beissel was just "warming up a thing that originated in the papacy."[98] This opposition reflected some anti-Catholic sentiment, an indication that Ephrata may not have sought explicitly to imitate medieval monasticism. The *Chronicon* reported that the "virgins of the first church" (*Jungfrauen der ersten Kirche*) wore their hair in this manner. It is just as likely that Ephrata sought to imitate the ancient church, not the medieval one. The ritual helped to dramatize obedience to the vows.

Fasting

Fasting figured prominently in the celibates' daily regimen, especially during the early years at Ephrata. Gottfried Arnold wrote that early Christians fasted often to tame the body for prayer, not to earn God's grace. Fasting, like all other forms of self-denial, acknowledged the need for repentance and faith as well.[99] Beissel and the celibates took this teaching to heart, for visitors often noted the thin, gaunt appearance of celibates.[100] Although not written until 1745, the sisters' rule, "Die Rose," allowed only one significant meal during the day and "a bit of bread" if one's "weakness" required it.[101]

If Ephrata's celibates ate as little as "Die Rose" prescribed, they ate less than other white colonial populations. However, many of Ephrata's population had fled southwestern Germany, where decades of warfare and bad harvests had accustomed them to a meager diet. As late as 1753, Brother Eleasar told the visiting Bishop Acrelius that Germans in the Palatinate were lucky to taste meat five times a year, whereas the English ate meat at every meal.[102] The diet of Ephrata celibates, while meager in comparison with those of other white populations in the colonies, was probably not much harsher than that of many commoners of southwestern Germany at the time.[103]

Beissel may have believed that spiritual rebirth and asceticism could create in the human body a paradisial state like the one he attributed to Adam. According to Sangmeister, Beissel claimed that he would "not die a natural death like other human beings," but would be "taken up like Enoch and Elijah."[104] In regard to Beissel's aging, Maria Eicher wrote in the 1750s that "perhaps divine youth will overtake age."[105] Beissel may have also sought to restrict elimination through reduced diet in an effort to attain a paradisial body. The *Chronicon* claimed that the celibates learned how Adam ate in paradise, and lived "without animal food and without evacuation of the bowels."[106] According to Boehme, Adam's paradisial body needed no bowels or elimination. It absorbed paradisial food without digestion and needed no sleep. It could have reproduced "magically," without sexual intercourse.[107] If Beissel held these views, they would partly explain the importance of fasting and restricted diet for celibates. It is unlikely that householders observed the dietary regimen.

The *Chronicon* recounted Johann Franz Regnier's attempt to restrict himself to a diet of acorns in 1734. Regnier induced the brothers to replace bread with acorns for food.[108] Sachse attributed this idea to Germanic mythology and Rosicrucianism, claiming that they made bread, coffee, and liquor from the acorns.[109] However, the Lenne Lenape (Delawares) used acorns in their diet. When properly roasted and ground, acorns lose their toxicity and become a food source.[110] Perhaps the Ephrata brothers attempted to copy this Lenne Lenape practice but failed to prepare the acorns properly, ending with wormy food.

Probably not all Ephrata celibates followed Beissel's regimen. Archaeological investigations at Ephrata have discovered dietary animal bones near the sites of monastic buildings. While fuller interpretations are in process, samples suggest that the dietary animal bones are fewer in deposits associated with the earlier periods of Ephrata's European occupation.[111] Acrelius reported that celibates permitted any who wished to eat meat to do so, although he found it in short supply.[112] Sangmeister noted that in later years Brother Agabus and Brother Philemon "roasted a lot of meat" for themselves and suffered indigestion.[113] Archaeological exploration confirms an increasing amount of dietary animal bones in the later colonial years, but even then the amount is still less than that found in contemporary sites in Philadelphia. As the years passed, Ephrata celibates moderated their dietary regimen.

In Beissel's treatise on music he prescribed a diet that he believed would lead to a better spiritual life.[114] He recommended bread and grains as primary foods and water for drink. He proscribed fatty and meat dishes and warned against leafy vegetables and legumes. His diet aimed at reducing sexual desire and purifying the body. His plan strikingly resembles the advice in a book titled *Diaetetica Sacra,* probably by Johann Samuel Carl (or Karl), the physician who reportedly treated Beissel during an illness in Europe. A photocopy of a manuscript copy of "Diaetetica Sacra" on Ephrata paper is in possession of the Ephrata Cloister. The provenance of the manuscript is unknown, so it is uncertain whether it actually has any connection with the Cloister.[115] Carl's diet, like Beissel's, advocates bread, grains, and water, although *Diaetetica Sacra* does advocate leafy vegetables and legumes. Carl's work also favors moderated periods of fasting.[116] Carl's work encouraged a healthy diet as a way to a richer spiritual life, and may have influenced Beissel. The diet Beissel proposed is stricter, in keeping with his stronger asceticism as a means to curb the desires of the flesh.

The frequent love feasts regularly supplemented the celibates' spare diet. The significance of the love feast as a Eucharistic ritual suggests that Ephrata developed a kind of "love feast piety." Feasting in messianic abundance at the love feast contrasted with fasting to control the body. For the celibates, fasting marked an abstinence and an absence. In place of eating, Beissel sought and admonished others to seek the presence of God. "My bread that I eat," he wrote, "is this, that I remain turned toward God and His pure Being without ceasing." Beissel's "water" to drink was "that I never more separate from God or His love."[117] Fasting and its opposite, the Eucharistic love feast, were ritual ways of enacting the absence and presence of God.

Monastic Dress

The Ephrata celibates gained a distinctive identity with their white hooded habits. However, they did not adopt monastic dress until after the Eckerlins arrived in 1728. They induced Beissel to abandon regular attire for Quaker garb, and the single brothers copied it, according to the *Chronicon.*[118] Sangmeister reported two different dates for the habit. He noted that soon after a few brothers joined Beissel at the Cocalico in 1732, they followed his lead in wearing "cowls and hoods." Whether this was a full monastic garment or only a hooded outer garment is unclear. Sangmeister also noted among events in 1738 that in the tenth month (December, old style) Beissel began to "burden" the celibates with "cloaks, cowls, and caps." However, Sangmeister would be in error if Martin Bremer indeed helped to design the habit, as Sangmeister claimed elsewhere, along with "Die Rose." Bremer died on the "third or fourth day" of the first month (March, old style) of 1738.[119] Sangmeister reported that Beissel took credit for designing the habit himself.

The *Chronicon* in its present form narrated the adoption of the habit in the context of events in 1738. Yet the chronicle also noted that celibates had worn the habits for about fifty years, suggesting an earlier date for their introduction, perhaps around 1735–36, since the *Chronicon* was published in 1786. According to the chronicle, the choice of a uniform habit symbolized in part a desire to demonstrate unity through dress. In noting the similarity to the Capuchin habit, the writers claimed that the Capuchin habit was closest to the garments of the first Christians. More important, the habit was designed as an outer hull to hide the male "body of death because of its shame," in contrast to the customary male dress, which is designed so that it "pleases the female gender."[120]

The male habit consisted of a robe (*einem langen Thalar*) reaching to the feet. A *Thalar* is typically a wide robe with wide sleeves worn by jurists, Protestant clergy, and professors to denote their offices. The habit had an outer garment (*Ueberwurf*) that had an "apron" (*Schurtz*) in front and a "veil"

(*Schleyer*) behind, covering the back. A "pointed monk's hood" (*zugespitzte Mönchs-Kappe*) was attached to the upper part of the outer garment. The habit included a belt (*Gürtel*). For worship the brothers also wore a waist-length cloak (*Mäntel*), also with a hood.[121]

According to the *Chronicon*, the sisters' habit was "like the brothers'," only the hood was rounded rather than pointed (*nicht spitzig sondern abgestumpfft*). The sisters' habit was designed to show little of the female body, the "terrible image that was revealed through sin." By no means did Ephrata writers consider the male body any better than the female body. The *Chronicon* described a large "veil" (*Schleyer*) that reached as far as the belt in the back but down to the feet in front. This garment symbolized the sisters' "spiritual betrothal" to Christ. The chronicle noted that Roman Catholics who saw it called it a scapular (*scapulir*).[122]

"Die Rose" adds more detail about the habit. The account credits Maria Eicher with first announcing to Beissel that she had "a strong drive to have a nun's dress" made for herself.[123] The sisters experimented first with wearing clothes of a uniform black. The black faded, however, so Maria consulted with Beissel and Martin Bremer, and eventually a white habit was designed.

According to "Die Rose," the veil (*Schleyer*), or outer garment that goes over the robe, should extend down to the hem of the robe in both front and back. "Die Rose" also added an interesting detail, which Sachse mistranslated. Attached to the hood were "little veils [*Schleyerlein*] that are ordered in front as a covering and hull for the body."[124] Sachse translated this as "two lapels" under the chin. What the scribe originally meant is unknown. Drawings of a sister's and brother's habits appear in a copy of the *Martyrs' Mirror* that belonged to Brother Amos (Figure 4). A similar but smaller illustration of a sister's habit appears in a lavishly illustrated music book created for Mother Maria Eicher by the sisters.[125] The householders wore a gray habit for a time, but abandoned it.

The habit identified members of the vowed celibate orders. It distinguished females from males, celibates from householders, and the Sabbatarians from the wider world. The similarities of the men's and women's habits represented a conscious attempt to conceal gender differences, visibly reinforcing Beissel's efforts to create a third gender (*Geschlecht*) of celibate androgyny. The habit cloaked the bodies that in Beissel's view were corrupted by bestial appetites. For the celibates, the white robes also pointed to the garments that the 144,000 virgins who would follow the Lamb on Mount Zion would wear (Rev. 7 and 14).

"HOLY CHURCH PRACTICES"

Fig. 4 Monastic habits worn at Ephrata, illustrated in Brother Amos's *Martyrs' Mirror.* (Courtesy of Pennsylvania Historical and Museum Commission, Ephrata Cloister.)

Prayer

Ephrata celibates devoted much time each week to prayer. Patterns of prayer changed through the years at Ephrata. Perhaps the most dramatic prayer time came at the midnight matins (*Nachtmetten*), or nightly worship services. Beissel shortened to two hours the four-hour service initiated before the completion of Kedar in 1736. The service featured preaching by Beissel and time for spontaneous prayer.[126] There is no evidence that Ephrata ever observed the canonical hours of prayer or that they recited fixed offices. For a time, householder families reportedly rose at midnight for prayer in their homes, copying the celibates' activities in the meetinghouses.

Christopher Saur, Sr., reported in 1751 that the celibates slept only three hours a night. "Die Rose," dated 1745, permitted two periods of sleep, each three hours long, interrupted by the two-hour midnight worship service. Sachse reported, with no documentation, that Ephrata's matins service imitated the previous practice of the Kelpius community.[127]

Beissel's desire to restrict sleep fitted with his regulation of diet in attempt to attain a paradisial body that would not tire, digest, or eliminate. Kelpius seems to have held this view also. Gichtel had complained that as he aged, he needed six hours of sleep rather than the two that had satisfied him earlier. He claimed to have spent the remaining hours in prayer.[128] Physical sleep represented for Gichtel and Beissel the sinful sleep of Adam, when he lost Sophia as a result of sexual desire. Holding the matins at midnight reflected their expectation that Christ would return at that hour.[129]

Beissel recommended frequent prayer during the day, preferring oral prayer, even in solitude. Ezechiel Sangmeister recounted his own desire for silent prayer, which would allow him to "go inside himself" for communion with God. Ephrata celibates typically knelt for prayer. In 1745 the brothers and sisters agreed to hold three special hours of prayer daily. The ringing of a bell signaled the beginning and end of one hour of prayer in the morning, one at noon, and one at night. This routine lasted only a year. Before the year ended, in June 1746, Beissel introduced a practice of perpetual prayer among the brothers. They set aside a certain room for prayer and one brother occupied it for an hour at a time, followed by another brother. How long the brothers observed this continual prayer is unknown.[130]

During the colonial years, Ephrata practiced prayer in various ways—private prayer in solitude, prayer in corporate worship, and sequential prayer. Israel Acrelius noted during his visit in 1753 that only Beissel prayed aloud in public worship, but other writers commented that members were free to pray or speak.[131] Probably the only certainty is that Ephrata never developed a fixed liturgy or calendar of prayer.

Beissel intended that prayer would fill the time normally given to sleep and eating. He called prayer "an unceasing, magical eating by our spirits of God's holy Being, through the fire-will of the drawing and magical desires of our souls." For Beissel, prayer opened a porthole into a mystical awareness of God's presence. Through prayer, wrote Beissel, "we are transfigured in Him with the glory [*Klarheit*] that has always been with Him."[132]

Other Practices

Ezechiel Sangmeister suggested that Conrad Beissel practiced flagellation. Christina Höhn told Sangmeister that she had often heard Beissel "lashing himself on his bare back" thirty-nine times, causing blood to flow. Sangmeister reported that in the final years of his life, Beissel would take "a rod with which he flogged himself," supposedly in remorse for drunkenness. Sangmeister even claimed that he scourged himself with stinging nettle to overcome sexual temptation.[133] While Sangmeister was often a credible informant, his bias against Beissel calls for caution in evaluating these reports.

Allusions in the *Chronicon* suggest that Beissel and others at Ephrata may have improvised spontaneous ritual practices of which no documentary descriptions remain. When Israel Eckerlin was at the peak of his power as prior, for example, he and Mother Maria Eicher served as priest and priestess for the community. Apparently at times he wore a specially embroidered outer garment in imitation of the breastplate of the Old Testament priesthood.[134]

CONCLUSION

Conrad Beissel and the Ephrata community developed rituals drawn from various sources to enact their ascetic pilgrimage toward the presence of God. Like the Dunkers, they expanded the reduced Protestant rituals based on practices they discerned in the New Testament and added others. Unlike the Dunkers, they expanded some of the interpretations of their rituals. Baptism included betrothal to Christ/Sophia and the quenching of sexual desire, and was administered on behalf of the dead.

Beissel drew on some Roman Catholic practices but redefined them uniquely. The monastic habit symbolized not only the poverty he prized but also the covering of the body in anticipation of its paradisial renovation in the presence of the Lamb. Tonsure signaled the celibate marriage to Christ/Sophia. The title of Father represented not just Beissel's status as minister but his superior role in leading converts to spiritual rebirth through Christ/Sophia. The more Roman Catholic these rituals appeared, the more opposition they seemed to arouse among the brothers and sisters. Thus Ephrata probably did not set out to "recover" medieval monasticism. Any apparent similarities of Ephrata's rituals to Catholicism's fade in the light of Beissel's anthropology and theology.

The most ascetic and the most elaborate rituals were performed by the celibates. Fasting and restricted diet, reduced sleep, and celibacy served to deprive the physical body and render it susceptible to the lost paradisial body. Christ represented the union of the two. Ephrata's ascetic rituals aimed to subdue the body and the will, pointing beyond appetites to what Beissel conceived as a transformation into a heavenly likeness of Christ. The celibates probably improvised or elaborated some rituals to demonstrate the grandeur of their anticipated world to come.

At the same time, these elaborate rituals undercut the very critique against the established churches on which Beissel embarked as a separatist. As he centralized his leadership in the performance of the rituals, he moved increasingly toward acting out ceremonies without the spontaneity of lively faith, for which he criticized the institutional churches. Beissel's prolific writings indeed underscore the need for faith. Such critics as Ezechiel Sangmeister, however, could attack the ritual life as lacking the inner devotion Beissel tried to create with his mystical language.

As Beissel aged and the number of celibates dwindled, mystical interpretations faded from the rituals and ascetic rigor abated considerably. Alternative interpretations within the community and some members' opposition to some of the rituals also helped to efface Ephrata's ritual life. Tonsure and baptism for the dead, which Beissel added only in the 1740s, seem to have largely disappeared by the end of his life, if not sooner. Similarly, probably before his death the celibates had moderated their diet and sleeping habits. The memory of asceticism was furthered obscured by William Fahnestock's report in 1835, which explained that the practice of sleeping on benches with wooden blocks for pillows merely reflected lack of money in the community's earliest years.[135]

Other rituals slowly lost their mystical significance as Beissel aged,[136] but remained as "church practices," not unlike those of the Dunkers. As Beissel's emphasis on the mystic death and identification with Christ's suffering faded, for example, the interpretation of baptism could stress cleansing from sin and entrance into the church. As Beissel's dietary restrictions relaxed, the love feast became less a counterpoint to fasting than a congregational Eucharistic celebration, like that of the Dunkers. Similarly, as Beissel's mystical and apocalyptic language lost currency, the Sabbath became more a literal obedience to a biblical command than an eschatological sign of eternal Sabbath.

Surely not every member or resident shared all of Beissel's views on the meanings of ritual practices at Ephrata. At times the rituals served as a corporate stage where Beissel acted out his control of the congregation. At times many members of the community found meaningful corporate identity as they performed the rituals that marked the transitoriness of the world they knew in Europe and Pennsylvania and served as a prelude to the paradise to come. Subject to baroque excesses, Ephrata's rituals marked important ways in which many of the Sabbatarians acted out the community's quest for the presence of God.

4

MANLY VIRGINS AND VIRGINAL MEN

Gender at Ephrata

"Woman is the lack of the man, and man is the lack of the woman," wrote Conrad Beissel to an unidentified woman sometime before 1745.[1] Ephrata's mystical language constructed unique gender concepts based on Beissel's belief that God possesses both female and male characteristics in perfect balance. Beissel also taught that God created the first human to possess both genders, "male and female" (*Männlein und Fräulein*), "not divided but in one person" (*nicht gezweyet sondern in einer Person*).[2] In his beliefs about an androgynous God and a savior figure of both genders, Christ/Sophia, Conrad Beissel accepted a traditional European view of subordinate women; he was unique in teaching that the trait of subordination was desirable for men as well as women. He prescribed a revolutionary notion of submission for men based on their lack of female characteristics.[3] He encoded this gender critique in his religious views, not in egalitarian views of gender. This concept, along with the celibate women's freedom from a husband's or father's rule, created some possibilities for women at Ephrata to achieve a degree of autonomy and exercise some power.

SOPHIA

The Context of Radical Pietism

Pietism within the established churches exerted a polyvalent influence on women and gender roles. On one hand, Pietism reinforced the Reformation's traditional view that women were subordinate to men. Each household was potentially a place of worship, where women were defined as daughters, wives, or mothers subordinate to their men.[4] However, Spener's small groups in Frankfurt included groups for women, and Francke's institutions at Halle offered education for girls. It was not equal to that for boys, but still it was an advance over earlier Protestant policies.

In Radical Pietism, women took more leadership in writing, teaching, and speaking, although outside the institutional Protestant churches. Johanna Eleanora von Merlau Petersen was in the Saalhof circle in Frankfurt, where Spener launched his small groups. After marriage in 1680, she helped to popularize the doctrine of the universal restoration of all things, which Jane Leade published ahead of the Petersens.[5] The couple defended the woman prophet Rosamunde Juliane von der Asseburg.[6] Prophets such as Anna Maria Schuchart of Erfurt, Katharina Reinecke of Halberstadt, and Anna Eva Jacobs typically called for repentance and moral improvement as they warned of God's judgment,[7] as the French Prophets of the same period did. In the role of prophet, a woman could claim authority to speak and at the same time defend such an "abnormality" as the result of an unusual state of prophetic inspiration.[8]

One of the most important women to challenge traditional gender roles in churchly Pietism was Anna Magdalena von Wurm Francke. She illustrates the difficulty of separating Radical and churchly Pietism too sharply. Familiar with Gottfried Arnold and Johann Georg Gichtel, she married August Hermann Francke, the pastor and administrator at Halle. From the spring to the fall of 1715 she refused to move with him into their new home. She resisted her husband's ostensible "authority," probably in protest of the marriage of their daughter Sophia (no accidental name) to Francke's assistant, the hymnist

Johann Anastasius Freylinghausen. Anna Magdalena Francke's correspondence with Gichtel suggests that she shared his views on the superiority of celibacy.[9]

Radical Pietist thought influenced Conrad Beissel. The women who acted as prophets, visionaries, writers, and leaders of small groups created models that would influence women at Ephrata. Using concepts of gender shaped by Radical Pietism, Beissel and his community challenged traditional social assumptions about gender, while in practice they often reinforced traditional assumptions of women's subordination.

The Virgin Sophia

The gender concepts of Beissel and Ephrata derive from a unique understanding of God based on Jacob Boehme's thought as transmitted by Gichtel, Gottfried Arnold, the Philadelphian movement, and related German Radical Pietist literature.[10]

For Boehme, God is not male or female, but has both female and male characteristics in divine balance. The male characteristic is fiery, wrathful, and dominating; the female is loving, submissive, merciful, and forgiving. Boehme personified the female aspect of God in the figure of the Divine Virgin, or Sophia.[11] She represents the female united to the male in the Godhead.[12] She was to be the spouse of Adam, whom God created androgynous. This androgyny reflected the full, divine image of God.[13] Thus Boehme partly rejected the prevailing interpretation of God as wholly male.[14]

According to Boehme, Adam faced testing in paradise to determine whether he would remain turned toward God's will or succumb to self-serving desire. Like Lucifer before him, Adam failed the test, and the Divine Virgin departed out of Adam when God opened his side to take a rib for creating Eve. While Boehme disparaged Eve and all women, he considered Adam more responsible than Eve for sin.[15] Boehme further worked out some Christological/Sophiological[16] and soteriological implications of Sophia as part of the Godhead. Boehme attributed Adam's fall to desire contrary to God's will and Adam's loss of Sophia, and he added a role for Sophia to the story of the crucifixion. When Christ's side was opened with a spear at the crucifixion (John 19), Sophia entered the wound and was reunited with humanity through Jesus, the second Adam. This created the possibility for redeemed believers to be restored spiritually to the image of God with a balance of genders. Because of the reunion of genders in Jesus Christ, consummated at his crucifixion, Christ is both bridegroom and agent of rebirth. Sophia is his bride, as is the Church. Yet the divine femaleness of Sophia has been restored to him so that Christ, the second Adam, has a divine womb by which to give spiritual rebirth.

Boehme described Jesus as born both of the Virgin Mary and of the heavenly Eternal Virgin (Sophia), without "male seed" (*Mannes Samen*). Thus while heavenly and earthly females (Sophia and Mary) have parts in the conception and incarnation of Jesus Christ, male biology does not. God, as divine Father, contributes the male "sign," or characteristics, to Jesus at his conception in Mary's womb. Christ is incarnated as the male Jesus, a hero "with male parts," who conquers the fire of God the Father's wrath.[17] The Virgin Sophia joins to a virginal Christ, the son of the Virgin Mary, to create a virginity from which sinners are spiritually reborn. Christ and the heavenly Virginity together beget "children" when believers come to faith through spiritual rebirth. Faith allows sinners to enter back into the will of God, which Adam had rejected. By faith, believers participate in a mystical incarnation (*Menschwerdung*) of Christ within them, whereby they attain a spiritual androgyny that mirrors the full image of the Godhead. In *De Signatura Rerum* Boehme expanded the Virgin Sophia's role by incorporating her into the seven qualities or source-spirits of God, described as "seven kingdoms of the mother of all being" (*sieben Reiche der Mutter aller Wesen*). In an alchemical reworking of themes from *Menschwerdung Jesu Christi,* Boehme recounted Christ's crucifixion as the sixth kingdom of the mother of all being and the resurrection from the dead as the seventh form of that kingdom.[18] Sophia thus plays a role in creation (mother of all being) and in redemption from sin (her union with Christ) through spiritual rebirth.

Gichtel further developed Boehme's concept of Sophia. Gichtel wrote that "she is not God, rather his mirror; she is not Jesus, rather his heavenly flesh and blood."[19] Sophia also mirrors what humans have lost: their androgyny. Gichtel altered Boehme's account of Adam's sin, attributing it to sexual desire rather than to self-will. Gichtel accepted Boehme's account of Sophia's reunion with Christ at the crucifixion. For Gichtel, this reinforced the need for believers to remain joined to Sophia in celibate lives.

Sophia figured in the English and German interconnections of the Philadelphian Society, with which Gichtel had contact. In England, John Pordage wrote *Sancta Sophia,* which was published in 1698, after his death.[20] Gottfried Arnold drew on it for his own *Geheimnis der Göttlichen Sophia oder Weisheit* (Mystery of the Divine Sophia or Wisdom), published two years later.

Arnold's work popularized among German Radical Pietists the concept of Sophia common to the Philadelphian Society and Gichtel, as Peter Erb has noted.[21] Arnold was more concerned with the journey to spiritual rebirth than with speculative theosophy. In his *Geheimnis der Göttlichen Sophia,* Arnold used citations from Scripture and writers such as Justin Martyr and even Augustine to argue that Sophia is a part of the Trinity. Anticipating charges of Valentinianism, Arnold stated that Sophia is "one with Christ [*ein mit Christo*]." Through her God gives new birth, but Sophia herself gives birth to no one and no thing. Yet, as Arnold portrayed her, Sophia plays an active role in the various steps toward rebirth.[22] She mourns as an abandoned widow over men who, like Adam, seek wives rather than Sophia.

The heavenly Sophia, according to Arnold, acts in many roles. She is a lover who arouses seekers. As a teacher, Sophia scolds and punishes her wooers with "an unpleasant sharpness" in the early phases of spiritual awakening. Sometimes she withdraws her love to test the resolve of her followers. Contradicting his earlier defense against charges of Valentinianism, Arnold claims that Sophia indeed gives spiritual rebirth "as a true mother" to the believer. She prepares the reborn for marriage to herself. She gives the "kiss of her mouth" (*Kuß ihres Mundes*) and lets her betrothed "lie then comforted at her breast and suck until he is satisfied." The two engage in "paradisial love play" (*paradiesiesches Liebesspiel*). Arnold insisted that the love play is all in "utmost purity and virginity" (*äusserst Reinigkeit und Jungfrauschaft*); the Song of Solomon is but a shadow of it. Only by renouncing "bodily desires, lusts, and sins of the flesh can men be joined to Sophia."[23] Writing from a male perspective, Arnold recast the medieval view of the soul as bride of Christ into a kind of gynocentric perspective. In the place of Jesus as bridegroom of the soul, Sophia becomes the bride of the soul for men. She, the bride, directs the relationship with souls of males. All this changed in 1701, when Arnold married. Duly scandalized, Gichtel wrote that Arnold had never truly understood Sophia and never would.[24]

The network of the English and German Philadelphian societies and their friends included a young scholar named Johannes Kelpius, who emigrated to Pennsylvania in 1694. He portrayed Sophia as mother in spiritual rebirth and spouse of the soul.[25] This transatlantic web of Boehmists cultivated an ascetic version of Sophia, the female aspect of the Godhead, who actively teaches, punishes, woos, and gives birth to new believers. In this sense, Sophia is by no means subordinate or passive. Yet Sophia is never fully independent of Christ or God. This network of writers on both sides of the ocean influenced Conrad Beissel.

Voices of the Turtledoves

Sophia at Ephrata

Beissel alluded to Sophia in the first of his surviving published works, *Mystyrion Anomias* (1728). Beissel identified the "pure, godly, and heavenly Wisdom" as the true spouse of Adam.[26] Their relationship prefigures the wedding of Christ the Lamb to the Church in Revelation. Beissel further worked out his views on Sophia in his *Dissertation on Man's Fall,* in his letters, and in the last of his spiritual speeches (*Geistliche Reden*).

In the *Dissertation* Sophia figures primarily as divine lover and spouse. Briefly Beissel mentioned the separation of the female and male characteristics in the Godhead at Lucifer's rebellion. When Lucifer stirred up a "fire ground" (*einen Feuergrund erweckte*), God had to leave the androgynous divine "unity and to awaken the hidden manhood [*Mannheit*] within himself, which is against his nature."[27] Because Lucifer's rebellion overcame "gentleness, which is divine femaleness [*die Sanfftmuth, als die Göttliche Weiblichkeit*]," God could no longer "keep house" [*Haus halten*] with female gentleness. God divided the whole creation into male and female, and decided to "subordinate femaleness, which is the gentle part, under the male [part], the authority [*Obrigkeit*]."[28]

Realizing that Beissel had created a major theological problem by dividing God, Peter Miller, Beissel's Heidelberg-trained editor, attempted to resolve it. Miller claimed that this division increased the dignity of Jesus Christ's mediation, because he "intervened in the cleft [or tear or rip, *Riß*] to restore the balance [or temperament] in the Godhead."[29]

Beissel tended to write in a more experiential way about Sophia, concentrating on the images of lover and mother. He claimed that in his "faded heavenly magic [*meine verblichene himmlishce Magia*]" he had not realized that "the fiery male will had an unchangeable rebellion against the heavenly femaleness."[30] Then God revealed the "secret [or mystery] of the cross" (*Geheimnuß des Creutzes*) and Beissel learned that maleness like Adam's had to be put to death like Christ on the cross. That would make Beissel virginal so he could partake of the heavenly femaleness.[31]

Sophia as mother helps to restore the gender division in God, bringing divine maleness into submission to divine femaleness, as a boy to his mother. In order for the divine manhood (*Göttliche Mannheit*) to be "released from the office of righteousness" and be "clothed in the female habit," the "heavenly femaleness must herself give birth to a man [*Mann,* or husband] from the eternal Motherhood [*ewige Muttserschafft*]." This man will have the "divine-male-female characteristic" (*Gott-mann-weibliche Eigenschafft*) balanced within himself.³² Obviously Beissel struggled to create words for his concepts. Little wonder that contemporaries found him so difficult to understand!

Through "heavenly femaleness, everything must be restored," Beissel wrote. "Everything that is brought to dying through death on the cross" will be delivered to "the eternal Spirit, or heavenly Motherhood for a glorious flourishing [*ausgrünen*]." Then even Jesus will "give himself up in his past manhood [*Mannheit*]" and surrender himself to "eternal Goodness."³³ The divine female gives ultimate birth in the restoration of all things after the last judgment. Then even judging, which Beissel perceived as a "male office," will be surrendered to the female.

In Beissel's account of Sophia, Jesus is important because he possesses both gender characteristics in perfect balance and remains virginal. Jesus was "begotten immaculate from the heavenly femaleness," born of a virgin who was "pregnant with the seed of the heavenly woman."³⁴ According to Beissel, Jesus had female and male characteristics, but "this man Jesus filled his office in the figure of a man, but the nature of his self was not male but female, because he went about in submission and obedience until death on the cross."³⁵

With his Christology/Sophiology, Beissel accepted the societal definition of women as subordinate but transferred it to men as a desirable trait, making Jesus the giver and primary example of it. Male domination, the corollary to male sexual desire, must be conquered. Thus Jesus is a virginal man, born of a virgin, not through the agency of male seed. The divine female participates in the conception of Jesus, reunites with him at the crucifixion, and acts to give spiritual rebirth to believers. Sophia acts decisively at every turn of Beissel's concepts of God, creation, and redemption.

In the last of his *Geistliche Reden,* Beissel created an allegory in which Sophia plays many roles that cannot be separated. Neither are they neatly separate from women in his own life. Throughout the sermon, an elusive virgin betrothed to the male author slips in and out of the story. At the same time, a seemingly kindly mother rejects the author and turns out not to be the author's true mother. An old, widowed mother with many children adopts him. Yet the old widow turns out to be a splendid bride, even as the youth awaits his impending marriage to another woman.³⁶ The divine female fuses several images. Sophia plays the role of betrothed, mother, and widow in various aspects of the mystical life, including spiritual rebirth and the soul's marriage. At the same time, all these figures represent important women in

Beissel's life, such as his mother, who was a widow, and women to whom Beissel found himself attracted.

In a letter to Peter Becker in 1756, Beissel expounded his gendered concept of God. Beissel urged him to abandon earthly marriage for Sophia and to seek the "heavenly and paradisial femaleness" (*die himmlische und paradisische Weiblichkeit*) and "the holy sinking into oneself" (*das heilige unter sich sinken*).[37] Beissel cautioned that in the war against sexual desire and male will, a male falls asleep, like Samson in Delilah's lap. Then Sophia "gives us a kiss, and thereby wounds our heart with an arrow of Sophian love." Her kiss gives "paradisial rapture [*Entzückung*], so that we think that we may be already resting in the lap of Wisdom or sleeping in her arms."[38] This image echoed Arnold's description of Sophia's "fiery love arrow."[39]

Sophia withdraws, however, and a man may think that she is punishing him for sin. He might also try to fight the male will by himself. Sophia, who tires of waiting, tears off the fetters and leads her suitor out of the battle with male will. She may cast the suitor on the sickbed, not the marriage bed, so that he will learn that Sophia herself "helps to soften the male fire-will." Sophia has the "holy Tincture in herself" to heal "Jacob's earthly venus spermatica [*sic*]."[40]

Here Beissel referred to Jesus' words about celibacy (Matt. 19:12) and to Gichtel's allegorical interpretation of Jacob's wrestling with an angel (Gen. 33). For Beissel, the wrestling represented the struggle to live in celibacy, which he called "spiritual castration for the sake of the Kingdom of Heaven." Jacob was made lame and his hip put out of joint.[41] Gichtel interpreted Jacob's wrestling as an allegorical metaphor for celibacy. According to Gichtel, because "God is disgusted with this earthly sleeping together," he touched Jacob's genitals (literally, *Schamm*). Gichtel believed that the Jewish custom of not eating meat from the thigh joint, although not expressly commanded in the Bible, implied that sex is unclean. Gichtel believed that "nature" settled the matter. "At the hind part of animals lie the genitals [*Schamm*] and Venae Spermaticae," and God "has no pleasure in these animal members."[42] In light of this conviction, Gichtel claimed, "I have circumcised [*beschnitten*] myself for the sake of the Kingdom of Heaven," renouncing further contact with women.[43]

Drawing on Radical Pietist writers, Beissel made separated genders the central problem of human evil and of the cosmos. That problem drove the evils of male sexual desire and male domination. In Beissel's mystical language, the figure of Sophia supplied the female part lacking in traditional theological images of God. Beissel also taught that Sophia was necessary to restore the lost female part to men. Beissel created a literature in which she fulfilled the mystical role of restoring the missing female characteristics as powerful lover and mother.

Aside from several hymn texts, few works by women at Ephrata survive. One of the most important works by women is "Die Rose," the so-called church book, or internal history of the sisters' order. Dated 1745, the work reinterprets the sisters' story in light of their reorganization that year into the Order of the Roses of Saron. "Die Rose" includes some devotions composed by sisters, at least one written before 1745. These devotions offer insight into how the vowed sisters viewed Sophia.

The Ephrata nuns offer a potential case with which to study Gerda Lerner's interpretive theory of women's history. Lerner proposes that the necessary preconditions for development of a feminist consciousness include women's access to "an economic alternative for survival other than marriage" and "large groups of single, self-supporting women." In such conditions women can "elevate sisterhood to a unifying ideal." They can seek the necessary "cultural affirmation" to challenge male repression and to "verify the adequacy, even the power of their own thinking."[44]

According to Lerner, a feminist consciousness consists of "(1) the awareness of women that they belong to a subordinate group and that, as members of such a group, they have suffered wrongs; (2) the recognition that their condition of subordination is not natural, but societally determined; (3) the development of a sense of sisterhood; (4) the autonomous definition by women of their goals and strategies for changing their condition; and (5) the development of an alternative vision of the future."[45] Admittedly, Lerner's concepts cannot be simply transposed to an earlier century; but since she offered the framework for interpreting women's history, the Ephrata sisters suggest a possible test case.

"Die Rose" praises five early sisters, Ketura, Föben, Efigenia, Sincletica, and Jael, as "founders, who were set together in the lap [or womb, *Schooß*] of the Upper Mother in this birthing work [*Gebährungs Werck*]."[46]

Sister Jael prayed that "the Divine Wisdom may lower herself longer and more" upon the sisters, in order "more to reveal her depths and secret ways"; for "Wisdom has her play in humility [*Niedrigkeit*], therefore there are so few who find her."[47] The entire manuscript ends with an anonymous benediction praising the virgin birth of Christ and the "foundress [*Anfängerin*], Mother and Queen of Heaven." This mother gives birth to the spiritually reborn.

From the "high, miraculous birth of the son of God and of the Virgin Mary" the work of the sisterhood was born, "without the doing of a man," just as they believed Jesus had been born without male intervention. The sisters will take pride in being "the gender [or race, *Geschlecht*] from the Mother of the Heavenly Virgin."[48]

Clearly the sisters believed that Sophia had acted in the founding of their order. They asserted female agency in declaring that just as Jesus was conceived without the help of a man, their order was founded without a man. While many passages in "Die Rose" flatter Beissel as the spiritual "father," the sisters may have considered him to be a man transformed by the heavenly Sophia, and thus not typical.

More frequently "Die Rose" speaks of bridal mysticism with Jesus Christ as the soul's spouse. Sisters Catharina, Paulina, and Sofia all long to share the heavenly bridal bed with Christ.[49] Sister Bernice, who died in 1744, wrote that after a sister has undergone many trials, "the complete union [*Vereinigung*] can happen with her holy husband Jesus, her heavenly bridegroom." Then such a sister will "be impregnated [*besamet*] through the overshadowing of the Holy Spirit and made fruitful [fertile, *fruchtbar*]."[50]

The author of "Die Rose" wrote that they all wished "to be daily and hourly married [*vermählet*] and joined [to Christ], in order to be and remain one [with him] and be solely his possession."[51] To attain this goal, their "entire life consists in a constant putting to death of both spiritual and bodily things."[52] Sister Efigenia recounted a vision of Christ proclaiming his love for her by letting himself be nailed to the cross.[53]

The sisters clearly learned the mystical language of Conrad Beissel. While their piety claims an important place for the divine female, Sophia, she is neither the sole nor the prevailing image for God in the sisters' writings that survive. The sisters prepared for and anticipated a unitive presence of Christ for which they used marriage as a metaphor.

One could easily attribute the persistence of male imagery for the mystical life among the sisters to Beissel's domineering supervision of their order. Certainly he wielded considerable power at Ephrata. Yet he also featured Sophia far more in his writings than the sisters did in what remains of theirs. While the *Chronicon* credited Beissel for Ephrata's strict regimen, "Die Rose" credited Mother Maria Eicher for setting the daily schedules and restrictions on visitors, entering and departing the house, and locking the doors. Thus while Beissel's domination may help explain hierarchy among the sisters, it does not explain their choice not to follow his stronger emphasis on Sophia in the images they used for their piety.

Sophia plays a mixed role in Ephrata's mystical writings. Certainly Conrad Beissel featured Sophia in his teachings. The female image for God, Sophia, even takes priority as the final restoration of all things unfolds. Yet solitary women, living together in their own space, did not claim Sophia as the sole or even primary divine image in their mystical lives. Conrad Beissel's dominating personality and the spirit of their times limited the sisters' ability to shape a gynocentric piety.

ATTITUDES TOWARD WOMEN, MEN, AND SEX

Attitudes Toward Women

Conrad Beissel described women as "the lack of the man." In examining the English language, Julia Stanley has noted male domination in phrases that define women only in negative comparison with men. Such phrases create a "minus male," in Stanley's view.[54] While neither Ephrata nor German literature was the object of her study, her work raises questions about how Beissel construed gender in his mystical language. He did identify women as a deficit of what is male. In that respect, he only perpetuated the long-standing legacy of Aristotle, who considered it self-evident that females were inferior because they lacked male attributes.[55]

Beissel, drawing from Boehme and Gichtel, illustrates the polyvalence of Radical Pietist men's attitudes toward women. Beissel devalued women because Eve was created from Adam after Adam lost Sophia, and thus was an inferior companion. Gichtel, more gynophobic than Beissel, warned that a woman can be the devil's tool. Women soften the male and "break the power of the will." They want to be "lord over the man's will and rule."[56] Gichtel conceded that by "putting on Jesus Christ," virginal women could become "manly virgins" (*männliche Jungfrauen*) and serve in the Priesthood of Melchizedek, but he thought this was "a rare thing."[57]

In the *Dissertation,* Beissel blamed Adam, not Eve, for sin in paradise, since Adam had sexual desire first. Beissel viewed Eve as inferior, because Adam's desiring was already active when she was created. However, Beissel also claimed that the woman was "a simple child" until she encountered the serpent. Again, Beissel blamed the serpent more than Eve for "poisoning" her through "serpent magic."

Translation errors in this portion of the *Dissertation* in Peter Erb's source book create a misrepresentation of Beissel's view of women. One passage about "the spirit of deceitfulness" was mistranslated, resulting in the implication that deceitfulness came over Adam, and that the "woman is a daughter of Lucifer, begotten by his magical will."[58] Beissel actually wrote that after the woman was made, "the spirit of deceitfulness and slyness came, which [the spirit, not the woman] was a daughter in the magic will of Lucifer, and it [the spirit] sought to corrupt completely the little remaining femaleness."[59]

Although Conrad Beissel envisioned the heavenly femaleness of Sophia as eventually triumphing in the cosmos, he did not advocate equality or superiority for women on earth. He counseled women "not to oppose the authoritarian office [obrigkeitlichen Amt] of the man" until they attained their paradisial bodies, presumably at the last judgment. According to Beissel, the more women try to come out from under male authority (Obrigkeit), the more danger of temptation they face from the serpent. Instead, they should seek the "lost God-femaleness" (verlohrne Gott-weiblichkeit) from above in celibacy and be espoused to Christ, their true husband.[60] While Beissel believed that Christ had commissioned Mary Magdalene as the first apostle to proclaim the resurrection,[61] he denied women leadership in public worship.

Despite Beissel's repressive implementation of his views, the sisters in Saron apparently gained some economic independence. According to the account book of a householder, Michael Müller, which starts in 1748, the sisters paid Müller to repair windows, doors, spinning wheels, and lanterns for them. Celibate brothers at Ephrata had the skills to do these repairs, but the sisters hired Müller to do them. The sisters also worked for Müller, a farmer and handyman. They often spun thread for him, and he paid with butter or other goods or services.[62] Müller's account book suggests that the sisterhood functioned as an organized economic unit, engaging in business, handling their own finances, contracting and paying for maintenance work. This finding raises the question of the extent of a communal economy at Ephrata.

This view of the sisterhood sheds light on Maria Eicher's apparent attempt around 1764 to separate the sisterhood from the brotherhood and have Peter Miller, their prior, deposed. At the time, Samuel Eckerlin had just returned with a group from the Shenandoah Valley, intending to press his legal claim to cloister land. Controversy also swirled over who would succeed Beissel. Mother Maria reportedly backed Brother Gideon (Christian Eckstein). Beissel, who favored Georg Adam Martin, deposed her before 1766. After Beissel's death in 1768, Peter Miller ultimately prevailed. Maria lived as a sister in Saron until her death in 1784.[63] For more than twenty years, Mother Maria's leadership as prioress helped the sisterhood to attain some degree of autonomy, yet always in Beissel's shadow.

Attitudes Toward Men

Beissel's mystical language radically defied traditional gender concepts. Not only did he define women as a lack of what is male, but he also defined men as deficient in what is female. While a similar view was implicit in some other Radical Pietists, Beissel alone sharpened it and created a communal way of life to remedy it through celibacy.

In order to restore the lack in men, Beissel prescribed that they become female and submissive to God. Only by rebirth through God's female aspect, Sophia, and betrothal to her could a man recover the missing part. Men should imitate the virginal celibacy of Jesus and be united to Sophia, their "manly Virgin."[64]

Beissel wrote to Peter Becker in 1756 that "we must bring our self-working and fire-masculine man's-will into a sinking, to become, to a certain extent, female."[65] Men must "present to the noble Virgin a pure matrix," because she already has "in herself the fire of the holy seed for heavenly fruitfulness." When the male will becomes feminized, Sophia "can quite easily come with her virginal man-fire to our matrix, healed in God."[66] Here Beissel portrayed Sophia with masculine terms (man-fire) and portrayed the men of Ephrata with female terms (as possessing a matrix, or womb), using his mystical language to reconstruct gender concepts.

Beissel's mystical language overturned the Aristotelian presupposition of male superiority: he defined men as deficient because they lack female attributes. Men lack a womb for spiritual rebirth until Sophia bestows it. Thus Ephrata's linguistic way to the presence of God mandated a restoration of the gender characteristics divided and lost by Adam's lust. Ephrata's general attitude toward women did not depart radically from traditional social definitions. Their concept of men as needing to recover the lost female aspect broke up traditional social constructions of male identity.

Attitudes Toward Celibacy, Sex, and Marriage

Conrad Beissel believed that the only redemptive way to the restoration of gender balance in each believer was through celibacy. Then would "Sophia or Jesus woo the soul of a person, in order to lead it to the chaste marriage bed." In union with Christ/Sophia, "nothing male is lacking from the female, and nothing female is lacking from the male."[67] Even some of the community's dissenters, such as Ezechiel Sangmeister, shared Beissel's view that celibacy is superior to marriage. Brother Ezechiel wrote that "God never wanted this [sexual] propagation" for humans. To awakened souls, "especially the masculine sex, involuntary seminal emission [*Samenfluß*] is an almost unbearable burden."[68]

Beissel's views on sex starkly contrasted with those of other Pietistic groups. He drew the opposite conclusion from Eva von Buttlar and her society, which indulged in free sex. Buttlar gathered a circle of followers first at Allendorf, in Hesse, in 1702, then at Sassmannshausen, in Wittgenstein, in 1704. She took two lovers, and claimed that together she and her lovers formed the Holy Trinity. "Mother Eva" drew on much of the Boehmist vocabulary that Beissel used, but with opposite conclusions. She taught men to curb their sexual desire by engaging in multiple liaisons rather than through celibacy. Apparently the group initiated some of the women by collapsing the uterus to purify them of sexual desire.[69] Spener and Francke denounced her, Gichtel called her a "public whore," and Hochmann von Hochenau criticized her "entirely sodomitic ways."[70]

Ephrata and the Moravians came into heated controversy in 1742 over conflicting interpretations of the metaphor of the soul's marriage to Christ. Ephrata set this metaphor in Gichtel's anthropology of primeval androgyny, warranting celibacy. The Moravians, however, encouraged marriage because it mirrored Christ's relationship with the Church. Little wonder that Johannes Hildebrand was horrified when Zinzendorf said during one of the synods of 1742 at Oley, "If I would die just at the time when I was sleeping with my wife, I could say to the Saviour, 'I am coming from this work.'"[71] For their part, the Moravians could never accept the Gichtelian anthropology that undergirded Ephrata's celibacy.

Ephrata's views on reproduction and spiritual rebirth spilled over into the controversy with the Moravians over salvation and baptism. One Ephrata tract denounced the Moravians' acceptance of marriage and childbearing as a way for the Church to grow. The Sabbatarians denied that "such a carnal way of increasing the Church could be pleasing to God." Instead, Christ instituted "a different birthing work" with the Spirit to fill the Church with "pure, virginal spirits."[72] As these polemics demonstrate, it is differences in beliefs otherwise similar that generate the most rancor.

Beissel's exhortation to dissolve marriage in favor of celibacy lent religious legitimacy to some women's resistance to the power of fathers, boyfriends, husbands, and even families. Anna and Maria Eicher defied their father to join Beissel in 1726, when Maria was sixteen.[73] Anna Landis attempted to leave her husband around 1731 and finally joined Ephrata after his death;[74] Christina

Höhn followed the same pattern. Sister Eunike (Eunice) left her husband and Maria Heidt (Sister Bernice) abandoned her betrothed to join the sisterhood.[75]

Perhaps the most famous wife to abandon marriage at Ephrata was Maria Christina Saur, wife of the Germantown printer. She joined the community in 1730, before it moved to the site of Ephrata. In Germany she had been widowed before she married Christoph Saur in 1720. Their only child, also named Christoph, was born the next year.[76] They arrived in Pennsylvania in 1724 and soon moved to the Conestoga region. She left her husband and nine-year-old son in 1730 to join Beissel's congregation, eventually taking the spiritual name of Sister Marcella. She left Ephrata in 1744.

Maria Christina Saur's reasons for leaving home to join Beissel are unknown. Ezechiel Sangmeister reported that she wanted to be with Jacob Weiss, who persuaded her to leave and became her "second husband" at Ephrata.[77] An anonymous book published in 1758, probably by the Saur press, *Ein Spiegel der Eheleute,* may offer a different explanation. The contents suggest that the *Spiegel,* cast as a dialogue between a master and apprentice, reflects the Saur household. The master explains that a wife should be subordinate to her husband on biblical grounds. A wife should not criticize if a husband has trouble finding and staying with a trade. Her contradicting the husband will "make life bitter and sour [*sauer*]" for both.[78] (Saur had tried several occupations before Maria left him.) The master criticizes women who desire to rule, insisting that married women obey their husbands. A woman who has a "ruling nature" (*herrschendes Wesen*) should remain single. It is also unbearable if "a wife rules over a husband because of child discipline." The author claims that discipline is good for children, even if "the rod went too hard, so that it [the child's skin] became red, or gave a few drops of blood." A wife who contradicts her husband has a "loose mouth."[79]

While some of Saur's early letters suggest marital harmony in Pennsylvania, a friend wrote in 1739 that Saur "lives now much more quietly than when she was with him."[80] If *Spiegel der Eheleute* mirrors the Saur family, Maria may have left over conflicts about her autonomy and child discipline. Saur's newspaper advertised *Spiegel der Eheleute* for sale on August 10, 1758. Late the next month he died.[81] Could he have left this as a final comment on a troubled personal life? While *Spiegel der Eheleute* cannot be conclusively traced to the Saur home, it certainly resembles their situation. It also illustrates male resistance to women's autonomy among Germans in colonial Pennsylvania.

Beissel taught his views in a Pennsylvania where the subordination of wives to husbands was still a serious matter, despite the presence of Quaker women who preached and enterprising women who ran the "caves" along the

Delaware River where sailors found entertainment. In 1731 Catherine Bevan of New Castle and the family's servant, Peter Murphy, were executed for murdering her husband. The servant was hanged; Catherine was burned at the stake. English law viewed a wife's murder of her husband as petit treason, deserving of harsher punishment.[82]

Beissel's teaching about celibacy could divide marriages, and it raised accusations that he was promiscuous. He reportedly had renounced women and "Adam's birthing work [*Gebährungswerck*]," or sexual reproduction, after an alleged clash with his master's wife when he was working in Mannheim as a journeyman baker.[83] In 1730 rumors about immorality among the Sabbatarians buzzed, but no charges were substantiated. The most serious accusation was Sangmeister's charge that Beissel had a sexual affair with Anna Eicher, producing a child, whom she killed.[84] Anna reportedly exposed the story, but retracted her accusation when she learned that her life was in danger as well as Beissel's.[85] Sangmeister placed this story in 1730, claiming that the charges came before Conrad Weiser as justice of the peace. But Weiser was not a justice of the peace in 1730 and had no acquaintance with Beissel's community at that time.[86] Sangmeister also accused Beissel of multiple sexual liaisons with the sisters in 1764, about some of which he heard from the wife of Johann Franz Regnier. The Regniers reportedly returned to Ephrata in the 1760s. She claimed that Beissel appeared "in a form similar to a shadow" and came through her window and into her bed "by means of magic."[87] While it is hard to imagine Beissel accomplishing such a feat at more than seventy years old, in declining health, the point of the story is the multiple accusations against him. Thus Sangmeister's accounts must be weighed with caution.

Beissel insisted that he maintained his celibacy.[88] No explicit information so far contradicts those claims. However, a curious piece of evidence appears in one of Israel Eckerlin's two surviving missives attacking Beissel. In 1755 Eckerlin wrote that Maria Eicher had Beissel "under the feet." She allegedly had such power because a certain woman who had died had cause to bring a case against Beissel, and now "her sister has totally weakened" him. The surviving sister "had you under the feet at the time," Eckerlin wrote to Beissel, and she was "priest not only in her own work but in the whole community."[89] Eckerlin said nothing about what the grievance was, however, or which sister's it was. Naema, the youngest of the Eicher sisters, was also a nun. The wrong may have been a sexual liaison. It may have been Beissel's decision to pass over Anna and make Maria prioress. If he had a sexual affair with Anna, Beissel might have acted more prudently to install her as prioress.

The number of sources reporting Beissel's trysts, especially with Anna Eicher, suggests that some actual events lie behind them. At the same time, Ephrata's rhetoric about celibacy made it and Beissel the perfect targets for charges of sexual license.[90] Beissel's persistent erotic imagery could only inflame passions. When sexually explicit rhetoric was often used to forbid sexual activity, some transgressions were unavoidable. To know definitively whether Beissel was one of the transgressors we must wait for better documentation.

CONCLUSION

Conrad Beissel's definition of the female as a person who lacked male attributes reflected traditional assumptions about gender in European Christendom. From it he drew the equally traditional corollary that women must be subordinate to men. However, Ephrata departed radically from traditional gender constructions in Beissel's parallel assumption that the male is deficient because he lacks female attributes. Equally revolutionary was Beissel's conclusion that male domination is the sinful result of Adam's fall. Ephrata's mystical language created a literature by which men could seek the missing female qualities through spiritual rebirth in Christ/Sophia, resulting in a celibate restoration of primeval divine androgyny. Beissel built a religious community and created a body of mystical literature to serve that radical reconstruction of gender.

At the center of the soul's mystical journey Beissel radically redefined Christ as a man not deficient but complete, with a female aspect, Sophia. Christ's redemption atoned for the sins of male wrath and domination. Beissel saw the crucifixion as both a redemptive event and an experiential event with which every Ephrata sister and brother must identify. The community's mystical language guided seekers to a mystical union with Christ or Sophia, who would restore the missing gender attributes and unify the soul in balanced androgyny, reflecting God's divine nature. Ephrata pursued a heterosexually oriented bridal mysticism of the soul.

Beissel's redefinition of maleness legitimated a woman's effort to be free of domination by her father or husband. Beissel advocated avoiding or dissolving marriage for celibacy, freeing women from the risks of childbearing. His ascetic regimen may have compromised some of the benefits of this freedom.

In the community Beissel created, the celibate sisterhood achieved a degree of autonomy, despite his efforts to curtail it. They had their own living and worship space, with their own leaders, and supported themselves financially. Ephrata's religious assumption that men should adopt the "female" trait of submissiveness provided at least rhetorical boundaries for men, of which the vowed sisters could take advantage.

It would be anachronistic to apply Gerda Lerner's theory to the eighteenth century, and in any case her attempt to create a model for interpreting women in history does not completely serve the women at Ephrata. The vowed celibate sisters had some economic independence, freedom from husbands and fathers, and a women's community within their house, Saron. Yet the sisters did not develop a primarily gynocentric expression of their piety that would have indicated a kind of women's consciousness, even though Beissel's writings frequently feature female imagery for the divine. Even more revolutionary was Conrad Beissel's reconstruction of male gender. The celibates journeyed on a path of alternative gender definitions, seeking union with the missing gender part through the aid of Ephrata's mystical language.

5

"GOD'S HOLY POINT OF REST"

Ephrata's Mystical Language in Space and Time

Ephrata's mystical language influenced some of the community's decisions about how to organize their space and time. Skilled commoners rather than professional architects created Ephrata's buildings, adapting familiar patterns from the early modern period rather than intentionally medieval styles.[1] These patterns in space and time contributed to Ephrata's anticipation and awareness of God's presence.

At least three distinct yet overlapping architectural periods developed among the Sabbatarians. In the first, or solitary, period, beginning in 1725, some members built hermit cabins on land belonging to Rudolf Nägele (Brother Jojada or Johoidah), formerly a Mennonite pastor.[2] This pattern continued after the move to the Cocalico in 1732. The cabin built in 1733 for Anna and Maria Eicher, the first women solitaries on the Cocalico, still stands in Ephrata Park, across the creek from the cloister site. The Eicher cabin was probably typical, although not necessarily a prototype. Julius Sachse claimed that dimensions in Brother Kenan's notebook for a cabin were the "uniform rule" for all the cabins. Because Brother Kenan joined only in 1744, the plans were not a rule.[3]

A transition toward a second architectural period of monastic community began in 1734. The hermits built a *"magazin,"* or storehouse, and a bakehouse for common use and charity.[4] The *"magazin"* has been identified as an extant stone building traditionally called the Almonry. Its considerable distance from the first cabins by the creek makes its location unlikely for an important storehouse. Alan G. Keyser, a specialist in Pennsylvania German architecture, has questioned the dating of the Almonry to the 1730s on the basis of construction details. The beams, visible from the cellar, are sawn and smaller than the beams in the extant buildings of the 1740s.[5] Four dendrochronology samples taken in 2000 were dated to the 1740s.[6] While the samples provided no conclusive dating, combined evidence strongly suggests that the stone building known as the Almonry is not the storehouse of 1734.

The members soon constructed a common house of wood and stone. Called the Berghaus (Hill House) for its construction "half against the hill" (later known as Mount Zion),[7] the house was home to four celibate men, including Israel Eckerlin and Peter Miller. The community lodged guests and held love feasts in it before 1735.[8] Julius Sachse wrongly claimed that the title page ornament in Ephrata's 1748 edition of the *Martyrer Spiegel* portrayed the Berghaus and Zion convent. The Ephrata printers merely copied the ornament from the title page of the 1685 edition. The ornament, with a different caption, was used again when Georg Zeissinger helped to reprint Alonso Barba's *Gründlicher Unterricht von den Metallen* in 1763.[9]

Ephrata's second distinct architectural phase began before the first ended. Some members continued to build hermit cabins up to and perhaps after 1740, when Beissel tried to gather the hermits into dormitories. The second phase, the monastic communal period, began as members erected buildings for communal use in 1735. This architectural phase ended in 1749 with the failure to build the last planned monastic house, Succoth. In the third architectural phase, after 1749, the community no longer built specific monastic dwellings or meetinghouses. The householders increasingly influenced this phase, up to their formal organization as the German Seventh-Day Baptists in 1814.[10]

The first monastic communal building was Kedar, a dormitory, built in 1735. According to the *Chronicon*, it contained "a room for the meetings, great halls [*Saale*] with every kind of equipment for the *Agapas,* or love feasts;

with them also cells were built for solitaries, according to the custom of the old Greek Church."[11] The decision to build cells in the house allegedly imitated what Gottfried Arnold reported about ancient monastic life.[12] With Kedar, Beissel's community shifted to monastic housing on a larger scale.

Kedar was the first symbolically named building. In Genesis, Kedar was one of the sons of Ishmael. A passage in a Kelpius letter suggests one possible reason for the building's name. Quoting Psalm 120:5, Kelpius claimed that he lived as an exile on earth, dwelling with those of Kedar. Kelpius noted that children of Kedar would not "inherit with Isaac, the son of Sarah," the promise of blessing. Kelpius wrote that "we desire this dark tabernacle of our earthly house to be dissolved, in order that we may obtain an edifice, bright and glorious," citing 2 Corinthians 5:1.[13] For Beissel, "Kedar" may have indicated a place where celibates could live ascetically to "dissolve" the appetites of the earthly body in preparation for paradise.

According to the *Chronicon*, four sisters lived in "the second story" of Kedar, four brothers in "the lower story" (*den untern Stock*).[14] If the chroniclers used the European convention of numbering the floor above the ground floor as the first, then a middle floor between two residential floors would have contained the meeting rooms, as Sachse claimed and others repeated.[15] No sources known to date describe Kedar's appearance in detail.

Archaeological investigations at Ephrata between 1995 and 1998 uncovered evidence for a post-built structure 84 feet by 30 feet on a north-south axis, with the northern end beginning in front of the two-story building traditionally interpreted as a "craft house" and more recently interpreted as Beissel's dwelling. Immediately to the west of the outline of the post-built structure, a stone footing runs at a 30-degree angle toward the west wall. Archaeologist Stephen Warfel has identified this post-built structure as Kedar and the adjacent stone footing as the foundation of the *Bäthaus*, or meetinghouse, attached to Kedar.[16] Although the post-built structure is the only evidence of a large structure so far discovered on the site that could be Kedar, it raises some questions. A more temporary, post-built construction only a year after the Berghaus was built of wood and stone seems out of sequence for a dwelling. The scarcity of evidence of hearths for heating and cooking is also puzzling.[17] If it is Kedar, it is an anomaly in Ephrata's monastic structures. All the monastic buildings after Kedar exhibit evidence of construction on stone footings.

Several writers have repeated Sachse's error in writing that Ephrata builders used no iron because of mysticism and "Rosicrucian theosophy."[18] Boehme related iron to Mars, which symbolized the "male fire will" to dominate.[19] But that did not prevent Ephrata builders from using iron. Sangmeister noted that Brother Darius did most of the iron work in Zion. Dale Biever found ample iron window hinges, spikes, and screws in excavations of the Zion complex in 1963.[20]

Soon after Kedar went into use, Sigmund Landert (Brother Sealthiel) proposed to join the community and donate a house of worship and a dwelling (*Wohnhaus* or *Wohnung*) for Beissel. The *Bäthaus*, or "house of prayer," was attached to Kedar, and Beissel's dwelling was attached to the *Bäthaus*.[21] Widowed for the second time in 1735, with two daughters (the older, Maria, was eleven), Landert was motivated by practical as well as religious considerations. He served as a skilled carpenter until his death in 1757.[22]

The new worship place was described as a "sightly building" with a "room [*Sahl* (sic)] for love feasts and a large room for meetings," with two *Port-Kirchen*, for the use of the solitaries, next to an *Altan*, a balcony or gallery, for the "gray-haired fathers."[23] Seidensticker interpreted *Port-Kirchen* as balconies.[24] By contrast, the Mennonites in Germantown had a log meetinghouse until they replaced it with a simple stone building in 1770. The Dunkers built their first meetinghouse in 1770 in Germantown, copying the small stone building style of the Mennonites. The Moravians, however, built large public structures at Bethlehem from 1741.[25]

Why did the Ephrata hermits build large monastic dwellings and meetinghouses? The *Chronicon* alluded to a need to accommodate a growing membership. Also in the autumn of 1735 Beissel called the solitary in to live on the grounds of the emerging community,[26] and may have planned to move them into dormitories. Building cabins for solitaries would have become impracticable if converts kept coming at the rate of arrivals in the 1730s. Stephen Warfel has also noted the regulating function of putting members to work on buildings, ensuring Beissel's control.[27] In a different light, the building projects might also serve to integrate new arrivals by engaging them in shared tasks. A very different view came from Christopher Saur I in 1751. He reported that Israel Eckerlin "ordered the erection of great buildings."[28] There is currently little other evidence to support this view.

By the winter of 1737–38, Conrad Beissel ordered a monastic house for the brothers, to be located near the crest of Mount Zion. Stephan Koch mentioned in a letter in 1738 that it was "some distance away" from the sisters' dormitory. Builders raised the frame in the spring of 1738, but work continued until 1743.[29] Beissel named it Zion and its residents the Zionitic Brotherhood. "Zion" occurs often in the Bible, and also refers to the mount of the temple in Jerusalem. What particular significance Beissel attached to the name is unclear.

Fig. 5 Vignette from the title page of "Der Christen ABC." (Courtesy of Pennsylvania Historical and Museum Commission, Ephrata Cloister.)

Sachse described a grandiose Zion of three stories with various chambers for secret rites, including one circular room.[30] Ernst and Alderfer simply repeated Sachse. Seidensticker said nothing of unusual arrangements.[31] Sachse played perhaps one of his wiliest tricks when he reproduced a vignette from the title page of a calligraphy manuscript, "Der Christen ABC": he altered it so that a large building on a hill appears to have a domed roof, which would support his theory of a circular upper story. Comparison of an enlargement of the original vignette (Figure 5) with Sachse's version (Figure 6) reveals the alterations. In Sachse's version, the bearded figure (whom he identified as Onesimus, or Israel Eckerlin) in the center sports a moustache, so that he resembles Julius Sachse himself.[32] This altered illustration demonstrates why his accounts require verification.

In late 1739 the Sabbatarians built a meetinghouse and school (*Bät- und Schulhaus*) to accompany Zion's dormitory. The community dedicated the meetinghouse on July 16, 1740.[33] The *Chronicon* described it as a "large, sightly building, below was a large room equipped with chairs, decorated with *Fraktur* writings." Within this space Beissel "had his chair, and behind him a

Fig. 6 Julius Sachse's altered view of Mount Zion in his *German Sectarians of Pennsylvania: A Critical and Legendary History of the Ephrata Cloisters and the Dunkers,* 2 vols. (Philadelphia, 1899–1900), 1:380.

choir [*Chor,* or chancel] was built, in which sat the solitary brothers below and the sisters above." A "large Saal" for love feasts (*Agapas*) was on the "second floor." In European convention, this would be two floors above the ground floor. In the "third floor," which by European custom would be the third above the ground floor (to Americans, the fourth), were rooms (*Wohnungen*) for eight solitaries.[34] If the description followed European custom, then Zion's meetinghouse closely resembled today's Saal (formerly called Peniel), still standing. On the floor above the second-floor balconies in today's Saal is a large open room with many windows. On the fourth floor is evidence of cells for celibates. Thus Zion's meetinghouse and Peniel may have been comparable in design.

Israel Acrelius, who visited in 1753, described the two-story worship room in Zion meetinghouse, with capacity for about a hundred people. Behind Beissel's seat in the center of the room was a chancel (*Chor*), raised "some steps higher." The chancel, where the brothers sat, took up the front third of the meeting room. The sisters sat in a gallery above them, apparently screened from view of the congregation in 1753.[35]

Stephen Warfel's archaeological investigations on Mount Zion, begun in 1999, challenge Dale Biever's interpretations of 1963. Biever believed that the parts of foundation walls he uncovered represented Zion's meetinghouse, measuring 40 feet by 40.³⁶ Warfel's more recent work suggests that these foundations are part of a larger structure with storage cellars beneath it. These details suggest that the structure may be Zion's dormitory, not its meetinghouse.³⁷

The Sabbatarians supposedly destroyed Zion's Saal in 1778, after its use as a hospital for Continental soldiers in the winter of 1777–78. The *Chronicon* reported that Zion's Saal "did not stand more than 38 years and was transformed to a hospital in the war of the Americans, and also afterwards was not built up anymore."³⁸ Seidensticker quoted the *Chronicon*,³⁹ but also quoted Ebeling's geography of Pennsylvania,⁴⁰ which in 1790 stated that members of the community met for worship in Zion. Another eighteenth-century source, Jedidiah Morse's *American Geography* (1789), described "three places of worship" at Ephrata: "Sharon," "Bethany" and a third "church, called Zion," for the whole community.⁴¹ Because Morse plagiarized this description from Morgan Edwards's history of the Baptists of 1770, it is of little help in efforts to discover conditions in 1789.⁴² A land indenture prepared in 1812 as the householders organized the German Seventh-Day Baptist Church also reserved "the Church called Sion" for the use of the last three celibate sisters.⁴³

Subsequent historians differed on which buildings were destroyed after the military hospital was closed. Sachse named Zion and Kedar. He apparently meant Zion's convent, although in describing its Saal, he indicated that it was used for the military hospital. Ernst wrote that both Zion and its Saal were destroyed. Alderfer held that only Zion's convent was sacrificed.⁴⁴ C. H. Martin wrote that Kedar and the Zion buildings were burned to halt disease.⁴⁵

An 1815 surveyor's map by Jacob Hibshman depicts three major buildings on Mount Zion (Figure 7). An uneven curve in the roof marks the central building; it differs from the roof lines of the other structures, which presumably were still standing. On the map, the structure with the sagging roof line appears to adjoin at a right angle another building on the east end. A third, separate building appears west of these two. Stephen Warfel has interpreted these details to mean that the structure drawn with a wavy roof line was Zion's meetinghouse, which was destroyed in 1778, and that Zion's dormitory survived into the nineteenth century.⁴⁶ The documentary evidence is conflicted. Some sources indicate that a building for worship stood on Mount Zion well after the American Revolution, while the *Chronicon* implies that it was not standing after 1778. Some buildings on Mount Zion clearly remained into the nineteenth century, and probably Zion's dormitory was one of them. The identity and uses of other buildings there is less certain.⁴⁷

In 1739 the "brothers built the Sisters' other house," as Ezechiel Sangmeister quoted from a now lost manuscript of the *Chronicon*. A letter from

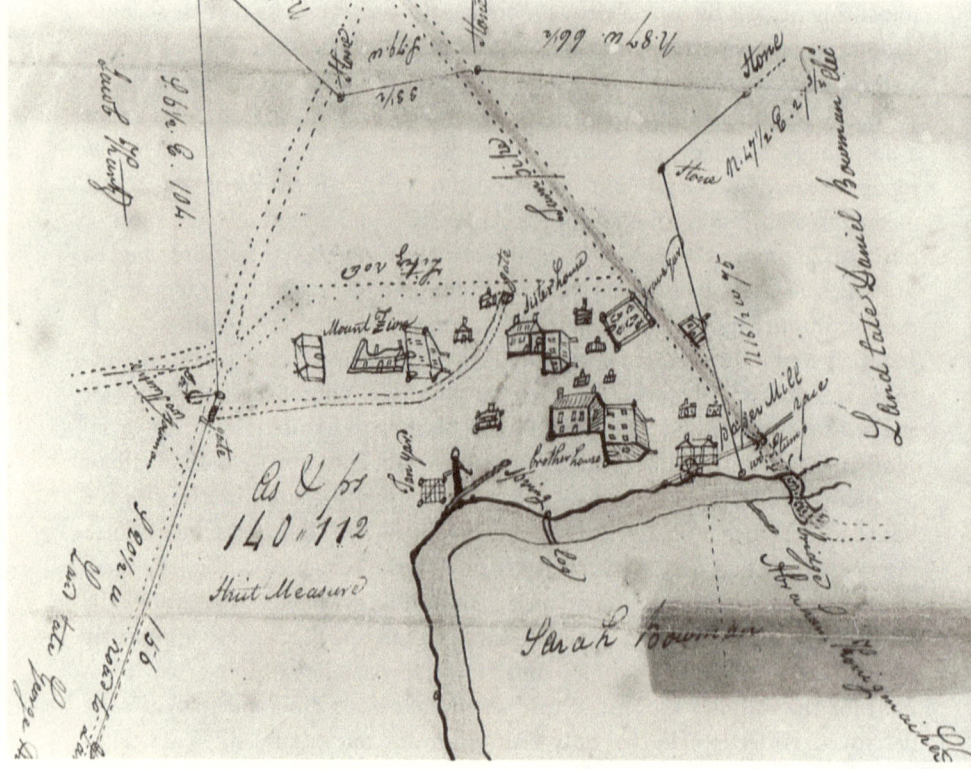

Fig. 7 Jacob Hibshman's survey of Ephrata, 1815. (Courtesy of Pennsylvania Historical and Museum Commission, Ephrata Cloister.)

Stephan Koch (Brother Agabus) confirms this second house. Writing in October 1739, Koch noted that "in two houses live 26 single sisters." They "eat at one table, and each one has a room alone."[48] The rooms probably resembled the cells of the other monastic houses. The size and location of the second house are unknown.

Why did the sisters have a second house? Kedar was large enough for at least thirty, according to a 1743 letter from Anna Thoma (Thommen) to Hieronymus d'Annoni, pastor of her former congregation in Switzerland. "About 30 of us solitary spiritual sisters" lived in Kedar, Anna wrote.[49] Perhaps one group of sisters was less willing to submit to Beissel. The *Chronicon* noted in the context of events in 1736 that "a special band of holy matrons and virgins" submitted to "no headship but that of Christ." The passage further alluded to a humbling of Conrad Beissel.[50] How long this second house was occupied is not known.

As Zion's meetinghouse neared completion, Beissel ordered the householder congregation to "build [its] own house of prayer [*Bäthaus*]" and ordered the destruction of Kedar's *Bäthaus*.[51] Although Stephan Koch's 1739 letter described "7 cabins in which live 1, 2, 3, 4, 5 brothers," located "a musket shot farther uphill" from Kedar.[52] Beissel commanded the hermits to move into the dormitories in 1740. Workers razed some cabins to build workshops with the lumber. Even the chroniclers puzzled over destroying the *Bäthaus*.[53] By ordering a meetinghouse for the householders and tearing down Kedar's *Bäthaus,* Beissel reframed the community's defining dichotomy from female/male to celibates/married couples. From 1740 until 1745 the celibate orders worshiped together in the brothers' meetinghouse, while householders worshiped apart from celibates from 1741 to 1745. Beissel may have wished to display his authority the way secular rulers of the time did, by launching building programs. Ephrata lagged only a decade behind the eighteenth-century peak of construction of new castles in Germany from 1710 to 1730, although the Sabbatarians built on a much smaller scale.[54]

In the bitter winter of 1740–41, workers began constructing a half-timber meetinghouse of four and a half stories for the householders. Ernst claimed without documentation that builders located it at "a mystical angle to Kedar."[55] When it was finished in 1741, Beissel named it Peniel. The structure, now known as the Saal, remains (Figure 8). Recent dendrochronology tests do not contradict this date, but also do not prove it irrefutably.[56] Reported to be the only worship house built free-standing originally, Peniel had cells on the top floor.[57]

Scattered references in Beissel's writings suggest what the name meant to him. The biblical Jacob gave the name Peniel (meaning "face of God") to the place where he wrestled with an angel and asked for a blessing (Gen. 32) while traveling to reconcile with his brother, Esau. In a letter of 1741 Beissel described the biblical story as a metaphor for the "renunciation of all things" and a "wrestling with God" for blessing.[58] Beissel also followed Gichtel's interpretation of the story. In a letter to Peter Becker he wrote that "the male willpower" must be overcome, just as Jacob was overcome by the angel as they wrestled. Then the angel "disjointed the joint of his hip, which is spiritual castration for the sake of the Kingdom of Heaven." With spiritual castration, Jacob has "overcome him [Esau] through the holy sinking into oneself."[59] Here Jacob is a metaphor for a man seeking to overcome sexual desire and the male will to dominate. With the name of Esau, Beissel has mixed the metaphor, because Jacob wrestled with an angel (or God) for a blessing, not with Esau. In Beissel's mixed metaphor, Esau represents a man

Fig. 8 Peniel (Saal) and Saron. (Courtesy of Pennsylvania Historical and Museum Commission, Ephrata Cloister. Photo by Craig A. Benner.)

who preserves the will to dominate and sexual desire. Jacob's disjointed hip typifies celibacy, or spiritual castration, to banish lust and male domination. Gichtel had written virtually the same points in 1697.[60] For Beissel, "Peniel" referred to the struggle to overcome sexual desire and domination by renouncing possessions and marriage. Peniel was to serve as the battleground where the householders advanced toward fuller monastic life.

Peniel's design may feature Boehmist symbols. Peniel measures 40 by 37 feet and is 47 feet high, nearly a perfect cube.[61] For Jacob Boehme, 40 represented the days of testing Adam endured in paradise, Israel's 40 days of testing at Mount Sinai, and Jesus' 40 days in the desert, all of which typified the inner testing each believer faced.[62] Boehme claimed that a "temptation tree" (*Versuchungs-Baum*) grew in the Garden of Eden, the tree of the knowledge of good and evil. As Adam succumbed to the desire for a mate and fell asleep, God took a rib from Adam's side and "the half-cross T" (*das halbe Creutz T*) from Adam's head to create woman. According to Boehme, the "half-cross T" symbolized the cross on which Christ would die and give rebirth to Adam and sinful humanity and to the Holy Trinity.[63]

Boehme's thought and other alchemical and Christian cabbalistic traditions helped to shape a little-known writer, Georg von Welling (1655–1727), and

"GOD'S HOLY POINT OF REST"

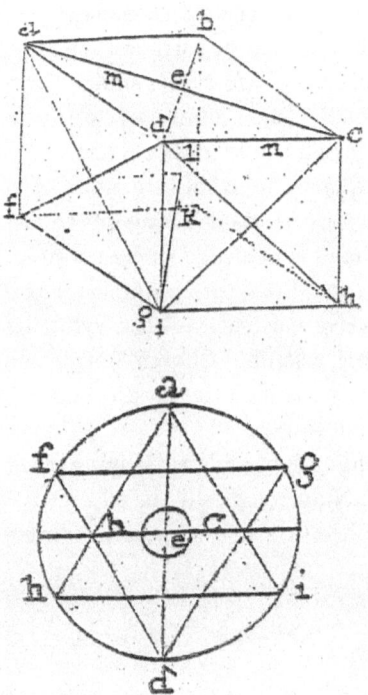

Fig. 9 Figures from Georg von Welling's *Opus Mago-Cabbalisticum et Theosophicum* (1754). (Courtesy of Pennsylvania Historical and Museum Commission, Ephrata Cloister.)

his *Opus Mago-Cabbalisticum et Theoreticum*. Welling, originally from southwestern Germany, worked for a time as director of mines for Margrave Karl Wilhelm of Baden Durlach before settling in Bockenheim, on the edge of Frankfurt, for his final years (1723–27).[64] The first part of Welling's *Opus* was published in Frankfurt in 1719 as *Opus Mago-Cabbalisticum et Theologicum,* under the pseudonym Gregorius Anglus Sallwigt, then again in 1729. The first complete edition of all three parts appeared in 1735, reprinted in 1760 and 1784. A certain "S.R." arranged the publication of the first part in 1719, against Welling's wishes. Most scholars believe S.R. was Samuel Richter, who wrote under the pen name Sincerus Renatus. Richter published the treatises that led to the revival of Gold and Rose Cross Rosicrucianism that flourished in the second half of the eighteenth century in Germany. Christoph Schütz (1693–1750), the Radical Pietist separatist, directed the publication of the expanded work in 1735.[65] Schütz and the Ephrata community were acquainted.

Welling's theosophy and his diagrams for it (Figure 9) may have influenced the design of Peniel. Welling believed that salt is the divine essence, or

Schamaiim. The geometric "signature," or outward characteristic, of salt is a cube. Welling also believed that the earth, although proved to be round, is in its "essential character" (*wesentliche Figur*) cubic. Thus "the true virginal figure of the earth is cubic."[66] Salt's numerical "signature" is also a cube, with the six surfaces representing the six days of creation. Thus the cube is "a sign of perfection which explains the whole creation." A cube can be subdivided into twelve bodies (*corporibus*), each having six surfaces. Welling illustrated his point with a line drawing of a cube with each surface bisected once diagonally, creating twelve triangles, with a point at the perfect center of the cube. For Welling, these twelve parts of the cube symbolize "the twelve foundational pillars of the true, invisible Church." Multiplying 12 by their 6 surfaces makes "72, the holy number, the mystical number, which is also the 24 elders of the first Church times 3."[67]

According to Welling, the triangle is "a figure of unity" (*eine Figur der Einheit*), a symbol for God. Numerologically the triangle is "3 from 1, and 4 is from 3 and 1." Three multiplied by 4 makes 12, which, multiplied by the 6 surfaces

Fig. 10 Ceiling beams in Peniel. (Courtesy of Pennsylvania Historical and Museum Commission, Ephrata Cloister. Photo by Craig A. Benner.)

of a cube, makes 72. A cube is made up of six pyramids, forming six days of work. The "Sabbath, the seventh day, is the center" (*Der Sabbath, der siebente Tag, ist das 'Centrum'*), signifying rest (*Ruhe*). According to Welling, the six equal pyramids in a cube symbolize the heavenly Jerusalem.[68]

Some of this numerological symbolism may be present in Peniel. Its dimensions create nearly a perfect cube. A massive chamfered pillar slightly off center rises from the floor to the ceiling of the meeting room (Figure 10). Four ceiling beams form a nearly equilateral cross, with the vertical pillar joining the ceiling at the center of the cross.[69] This creates the optical illusion that the pillar rises through the center of the building, although it does not. Because the pillar reaches the ceiling at the top of the second level, it creates the appearance of a center point in a cubic building. In other words, the pillar disappears into the ceiling at what appears to be the center of a cube, which for Welling represented a point of rest, symbolizing the Sabbath.

Support for the importance of cabbalistic thought such as Welling's appears in Ephrata's large *Fraktur* labyrinth, popularly known as "The Crooked and Narrow Way." A portrayal of the New Jerusalem appears in the center. Part of the text reads, "In the midst of these four parts of the world is God's holy point of rest, upon the same point is built the city of peace, or the holy Jerusalem."[70] This undated text demonstrates Christian cabbalistic symbolism in some of Ephrata's material culture.

The present floor plan of Peniel differs from the original. A kitchen later added to the east wall obliterates a wide, formerly exterior doorway, corresponding to the western doorway in the meeting room. An open space behind the eastern wall of the meeting room was originally divided into three chambers.[71] A Star of David (hexagram) imposed upon the present floor plan creates the points for the eastern dividing wall, as well as points for the vertical pillars in the meeting room (Figure 11). O'Bannon suggested a Masonic symbol called the "sacred cut" as the outline for Peniel's floor plan, but the Star of David fits better.[72]

The exact dimensions of the three chambers along Peniel's eastern wall are not completely known, although architectural evidence suggests that dividing walls may have created three chambers of equal size. In 1753 Israel Acrelius observed in Bethania's Saal a curtained entrance to a chamber behind the back wall of the meeting room. The brothers told him that this was the "sanctuary," which only Beissel could enter. Acrelius stated that the interior of the sisters' Saal (Peniel) was arranged the same as the brothers' meetinghouse.[73] If this had been the case before the sisters took over Peniel in 1745, the chambers behind the eastern wall of Peniel's worship room would be corroborated.

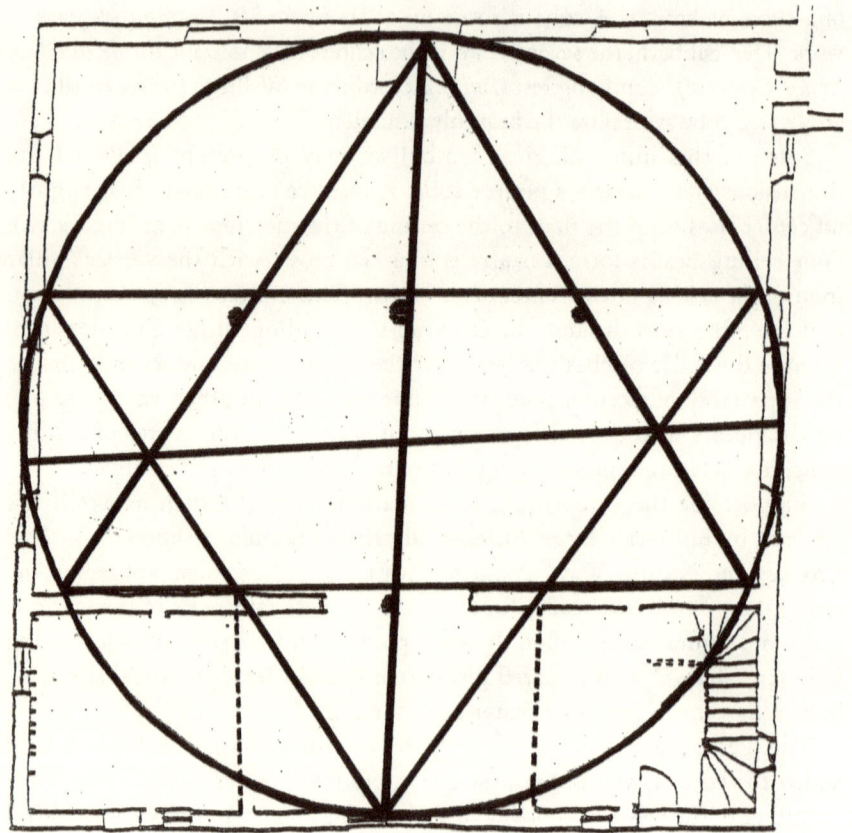

Fig. 11 A hexagram on the reconstructed floor plan of Peniel. The scored lines suggest possible locations of three chambers behind the interior wall. (Patrick W. O'Bannon et al., "Ephrata Cloister: A Historic Structures Report," vol. 1, "The History and Archaeology of Ephrata Cloister," Figure 3. Courtesy of Pennsylvania Historical and Museum Commission, Ephrata Cloister.)

The hexagram would indicate the appropriate locations for the partitions that created three chambers of equal size.

The *Fraktur* labyrinth placard again suggests at least corresponding metaphors for a special chamber in the meetinghouse. Another part of the text reads, "In the middle of the inward Holy Place the priests and Levites go in," and "in the Holy of Holies the eternally flourishing priesthood will govern." Only one enters, the "High Priest," who has "a golden censer in [his] hands." This passage may well refer to Beissel and the ministry of prayer.[74]

The Star of David in a circle with an imposed equilateral cross is an important symbol for Welling. It unites Boehmist, cabbalistic, and alchemical symbols. The six points of the hexagram represent the six days of work, with the center point for the Sabbath, or rest. Other components of the hexagram with cross create the symbols for the four elements: △ represents fire (and God); ▽ is for earth; $\triangle$ is for air; $\overline{\nabla}$ is for water. The symbols for fire and earth together create a horizontally bisected diamond, symbolizing the earth emanating from God. The entire circle bisected by the central horizontal diameter creates Welling's symbol for salt (or *schamaiim*), θ.[75]

The placement of the vertical pillars in Peniel may be interpreted on the floor plan as outlining a T shape. It may represent Boehme's "half-cross T," which symbolized the cross on which Christ died for Adam's rebirth through Sophia's union with Christ. The vertical, chamfered pillar rising to the cruciform ceiling beams also creates visually the "half-cross T" and a center point of rest.

Thus Peniel may express important symbols for Ephrata's mystical language. The 40-foot cube could symbolize the testing of the married householders, to see if they will remain with their earthly mates or desire Christ/Sophia. The massive vertical pillar rises both as Boehme's "temptation tree" and the "half-cross T" for Christ's cross and spiritual rebirth to restore paradisial androgyny. The cubic place of worship could symbolize a foretaste of the heavenly Jerusalem coming down, in which God is present, making all things new and restoring virginity to marriage partners. If, as O'Bannon suggested, Beissel preached from the very center of the nearly square floor plan,[76] the spot would be in the center of the cross imposed on the Star of David. This would be the perfect location for Beissel to encourage celibacy.

How well Beissel knew Welling's work, if at all, is unclear. The connection of Christoph Schütz with Beissel and Welling suggests that at least similar interests influenced all three.[77] Welling's concepts came from a broader pool of Christian cabbala and numerology familiar to many Radical Pietists. The influence of Welling, or any other cabbalistic symbolism, does not automatically mean that Beissel was a practicing Rosicrucian. As will become clear in the final chapter, Beissel's religious views developed in a direction different from that of the later Rosicrucian revival. However, some common esoteric interests lie behind both Beissel and Welling, and they may have influenced the design of Peniel.

On the other hand, Peniel's design may have derived simply from a circle with its diameter and a triangle imposed on it, a conventional pattern that Lauren Stevens and Eugene George have identified.[78] This and other such patterns would have allowed commoners to construct large structures with simple measuring devices and without drawn plans. Whether intentional mystical symbols shaped Peniel remains an open question. However, symbolic metaphors and shapes clearly existed in the literature that influenced Beissel and Ephrata and could have contributed corresponding design elements to Peniel. Those metaphors appear in the literature that Ephrata created.

Several householder couples turned to celibacy soon after Peniel's completion in 1741. The *Chronicon* alleged that Israel Eckerlin wished to acquire their land for the community,[79] but the couples may have tired of marriage, or the responsibilities of child rearing. At any rate, the community built a new dormitory, attached at a right angle to Peniel. Workers finished the three-story log and half-timber structure with attic in 1743, the date carved into one of the lintels. Dendrochronological tests confirm this date.[80] Beissel named the building Hebron, although it is known today as Saron (seen in Figure 8). The name Hebron probably alluded to the biblical place where Sarah died (Gen. 23:2), leaving Abraham a widower. As Sachse indicated and Ernst and Alderfer repeated,[81] the name probably symbolized the end of married life for its residents.

Beissel's numerology may have influenced Hebron's (Saron's) dimensions. Hebron measures about 30 by 70 feet, rising 68 feet to the peak of the roof gable.[82] Seven is the sabbatical number. According to *Mystyrion Anomias,* 10 signifies completion, in which a beginning (signified by the numeral 1) reaches its end (the numeral 0). This symbolic meaning of 70 (7 "helped" by 10) appears in Beissel's speeches.[83] Three squared signifies the undesirable number of division.[84] However, 3 times 10 gives a number of completion with the Trinity. Additionally, Beissel gave symbolic importance to 30 as the number of years before Jesus entered his public ministry.[85] By implication, 30 could signify the entry of newly celibate householders into the Priesthood of Melchizedek. Hebron's dimensions could show the completion signaled by the Sabbath (7 × 10) and the completeness of the trinity (3 × 10), or the fulfillment and ending of the married life of the householders and the beginning of a new, priestly vocation as celibates.

Hebron consisted of two large "houses" joined with a central area between them.[86] O'Bannon suggested that this arrangement was an adaptation of a typical simple German house, consisting of two rooms: a *Stube* (sitting or work room) and a *Küche,* or kitchen. Hebron's builders simply added a series of cells around the *Stube.* A central bay joined the kitchens of the respective sides.[87] Several cells (Figures 12 and 13), with low doorways opening onto very narrow hallways lined two sides of each common room. The narrow cells, halls, and low doors express spatially Beissel's teaching that "the door of heaven is small," and whoever wants to enter must be a little child.[88] The

Fig. 12 An unrestored cell in Saron. (Courtesy of Pennsylvania Historical and Museum Commission, Ephrata Cloister. Photo by Craig A. Benner.)

narrow hallways suggest the narrow way to paradise through ascetic living. The number of cells in each half of the dormitory may have been six or seven, both symbolic numbers. Six could represent the Philadelphian age of brotherly love; or seven could represent the sabbatical number of rest. Remodeling through the centuries has obscured the original number of cells on each floor. The organization of cells around the common rooms and the low doors and narrow halls were used in Bethania[89] and were probably typical of Ephrata's monastic houses.

In 1741, funds from Benedict Jüchly (Brother Benedict) allowed the Zionitic Brotherhood to buy a mill on the Cocalico.[90] The brothers soon added an oil mill, sawmill, fulling mill, and paper mill. Sangmeister reported that much later, around 1764, the community obtained money to expand the paper mill from Johann Franz Regnier and his wife, who apparently returned to the community temporarily.[91] Cheap, reliable labor from the brothers, a swelling rural population, and access to roads poised Ephrata for prosperity in the 1740s. But wealth contradicted Beissel's teachings. Whether Israel Eckerlin

Fig. 13 A restored cell in Saron. (Courtesy of Pennsylvania Historical and Museum Commission, Ephrata Cloister. Photo by Craig A. Benner.)

masterminded the economic expansion alone or with Samuel, his brother, Beissel rejected it. As tensions mounted, the householders left Hebron for their farms around 1744–45, after attempting celibacy for about eighteen months. Beissel expelled Israel Eckerlin in 1745.[92] Poor widows and widowers temporarily moved into Hebron.

Beissel moved the brothers to Kedar in 1745 and moved the indigent out of Hebron to Zion, and the householders worshiped in Zion's meetinghouse.[93] The sisters' order, reorganized as the Roses of Saron, moved into Hebron and renamed it Saron. Workers removed the original interior walls dividing the two halves of the building. They also removed the west stairs and closed off the west front door.[94] Ann Kirschner proposed that Hebron's original design reflected an architectural symmetry symbolic of prosperity, and Beissel wanted to erase it. However, Hebron's renovation may just as well have been undertaken to ease movement across each floor, once the separation of men and women in the same house was unnecessary. The celibate sisters took over Peniel (later known simply as the Saal) as their house of worship. Carpenters completed a floor spanning its two balconies, reducing the worship room to a single-story space until the restoration in 1968.[95]

Beissel ordered a new dormitory and meetinghouse for the celibate brotherhood, reorganizing them as the Brotherhood of Bethania. The builders began work on March 31, 1746, and raised the structure in May. They started the meetinghouse (*Bäthaus*) in November and finished it five weeks later.[96] The builders located the three-and-a-half-story half-timber dormitory in the meadow near the Cocalico. Bethania, the only house with a distinctly New Testament name, recalled Jesus' raising of Lazarus from the dead (John 11). The new convent perhaps symbolized a resurrection of the brothers' order.

Bethania was 72 feet by 36 feet, just a little larger than Saron. These were also special numbers for Beissel. Six could represent the age of Philadelphian love, or the six days' work awaiting completion of the Sabbath. Twelve represented the number of apostles and tribes of Israel. The dimensions could portray the holy number of Israel multiplied by the number of brotherly love, or by human toil awaiting rest. Seventy-two was Welling's number for the New Jerusalem. The width of the building might represent the squaring of the number for brotherly love or of the time of toil.

Seidensticker claimed that ten cells had lined the southern side of the long corridor.[97] Ten, as we know, was Beissel's number of completion. But the actual number of cells and their arrangement is unknown. They may have been remodeled, like the ones in Saron, long before Seidensticker saw the building.

Fig. 14 Bethania. (Courtesy of Pennsylvania Historical and Museum Commission, Ephrata Cloister.)

Photographs reveal that Bethania's two lower floors were wider than the upper floors, with lean-to roofs on the extensions on both sides of the building (Figure 14). Lawrence Kocher speculated that these features imitated medieval buttresses.[98] O'Bannon observed that it was a simpler way to expand floor space without the problems of a larger roof. Dale Biever proved that the long central corridor was actually off center. This contradicts the erroneous account of a centered hallway by Sachse, who supposedly actually observed Bethania.[99]

Bethania's Saal measured approximately 40 by 30 feet.[100] The numbers could symbolize testing (40) combined with 30, Beissel's number of completion (10) times the Trinity. This Saal resembled Peniel. The *Chronicon* stated that Bethania had "a meeting room for the congregation" and "galleries and halls for the love feasts." Acrelius reported a worship room on the first floor, a refectory on the second, and storerooms on the third.[101] Sachse wrongly claimed that Bethania's meetinghouse was 99 feet long. He recounted a tale, reportedly from the Moravian bishop Cammerhoff, about a debate among the brothers as to whether to build it 66 or 99 feet long.[102]

Bethania's location probably indicates intentional design in the overall placement of buildings at Ephrata (Figure 15). Bethania's and Saron's closest walls are about 300 feet apart. Beissel described the "Enochian age" as lasting 300 years. Three represents the "mystery of the Holy Trinity" and the "humbled human nature of the Son of God unified with the Father and Holy Spirit." The zeroes in 300 portray the "household of the Son of God" followed by the "household of the Holy Spirit."[103] Furthermore, Bethania, Saron, and Zion form a triangle, the cabbalistic shape of perfection, according to Welling and others. Thus the most significant final outline of the Ephrata community was triangular, although only after the completion of Bethania.[104]

The eastward orientation of the meetinghouses attached to Saron and Bethania probably also reflects intentional design. European churches were oriented toward the east. Beissel may have had additional thoughts. He wrote, "At night, when it is cloudy and dark, turn your eyes continually toward the [sun]rise." Pilgrims should not look to the sunset and darkness. "Turn your face to the [sun]rise," where "clear light will again surround you."[105] For Beissel, night symbolized spiritual darkness, and the dawn in the east represented hope for a new age of the Church, the *Aurora* (Latin "dawn") of Boehme's first work.

After 1745, Conrad Beissel continued to erase all vestiges of Eckerlin leadership. In 1746 he ordered that a wash house built by the Eckerlins be destroyed, because it was rumored to be a trysting place. In 1747 he ordered the razing of the Berghaus, the Eckerlins' former residence.[106] On December 5, 1747, a suspicious fire broke out around midnight, destroying the gristmill, the oil mill, and the fulling mill. The *Chronicon* insinuated that Beissel's wishes had a part in it. Members and neighbors quickly rebuilt the gristmill, but the economic muscle of the celibates never recovered.[107]

Ephrata entered a third architectural period after 1749. As a new religious awakening spread to the youth and new arrivals from Europe, Beissel planned a dormitory for boys, Succoth. Fervor dissipated within eighteen months and the plans were abandoned.[108] Beissel's efforts for communal monasticism had peaked. Ephrata's literature reveals little about structures in the second half of the eighteenth century. Archaeological evidence may reveal more about this later period.

After Samuel Eckerlin and Ezechiel Sangmeister and their group returned from Virginia in 1764, they eventually won housing on Mount Zion. Between Sangmeister's perch there and the aging celibates down the hill lay the rift in Beissel's views about pursuing the mystical life as a hermit or in a

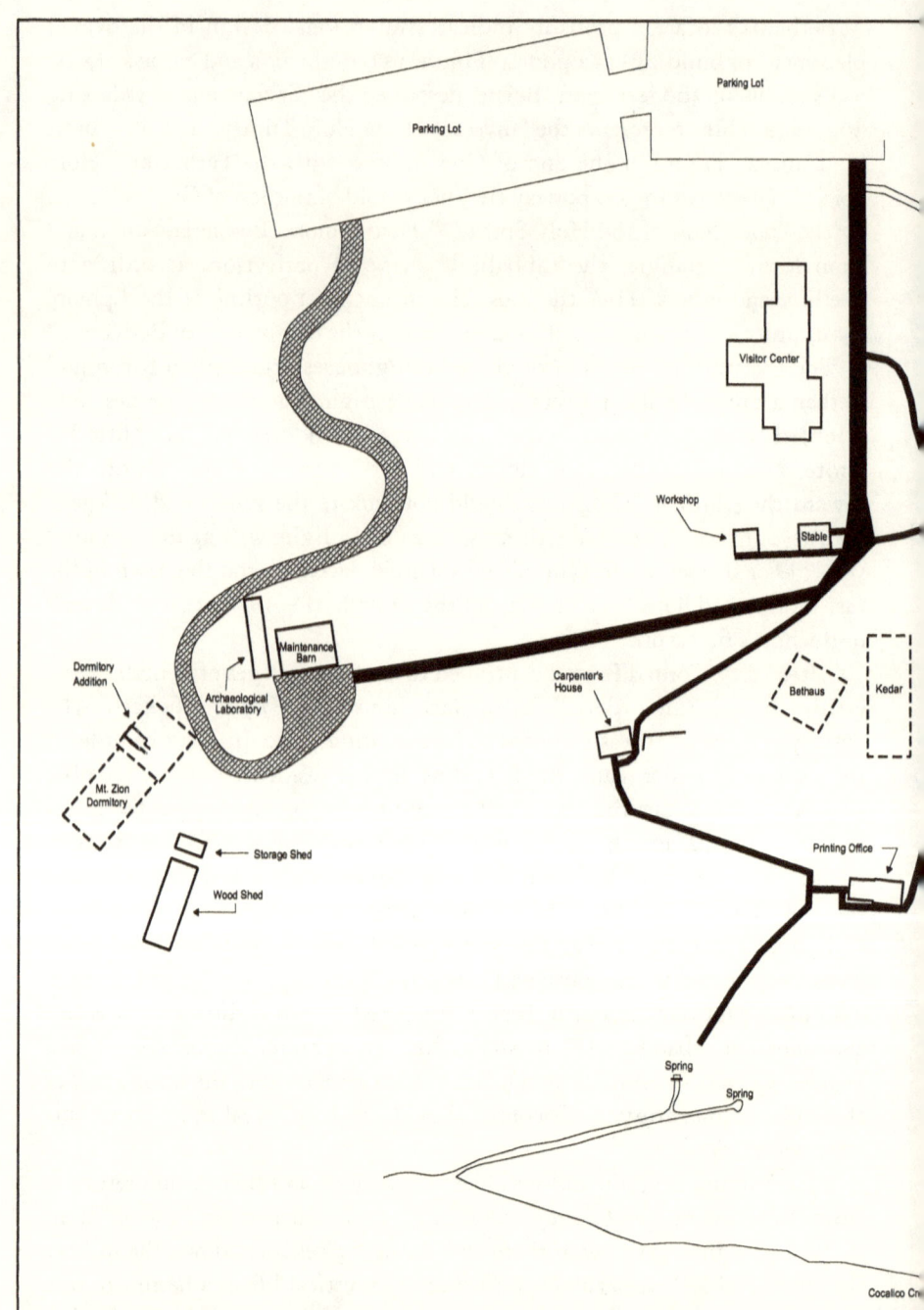

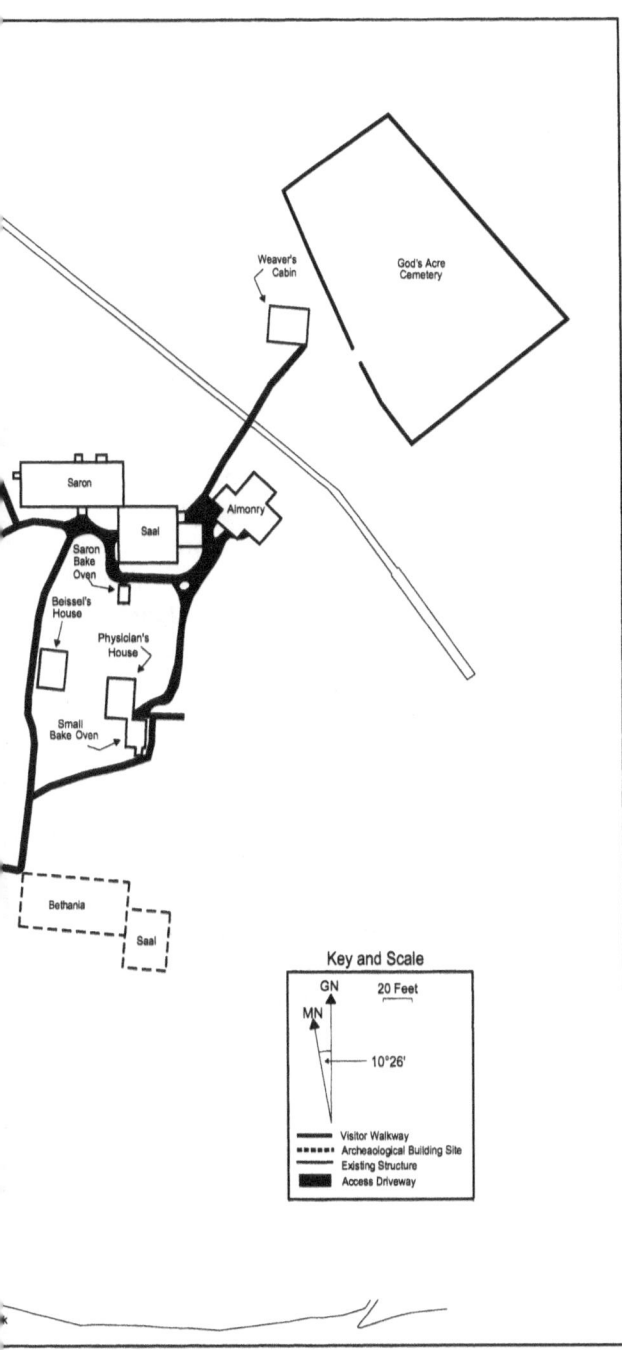

Fig. 15 Partial site map of Ephrata, showing buildings and archaeological remains. (Courtesy of State Museum of Pennsylvania, Pennsylvania Historical and Museum Commission. Created by Stephen G. Warfel.)

gathered church. Ephrata's final dichotomy counterposed not female and male or celibate and married but hermits and a gathered community. Indeed, Beissel probably never fully eliminated hermits from Ephrata.[109] Ultimately, Sangmeister's friends the Kelps outlived the last vowed sisters by a few years. Ephrata's mystical language disappeared as it had begun, in the contemplation of solitary hermits.

TIME AT EPHRATA

Israel Acrelius noted in 1753 that the Sabbatarians "count their hours after the Jewish fashion, from the beginning of the day, so that our six o'clock is their one, and our twelve their seven."[110] Besides breaking the night with worship and shifting their day of worship to Saturday, the Ephrata brethren altered their numbering of hours, beginning the day in the evening.

A death record confirms Acrelius's observation. Two entries note that Beissel died toward the end of the eighth hour, "commonly known as about 1 o'clock in the afternoon."[111] If Acrelius was right, noon was the beginning of their eighth hour. Beissel expired as the eighth hour ended, about 1:00 P.M.

Israel Eckerlin's letter to Ephrata in 1755 suggests some of the significance behind their altered measuring of time. Reminding them that everything must end in God's "rest center" (*Ruhe Centrum*), the hour hand (*Zeiger*) shows each hour until the twelfth hour of the night (i.e., 5 A.M.), symbolizing the beginning of Christianity through the twelve patriarchs of "the Old Testament Church" (*alt testamentliche kirge*). With the first hour (i.e., 6 A.M.) a new period begins with twelve hours for the apostles of the New Testament. Then the hour hand "has climbed the twelve hours" and moved into the one full day, "the entire perfect number" (*das gantze volkomene numer* [sic]) of twenty-four hours. Therefore "out of evening and morning the entire day of God is revealed."[112] Together the two portions of a day constitute the fullness of God's reign, symbolized in the twenty-four elders of Revelation. The sabbatical number, seven, came at the midnight worship service, and again at noon.

Although odd to the uninitiated, Ephrata's system of time expressed Beissel's allegorical harmonization of Old and New Testaments. The fulfillment of the old would come in Beissel's church, which was preparing for the eternal Sabbath through ascetic living. Thus Ephrata used its mystical language to count the hours until eternity,

"GOD'S HOLY POINT OF REST"

CONCLUSION

Most of the building of the Ephrata community probably differed little from that of their German immigrant neighbors. At the beginning the Sabbatarians built typical hermit cabins and farmhouses, first at Rudolf Nägele's farm, then at the Cocalico. At some point Beissel's congregation decided to establish a lasting community, choosing to build durable structures shaped partly by religious interests. Although they worked without a master plan, the Sabbatarians organized some of their space and their time around Beissel's mystical language. In design and eventually in placement these structures created a holy space, matching Ephrata's holy time with its altered counting of hours. In this holy space, Beissel localized the pilgrim journey of testing and sanctification to his spot beside the Cocalico. Yet even spatially, the divide between the hermit's private quest for God and the gathered Church as the visible bride of Christ cut through Ephrata's architecture.

In the building period, Ephrata built on a scale and at a rate unsurpassed by any other segment of the colonial German population except the Moravians. For nonprofessionals, these buildings were extraordinary, and required intense labor during the ten to twelve years of their construction. No other religious community in the colonies matched their integration of unique religious symbolism with space and time. Surely not every resident saw these symbols. However, the monastic buildings and organization of time witnessed to Ephrata's effort to express their mystical language for God in holy space and holy time.

6

ROSES IN THE WILDERNESS

Ephrata's Manuscript Art

William Fahnestock described the buildings at Ephrata in 1835: "The walls of all the rooms, including the meeting room, the chapels, the saals, and even the kammers, or dormitories, are hung and nearly covered, with large sheets of elegant penmanship of ink-paintings . . . in ornamented gothic letters, called in the German *Fractur-schrifften*."[1]

Long before Fahnestock, Ephrata's calligraphy impressed visitors. A Maryland governmental official who visited in 1744 offered to purchase "at any price" a "rare piece."[2] According to the *Chronicon, Fractur-schrifften* already adorned the walls of Kedar's *Bäthaus* in 1736.[3] Fahnestock was among the first to relate the art form *Fraktur* to Ephrata's religious life.

For the Sabbatarians, the calligraphy "served them on the path to sanctification for the crucifixion of nature." At the same time, the "writings were hung up in the chapels as decorations [*Zierde*], or distributed to admirers."[4] In the "writing school" (*Schreib-schule*) the scribes lavished hours on manuscript art more as religious discipline than as aesthetic creation, in parallel with the purpose of singing.[5] Ephrata scribes created text, letters, and illustrations from familiar images in the weaving, printed works, and folk art they knew, adapting these images to construct further the sacred space of their mystical language. Beissel intended that the discipline of calligraphy would advance the scribes toward God. Other motivations mingled with spiritual purposes. Scribes sold some pieces, such as bookplates, for income. By creating elaborate music manuscripts for Beissel and Maria Eicher, the artists sought favor from leaders. The Ephrata scribes, celibates of both genders, created *Fraktur* pieces in four major surviving genres: bookplates, wall placards, music books, and a unique massive pattern book, "Der Christen ABC."[6] A few other occasional pieces survive, but they are too few to assess. This chapter samples two genres, the wall placards and the music manuscripts, for religious symbolism. The sampling of music books is confined to better copies of manuscripts for the *Zionitischer WeyrauchsHügel*. It is not comprehensive, only suggestive.

Donald Shelley defined *Fraktur* as "the large Gothic initials which appear so prominently in the Pennsylvania German manuscripts and which frequently employ strapwork, interlace, or other ornamentation associated with this early typeface." The term generally refers to "the Pennsylvania German illuminations which usually are drawn with pen and ink, and then embellished with vigorous colors."[7] Most commentators agree that Ephrata scribes were the first in Pennsylvania to practice this art.[8]

Julius Sachse interpreted Ephrata's "writing school" as an "educational department" of the cloister for instruction in fine art.[9] However, Ephrata writers never used the term "school" for academics or the arts. It referred rather to the way one learned spiritual wisdom. Beissel's "curriculum" in the "inward school of suffering"[10] featured discipline to prepare the soul for paradise. Calligraphy aided that discipline.

Thus Ephrata's art was aesthetics designed for ascetics on a pilgrimage toward God. The artists were not representing the visible world around them. Often mistaken for medieval manuscript illumination,[11] Ephrata's manuscript art was Baroque. It offered common people a process for seeking the presence of God and images to express the quest. Ephrata's art immediately reveals that its creators were not artists. At times crude, even bizarre, the cloister's art may disclose beauty in the eye of a beholder informed by Ephrata's story of paradise opened through Christ/Sophia.

Interpreters of Ephrata's *Fraktur* cluster around two theories, often set somewhat as opposites. On one hand, John Joseph Stoudt proposed in 1937 that all Pennsylvania German folk art was religiously motivated. Religious motifs flowed from a collective social subconscious at the Ephrata fountainhead to later artists. Stoudt saw the decorative motifs as "artistic representations of Scriptural phrases and metaphors" that became "mystical images descriptive of this quest for reality."[12]

Guy Tilghman Hollyday explored Stoudt's thesis by researching Ephrata's "wall-charts" (or placards) and the relationships between text and art in the so-called Ephrata Codex, an elaborate music manuscript presented to Conrad Beissel.[13] Virtually no other writer has examined the marriage of text and art in the music books, and Hollyday worked with only one exceptional volume.

Donald Shelley, in contrast to Stoudt and Hollyday, saw Ephrata's art, along with all other Pennsylvania German folk arts, as "a creation of the peasant," expressing "his great love for the beauty of nature." While conceding some religious significance, Shelley held that Pennsylvania German folk art, including Ephrata's, was done for aesthetic pleasure.[14]

Frederick Weiser and Howell Heaney, who have continued Shelley's interpretive approach, note that "printed visual sources for motifs" betray the *Fraktur* artists as "copyists." They hold that with few exceptions, "the motifs of *Fraktur* are simply embellishments and have no esoteric meaning or function beyond the beautification of the piece." Yet they admit that often Ephrata *Fraktur* is "a law unto itself."[15]

Shelley and Weiser and Heaney have demonstrated persuasively the influence of European manuscript art on Ephrata and other Pennsylvania German manuscript artists, who copied from books and from one another. Yet this interpretation offers little explanation of the specific context in which Ephrata artists chose their designs and organized them. Did all choices of design at Ephrata depend solely on the untutored taste of peasants?

Stoudt's and Hollyday's work asks seriously the question of religious significance in Ephrata's *Fraktur*. Stoudt certainly overargued some of his points, especially by crediting Ephrata as the model and inspiration for all later creations. Stoudt correctly pointed toward Boehme as fundamental for understanding the Ephrata community. Yet Hollyday continually found in the Ephrata Codex no ready explanation for the relationship of art and text. Do specific designs carry a consistently fixed correlation to religious concepts at Ephrata?

Another possibility lies between these two nearly polar opposites. At Ephrata, manuscript art was steeped in an alternative religious worldview. The creation of this art was considered a religious discipline to reinforce this worldview. The scribes drew on familiar decorative motifs, but employed them in a context where at times some specific images also corresponded with important metaphors in their religious life. Some, but not all, of Ephrata's *Fraktur* helped to shape the community's sacred world.

Fraktur, the ornamental "breaking," or fracturing, of letters, as the name suggests, was metaphorical for the purpose of the manuscript art at Ephrata. Like the letters they drew, the scribes' wills were to be broken, in order to be freed from the self for union with Christ. According to the *Chronicon,* Beissel also said that *Fraktur* was possible because "each [scribe] has the birthing

Fig. 16 The letter V in "Der Christen ABC." (Courtesy of Pennsylvania Historical and Museum Commission, Ephrata Cloister. Photo by Craig A. Benner.)

Fig. 17 The tailpiece (enlarged) in Christoph Schütz's *Güldene Rose*. (Courtesy of Rare Book, Manuscript, and Special Collections Library, Duke University.)

work in himself [*ein jeder das Gebährungswerck in sich hätte*]" after spiritual rebirth.[16] Thus *Fraktur* was a fruit born of spiritual rebirth. From the scribes' breaking and rebirth a florid paradise sprouted in many Ephrata calligraphy pieces. With these pieces, especially the placards and the music books, the solitaries constructed space for the sights and sounds of paradise to communicate God's presence. Yet not every piece or every design was devoted solely to the religious life. The scribes sold some pieces, such as bookplates, and sought status through elaborate presentation books for their leaders. Ephrata's *Fraktur* sprang from mixed motivations and carries mixed meanings, and perhaps sometimes no specific meaning.

One sample from the manuscript calligraphy book "Der Christen ABC" illustrates well how an Ephrata artist created from a familiar European design a symbol significant in Ephrata's mystical piety. An uppercase V contains a winged head in a night sky (Figure 16). The winged head resembles a printer's tailpiece at the close of Christoph Schütz's *Die Güldene Rose* (Figure 17), a book familiar at Ephrata. By inserting the design against a starry sky in the letter V, the Ephrata artist has created a symbol for the divine Virgin Sophia, whom Beissel called "the heavenly Venus."[17] The artist chose a familiar image but placed it in a context that gave it religious significance to express part of Ephrata's mystical language. By choosing the letter V rather than the obvious S for Sophia or J for *Jungfrau* (virgin), the artist partly reveals and partly conceals the symbolism of the motif. Other interpretations for this image are possible. Yet knowledge of Ephrata's religious concepts and language reveals that this design and its placement are more than merely decorative whims. This image illustrates one way in which some of Ephrata's manuscript art operated like their mystical language. Both can at times hide seemingly apparent meanings and draw observers into a hidden meaning related to their understanding of God's presence.

ELEMENTS OF EPHRATA'S SYMBOL VOCABULARY

As Hollyday observed, not every design in Ephrata's *Fraktur* has symbolic significance. Of the designs that probably do, most also have precedents in European folk art, calligraphy, or textile patterns. Since Shelley's work, Cynda Benson has suggested that many patterns circulated internationally in textile pattern books in the early modern period.[18] Thus the attempt to trace any given Ephrata design uniquely to one region of Central Europe or one type of folk art is neither possible nor informative. Emblematic illustrations in Pietist publications contributed another source of motifs, as Peter Erb has noted.[19] Before examining Ephrata's placards and music books, let us explore some common images in the repertoire of their manuscript art and the vocabulary of related metaphors in Radical Pietist literature. The illustrations used here are representative. All of the designs at Ephrata have variations.

Ephrata artists often chose designs that resemble roses and lilies (Figure 18). Common in Christian art in the Middle Ages and before, the rose appeared in a design for the Lutheran Church and in Johann Valentin Andreae's Rosicrucian tracts. Jacob Boehme used the rose as a symbol for Christ. Menno Simons likened the work of "pious ministers" to "seven unmeasured mountains whereon roses and lilies grow in whose scent and beauty all who fear the Lord rejoice."[20] In Heinrich Horch's *Mystische und profetische Bibel*, the beloved woman of Song of Solomon 2:1, the rose of Sharon, symbolizes the soul betrothed to Christ (Horch's mystical interpretation). It also represents the regenerate Church betrothed to Christ (Horch's prophetic interpretation), a criticism of the territorial churches.[21]

Christoph Schütz, one-time Inspirationist and then separatist, titled his devotional booklet *Die Güldene Rose* (The golden rose). Schütz stated that Micah 4:8 "names with express words a 'golden rose,'" the coming "golden and lovely blooming time" of Christ's return. Older versions of the Luther translation of the Bible did refer to a golden rose in Micah 4:8. Schütz hoped that "the beautiful flower of Saron and rose of the valley, Jesus Christ," would

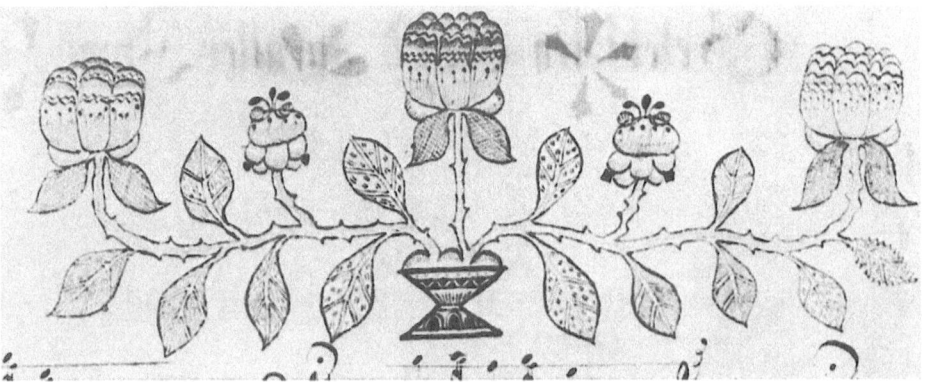

Fig. 18 A rose design. (Courtesy of Pennsylvania State Library.)

impart its sweet fragrance to the booklet's readers. He hoped that "all of God's little bees" would find refreshment in the rose.[22]

Similar imagery appears at Ephrata. Conrad Beissel called Ephrata "something of the golden rose [*etwa der güldenen Rose*]" emerging in Pennsylvania. In the spiritual speeches, Beissel noted that "roses break forth here and there" out of the briars, and "the bees of Paradise get the honey from the flowers."[23] On the dedication page of an elaborate music manuscript known as the Ephrata Codex, the brothers called Beissel "a golden rose planted in God's Paradise."[24] Thus Beissel and the community knew and used some of the Pietist meanings for the rose.

The lily also has much symbolic meaning in Christianity. Besides frequent references to lilies in Song of Solomon, Heinrich Horch related it to Isaiah 35:1, describing a desert (or wilderness, *Wüste*), which will blossom like a lily (according to Luther's translation). Horch interpreted it to mean a time when believers reach sanctification, revealing God's paradise, and fields will "bloom like a rose."[25]

Jacob Boehme used the lily as a metaphor for rebirth in Christ. "God's sun draws the human lily, the new person, always in His power, forth out of the evil essence." According to Boehme, this is the fulfillment of the seventh form or quality of God, which is a Sabbath rest and paradise.[26] In comparing spiritual rebirth to an alchemical transmutation, Boehme noted that when rebirth occurs, "the lily time will [become] a rose [time], which will bloom in May when winter passes."[27] Boehme's allegorical linkage of rebirth and Sabbath rest to a lily (Figure 19) gave central metaphors to Ephrata.

Fig. 19 A lily in "Der Christen ABC." (Courtesy of Pennsylvania Historical and Museum Commission, Ephrata Cloister.)

Thus in Radical Pietist literature that profoundly shaped Ephrata's piety the rose and the lily each symbolized a nexus of concepts combining love for Christ and spiritual rebirth through Christ, joining the minority of the faithful and the imminent millennium of Christ. One cannot identify separate meanings in these metaphors or conclude at all times whether a given drawing represents a symbolic meaning or merely a decoration. Clearly Ephrata scribes could have seen lily and rose motifs in a host of contemporary folk art and textile patterns. Yet they drew their lilies and roses in a community that used these two floral images as central spiritual metaphors. Thus Ephrata artists used familiar decorative patterns at least in part to create a symbol world laden with religious meaning.

Another common floral design at Ephrata with possible religious symbolism is the sunflower (Figure 20).[28] Johannes Kelpius, the hermit on Wissahickon Creek, described the sunflower as turning its "face" toward "the most beloved," playing on the sunflower's movement to follow the sun during the day. Christ represents the sun, the Son of God, the soul's beloved, whom a faithful soul will follow constantly. Kelpius prayed to Christ to be able to "stand silent in You, I, Your sunflower."[29] Kelpius may have drawn from medieval mystical literature such as John Ruusbroec's work,[30] popularized by Gottfried Arnold. The remnants of Kelpius's group influenced Beissel.

The most common animal design in Ephrata's folk art is the dove, which occurs in two forms. The frontal image of a descending dove (as in Figure 4) often portrays the Holy Spirit, as in the baptismal scene in Ephrata's ABC book. The depiction of a dove or a pair of doves in profile usually represents the soul, the Church, or both espoused to Christ (note the birds in Figure 21, and see Figure 22), a metaphor pervasive in Radical Pietist writings, among others.[31]

Frequently trees with many branches appear in Ephrata manuscript pieces as in Figure 21. They might merely portray the forested expanse surrounding Ephrata. However, Boehme also used the branching tree metaphorically for the joining of believers to Christ "as a tree with many branches and limbs" through spiritual rebirth. Boehme even wrote, "I am the same as Christ, as a branch on the same tree."[32] Thus branching trees were familiar metaphors in the religious literature that shaped Ephrata.

Variations on the cross and the heart appear frequently in Ephrata art, as in Figure 22. Boehme consistently identified Jesus as "the heart of the Father" (*das Hertz des Vaters*). As the heart, Christ works the love that quenches God's wrath and forgives sinners. The cross represents the suffering death by which Christ redeemed humanity.[33] A crown appears at times within a flower or over a flower or heart, again as in Figure 22. The crown can refer both to the victory of those who persevere in the virginal life and to the wedding wreath (*Hochzeitskranz* or *Blumenkranz*) worn by virginal souls espoused to Christ. Boehme described angels as being like children at a Mayfest, "picking lovely rosettes, giving them to each other" to make "beautiful flower crowns in God's beautiful May."[34] In the Bible a "crown of life" (Rev. 2:10) is promised to martyrs who are faithful unto death.

A few floral images frequent in Ephrata art appear to have little or no connection to floral images in Radical Pietist literature. Ephrata artists

Fig. 20 An Ephrata sunflower. (Courtesy of Music Division, Library of Congress.)

Fig. 21 An Ephrata pilgrim pictured among branching trees in a songbook prepared for Mother Maria Eicher. (Courtesy of Guy Oldham, London.)

Fig. 22 A cross flanked by doves within a heart surmounted by a crown in a songbook prepared for Mother Maria Eicher. (Courtesy of Guy Oldham, London.)

frequently used tulip designs (Figure 23). Tulips are not prominent images in the Pietist literature that influenced Ephrata. Scribes may simply have borrowed them from decorative folk arts, or the tulips may represent a variation on the lily design.

Ephrata artists often drew a large design of three interpenetrating circles, which most commentators identify as a pomegranate (Figure 24). If it is a pomegranate, its use at Ephrata may refer to fruits in the Song of Solomon. Because the design often appears on a flower stem, it may also represent a poppy, which seems more plausible. However, a poppy is rarely a metaphor in Radical Pietism. Commentators have identified another frequent floral design as a thistle (Figure 25). Typically the petaled blossoms alternate in color between blue and uncolored. Some have called this design a carnation, which may be the German *Nelke* (flowers of the genus *Dianthus*). It may be a cornflower (*Kornblume*), which would account for the blue color. If the design represents a thistle, which seems more likely, it could refer symbolically to thistles as the opposite of roses, as in Horch's comments on Song of Solomon 2:2. If it is a *Nelke* or cornflower, it seems to have little, if any, corresponding literary image in Radical Pietism.

Many other design elements appear throughout Ephrata manuscript art, but these are the most common among the surviving pieces. Ephrata's productions conspicuously lack the fanciful images of later Pennsylvania German *Fraktur*, such as unicorns, eagles, and parrots. Ephrata art has no human figures other than religious characters.[35] Cloister artists preferred more muted colors than the sometimes garish ones seen in later *Fraktur*. Ephrata scribes loved green, which abounds especially in manuscripts of the 1754 *Paradisisches Wunder-Spiel*.

The appearance of images that have metaphorical religious associations does not prove that the artists intended to express or evoke a specific religious meaning. However, Ephrata scribes chose to work within a somewhat limited range of images, many of which correspond to religious metaphors they knew. Ephrata's wall placards and manuscript music books offer two genres in which to explore scribes' use of symbolic images to construct holy space with their manuscript art.

WALL PLACARDS

Ephrata scribes reportedly created the first large *Fraktur* works for the walls of the first worship building, Kedar's *Bäthaus,* in 1736. One commentator

Fig. 23 A tulip design. (Courtesy of Music Division, Library of Congress.)

Fig. 24 A pomegranate or poppy pictured in a songbook prepared for Mother Maria Eicher. (Courtesy of Guy Oldham, London.)

Fig. 25 A thistle pictured in a songbook prepared for Mother Maria Eicher. (Courtesy of Guy Oldham, London.)

noted in 1752 that the Ephrata brethren "delight much in scrouls [*sic*] of writing on religious subjects, stuck up in their halls and cells," with the initials "beautifully illuminated with blue, red and gold."[36] While Fahnestock reported in 1835 that the walls of the cells and chapels were "nearly covered" with placards,[37] he seems to have visited only some cells and Saron's meetinghouse, which was then reduced to a one-story room. At any rate, only thirteen large placards are currently known to survive and all are at the Ephrata Cloister. How many placards were lost is unknown.[38]

Of the twelve large placards and the smaller thirteenth, two present verses from the book of Revelation. Nine more illustrate religious poetry. Hollyday noted that the texts of two of those nine came from the "Theosophischen Gedichten" in the *Theosophischen Lectionen* (1752).[39] The sources for the seven other placards are unknown, although they may be from Beissel or an Ephrata poet. Two placards are unique in being mainly pictorial. One portrays a spiritual labyrinth, the other a scene of Christ as the good shepherd.

On the eleven placards with biblical or religious poetic texts, large gothic letters dominate the space. Occasional illustrations of tulip, lily, thistle, and pomegranate (or poppy) motifs decorate the placards, along with varying patterns of ornamentation. No apparent pattern in the choice of floral designs or their placement is conspicuous. Text dwarfs the floral images on these eleven placards. As Frederick Weiser and Howell Heaney have pointed out, text, more than image, dominates *Fraktur*, showing the Protestant origins for this form of art.[40]

Some of the poetry admonishes readers to faithfulness in the virginal life. One placard exhorts, "God and the chaste Lamb must always rule in us, and never let us grow cold in eternity."[41] Another text reads, in part: "So the Temple stands there filled with pure souls whom the chaste Lamb weds to himself."[42] Part of the text on another placard announces that the door at the entrance of the house where the unified souls live will let in nothing more from outside, for God himself is enthroned in their midst.[43] These placards illustrate how Ephrata scribes defined the interior space with manuscript art to prepare the people in the space for the immediate presence of God.

The labyrinth and the good shepherd placards depart from the overwhelming textual style of the other eleven. According to William Fahnestock, the labyrinth "represents the narrow and crooked way," a name that stuck with the placard, even though it does not depict a narrow and crooked way. Rather, it portrays a labyrinth of text, like the popular mazes of print, calligraphy, and gardens of the seventeenth and eighteenth centuries.

Beginning at the lower left, the text winds around a representation of the New Jerusalem (Figure 26). The whole piece is divided into four squares, and the New Jerusalem sits approximately in the center. At the top center, the "path" passes beneath a sun done in gold leaf, the only known instance of gold leaf at Ephrata. Beneath the New Jerusalem stand myriad trees. Amidst them are faded images of celibates in habits. Most of the text on the path is legible. The entire work is framed by additional texts in the surrounding border. Some text in the frame is legible and some is lost.

Fig. 26 An Ephrata *Fraktur* labyrinth. (Courtesy of Pennsylvania Historical and Museum Commission, Ephrata Cloister.)

The text on the path describes the "holy Jerusalem" at the center point, or "point of God's holy rest" (*Gottes heiliger Ruhe Punct*) in the middle of the four parts of the world (*In der Mitte dieser vier Welt Theilen*).[44] In the middle of the New Jerusalem is God's temple, where "priests and Levites" in their priestly vestments (*die Priester und Leviten in priesterlichem Kleiderschmuck*) "slaughter the willing sacrifice" (*schlacthen die willige Opfer*). These ministers belong to the Priesthood of Melchizedek, who, according to Gichtel and Beissel, offer sacrifices of self-will and yield themselves to God.

The text states that a high priest offers in the Holy of Holies incense from a golden incense vessel. A drawing depicts a priest wearing a special breastplate, apparently the high priest, at the temple in the New Jerusalem. The priesthood "reconciles all the lands and peoples around Jerusalem," another reference to the Priesthood of Melchizedek, who give themselves spiritually in prayer for the forgiveness of others.[45]

Ephrata's *Fraktur* labyrinth used the common genre of calligraphic labyrinth to lead readers on a visual pilgrimage to the New Jerusalem. Text and images unite to create a visual allegory for the intended religious life of Ephrata. The labyrinth invites readers to lose themselves from their visible world and reason in order to find their way into God's presence and become priests. Only then can they find the true Sabbath rest and the abiding presence of God at the center of their lives. The process of creating such a piece supposedly helped the scribes themselves to undertake this journey.

The placard of the Good Shepherd, dated 1755, has deteriorated badly. A large central image of a shepherd with sheep forms the apex of a triangle created by calligraphic text descending toward the bottom left and right corners, joining a large base once filled with text. On either side and above the shepherd, three tiers of scenes rise to the top, for which reason Fahnestock named this placard "The Three Heavens." The name has persisted, even though the texts, of which only about a third remains, say nothing of three heavens.

Guy Hollyday used a photo from the 1930s in the Library of Congress and a Sachse photo of the placard to recover text that has not been visible for years. During the painstaking restoration, photographs were made of some of the detailed vignettes around the shepherd. The placard depicts sheep closest to the now lost image of the shepherd, and apparently sisters dressed in habits in the rising tiers at the sides of the sheep and shepherd. The text describes sheep pasturing with their shepherd as throngs of virgins ascend the mount to drink of the water of life. Singing "a new song," the virgins "follow the Lamb wherever it goes,"[46] an allusion to Revelation 14. The text and pictures portray a pastoral image of the New Jerusalem, a counterpart to priestly images in the labyrinth.

The text describes "a paradisial field of flowers (*Blumen-Feld*)" where the "children of the new world embrace each other" and "rejoice over the beauty of the flowers."[47] Some scenes depict women in the monastic habit embracing, giving flowers to one another, and placing a crown on one another's head. These images resemble Boehme's description of angels like children at a Mayfest, picking rosettes and giving floral crowns. Several vignettes in the Good Shepherd placard depict the paradisial life of Beissel's teachings. Although using metaphors quite different from the labyrinth, the artist or artists of the Good Shepherd placard also sought to construct visually the world of Beissel's mystical language, in which the spiritually reborn become like angels in paradise.

The shepherd and the high priest of the two placards could well represent Christ, who is called both in the New Testament. However, some Ephrata residents, perhaps even the scribes, may just as likely have thought of Beissel as the shepherd or pastor of the flock and the leading priest of the Priesthood of Melchizedek at Ephrata. Thus the placards may also pay tribute, even flattery, to Beissel.

The remaining wall placards helped to define some of Ephrata's public space with their mystical language. In two cases, prolific vignettes illustrate the florid beauty of paradisial life in the presence of Christ. Joined in mutual love, these seekers of Beissel's mystic way served as priests of worship and atonement. They anticipated a heavenly Jerusalem and rest while they observed a literal Sabbath and ascetic life at Ephrata. Certainly not everyone found such a life there. Yet the surviving placards suggest that Ephrata scribes used manuscript art to help construct the world of Beissel's mystical language. The art disciplined the spirits and bodies of the artists to receive what the text and images announced from God.

MUSIC BOOKS

Illustrated manuscript music books are hardly surprising at Ephrata, given the love for floral metaphors and for song in Radical Pietism. Gichtel wrote that "Sophia opens paradise to the will [*Gemuth*], and out of the harmony gives beautiful, lovely, fragrant little flowers."[48] Flowers, doves, and hearts adorn many Ephrata music manuscripts, along with geometric patterns similar to weaving patterns. A sample alphabet (Figure 27), now in the possession

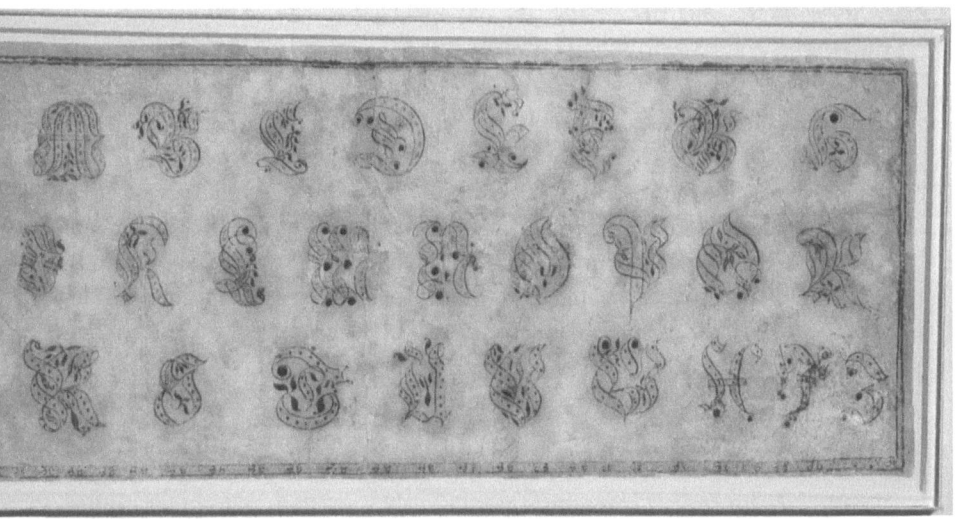

Fig. 27 A sample alphabet. (Courtesy of Pennsylvania Historical and Museum Commission, Ephrata Cloister.)

of the Ephrata Cloister, shows the small scale of work done in the music books, in contrast to the large lettering of the placards.

Celibate women and men created music manuscripts, but the actual scribes are largely unknown. Fahnestock's identification of Sisters Anastasia and Efigenia as two of the artists of the ABC Book has found no confirmation so far. Sister Athanasia is known to be the artist of a floral design in one manuscript, as Dorothy Duck has pointed out.[49] A drawn cross-stitch pattern in another manuscript creates the name Naema, probably for Naema Eicher, a younger sister of Mother Maria Eicher.[50] Whether the name indicates Naema's work or her ownership of the book is unclear. The dedication page of the Ephrata Codex bears the names of Brother Theonis, Brother Nehemiah, Brother Jonathan, Brother Jethro, and Brother Jaebez, perhaps the copyists and artists.[51] Otherwise, the artists are anonymous. Nearly every remaining music book evidences the work of more than one hand.

Ephrata scribes created music manuscripts primarily for three hymnals: the *Zionitischer WeyrauchsHügel* (1739), *Das Gesäng der Einsamen und Verlassenen Turtel-Taube* (1747, 1749, and multiple variations), and *Paradisisches Wunder-Spiel* (1754 publication). Scribes created a few presentation manuscripts for various hymnals to honor Beissel. One exquisite book for Mother Maria Eicher survives. I shall refer to it as Mother Maria's book.

Almost no researchers have explored the correlation of hymn texts with illustrations, except for Guy Hollyday's work on the Ephrata Codex. Samples of better manuscripts for the *Zionitischer WeyrauchsHügel* provide a test case here for exploring the correlations, if any, between text and art.[52] The manuscripts for the *Turtel-Taube* were eliminated from this book because variations appear in several manuscripts prepared for the printer. Several copies of the printed *Paradisisches Wunder-Spiel* of 1754 survive with *Fraktur* ornamentation. However, no apparently consistent patterns emerged in the choice of motifs and their placement in the few samples examined for this study. Thus the *Zionitischer WeyrauchsHügel* seemed to offer the best set of manuscripts for comparison. The manuscripts used here are not a scientific sample but random choices of amply illustrated manuscripts easily accessible.[53] The results are suggestive but not conclusive.

Examination of six of the better manuscripts for the *Zionitischer WeyrauchsHügel* reveals seven instances of fairly consistent placement of illustrations in each volume. In two instances, illustrations appeared on exactly the same page in all six manuscripts. In two more instances, illustrations appeared on exactly the same page in five of the six. In two more instances, illustrations appeared on one of two adjoining pages in all six volumes. In one instance, illustrations appeared on one of two adjoining pages in four of the six manuscripts. These findings suggest a pattern of seven chosen placements, with minor variations, for major illustrations.

The illustrations appear on pages 3, 22 or 23, 36, 60 or 61, 87, 88 or 89, and 121, with only a few exceptions.[54] One of the hymnals in the sample contains no large floral or heart illustrations; it is ornamented with geometric patterns created in the music staves, and simple flowers are added to these patterns.[55] However, very complex geometric ornamentations with more floral designs occur on six of the seven pages where locations of illustrations are shared with the other five manuscripts.

Of the six manuscripts, one lacks an illustration on page 3.[56] Only one manuscript has no major illustrations on either page 60 or 61.[57] Only Mother Maria's book lacks a distinctive illustration on page 121.[58] All six have either an illustration or space left for one on pages 22 and 23. It is unclear whether the variations on pages 22–23, 60–61, and 88–89 were intentional or accidental.

This similarity in placement raises questions about the reasons for these choices. Perhaps illustrations were placed in conjunction with hymns whose authors were significant to Ephrata. Altogether, the pages involved in these seven rather consistent instances of illustration contain twenty-nine hymns. Of the twenty-nine, five hymns are known to be by Conrad Beissel and had appeared in earlier printed hymnals. Although his hymns represent less than 20 percent of those in the sample, he is the author whose hymns appear most frequently in this sample. Michael Wohlfahrt (Brother Agonius) contributed two on the illustrated pages. Angelus Silesius wrote three, Gottfried Arnold wrote two, and Joachim Neander wrote two. Four hymn texts are by unknown European authors, one by an unknown Ephrata author. No texts known to be by sisters or by European women appear on these elaborately ornamented pages, unless women are among the writers of the hymns of unknown authorship. Thus authorship is an inconclusive factor on seven pages and their variations, except that Beissel is understandably the most represented single author.

These seven instances of illustration also raise questions about the relationship between the poetic imagery in the texts and their accompanying illustrations. The hymns on pages 3 and 36 contain basically no floral metaphors, although flowers dominate all but one of the illustrations. All three hymns on page 36 are by Beissel.

On page 3, two hymn texts are by Beissel. One of them, "Ich lauf den schmalen Himmelsweg," speaks of the narrow way to heaven, the ascetic life. In the other hymn, "O Jesu meiner Seelen Lust," Beissel declares to Jesus, "You kiss me with your kiss" and water me with your Wisdom's stream of love.[59] In one manuscript only, an illustration on page 3 contains a large heart with a pair of facing doves perched on the cross in the center of the heart.[60] This image corresponds to the text's expression of love for Christ.

Large illustrations appear on page 22 in five of the six manuscripts. One has a large empty space for an illustration on page 23.[61] Two other manuscripts have illustrations on page 23 in addition to those on page 22.[62] The hymn texts on page 22 are virtually devoid of floral imagery but speak of love for Jesus. Particularly the first hymn on page 22, "Ich will mit Liebesfurcht anbeten," by an unknown European author, has sensual language similar to Beissel's "O Jesu meiner Seelen Lust." The unknown poet longs to drink from Jesus' breasts in silent quiet.[63] One manuscript has an illustration of three large trees,[64] which might allude to Boehme's imagery of being joined to Christ like a branch to a tree. Another manuscript has an illustration of a large sunflower,[65] which might allude to Kelpius's sunflower metaphor for always turning to Christ.

The texts on page 23 (for which two of the manuscripts provide illuminations in addition to p. 22) offer floral poetic imagery, although none of the authors are Ephrata poets. Angelus Silesius's "Ihr Töchter Zions die ihr" alludes to the beloved in Song of Solomon, stating that "My friend is a little rose" and "My friend is like a little dove, meek, loving, white and pure."[66] The next hymn on the page, Johann Feuchter's "Ihr Töchter Zions kommt," praises the Son of God, claiming that all earth and heaven "bow before his scepter, kingdom and crown," and speaks of the Bride who honors him in his kingly crown.[67] Gottfried Arnold's "Laß mich dich mein Heiland" implores the divine Word to grant that the worshiper "drink from the sweet sea of love."[68] One manuscript has a large tulip design with a heart in the stem and flowers at the bottom whose blossoms consist of five hearts joined at their points.[69] The heart-flowers in this motif express love. Mother Maria's book depicts two sisters among flowers, one of them a rose, with a dove (Figure 28). The rose could represent the rose of Sharon, and the dove could portray the rose of Sharon's beloved mate, Jesus Christ.

Two manuscripts contain on page 60 virtually identical illustrations of a large pomegranate (or poppy) with three pairs of varying blossoms branching from the stem.[70] Probably the same artist has done these. Similarly, in two manuscripts page 61 has nearly identical illustrations of a heart with a cross on the center and a pair of facing doves, augmented with floral motifs.[71] Again, the similarities suggest the same artist. Mother Maria's book has illustrations on both pages 60 and 61 (as does HSP Ac. 1891), but completely different designs appear. In Mother Maria's book, page 60 contains a large thistle, while page 61 displays a stylized lily. The manuscript with geometric patterns (LC M2116.E6 1745[B]) has no illustration on page 60 or 61.

The hymns on page 60 use much bridal imagery. The second, "Der das Wort hat ausgebohren," by an unknown European poet, describes the need for believers' hearts to be virginal, so that "we may become mothers and give birth to this Child"[72]—that is, to Christ's coming in the mystic's heart. Interestingly, page 60 has no explicit heart or dove motif, as the texts might lead one to expect. Similarly, the illustrations of hearts and doves on page 61 accompany hymn texts by Michael Müller that speak less of love than of the majesty of the Lord, who is king and priest like Melchizedek.[73] Page 61 also contains Michael Wohlfahrt's hymn "Der Glaubens Grund ruht auf dem Gnaden Bund," which proclaims the foundation of faith as God's covenant of grace, sealed in baptismal identification with the death and resurrection of Christ. This hymn alone alludes only slightly to Christ's cross.

On these two pages the crossing of design motifs against texts is almost maddening to anyone who seeks fixed correlations between poetic metaphors and illustrations. The hymn texts about love for Christ have no heart designs. The heart and cross designs appear with hymns lacking overt expressions of

Fig. 28 Sisters in habits pictured among flowers in a songbook prepared for Mother Maria Eicher. (Courtesy of Guy Oldham, London.)

love for Christ. Whether the crossing is accidental or intentional is unclear, for either is possible in the Ephrata scriptoria.

Illustrations decorate page 87 in all six of the manuscripts. All except one contain some large floral design. The Library of Congress manuscript (LC M2116.E6 1745[B]) is decorated with half a tree running from top to bottom of the right border. In two manuscripts a very large thistle suggests that the same artist illustrated both pages.[74]

A significant hymn appears on page 87, Angelus Silesius's "Reinste Jungfrau." The Ephrata context suggests that Sophia would be as important as the Virgin Mary. The poet describes the most pure Virgin as "a chest of pearls" and "a closed spring garden." The hymn invites all virgins and daughters of God to see the "Mother, Bride and Queen whom God himself has wed."[75] Bold floral images are wedded to poetic metaphors of a spring garden in the quest for paradisial life.[76]

Illustrations appear on page 88 in three manuscripts[77] and on page 89 in four.[78] In one manuscript, page 88 contains lettering more elaborate than elsewhere, but no large illustrations.[79] Mother Maria's book is the only one with illustrations on pages 87, 88, and 89.[80]

On page 89, Ernst Lange's hymn "Seyd froh ihr unbesteckte" exhorts believers to rejoice in their virginity, to follow the Lamb "in chaste flames of innocence," and to bring "new wedding songs."[81] On the same page appears Paul Gerhardt's paraphrase of Isaiah 53, "Siehe mein getreuer Knecht." This hymn compares the Son of God on the cross to a little lamb led to the slaughter. The large sunflower in one manuscript may illustrate the desire to follow the Lamb in innocence.[82]

The last major illustration in all but one of the music books surveyed appears on page 121. Mother Maria's book has no distinctive illustration, although its wide margin ornament has the only border of roses in this manuscript. One other manuscript contains a vertical right border of flowers from top to bottom of page 121, the only such border in this book.[83]

Three of the manuscripts contain on page 121 variants of a large, highly stylized lily outlined but unfilled on a stippled background.[84] These three resemble strongly the lily motif with the name Athanasia on page 121 of the manuscript in the Winterthur Library.[85] In Mother Maria's book, however, a virtually identical illustration appears on page 73 with three different hymns. Dorothy Duck has proposed that this may be a "signature" illustration by Sister Athanasia.[86] While very plausible, this theory awaits further research.

Two hymns appear on page 121. The first is a text by a European author, Johann Daniel Herrnschmidt, "Liebster aller lieben," scored antiphonally here; the other is Joachim Neander's "Meine Hoffnung stehet fest." Herrnschmidt's text is a dialogue between the Bride (the Church or the soul or both) and Christ, emulating the Song of Solomon. The Bride calls her most beloved a "flower of Saron," which the lily may represent. Christ answers her as "my dear dove, my elect bride," and bids her "wait in the garden of the cross" for him.[87] One manuscript (LC M2116.E6 1745[B]) contains a different floral motif, which has a pair of facing doves, perhaps symbolizing the beloved and his bride.

Because variants of the same motif appear with different hymn texts in various manuscripts, there is no conclusive evidence that a given design was created to illustrate a given text or texts. In some cases, however, the floral design corresponds to metaphors in the hymn. Yet the same metaphors may occur in many hymns at Ephrata, and in other cases no link between illustration and text is obvious.

Occasionally an isolated illustration in some manuscript neatly fits its page of hymns. In Mother Maria's book, for example, a crucifixion scene appears at the end of the hymn "Christi Tod ist Adams Leben" (Christ's death is Adam's life], by the European writer Adam von Frankenberg.[88] In the same manuscript, a grape arbor with fruit (Figure 29) appears at the end of the hymn "Wohlauf zum rechten Wein[berg]" (Up to the true vineyard), of unknown authorship.[89]

Thus no consistent pattern emerges in the way artists paired design with text in the seven recurring sets of illustrations in this suggestive sample of *Zionitischer WeyrauchsHügel* manuscripts. A pattern does emerge of seven fairly consistent places where artists inserted some kind of substantial decoration. These choices were not based on a decision to match art explicitly with text or with authors. It is impossible to know whether the seven pages contain hymns that were popular or sung often, or if some other factor motivated the placement. This small survey only suggests some consistent intentionality in choosing seven particular places for illustration.

Virtually every music manuscript surveyed for this project (and many beyond those cited) is incomplete. Perhaps the manuscripts, like some of the buildings, were never fully completed. Probably completion should not be expected. The primary purpose of the music books, like that of the singing, was not aesthetic creativity. Rather, the *Fraktur* was intended to discipline the scribes' bodies and wills for virginal betrothal to Christ/Sophia.[90] The decorated pieces were "fruits" of the spiritual birthing work of the celibates. As from hands pierced by quills, ink flowed from the scribes' spiritual wounds across the pages, their efforts finally dissolving in incompletion. Perhaps they

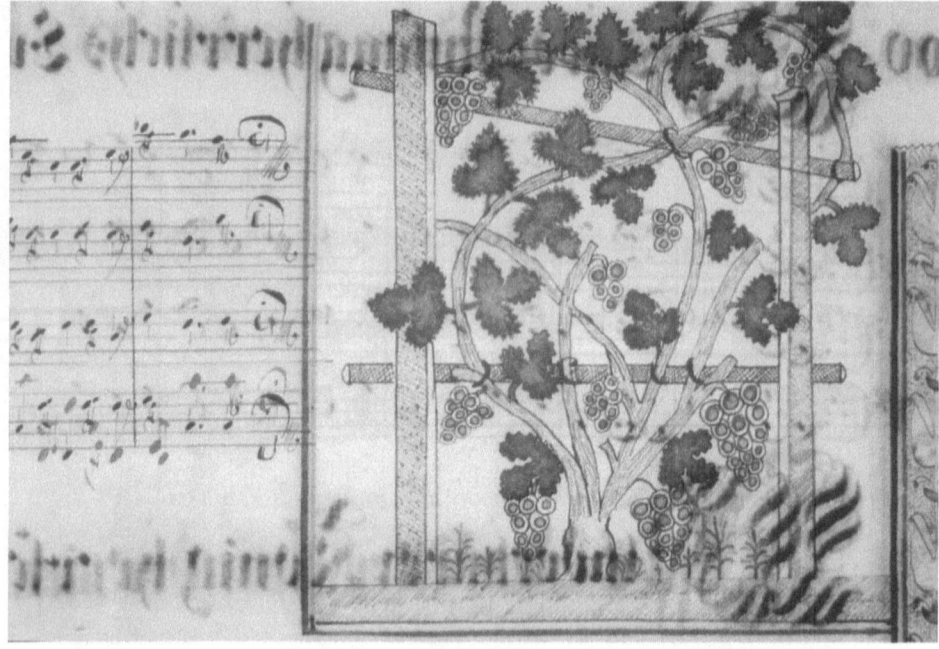

Fig. 29 A grape arbor pictured in a songbook prepared for Mother Maria Eicher. (Courtesy of Guy Oldham, London.)

stopped from boredom or the limitations of old age. Perhaps some were stopped when Beissel's spiritual alchemy attained its goal and their mortal lives were dissolved into immortality in the presence of the Lamb.

CONCLUSION

While countless other immigrants used these motifs in embroidery, weaving, pottery, wood, iron, and glass decoration as well as in *Fraktur,* no other decorators used these motifs within an organized community shaped by the religious metaphors of Ephrata. Within the quest for an androgynous paradise through ascetic living, calligraphy at Ephrata took on a significance beyond mere decorative whim. Ephrata scribes devoted hours to their art, in part because Beissel taught them to train the appetites to desire Christ rather than the pleasures of sex or food. Not all followed the training at all times. Not every picture bears a religious metaphor. Whim and fancy still find a place. Sometimes devotion focused not on God but on Father Friedsam or Mother

Maria. Yet in its folkish way, Ephrata *Fraktur* breathes a splendor of delight that the scriveners sought, and perhaps at times found. The process of creating *Fraktur* was a religious discipline to make the scribes' bodies living temples, even as the placards helped to make some of the buildings into temples for God's presence, while the members anticipated the New Jerusalem, for which the music books and hymns provided practice for an eternity of praising God. At least Conrad Beissel hoped so.

This limited sample of some important pieces of Ephrata's *Fraktur* evidences the fusion of ascetic regimen with folk art, tempered at times by the artists' whims. The pictures, whose motifs the artists borrowed from a variety of familiar sources, did not portray the world they saw or consistently convey allegorical messages. Rather, the process of creating the art offered ways to portray Ephrata's religious language while disciplining the flesh. What the artists left behind, incomplete as it is, represents a significant early achievement in colonial manuscript art in a community that could have flourished nowhere else at the time.

"HEAVENLY MAGIC"

Hidden Knowledge at Ephrata

If Radical Pietism were likened to a pot of simmering soup, we could say that some of its unusual flavors came from a scattering of diverse ingredients, including disciplines of hidden knowledge such as alchemy, astrology, numerology, magic, and Christian cabbala. Jacob Boehme distilled his theosophy from these and other elements within the popular worldview of spirits. From the seventeenth century into the nineteenth, various individuals and groups, among them Conrad Beissel and Ephrata, ladled out generous servings from the Radical Pietist stock, rich in arcane disciplines. Each individual or group further seasoned its own serving; the result was a multitude of developments in differing directions. Yet all of them shared commonalities that overlapped at times but never completely coincided. Conrad Beissel and Ephrata took their borrowings from Boehmist hidden knowledge and fused them with the spirit world of popular religion, inhabited by ghosts and spirits. These esoterica served Ephrata's mystical language at times in its efforts to describe what for them was too great for words, the unmediated presence of God, and to warn when God seemed absent.

In an effort to define magic, Keith Thomas proposed that magic "postulated occult forces of nature which the magician learned to control," whereas "religion assumed the direction of the world by a conscious agent who could only be deflected from his purpose by prayer and supplication."[1] Revisiting the relationships of religion, magic, and science, Stanley Tambiah proposed that seventeenth-century Protestants would view magic as "a class of acts ranging from sacramental ritualism to false manipulations of the supernatural and occult powers." Meanwhile, during the seventeenth century, religion became a "'rational' belief system in a sovereign providence."[2] Jon Butler has challenged Thomas's thesis by exploring how folk beliefs continued alongside church teachings.[3] While none of these definitions fully covers the range of issues and problems invoked by discussion of magic and religion, they serve as beginning points. As Tambiah cautioned, esoteric fields of knowledge are not reified, "well-defined bounded systems," amenable to a context-free approach. Rather, the practitioners of disciplines of hidden knowledge attempted to explain, often in a quite complex manner, the realities of the universe as they conceived them.[4] These insights help to explain the persistence of magic, alchemy, and astrology as parts of Ephrata's deeply held religious beliefs.

Ephrata emerged at a time when both Protestant clergy and empirical scientists dismissed magic. In intellectual circles far from Ephrata, secular philosophers and scientists widened the gap between religious faith and a mechanistic view of a universe ruled by unbreakable natural law. Philosophers such as John Locke and Immanuel Kant sought similar universal ethical laws. The distance between the views of common people and those of the intellectual elites grew even as occult knowledge persisted for a time alongside Enlightenment science.[5] Among the people at Ephrata, arcane disciplines survived as tools for describing the workings of a God whom philosophy and emerging science saw as increasingly distant and static. Ephrata thrived with a worldview both mystical and magical.

MAGIC AND SORCERY

Conrad Beissel viewed magic as a divine power related to faith. The Word of God, revealed by Jesus, effects a power born of faith beyond sheer human ability. Beissel wrote, "[This] word is magic and an in-speaking of essence into all humanity: spirit, soul, and body."[6] In his *Dissertation on Man's Fall*, Beissel praised the "holy and heavenly magic [*Magia*]" by which a "child of eternity might be born." This divine power restores the androgynous union of female and male "tinctures" after spiritual rebirth.[7]

Jacob Boehme incorporated magic (*Magia*) into his writings, along with concepts from alchemy, astrology, and cabbala. Boehme wrote that "in magic lie all the forms of the Being of all Being." Magic is "a ground and keeper of all things." Magic is "the mother toward nature, and understanding (*Verstand*) is the mother out of nature." Yet "magic is not understanding [*Verstand*], rather it is an artificer according to understanding."[8] Through "magic, everything is completed, both good and evil." Magic's "own working is necromancy." Magic manipulated with evil intent was sorcery. Magic serves "the children of God's kingdom, and the sorcerers of the devil's kingdom."[9] For Boehme, magic was a supernatural power that could generate godly results.[10] It is a "master and mother" of philosophy. "Magic is the best theology, for in it true faith is grounded and found." Boehme wrote that "Mysterium is the magic will," and the "Magnum Mysterium is the hiddenness of the Godhead, with the Being of all Being."[11]

Johann Georg Gichtel drew on Boehme's thought and accepted much of the magical worldview of common people. Gichtel believed that the devil afflicted so many because so few understood spiritual rebirth. In 1697 Gichtel recounted a so-called devil's wedding, during which a mother supposedly betrothed her daughter to Satan. Gichtel claimed to have battled incubi occasionally, but "turned away the devil" by prayer. He wrote that while he was working in Speyer in 1665, werewolves prowled the Electoral Palatinate, eating cows, swine, and children. When pursuers shot one werewolf and followed the blood trail, they found that he was a local smith.[12]

The "magic of faith" is superior to the evil "magic of necromancy," Gichtel believed, and cannot be understood with reason. "The magic of darkness, through a poisonous sorcerer, with his poisonous imagination, can introduce evil in body and soul" in a person not spiritually reborn. Likewise, "the good faith magic can stir the tincture in a holy person with the Light-Imagination and make it [the tincture] receptive."[13] Like Boehme, Gichtel stressed not a manipulative magic for personal or evil advantage but magic as the power of God's working through Christ and faith in believers' lives.

Conrad Beissel similarly distinguished between the evil magic of sorcery (*Zauberey*) and a good magic, or faith magic, which he often called simply "magic" (*Magia*). For Beissel, magic was not a manipulation for personal benefit. He wrote in a letter before 1745 that disobedience to God's will is "the sin of sorcery." God brings about good from "our being Nothing, or annihilation [*Ent-seyn*]."[14] Andrew Weeks has pointed to a similar concern at the center of Boehme's concept of magic.[15] Beissel stressed not necessarily self-annihilation for its own sake but obedient surrender of the will to God, so that God could work in the soul. This transcendent, transforming power of the divine is magic. According to Beissel, God gives a kind of prayer that is an "unceasing and magic eating by our spirit." This magic transforms souls so that "we live in God and His holy Being; his life is our life."[16] One who prays should "penetrate with your will outside of the world and time and you shall come to the divine magic" and reach the will of God.[17] Meanwhile, Beissel was often accused of working sorcery, not divine magic. Ezechiel Sangmeister reported that "it was always believed by many and especially by Br. [Daniel] Eicher and Br. Israel [Eckerlin] that Conrad practiced magic." Sangmeister often blamed his own misery on Beissel's alleged magic.[18] Yet clearly Beissel drew from Boehmist thought to describe magic as a power of God to work beyond human power, in a way that was accessible by faith.

ASTROLOGY

Jacob Boehme used astrology, widely popular in his time, in his quest to synthesize all knowledge with his understanding of God. In *Aurora*, Boehme explained how the seven planets represent the seven qualities of God. The work ends with an astrological compendium of the meanings of the stars and heavens.[19] In *De signatura rerum*, Boehme reworked his astrological metaphors as "signatures," or outwardly visible signs of the essence of rebirth in Christ.[20] As Andrew Weeks has pointed out, Boehme was less concerned with interpreting what the stars predict (judicial astrology) than with "reading" the unfolding of the "inner essences" of God's will through them (a spiritualized "natural" astrology).[21]

Radical Pietists had mixed opinions on astrology. Gichtel concerned himself far less with it than did his spiritual guide, Jacob Boehme. In Gichtel's opinion, no matter how "anxious we poor worms make ourselves to comprehend God's mysteries in the stars, it is not possible."[22] Johannes Kelpius and his hermits near Germantown hoped that astrology would reveal the time of Christ's return. Kelpius's mentor, Johann Jakob Zimmermann, had predicted that the millennium would come in 1693, on the basis of the appearance of a comet in 1680 and other astrological calculations and Scripture.[23] Zimmermann and

Kelpius supplemented astrology with cabbalistic thought imbibed from Christian Knorr von Rosenroth.[24] Kelpius's travel journal evidences familiarity with astronomy. Letters from him and his associate Johann Gottfried Seelig occasionally warned of the dangers of sexual desires aroused by the "astral Venus." They saw the stars as portents of the return of Christ.[25] Zimmermann and Kelpius were not the only educated men to find astrology credible in the late seventeenth century. By contrast, Pierre Bayle, the French Protestant philosopher, wrote in 1682 that the comet of 1680 and all other comets bear no divine messages.[26] Bayle's path eventually prevailed, but astrology has not yet disappeared.

Conrad Beissel apparently used astrology mostly metaphorically, and then only seldom. Scattered references in Beissel's writings allude to the magic of the constellations. Like many Boehmists, Beissel often referred to the divine Sophia as the "heavenly Venus" (*himmlische Venus*).[27] The *Chronicon* alluded to Emmanuel Eckerlin's being formed by the stars for the Priesthood of Melchizedek.[28]

Among the writers at Ephrata, Johannes Hildebrand and Jacob Martin showed the most interest in astronomy and astrology. Comets that appeared in 1742 and 1743 inspired an anonymous hymn from the Ephrata Press in 1745, warning of God's impending judgment and calling for repentance.[29] A year later the Saur Press published a treatise about comets by Johannes Hildebrand.[30] Julius Sachse claimed that the community reacted to the first comet by reciting a prayer supposedly from "the Cabbalistic ritual of the Zionitic Brotherhood." He printed a chart correlating days of the week with zodiac signs, angels, and planets with their "cabbalistic" names. This material has not surfaced in literature from Ephrata known so far, and Sachse gave no citations.[31]

The comet song (*Cometenlied*) from Ephrata begins with a preface warning against material comforts and calling for self-denial. Desire for worldly pleasure originates not from God but from the "fire source of God's kindled wrath."[32] One stanza lamented war in Europe. Another warned that unless people repented the sins of drunkenness, whoring, lying, greed, envy, and pride, God would punish the new land. The "star" warned of evil to come.[33]

In his comet booklet Johannes Hildebrand responded to a treatise by a man from Augsburg who held that comets, like planets, follow orderly paths around the sun. The scholar asserted, as Pierre Bayle had done a half century earlier, that "the comet means nothing."[34] Hildebrand's tract reproduced a diagram from the original treatise depicting the comet's orbit around the sun.

Hildebrand argued that the comet was not a star that had existed from the beginning of creation. Echoing Boehme, he wrote that a comet, like an angel, is a "spirit that puts on a body through its magic magnetic power from the chaos from Prima Materia."[35] Both comets and angels can appear as messengers of God's judgment and disappear upon fulfilling their mission. Hildebrand envisioned the Prima Materia as sulfuric, saline drifts of dust soaring through chaos (*ein Sulphureo Salinisches Gestiebe im gantzen Caos in allen Lufft-Sphaeren schwebend*), coagulating into material bodies at God's command.

Astonishingly, Hildebrand reverted to a geocentric view of the solar system: "The earth is the middle point of all creation, not the sun."[36] According to Hildebrand, all planets revolve around the sun and draw power from it. But the sun orbits the earth, which also rotates on its axis every twenty-four hours. This rotation exposes all of the earth's surface to the sun, whose rays generate animal and vegetable life and precious metals and stones beneath the earth's surface.

In the seventeenth century some writers still maintained a geocentric view. Among them was a Jesuit, Gaspar Schott, who taught at Jesuit colleges in Mainz and Würzburg.[37] He had explained that magnetism keeps the earth properly tilted so that it can receive from the stars the *semina rerum,* or "seminal matter," from which all living substances are generated.[38] Hildebrand probably did not know Schott's work, which was written in Latin, but Schott demonstrates the survival of a geocentric worldview even among some educated people.

Hildebrand worried most about the motivation behind claims that comets are merely predictable occurrences with no further significance. Such a "false premise was contrived for the service of Satan," Hildebrand railed. Like false prophets, "such atheistic astronomers" would perish in the coming judgment that the comet portended.[39] Hildebrand's geocentrism appears to be unique at Ephrata. While Ephrata writers declined to use judicial astrology to predict the future for individuals, the Sabbatarians believed that the stars and comets disclosed some of God's hidden will to those who could read them.[40]

In contrast to Hildebrand, Jacob Martin was interested in scientific observation, arcane disciplines, and their religious significance. Little is known of Jacob Martin before his association with Ephrata, which so far can be documented no earlier than 1761.[41] His tombstone states that he was born in Europe June 10, 1725, and died as a "good Christian" July 19, 1790. The epitaph calls him a "high Philosopher." He and his wife, Elizabeth, had at least five children.[42]

Martin either created or collected observations about the movements of planets, the sun, and the moon. His papers include a chart for calculating longitude and the declination of the sun. At the end of the table are stanzas from two hymns. The second is Conrad Beissel's "Wer kan verdenken mir," first published in 1736.⁴³ The papers include a table of logarithms to help with calculations, all apparently by Martin.

In one incomplete treatise, Martin also used astrological concepts as metaphors for the process of mystical union with God.⁴⁴ Martin's papers also witness to the only attempts at Ephrata known so far to measure and record astronomical observations. In some respects, Martin shared the world of the colonial astronomer David Rittenhouse, who had no use for piety or magic. Yet Martin lived partly in Ephrata's older worldview, from which the magical powers of stars had not yet faded.

ALCHEMY

Alchemy provided Ephrata's most frequently used metaphors from arcane disciplines to describe the soul's transformation in spiritual rebirth and union with God. Israel Eckerlin once described Conrad Beissel as a "spiritual alchemist," who dissolves words and "brings forth the spiritual body," or the "gold of faith," but who also deceives people.⁴⁵ Besides taking metaphors from alchemy, a member of the Ephrata community, Georg Zeissinger, helped to reprint Alonso Barba's *Gründlicher Unterricht von den Metallen* in 1763. This work was a hybrid of alchemical and metallurgical information.

Given their dependence on Boehme, Ephrata understandably employed alchemical imagery for the spiritual life. The alchemical process of breaking down base elements, applying tinctures or other treatments to transmute them into precious materials, corresponded to Boehme's view of sinners experiencing repentance and rebirth through Jesus Christ to become children of God. Boehme's *De incarnatione verbi* and his *De signatura rerum* treat the spiritual rebirth as an alchemical process.⁴⁶ Boehme saw a divine essence hidden in all people, like veins of gold in course stone. Only through the right tincture—namely, Jesus Christ—and through total self-denial could the coarse be transmuted into the precious. As Andrew Weeks observed, Boehme stressed alchemy as spiritual allegory more than laboratory work.⁴⁷

Gichtel intensified the spiritual interpretation of alchemy. He dismissed practicing alchemists as money grubbers. Concerning alchemy in Boehme's works, Gichtel noted, "I do not say that to work in metals is sinful, rather that one must be equipped by God and be gifted with wisdom from God, otherwise you will err manifoldly in this labyrinth."⁴⁸ While admitting an earlier interest in alchemy, he wrote, "I consider the spiritual chemistry and magic much higher than outward chemistry and magic," without rejecting the physical practices.[49] Like Boehme, Gichtel labored in alchemy for verbal transmutations that would lead to spiritual rebirth.[50]

The most likely practitioner of alchemy at Ephrata, if there was one, was Jacob Martin. His papers include notations about experiments, suggesting that he actually dabbled in the craft. A manuscript that he signed and dated includes a few astronomical observations, then several pages of observations from experiments and notes from alchemical manuals, primarily those of Basil Valentine. Martin recorded steps for using a red tincture with lead for gold, according to the alchemist Isaac Holland:

> Afterward take a glass, called a vial [Martin here sketches a little vial with a globe-shaped base and narrow, tubular neck], and put in it half of your purified ♄, and keep the other half in storage, until you need it; place a small closed glass upon the likewise closed mouth of the glass [i.e., the vial], [and] set the glass on a stove in an enclosure with sifted ashes, or set it in a tripod arcanorum (described in the third part of *Operis Mineralis*, p. 29), or set it on the stove in which you calcine vapors; and apply heat as hot as the sun shines in midsummer, and no hotter, or just a little hotter, or a little cooler, as best as you can hit on it; if you give it greater heat, so that thereby the lead becomes fluid, then your material will be melted.[51]

He recorded observations of the processing of various raw materials in the search for gold.[52] In another manuscript Martin noted his theory that he could extract sal amoniac (ammonium chloride) by distillation and extraction.[53]

The sources Martin copied included typical sixteenth- and seventeenth-century alchemists such as Basil Valentine, Isaac Holland, Michael Sendivogius, Abraham the Jew, and Rudolf Nied. Martin often quoted Georg von Welling's *Opus Mago-Cabbalisticum et Theosophicum*.[54] Martin corresponded with Jacob Sennsnig about alchemy and referred to a Dr. Land of Lancaster, who apparently had written a treatise on alchemy.[55] In one letter Martin quoted a "great secret" from Welling: mercury and its vapors were dangerous.[56]

Jacob Martin's copious notes suggest that some observations came from actual experiments. Sachse claimed without documentation that in 1762 Beissel had authorized Martin to try to produce gold to provide new income. This is probably only Sachse's interpolation.[57] Dale Biever suggested that pieces of glass tubing found during his excavations of Bethania might point to alchemy, but no conclusive physical evidence has been found at Ephrata.[58] Jacob Martin's will lists no items that can be specifically identified as equipment for alchemy. But despite the lack of material evidence, Martin's papers offer literary evidence suggesting that he experimented in alchemy.

Jacob Martin seems to have pursued the mystical life as diligently as he did alchemy and astrology/astronomy. Martin was an abler student of Jacob Boehme than Conrad Beissel, judging by the fuller use of Boehme's concepts. In a treatise on divine union, Martin used the concepts of the seven qualities, or "source spirits," of God, drawn primarily from the list in Boehme's *De signatura rerum*. Except for Martin's first and third qualities, his list corresponds closely to Boehme's.[59]

Martin followed Boehme in describing Adam's sin as causing a break in the harmony of the seven qualities. Adam fell out of the divine Sabbath rest into the six days of work, which lack the perfect Sabbath. However, a little spark of the divine image remains in the innermost ground of the soul. Martin held Boehme's view that the corruption of humanity reflects in microcosm the evil of the fallen Lucifer in the macrocosm. Jesus Christ, the redeemer, introduces the *lapis philosophorum* or philosopher's stone to humanity. In alchemy, the *lapis* is the substance (not always a rock) that completes the transmutation from base metal to gold. The stone allegorically represents Christ, who forgives sins.[60] The transformation results in spiritual rebirth, which Martin described as union with God.

Martin gives a distinctly Sabbatarian tone to his description of union with God. Through Christ "one comes again into rest and the Sabbath, as the uniting with and in God." All "motion of the senses and will [*Gemuth*]" becomes "still and yielded [*gelassen*] through daily dying." Whoever undergoes this process (as in an alchemical reaction) "is united with God through Christ" and has found the "treasure," or the "pearl." Such people have penetrated into "the center of rest, the middle point and innermost ground, where Jesus is found." Through "the sacrifice of reconciliation of Jesus Christ" (*durch daß versöhn opfer Jesu Christe*) God brings about this union, which restores the faded divine image in which Adam was created.[61] In this treatise Martin used Boehmist concepts more systematically and explicitly than Beissel did, but with a Sabbatarian imprint. Martin's description of union with Christ as a restoration of humanity's paradisial state echoes Beissel's *Dissertation*.[62] Yet Martin did not adopt Beissel's concept of two conversions or that of the mystic death.

In a treatise on the creation of angels and the fall of Lucifer and Adam, Martin recounted Boehme's concept of three worlds, the angelic light world, the dark fire world, and the outwardly visible world in which people live, which is penetrated by both other worlds.[63] The incomplete treatise deals more with Christ and his incarnation than with the fall of Lucifer and Adam. Mixing alchemical and astrological metaphors, Martin describes Christ as "the heart of God, the divine Sun. According to His angelic creatureliness, He is the heart of the angels and the angelic sun . . . with and through these same He flowed out and fills everything, whether according to His pure, fix Tinctural Body [or] according to His angelic creaturely Length, height and breadth . . . [and] the entire system fills everything [with] pure solar being."[64]

In an essay on spiritual rebirth, Martin describes the death to self as being "divided and dissolved" in preparation for Christ's "tincture." One tears loose of all visible things in order to penetrate "with one's faith-magic through Christ into God (*mit seiner glaubens-Magia, durch Christo in Gott eintringt* [sic]). Here "the Virgin Sophia leads the soul into the Paradisial Rose Garden and shows the soul the many various sorts of roses and flowers," all of which were "born out of the Light Schamaiim."[65] The cabbalistic term *Scha'maiim* signifies the heavenly essence from which flow the delights of spiritual rebirth.

Martin shared much of Beissel's mystical piety, even though Martin reportedly once told Ezechiel Sangmeister that Beissel "has an evil, quarrelsome nature and has no God within him."[66] Martin employed alchemical, astrological, and some cabbalistic terms more explicitly than Beissel. Both used a mystical language, derived through Boehme partly from astrology, alchemy, and elements of cabbala, to transmute seekers with the tincture of Christ/Sophia for rebirth into the paradisial divine image. In Ephrata's declining years, Jacob Martin represents the most significant remnant of a magical worldview.

GHOSTS

Ezechiel Sangmeister reported other allegations of the magic world related to Ephrata. A certain widow, Mrs. Good, was suspected of being a witch. Sebastian Keller, Sangmeister's former roommate at Ephrata, supposedly owned a copy of *The Key of Solomon,* the famous medieval magic handbook. Sangmeister wrote of the Funks' divining for ore in Virginia in 1763, when Ephrata reprinted Barba's handbook on metals. Sangmeister himself was accused of being an alchemist. He claimed that Georges de Benneville once showed him a bottle of a golden fluid that supposedly gave off sparks and was a "universal gold tincture."[67]

Sangmeister frequently recounted the appearances of ghosts, especially in the closing sections of his autobiography. He reported that the ghost of

Conrad Beissel appeared to many people at Ephrata, and once allegedly attacked Christian and Christina Luther.[68] In Sangmeister's view, the restlessness of Beissel's ghost indicated that he was troubled in eternity.

The most famous ghost story at Ephrata involved Eliseba Böhler (Beeler), born Henrietta Wilhelmina von Höning, and her husband, Christoph. In the winter of 1761, the ghost of Christoph's second wife appeared to Eliseba to disclose the location of hidden money that the departed had taken while alive.[69] This second wife, the widow of Hans Schule, had moved with Böhler to the Shenandoah Valley, and his first wife, Catherine, joined the celibate sisters at Ephrata in 1740. Sangmeister claimed that Böhler was having an adulterous affair with the widow Schule and impregnated her, precipitating Catherine's move into the sisters' house.[70] After Catherine died in 1741, Böhler married his companion, who then died in 1758. The ghost of the second wife and eventually also of the first wife continued to appear. The ghosts told the couple to go to Beissel for help. In a late-night seance with the couple and one daughter of each of the first two wives, Beissel effected a reconciliation.[71] Eliseba Böhler wrote an account of the events, to which Beissel added his thoughts on ghosts.

For many at Ephrata, as for many common people in the eighteenth century, the ghosts of the dead remained a reality of daily life. Ephrata was not unusual in this respect. The Saur Press printed a collection of ghost stories three times in the eighteenth century. One of the stories was by Stephan Koch (Brother Agabus), who reported seeing in 1732 the ghosts of Hochmann and the widow Benz, a Dunker who died in Germantown.[72] For some Pietists, these apparitions encouraged the living to faithfulness.[73] At Ephrata, the boundary between the worlds of spirits and flesh was porous.

ROSICRUCIANISM

Julius Sachse introduced the theory that the Zionitic Brotherhood was a Rosicrucian order. While many historians after Sachse simply accepted his word, Oswald Seidensticker, writing almost twenty years earlier, attributed "the essential components" of Beissel's thought to Jacob Boehme. Seidensticker saw no evidence of Rosicrucianism, even in Jacob Martin.[74]

Rosicrucianism itself is an amorphous succession of texts, seekers, and sometimes societies, partially veiled in rumor, partially revealed in printed rules. The legend began with three Rosicrucian tracts, probably by Johann Valentin Andreae and his associates, that appeared starting in 1614. To complicate matters, some elements of Rosicrucian thought resemble the ideas of Boehme, who was writing at the same time. Ever since Andreae's tracts, waves of inquiries about and organization of Rosicrucian groups have alternated with periods of silence and apparent inactivity.

At Ephrata, elements of Rosicrucian vocabulary surfaced amidst all the other Radical Pietist literature that shaped Beissel. There is no convincing evidence that either Beissel or Ephrata was actively seeking to organize a Rosicrucian order. Much of what Julius Sachse presented as "Rosicrucianism" simply does not appear in surviving Ephrata literature. Near the end of Beissel's life, some possible influences similar to Rosicrucianism appear, but associated primarily with Jacob Martin. By this time, however, the cloister was fading fast.

Before we closely examine the question of Rosicrucianism at Ephrata, a brief review of Sachse's account of a supposed Rosicrucian initiation ritual in 1734 will reveal why his interpretations must be questioned against primary sources. Sachse placed an autobiographical account of Johann Franz Regnier's attempt in 1734 to join Beissel's group next to a description of a chemical initiation rite not found in Ephrata sources. Sachse did not claim that the initiation description was in Regnier's account, but he created that impression.[75] Ernst, Alderfer, and Erb all repeated it.[76] J. J. Stoudt noted in Ernst's history that there was no evidence for such a ritual at Ephrata. Sachse actually altered the words of Regnier's account to create the impression of a pharmaceutical initiation administered to Regnier.

Regnier's story appeared in Johann Philip Fresenius's anti-Moravian polemic, *Bewährte Nachrichten von Herrnhutischen Sachen*. A Pietist separatist from Switzerland who arrived in Pennsylvania in 1728, Regnier sought out the Sabbatarians in July 1734. The community was small but growing. The Berghaus was completed that summer, and the celibates had not yet organized into distinct orders.

After describing his efforts to live a sanctified life, Regnier wrote that when he arrived at Ephrata, the Sabbatarians told him that "one could grow and increase very much in sanctification [*Heiligung*] through a strict life and bodily denial." Then the Eckerlins "described it, how we would do it,"[77] meaning a life of bodily denial and sanctification. Here Sachse inserted the words "the rite and observance," which do not occur in Regnier's account.[78] Regnier referred only to sanctification and asceticism.

When the Eckerlins postponed beginning the strict life and bodily denial, Regnier insisted. "Because I had on me the sign [*Kennzeichen*] that belongs to brotherhood," Regnier wrote, he was "viewed as a genuine [*ächten*] brother."

The sign of brotherhood he referred to, as he had explained earlier, was a living faith. The Moravians, he complained, could not decide whether one was truly converted or not. He questioned whether they had any better touchstone (*Prufstein*) to indicate a living faith.[79] Sachse, however, translated *Kennzeichen* as "countersign," which he implied pertained to a secret brotherhood.

Although considered a "genuine brother," Regnier noted that none of the Sabbatarians ever examined him to ascertain whether he considered himself "converted." Beissel welcomed him to participate in love feasts without his ever receiving a believer's baptism. Without Sachse's term "countersign" and with Regnier's previous context, the whole passage turns not on a secret brotherhood but on Regnier's desire for a living faith and the Sabbatarians' neglect to ask about it.

After the Eckerlins put him off, Regnier resolved to begin "the matter" (*die Sache*) on his own. Sachse replaced "the matter" with "the observance of the ritual," words that do not appear in the original. The "matter" was simply the life of bodily denial for further sanctification, as Regnier stated at the opening of the account. He also asked the Sabbatarians to help him build a hermit cabin (*Einsiedlers-Hütte*), something they often did for new arrivals at that time. Sachse fabricated another phrase indicating that Regnier wished "to obtain physical regeneration" in the cabin. Again, Regnier wrote nothing about physical regeneration.

As the Eckerlins stalled in beginning "the matter," Regnier asked "whether they would acknowledge that it was not therefore right." The only antecedent for "the matter" in Regnier's account is sanctification and the life of bodily denial. However, Sachse inserted the phrase "the ritual or process as communicated by him," presumably by one of the Eckerlins. According to Regnier, they answered that "one should simply live thus, if one wants to be sanctified, only no one could endure [*ausstehen*]."[80] If Regnier were writing about ascetic self-denial, he could mean the fasting and sleeplessness that Beissel himself practiced. In such a context, the Eckerlins could be revealing their reluctance to live as ascetically as Beissel, which rings true in light of Israel's economic enterprises in the 1740s. However, Sachse again added words: it was "the trial, the rigorous requirements of the ritual," that he implied the Eckerlins could not endure. Sachse reinforced the impression of a "ritual" that did not exist.

Regnier recalled, "I then exercised myself in the cabin according to all the rules which they had previously described to me." Sachse translated it thus: "I subjected myself in my cabin to all the rules and requirements of the ritual." Clearly Sachse changed the words to suggest a ritual of which Regnier wrote nothing. When Regnier tried to live even more ascetically, he lost his mind.[81] After confinement in various rooms (*cammer*), he was beaten. This was sadly not an uncommon treatment for mental illness then. Regnier regained his mind and attempted to join the brotherhood a few more times. He left in July 1735 for Georgia "to learn the way to sanctification" with the Moravians.[82] As noted above, he apparently returned with his wife about thirty years later for a brief time. Thus the full context of Regnier's account indicates that he sought a life of sanctification among Beissel's Sabbatarians, not a secret pharmaceutical ritual of physical regeneration.

Sachse, however, described an initiation allegedly performed over forty days in a circular room in Zion's convent. The ritual required fasting and taking an elixir that would cause the loss of hair and teeth, which would later grow back. No such accounts exist in any Ephrata writings known so far. The Zionitic Brotherhood was not organized until the convent was built in 1738. Sachse claimed that in the Berghaus the Eckerlins founded a renegade Rosicrucian order whose teachings were "similar to what are now known as the 'strict observance' or the Egyptian cult of mystic Freemasonry."[83] Sachse alleged that the "speculations and mystic teachings of Beissel and [Peter] Miller," from which the Eckerlins supposedly distanced themselves, "were nothing else than the Rosicrucian doctrine pure and undefiled." But Peter Miller lived in the Berghaus with the Eckerlins. Also, Israel did not move into Zion until 1740, over a year after the first brothers moved into it. Sachse's account of a secret order in Zion with a chemical initiation is merely interpolation.

The Rosicrucian movement derives primarily from three short treatises announcing the brotherhood in the early seventeenth century. The *Fama fraternitatis*, written in German, was published in Cassel in 1614. The *Confessio fraternitatis* followed in 1615, also published in Cassel, first in Latin, later in German. The first volume announced a universal and general reformation and introduced the Fraternity of the Rose Cross. Its alleged founder, Christian Rosenkreutz, had learned magic, cabbala, Arabian wisdom, and astrology and alchemy in the Near East. The *Fama fraternitatis* announced the recent discovery of Rosenkreutz's tomb and six rules of the fraternity. The *Confessio fraternitatis* continued the story, revealing that Rosenkreutz was supposedly born in 1378, lived for 106 years, and was buried in a tomb constructed to portray all his secret knowledge. In 1616 an allegory titled *The Chemical Wedding of Christian Rosenkreutz* was published in Strasbourg. The *Chemical Wedding* detailed a seven-day celebration of the marriage of a king and queen. The week was filled with music, plays, alchemical work, and strange occurrences.[84]

Johann Valentin Andreae later took credit for writing this allegory, yet claimed that all three treatises were a *ludibrium,* a joke or farce.[85]

The Rosicrucian treatises set off an international clamor. Many people, even among the most learned, sought to associate with the Rosicrucians, eventually including René Descartes. Just as frequent were denials of any association with such a group. Periodically various countries banned the Rosicrucians. By the end of the seventeenth century, interest in their teachings abated. Christopher McIntosh has suggested that the Rosicrucians persisted at the end of the century among a few secretive adepts, only loosely associated, if at all, and widely scattered.[86]

With Johannes Kelpius the question of Rosicrucian influence at Ephrata becomes controverted. Gottfried Arnold mentioned Rosicrucians in his history of the Church and heretics. Quoting a professor at Kiel, Arnold wrote that the Rosicrucians were a secret order that did not and would not publish books under that name. The books issued under the Rosicrucian name were not truly Rosicrucian. He claimed that Rosicrucians were Lutherans who held to the unaltered Augsburg Confession, not Weigelians or heretics. Arnold also recorded that Kelpius's mentor, Johann Jakob Zimmermann, lost his pastorate in Bietigheim under charges of being a Boehmist, not a Rosicrucian. Arnold did not associate Zimmermann or Kelpius with Rosicrucianism.[87] Kelpius, although Lutheran, by no means conformed to the unaltered Augsburg Confession, as he himself stated.[88]

Willard Martin, in a dissertation on hymns by Kelpius and Johann Seelig, carefully rehearsed the literature up to his writing in 1973 and concluded that there was no proof that Kelpius and the hermits intentionally organized and operated as a Rosicrucian group.[89] A. E. Waite thought that Kelpius and a few in his group were in "some manner integrated into the Order." Waite recounted a tradition that Kelpius and his friends brought and followed "a priceless Rosicrucian MS" that "represents an early stage of the Secret Symbols, published in Altona in 1785–8." He finally concluded, however, "I have searched in vain for traces of . . . any characteristic Rosicrucian vestiges in the letters of Kelpius."[90] Sachse, of course, considered Kelpius a Rosicrucian.[91] Ernst Benz called Kelpius a Rosicrucian without explaining what he meant by the term or citing documentation.[92] Elizabeth Fisher claimed that Kelpius's writings show that he was "well acquainted with the Rosicrucian *Confessio.*" She noted the overlap between Boehme's and Rosicrucian thought, however, as well as commonalities with cabbala.[93] Willard Martin pointed out that R. Swinburne Clymer, once head of the Rosicrucian fraternity in America, believed that Kelpius and his hermits were not at all Rosicrucians, partly because the hermits expected the coming millennium. Martin quoted a personal letter from Ralph M. Lewis, at the time "imperator" of AMORC, who claimed that Kelpius was a "true Rosicrucian," but Lewis cited Sachse for support.[94]

Kelpius is difficult to assess. Unlike the early Rosicrucian treatises, Kelpius's surviving writings claim no knowledge of or interest in Oriental arcana. His concern was not to reform church or society but to prepare a small remnant for Christ's return and the millennium. Kelpius shared Zimmermann's fascination with the stars, which was similar to the traditions of both Boehme and Rosicrucianism. Kelpius's thought seems to derive primarily from Boehme, shaped by connections with the German and English Philadelphians. Other influences, such as Christian Knorr von Rosenroth's cabbalism and perhaps some Rosicrucian concepts, enter into the mix. If Kelpius were a practicing Rosicrucian using a specific rule, there is no concrete evidence indicating which rule he used. His thought reflects the eclectic range of esoteric literature simmering in Radical Pietism in the late seventeenth and early eighteenth centuries.

A small revival of interest in Rosicrucianism began in Germany in the early eighteenth century, according to McIntosh, and bloomed in the last decades of the century.[95] On the margins of Pietism, the revival accompanied the interest in Boehme. This does not mean that Pietism or its radical forms precipitated the revival. Rather, renewed interest in Rosicrucianism often appeared in proximity to Pietists and their literature. The best example is Samuel (Sigmund) Richter, a Lutheran originally from Nimptsch in Silesia, who studied at Wittenberg, then Halle. He worked as a tutor for noble families and served as a preacher in Hartmannsdorf, near Landshut. He seems also to have practiced as a physician. Under the pen name Sincerus Renatus ("truly reborn") Richter published in 1710 a book titled *Die wahrhafte und volkommene Bereitung des philosophischen Steins der Brüderschaft aus dem Orden des Gulden und Rosen Creutzes* (The true and complete preparation of the philosopher's stone of the Brotherhood of the Order of the Gold and Rose Cross).[96] Richter's introduction to the book claimed that all Rosicrucians had left Europe and gone to India, yet he presented rules and plans for the organization of a brotherhood of the Gold and Rose Cross. A spate of books associated with a fraternity of the Gold and Rose Cross proliferated at the end of the eighteenth century.

When Richter's book is compared with Beissel's writings, one can see little of Richter's kind of Rosicrucianism at Ephrata. This finding undermines Sachse's claim that Beissel's conversion in 1715 was an initiation into a

Rosicrucian group in Heidelberg. One very striking difference is that Richter's fraternity admitted no women. Richter published a greeting formula in Latin for the brotherhood.[97] No Ephrata literature mentions a special greeting, especially not in Latin. Richter also organized his brotherhood in a progression of grades, each with a name. The "imperator" headed the order, which was restricted at first to sixty-three members.[98] The Ephrata community had no titled grades and never restricted membership. After 1745, the Roses of Saron had seven unnamed classes, but it is unclear whether these were grades or ranks. Beissel held only the titles "father" and "superintendent" (*Vorsteher*). Richter's rule for the Gold and Rose Cross order permitted that "each might live freely in whatever religion" he wished.[99] Beissel never accepted this rule, as Ephrata's polemics against other religious groups attest.[100]

Richter's rules assumed that the brothers would travel, have no permanent home (rules 27, 31, 35), and change their "secret" names when they reached each new place so they would not be recognized (rules 25, 26).[101] Beissel changed Sister Tabea's (Anna Thommen's) name to Sister Anastasia, but she stayed in the community, where her name was well known.[102] While metaphors of wandering pervade Ephrata's literature, after 1732 the members indeed had a permanent home in the community.

A few of Richter's rules echo some of Ephrata's piety. Brothers should not talk much and should not seek a wife. In seeming contradiction, Richter's rule 17 instructs a brother with a wife not to bring her around the younger brothers often.[103] Rule 42 forbids any married man to join the brotherhood. Richter's rules are much milder than Ephrata's celibacy requirements.

In 1714 Richter published another work titled *Theo-Philosophia Theoretico-Practica*. Here he identified himself as a Lutheran, yet condemned Lutheran theologians. Some of Richter's theosophical beliefs resemble Beissel's teachings, but important differences separate the two. Richter described the creation of an initially androgynous Adam espoused to the virgin Sophia, very similar to Beissel's views.[104] Richter attributed Adam's fall into earthly desire to Satan only, however, and made no mention of Adam's sexual desire for a mate after watching the animals, as Beissel taught.[105] Richter lacked Beissel's account of two conversions to reverse Adam's two distinct falls and a concept like Beissel's "mystic death."[106] Richter's Christology/Sophiology is far less developed than Beissel's. Richter blamed part of the "disease of sin" (*Sündenkranckheit*) on food, but suggested that proper medicines could heal it, rather than fasting or restricted diet. Richter's book concluded with eleven experiments for extracting or purifying gold and silver.[107] Indeed, the whole work contains much more explicit alchemy than Beissel's writings. All of these differences reveal that Beissel was more strongly influenced by Gichtel's transmission of Boehme.

Christopher McIntosh suggested that part of the Rosicrucian legacy concerned secrets of sexual performance couched in metaphors of the "alchemical wedding," in which female and male sexual fluids were mixed in a union of "vital forces."[108] Beissel held that the "watery female characteristic" should soften the "fiery" male characteristic. But he insisted that it could do so only through celibacy in imitation of Jesus. Here he concurred with Gichtel, in opposition to Eva von Buttlar's promiscuous group.

If the Lutheran Richter and his Order of the Gold and Rose Cross mark the early eighteenth-century revival of Rosicrucianism, then it probably had no direct influence on Conrad Beissel. The similarities between Richter and Beissel can be attributed to Boehmist thought circulating among Radical Pietists. The points unique to Beissel—Sabbath observance, celibacy, ascetic diet, twofold conversion, an organized church with rituals, the Priesthood of Melchizedek—all are absent from Richter. Conversely, Richter's obsession with alchemy far outweighs Beissel's allusions. Furthermore, few, if any, Ephrata members came from the areas McIntosh identified as centers for the Rosicrucian revival, such as Sulzbach (Christian Knorr von Rosenroth's old center), Marburg, Berlin, Hamburg, and Austria.[109]

Good evidence against Ephrata as a Rosicrucian order comes from Stephan Koch (Brother Agabus). In a vision in 1732, a handsome man appeared to him who revealed several things to him. Eventually the man asked if Koch had "heard or read of people in old England whom one called Rosicrucians [*Rosen-Creutzer*]." Koch replied that he had "never read anything about it, but he had heard that such people were there and could make gold." The man then said that he was one of them, and took Koch to his house, which was full of gold and gems.[110] Koch's account makes clear that he thought Rosicrucians were English, not German, that he knew none personally, and that he had only hearsay information about them. His account in the *Chronicon* of how he came to Ephrata made no mention of seeking or finding Rosicrucians there.[111]

Altogether, evidence seems insufficient to identify Ephrata as an organized Rosicrucian group. Rather, from the esoterica in Radical Pietism, Conrad Beissel and his community developed in a different direction than the Rosicrucian revival of the latter eighteenth century. The two groups, however, shared many Boehmist elements.

If Ephrata had any link to the Gold and Rose Cross revival of the second half of the eighteenth century, it was through Jacob Martin. He evidenced the greatest interest in alchemy and astrology. He frequently cited Georg von Welling's *Opus Mago-Cabbalisticum et Theosophicum,* a work that McIntosh associates with the Gold and Rose Cross fraternity. McIntosh estimated that the brotherhood was reconstituted in 1747 or 1757 and expanded significantly in the remainder of that century, nurtured partly through Freemasonry. Jacob Martin's earliest confirmable date at Ephrata is 1761. If he had arrived recently from Europe, he could have been exposed to renewed activity of the Gold and Rose Cross before coming to Ephrata. But Ephrata's formative years were past by that time.[112]

Welling's *Opus Mago-Cabbalisticum* consists of three main parts, each assigned to one of the three main principles, salt, sulfur, and mercury. The first part contained six chapters about creation and the six days' work, then another about the Sabbath, the completion of all times, the eternal rest and its soft, silent joy.[113] Obviously these themes resonated with Beissel and Ephrata. Part I was published in 1719, the only section published before Beissel founded his movement. Parts II and III were published in 1735, a good ten years after Beissel's congregation formed.

In Part II Welling took up Lucifer and his rebellion, the last judgment, the book of Revelation, and how to work with sulfur. Part III, devoted to the heavenly mercury, gave detailed directions for astrology and a chapter on Sophia as a commentary on Proverbs 8:27. The book concluded with miscellaneous materials, including three devoted to Eternal Wisdom (Sophia); a discourse by a Dr. Hensing, of the university at Giessen, on the philosopher's stone (1722); and a tract, *Non plus ultra veritas,* outlining various pharmaceutical procedures.[114]

Some of the similarities between Welling's Part I, particularly the Sabbath and cabbalistic diagrams that may have influenced Ephrata's architecture, raise the question of possible Rosicrucian ties at Ephrata. However, the differences between Beissel and Sincerus Renatus argue against an explicitly Rosicrucian connection. More probably, the first part of Welling emerged from a matrix of Radical Pietist and esoteric literature with common themes. The expanded editions of Welling after 1735 may have stimulated separate development of renewed Gold and Rose Cross groups under the influence of Sincerus Renatus. By that time, however, Ephrata was developing in a different direction. It is unclear how much Jacob Martin was influenced by the Gold and Rose Cross movement in Germany, if at all. More likely, Martin found a home at Ephrata because of the Boehmist commonalities between Ephrata and Welling.

The interest in alchemy in Germany may be seen as resistance to the Enlightenment. McIntosh has described a "matrix" of hermetic, alchemical,

Rosicrucian, and Pietistic thought parallel to the Enlightenment, all of which resisted the authority of the established churches. He suggests that the Rosicrucian thread could go for or against the Enlightenment, depending on place and time during the century. While the matrix produced many similar individuals and groups, they followed different trajectories.

From this matrix of nonconformist thought the Ephrata community drew selected ingredients to shape their mystical language of words and ritual. Similarities between Ephrata and eighteenth-century Rosicrucianism derive from a wider pool of esoteric thought, some of it taken from Boehme, transmitted in part through Radical Pietism. These overlapping connections through Radical Pietism help to explain how a separatist like Christoph Schütz could know of Ephrata and Samuel Richter (Sincerus Renatus) while each pursued a separate path. Ephrata and eighteenth-century German Rosicrucians followed different courses, partly because they flourished in different times and places and attracted different social classes. The Gold and Rose Cross Rosicrucians remained a secret, limited order indifferent to organized religious life. Beissel and the Ephrata brethren developed a visible, public Christian community.

CONCLUSION

Esoteric disciplines of hidden knowledge thrived for a time in the eighteenth century in Europe and in the American colonies. They served as alternative bodies of knowledge. During the eighteenth century, the boundaries hardened between natural and supernatural, religious and empirical, scientific and superstitious. Still, the Enlightenment did not prevail overnight. Isaac Newton labored in alchemy. Despite Robert Boyle's theory of gases, only Lavoisier's theory of combustion in 1777 conclusively eliminated phlogiston and remnants of alchemy.[115]

As arcane disciplines faded with the emergence of a scientific worldview, vestiges of esoteric thought lodged in some folkways. The Ephrata community was one place, but not the only place in the colonies, where hidden knowledge survived. John Brooke has demonstrated Ephrata's connections to New England centers of esoteric thought, evidenced in the journey of Israel Eckerlin and Peter Miller in 1745. Fragments of early modern magic from Ephrata eventually reached Joseph Smith and Mormonism.[116]

From Beissel's earliest years, alchemy, astrology, and magic offered metaphors for Ephrata's mystical language, which was much more concerned with the disciplines and devotions needed for spiritual rebirth and its hoped-for regeneration than with manipulating chemicals or predicting the future by the stars. Virtually no one at Ephrata had any interest in hidden knowledge for its own sake, and none was adept in the complexities of the various hidden disciplines. For the Sabbatarians, such arcana provided alternative categories for seeking and sensing an unmediated presence of God, whom they believed was increasingly disregarded in the surrounding culture.

Conrad Beissel and especially Johannes Hildebrand illustrate well the enchanted world of German commoners in the early modern era. Ezechiel Sangmeister represents the persisting magical worldview of commoners as the complexities of arcane knowledge disintegrated. These common folks did not necessarily see a conflict between insights grasped from hidden knowledge and the teachings of Christianity. Jacob Martin, nearly the same age as Sangmeister, illustrates how a few at Ephrata lived in two worlds for a brief time. Martin belonged to a shrinking minority who attempted to retain astrology, alchemy, and perhaps magic as means to understand the natural world, and to use them in the inward spiritual life. Ephrata thrived as a community where hidden knowledge provided metaphors by which believers transmuted language, dissolving their apparent meanings in order to speak of that which eludes words: the life of the soul in the presence of God.

EPILOGUE

As early as 1762 Peter Miller wrote that only a few remained who could speak the "language of the Spirit," and that they were hard to understand. Between 1764 and 1768 two nasty battles convulsed the aging community of celibates. The first was over Beissel's successor. Peter Miller hoped to take Beissel's place; Maria Eicher backed Christian Eckstein (Brother Gideon). Beissel himself chose Georg Adam Martin to succeed him—not at Ephrata but at Antietam, where Snow Hill flourished in the next century. Beissel deposed Maria Eicher and Eckstein moved to Germantown; he returned about a decade later. The second battle, concerning ownership of cloister land, erupted when Samuel Eckerlin returned from Virginia in 1764, threatening to claim legal right to the property. Beissel died in 1768; the land dispute was resolved in 1770, but not before petitions had reached the Pennsylvania Assembly. Peter Miller became "superintendent" at Ephrata in 1768. He had the sweet pleasure of outliving Georg Adam Martin and Ezechiel Sangmeister, who predeceased Miller by twelve years. Yet Ezechiel's separatist household outlived the last vowed sisters. The last Ephrata nun died in 1813; the Kelps, Ezechiel's compatriots, died a year or so before 1820. Ephrata's celibate piety ended in the kind of eremitic separatism in which Beissel first came to Conestoga. Neither the aging nuns nor Sangmeister's household successfully passed on the language of the Spirit at Ephrata. There the voices of the solitaries murmured ever more faintly for a half century after Beissel's death before the silence of eternity swallowed them.

Conrad Beissel spoke and wrote in an idiom that he wished to have understood in a mystical sense. He developed a language to portray God's presence in the intimacy of loving spouses, in the nothingness of dissolution into God, in the holiness of theophany in an inner sanctum. Beissel saw the hindrance to this presence of God in a fundamental bifurcation of gender that he believed cuts through the cosmos, having originated in rebellious divine beings that stirred God's androgynous balance into separation and finally spread to the first human. What Beissel saw as the tragedy of gender division played out again as the primal human was aroused by sexual desire, suffering a break in the unity of gender that alienated people from God and from one another. Access to the unitive presence of God was restored through the redemptive death of Jesus Christ on the cross, where the divine female, Sophia, was reunited with the divine male in one human. Through the union of Christ and Sophia, God offers resolution of gender division to people. The redemptive restoration of genders and restoration of access to God are gifts of grace through Christ and Sophia, evoking a life of self-denying discipleship. For Beissel they anticipated a glorious consummation in the rest of the Eternal Sabbath, when all hindrances to God's presence would disappear.

Conrad Beissel began his religious pilgrimage as a separatist, exposed to many groups but alienated from the established churches and joining no other. Periods of solitude alternated with leadership of the Ephrata community. He wrote prolifically, but many people shared in creating the mystical language of Ephrata, even detractors such as Ezechiel Sangmeister. The individual quest for God always stood in constant tension with the life of a gathered religious community at Ephrata; it found resolution only after all the celibates had died.

Ironically, the successors to Penn's government have become the preservers of Ephrata. After the last nun died in 1813, the householders reorganized as the German Seventh-Day Baptist Church in 1814. Snow Hill carried on

Ephrata's legacy with its nunnery near Waynesboro, though it was never as large as Ephrata and never ascetic. The last of Snow Hill's celibates died at the end of the nineteenth century, and the church survived among the married members. A congregation is located at Salemville, Pennsylvania; it has never had monastics. The church at Ephrata continued, although much of Beissel's unique teachings were forgotten. Declining membership in the early decades of the twentieth century and inadequate resources for maintenance pressed the members to consider the future of the site. In 1941 the Commonwealth of Pennsylvania officially completed the purchase of the grounds and buildings of Ephrata, despite some contention after 1934, when the German Seventh-Day Baptist Church congregation at Ephrata dissolved. Through restoration, preservation, and further study and interpretation at the site, the memory of Ephrata lives on.

From familiar and obscure sources in Radical Pietism, the Bible, and Christian belief, Conrad Beissel and the Ephrata community created unique ways to speak about the presence of God. They inscribed it in their manuscript art and voiced it in voluminous hymn texts and unique musical settings. They prepared for and celebrated it in corporate ritual and private contemplation. Beside the Cocalico, Conrad Beissel, his supporters, and even his detractors created a unique monastic community founded on religious concepts of the Old World but made possible only in the freedom of Penn's colony.

BIBLIOGRAPHICAL ESSAY

The most important way to begin any bibliography of Ephrata is to warn that most of the secondary literature depends too uncritically on Julius F. Sachse's two-volume history, *The German Sectarians of Pennsylvania: A Critical and Legendary History of the Ephrata Cloister and the Dunkers* (Philadelphia: Printed for the author by P. C. Stockhausen, 1899–1900; rpt. New York: AMS Press, 1970–71). For reasons already demonstrated, his work is not reliable, although it is valuable for its preservation of much source material. Sachse was not above altering material to suit his purposes. All work that depends primarily on Sachse must be approached cautiously. James E. Ernst's *Ephrata: A History*, Pennsylvania German Folklore Society, vol. 25 (Allentown: Schlechter's, 1953), and E. G. Alderfer, *The Ephrata Commune: An Early American Counterculture* (Pittsburgh: University of Pittsburgh Press, 1985), demonstrate the problems of depending on Sachse.

PRIMARY LITERATURE

Ephrata's primary sources, too, must be approached with caution. The main primary source narratives of Ephrata's story are its internal history, the *Chronicon Ephratense*, along with the autobiography of a disgruntled member and critic, Ezechiel Sangmeister, and the internal history of the reorganized sisters' order, "Die Rose." The Ephrata chronicle, edited by Peter Miller, or Brother Agrippa, was based on a manuscript reportedly kept by Jacob Gaas, or Brother Lamech, who died in 1764 (see *LuW* 9:50 for Lamech's death and identity as a signatory to the original and deed to Ephrata, which reveals hs name), under the names Lamech and Agrippa. The chronicle overpraised Beissel and consistently criticized the Dunkers. The original was in German: *Chronicon Ephratense, Enthaltend den Lebens-Lauf des ehrwürdigen Vaters in Christo Friedsam Gottrecht, Weyland Stiffters und Vorstehers des geistl. Ordens der Einsamen in Ephrata in der Grafschaft Lancaster in Pennsylvania. Zusammen getragen von Br. Lamech u. Agrippa* (Ephrata, 1786). J. Max Hark's translation, *Chronicon Ephratense: A History*

BIBLIOGRAPHICAL ESSAY

of the Community of Seventh-Day Baptists at Ephrata, Lancaster County, Penn'a by Lamech and Agrippa (Lancaster: S. H. Zahm, 1889; rpt. New York: Burt Franklin, 1972), is readable, with only occasional errors. Hark's limited understanding of Boehme skewed some of the translation, but usually only in technical religious passages.

Ezechiel Sangmeister criticized Beissel caustically and indulged in rumor and interpolation, yet his is a necessary critical voice to accompany the *Chronicon*. Sangmeister also quoted several excerpts reportedly from Lamech's manuscript version of the *Chronicon* before it was printed. They provide helpful information on some aspects of the early years, although one must use them carefully. Sangmeister's autobiography is *Das Leben und Wandel des in GOTT ruhenten und seligen Br. Ezechiel Sangmeisters; Weiland ein Einwohner von Ephrata. Dessen höchst sonderbare, und bemerckungswürdige Laufbahn, Unter der Leitung und Führung Göttlicher Vorsehung! Mit allen Merckwürdigkeiten, womit seine Laufbahn begleitet, bis zu seiner Seligen Vollendung; Von ihm selbst beschrieben. Bestehend in 6 Theile. Welchem vorangehet, ein kurzer Entwurf einer Chronick, von der Stiftung und Grundlegung des Ephrataner-Wercks; bis auf des seligen Autores Ankunft daselbst: Wo alsdann die Chronick nebst seiner Laufbahn, gelegentlich mit fortgeführt, und aus dem Grunde der Wahrheit, mit Unverfälschter Treue, Ohne einige Partheylichkeit; Frey und offen ans Licht gestellt wird,* 3 vols. (Ephrata: Joseph Bauman, 1825–27). Only three of the projected four volumes were published by Bauman. Its fine translation by Barbara M. Schindler is in *Journal of the Historical Society of the Cocalico Valley* 4–10 (1979–85).

The internal history of the reorganized sisterhood is "Die Rose oder der angenehmen Blumen zu Saron geistlichen ehe verlöbnüs mit ihrem himmlischen Bräutigam Welchen sie sich als ihrem König Haupt, Herrn und Bräutigam aufs ewig hin verlobt (Ephrata den 13: des 5: Mon 1745)," a variously paginated manuscript in the Cassel Collection, Ac. 1925, Historical Society of Pennsylvania, Philadelphia. It praised Beissel in glowing terms and flattered Maria Eicher. Still, its importance cannot be overestimated as a source in women's voices, describing the reorganized sisters' order. The Historical Society of Pennsylvania also has a nineteenth-century manuscript copy, Ac. 1924, probably copied at Snow Hill, which has some copying errors.

An essential collection of contemporary sources outside of Ephrata can be found in Felix Reichmann and Eugene E. Doll's *Ephrata as Seen by Contemporaries,* Pennsylvania German Folklore Society, vol. 17 (Allentown: Schlechter's, 1953). All the documents they have chosen for the volume have been translated into English. Most of the accounts offer valuable eyewitness information. Unfortunately, the account by Johann Franz Regnier was taken from Sachse's faulty translation. More sources related to the early members of the Ephrata community and their interactions with the Dunkers can be found in Donald F. Durnbaugh's edited volume *The Brethren in Colonial America* (Elgin, Ill.: Brethren Press, 1967) and his *European Origins of the Brethren* (Elgin, Ill.: Brethren Press, 1958).

BIBLIOGRAPHICAL ESSAY

An anonymous polemic against communal Ephrata was published in the second decade of the nineteenth century. Clearly favoring the faction of Samuel Eckerlin and Ezechiel Sangmeister, the book also gives a few brief biographical descriptions of some other Ephrata members. Although late, this source is important: *Das Heutige Signal, Oder Posaunen-Schall!Dem Freyen Abend-Lande zur Warnung und zum Trost/zum Feyerabend sich vor-zu-bereiten; wie solches im Rath der Wächter beschlossen, und worauf mit Fleiß zu merken ist!/Denen Liebhabern der Weisheit, und zu dero Dienst fürnemlich, wird also hiemit, ein Schlüssel aus dem Arcano gereicht, So zur Eröffnung Der Geheimniß-vollen Wunder-Pforte!Imanuelis, Hauptsächlich gewidmet ist. Wie solches zwar (nach der mit unserm Freyen Abend-Land, hiemit angemessenen Uebereinkunft zufolge) in einem unpartheyischen und ungezwungenen Stilo; also, nach dem Sinn des Geistes H. Schrift, als aus dem Centro verfaßt, befindlich* (Ephrata: Jacob Ruth, 1812).

Some data come from Jacob Funk's notebook, an untitled, unpaginated manuscript now known as "Brother Kenan's Notebook," in the Sachse Collection, Seventh-Day Baptist Historical Society, on loan to Pennsylvania State Archives, Harrisburg. It is not thorough, but it, too, is important. So is the anonymous "Register vor die Bruder und Schwestern die in und ausser Efrathaer (Gemeinschaft) gestorben sind," a variously paginated manuscript in the Cassel Collection, Ac.1926, Historical Society of Pennsylvania, Philadelphia, which lists some important events along with the deaths of Ephrata's members.

Peter Erb's *Johann Conrad Beissel and the Ephrata Community: Mystical and Historical Texts*, Studies in American Religion, vol. 14 (Lewiston, N.Y.: Edwin Mellen Press, 1985), attempts to present some of Ephrata's primary sources in English. However, it contains some serious translation errors that alter the meaning. Readers should check anything in that collection against the German originals. A small translation by Michelle Long of Beissel's maxims, *Some Theosophical Maxims or Rules of the Solitary Life*, edited by Nadine A. Steinmetz (Ephrata: Ephrata Cloister Associates and Pennsylvania Historical and Museum Commission, 1991), is generally good, in spite of a few translation errors.

Most other primary sources are available only in German. An essential tool to get started is Eugene E. Doll and Anneliese M. Funke's *Ephrata Cloisters: An Annotated Bibliography* (Philadelphia: Carl Schurz Memorial Foundation, 1944), which should be used in conjunction with the fine bibliography on early German imprints in America by Karl John Richard Arndt and Reimer C. Eck, *The First Century of German Language Printing in the United States of America: A Bibliography Based on the Studies of Oswald Seidensticker and Wilbur H. Oda*, Publications of the Pennsylvania German Society, n.s. 21–22 (Göttingen: Niedersächsische Staats- und Universitätsbibliothek Göttingen, 1989). One important early work in English is Cunrad Beysell, *Mystyrion Anomias: The Mystery of Lawlessness; or, Lawless Antichrist Discover'd and Disclos'd* (n.p., 1729), which survives only in Michael Wohlfahrt's 1729 English translation, fortunately copied and preserved by Sachse. Among the German sources, an important early example of Beissel's mystical literature is *Mystische und sehr geheyme Sprueche, Welche in der Himlishcen schule des heiligen geistes erlernet* (Philadelphia: B. Franklin, 1730).

The bulk of Beissel's known writings were published. His single most important piece, judging from the number of times it was printed, was the so-called *Wunderschrift*, or, as it is known in Peter Miller's English translation, *A Dissertation on Man's Fall*. The only known self-contained German publication of this work appeared in 1789. It contains minor word or spelling changes and lacks all of Peter Miller's earlier footnotes from the version printed in *Deliciae Ephratenses, Pars I* in 1773. The 1789 edition appeared as *Göttliche Wunderschrift, Darinnen entdecket wird, wie aus dem ewigen Guten hat können ein Böses urständen. Desgleichen Wie das Böse wieder in das Gute vergestaltet, und der ewigen Mutter, als die vor den Zeiten des Abfalls das Ruder geführt, in den Schoos geliefert wird. Da dann alle Amtsverwaltungen, die im Abfall durch den Willen des Manns entstanden, wieder aufgehoben werden. Denen Irrthümern des Naturalismi und Atheismi entgegen gesezt, und zum Heiligen Nachsinnen den Kindern der Obern Weisheit* (Ephrata, 1789).

Many of Beissel's letters have been preserved. A large volume of theosophical epistles was published in two versions in 1745, the first as Irenici Theodicäi, *Zionitischen Stiffts I. Theil Oder eine Wolrichende Narde* (Ephrata: Drucks und Verlags der Brüderschaft, 1745). The second version, reformatted upon the expulsion of Israel Eckerlin, was *Urständliche und Erfahrungs-volle Hohe Zeugnüsse Wie man zum Geistlichen Leben und dessen Vollkommenheit gelangen möge* (Ephrata: Drucks der Brüderschaft, 1745). The letters were reprinted in 1773 in Peter Miller's two-volume edition of some of Beissel's works (see below). Beissel's speeches or sermons, some of which appeared to be intentionally composed for publication, appeared under the pseudonym Friedsam Gottrecht: *Deliciae Ephratenses, Pars I. Oder des ehrwürdigen Vatters Friedsam Gottrecht, Weyland Stiffters und Führers des Christlichen Ordens der Einsamen in Ephrata in Pennsylvanien, Geistliche Reden* (Ephratae: Typis Societatis, 1773). Part II contained the reprinted theosophical epistles: *Deliciae Ephratenses, Pars II. Oder des ehrwürdigen Vatters Friedsam Gottrecht, Weyland Stiffters und Führers des Christlichen Ordens der Einsamen in Ephrata in Pennsylvanien, Theosophische Episteln* (Ephrata: Typis Societatis, 1773). Miller also edited a small volume of a few letters, most of them to Georg Adam Martin: *Geistliche Briefe eines Friedsamen Pilgers, Welche er von 1721. bis an seine 1768. darauf erfolgte Entbindung geschrieben* (Ephrata, 1794). A very important set of manuscript letters by Beissel survives in two copies: "Conrad Beissel Letterbook," paginated manuscript in the Borneman Collection, B. Ms. 22, Free Library of Philadelphia, and "Letter Book of Conrad Beissel, 1755," paginated manuscript in the Cassel Collection, Ac. 1923, Historical Society of Pennsylvania, Philadelphia. These books contain virtually the same letters, except that the one in the Free Library of Philadelphia contains a fragment of a letter to Ezechiel Sangmeister. Both books are copies, not in Beissel's hand. An additional manuscript collection of late eighteenth-century letters between Snow Hill and Ephrata survives in a copybook in the Pennsylvania State Archives. It is catalogued as "Letter Book," untitled, paginated copybook of correspondence between Snow Hill and Ephrata, and excerpts from books received from Ephrata, in the Sachse Collection, Box 14, no. 15, Seventh-Day Baptist Historical Society, on loan to Pennsylvania State Archives, Harrisburg. A small collection of a few miscellaneous Ephrata letters is in "Copies of Letters, etc.," collection of manuscript letters and other miscellanea in the Cassel Collection, Ac. 188, Historical Society of Pennsylvania, Philadelphia. One letter, headed "Cobia eines briefes von einem Längst verstorbenen Bruder in Ephrata," was written as if by Beissel if not actually by him, denouncing Samuel Eckerlin's attempt to claim Ephrata property in 1764.

Two rich sources, although difficult to read, are the lengthy manuscript "letters" that Israel Eckerlin, under the name Onesimus, wrote to Beissel and Ephrata from the Alleghenies in the mid-1750s: "Ein Evangelisches Zeugnüß, und geistliger bericht, An . . . Verfasser der Ephratanischen Gemeinschafft, und Haubt Regierung . . . ihrer auferbauung. Geschrieben und verfertiget von Onesimuß . . . In dem groß, und weit umliegenden Eligenischen Gebörgen. Im Jahr unseres Herrn und Heilandes 1755," unpaginated manuscript, Pennsylvania Historical and Museum Commission, Ephrata Cloister. The second item is listed as "A Sermon by Israel Eckerlin," unpaginated manuscript in the Cassel Collection, Ac. 1927, Historical Society of Pennsylvania, in Philadelphia. The work is actually a letter addressed to Peter Miller in 1756.

Among Beissel's other published works is a collection of devotional materials very difficult to assess: *Erster Theil Der Theosophischen Lectionen, Betreffende die Schulen des einsamen Lebens* (Ephrata, 1752), contains theosophical readings composed by members of the community but reviewed by Beissel for publication. The authors are not identified, and it is unclear how much editorial control Beissel exercised. The volume also contains a reprint of Beissel's original mystical and secret sayings and additional theosophical maxims.

Larger-scale writings by Ephrata authors are important for the light they shed on Ephrata and for revealing that even Beissel's enemies shared many of his religious views. Judging from the works that survive and were published, Johannes Hildebrand was the most important writer related to Ephrata next to Beissel. This evaluation is based on the working assumption that most of Israel Eckerlin's writings, which may have been more numerous, were lost or destroyed after his expulsion in 1745. Hildebrand's works include *Gründliche und Natur-gemäße Verhandelung von den Cometen und deren Erscheinung; Darinnen die Frage umständlich erörtert wird: Ob sie nur bloß Phaenomena der Natur sind oder ob sie Gerichts-Botten der zukünfftigen Straff seyen,*

Ausgeführet nach den Principien beydes der natürlichen Astronomie und Theosophia durch Johannes Hildebrand. Bey Veranlassung einer aus Teutschland übersandten Schrifft betreffend den letzt erschienenen grossen Cometen (Germantown: Christoph Saur, 1746); *Schrifftmässiges Zeuchnüß Von dem Himmlischen und Jungfräulichen Gebährungs-Werck, Wie es an dem ersten Adam ist mit Fleisch zugeschlossen, aber an dem zweyten Adam bey seiner Creutzigung durch einen Speer wiederum geöffnet worden. Entgegen gesetzt Dem gantz ungegründeten Vorgeben der Herrenhuthischen Gemeine von einem heiligen Ehestand, daraus Sie das Ebenbild Gottes auszugebähren vorgeben. Ans Lichte gegeben durch Johannes Hildebrand, Einem Mitglied der Gemeine Jesu Christi Ephrata Hausväterlicher Seite* [Germantown: Christoph Saur, 1743]; and *Ein Gespräch zwischen einem Jüngling und einem Alten von dem Nutzen in Gottseeligen Gemeinschafften* [Germantown: Christoph Saur, 1754]. In addition, the Moravians published a harsh letter against Hildebrand that Saur printed, *Ein Schreiben der Herrnhutischen Gemeine aus ihrer Conferentz an Mstr. Johann Hildebrand in Ephrata* [Germantown: Christoph Saur, 1743]. A manuscript letter by Hildebrand to Sander Mack and Christoph Saur, 1757, survives in Juniata College Library, Huntingdon, Pa. In addition, Hildebrand was probably the main author behind *Mistisches und Kirchliches Zeuchnüß Der Brüderschaft in Zion, Von den wichtigsten Puncten des Christenthums Nebst einem Anhang Darinnen dieselbe ihr unpartheyisches Bedencken an Tag gibt von dem Bekehrungs-Werck der sogenanten Herrenhutischen Gemeine in Pennsylvanien, und warum man ihnen keine Kirche zustehen könne* (Germantown: C.[hristoph] Saur, 1743).

Ezechiel Sangmeister presented his religious views in his *Mystische Theologie, oder Wahrer Wegweiser nach unserm Ursprung und Vaterland! Bestehend in 3 Theilen, 1. Theil, von den Irr- und Abwegen gutmeinender Frommen. 2. Theil, ist eine Erklärung über Mathäi 24. 3. Theil, ist eine Erklärung der sechstägigen Schöpfung und den Zeitlauften dieser Welt. Gestellt nach dem hohen Licht und Erkenntniß durch Ezechiel Sangmeister* (Ephrata: Joseph Bauman, 1819–20). Another witness to Ephrata's religious views, the work of Brother Philemon (Johann Conrad Rissmann or Reissmann), evidences a quietist strand in Ephrata's religious thought. This untitled, paginated copybook containing voluminous excerpts from Madame Guyon's letters is in Muddy Creek Farm Library, Denver, Pa.

Georg Adam Martin became the leading minister at Antietam (which grew into Snow Hill) and Beissel's handpicked successor, although not at Ephrata. Martin's most significant work is his *Christliche Bibliothek, Enthält dasjenige was allen Pilgern auf der Reise nach der verlornen Herrlichkeit zu wissen nöthig ist. Herausgegeben durch deinen Getreuen Aufrichtigen Mitbruder* (Ephrata, 1792). Although published late in the eighteenth century, it illustrates the evolution of Ephrata's thought after Beissel and most of the other early writers were gone.

Another late but important eighteenth-century source is Jacob Martin. Except for one printed broadside, Jacob Martin's known writings are all short manuscript essays.

BIBLIOGRAPHICAL ESSAY

The broadside is "Copie Eines Briefs oder eine Antwort auf die Frage: Ob alle Menschen die zur Seelichkeit gelangen, zuvor ins inwendige Leben müssen versetzt werden?" (1760). The work is attributed to the Ephrata Press on the basis of typographical evidence, although Clarence Spohn has demonstrated that the type was not in use as early as 1760, so the date is probably inaccurate. The manuscript papers of Jacob Martin in the Pennypacker Collection are catalogued at Ephrata as Ephrata Collection no. 52 Mss.46, Ephrata Cloister, Ephrata, Pennsylvania. The collection contains other miscellaneous items as well.

The Ephrata Press published a number of volumes that offer insights into the overall interests at the community. Some authors were from Ephrata, others were not. Among these works are *Ernstliche Erweckungs-Stimm In ein Lied verfasset Ueber den so lang gestandenen und grosen Cometen Welcher sich im X Monast des Jahrs 1743 das erste mal sehen ließ, und 10 Wochen lang gestanden* (1745); *Von der Historia Des Apostolischen Kampffs, Zehen Bücher Wie sie der Abdias anfänglich in Hebräischer Sprache beschrieben, Eutropius aber ins Griechische, und Julius Africanus ins Lateinische übersetzet haben. Welchen dann Wolfgangus Lazius aus alten Scribenten auch beygefüget hat Das Leben des Apostels Matthäi, und des heiligen Marci Clementis Cipriani und Apollinaris; Nunmehro für einige unpassionirte Liebhaber der Wahrheit ins Deutsche übersetzt; Nebst etlichen Merckwürdigen Reden Jesu die man zwar nicht in den Evangelien, aber bey andern bewährten Scribenten findet: Auch der Marter-Geschichte der heiligen und hochberühmten ersten Märtyrin und Apostolischen Jungfrau Theclä* (1764); *Erster Eingang und Gebät. Im Namen deß Herren Jesu Amen.* [1754]; [Anthony Benezet], *Eine kurtze vorstellung des theils von Africa, Welches bewohnt wird von Negroes, Darinnen beschrieben wird die fruchtbarkeit desselben landes, die gutartigkeit dessen einwohner, und wie man daselbst den sclaven-handel treibt* (1763); Eliseba Böhler, *Abgeforderte Relation der Erscheinung eines entleibten Geists Dem Publico zur Nachricht getreulich aus dem Mund derer, die von Anfang bis ans Ende mit interessirt, aufgeschrieben* (1761).

Two interesting works seem to have been published at Ephrata through other agencies: Alvaro Alonso Barba, *Gründlicher Unterricht von den Metallen, Darinnen beschrieben wird, wie sie werden in der Erden generirt; und was man insgemein dabey findet. In zwey Büchern. Vormals im Spanischen beschrieben durch Albaro Alonso Barba, Pfarrherr zu St. Bernards Kirchspiel in der Kaiserlichen Stadt Potosi, in dem Königreich Peru, in West-Indien; im Jahr 1664. Hernach in das Engländische übersetzt durch Edward Graff von Sandwich. Anno 1669. Und nun um seiner Vortrefflichkeit willen zum erstenmal ins Hoch-teutsche übersetzt, und zum Druck befördert durch G. R. Dieser Kunst befliessenen. Nebst einem Anhang betreffend obige Materie* (Ephrata: J. Georg Zeissinger, 1763); and *Die Beschreibung Des Evangeliums Nicodemi. Von dem Leyden unsers Herren Jesu Christi, Wie er von den Juden, als ein Uebelthäther Zauberer, ect: vor Pilato fälschlich verklagt, und unschuldig zum Tod verurtheilt worden. Wie auch Von seiner Begräbnuß, Auferstehung u. Himmelfahrt ect:*

Welches beschrieben worden in dem dreysigsten Jahr des Kayserthums Tyberii (Ephrata: Verlags M[ichael] M[iller], 1748). Apparently Georg Zeissinger (or Zeisinger), an Ephrata member, provided some kind of primary support for the publication of the work by Barba. Michael Miller (or Müller) was the loyal member whose "Debt Book" gives insight on some of the financial dealings of the sisterhood. Apparently he helped to support the publication of the *Evangelium Nicodemi* (Gospel of Nicodemus). A similar case appears in a schoolbook by Ludwig Höcker (Brother Obed), *Kurz gefasste* [sic]. *Nützliche Schul-Büchlein Die kinder zu unterrichten in Buchstabieren, Lesen und auswendig lernen, Deme angehänget ein kurzer doch deutlicher, und gründlicher Unterricht Zur Rechenkunst. Aufgesetzt zum Nutz und Gebrauch vor Kinder* (Ephrata: Gedruckt und zu bekommen bey dem Schulmeister, Drucker und Buchbinder, 1786). Apparently Höcker produced this work on his own. No copy of the first edition is known. Tamara Groff's English translation is well done: Ludwig Höcker, *Ephrata Cloister School Booklet,* edited by Nadine A. Steinmetz (Ephrata: Ephrata Cloister Associates and Pennsylvania Historical and Museum Commission, 1988).

Ephrata published several religious works by Mennonites, perhaps for Mennonite readers, but they also contributed to the devotional life at Ephrata. A few representative Mennonite works are *Die Ernsthaffte Christen-Pflicht Darinnen Schöne Geistreiche Gebetter Darmit Sich fromme Christen-Hertzen zu allen Zeiten und in allen Nöthen trösten können Nebst einem Anhang Einer Aus dem blutigen Schau-Spiel übersetzter Geschichte zweyer Blut-Zeugen der Warheit, Hans von Oberdam u. Valerius des Schulmeisters* (1745); *Güldene Aepffel in Silbern Schalen Oder: Schöne und nützliche Worte und Warheiten Zur Gottseligkeit. Enthalten in Sieben Haupt-Theilen die in diesem Buch zusammen gestellet sind; Mit sonderbarem Fleiß von denen in der vorigen Edition häufig eingeschlichenen Druckfehlern gereiniget. Nebst angehängten Vorreden und einem zweyfachen Register* (1745); Tieleman Janszoon van Braght, *Der Blutige Schau-Platz oder Martyrer Spiegel der TauffsGesinnten oder Wehrlosen-Christen, Die um des Zeugnuß Jesu ihres Seligmachers willen gelitten haben, und seynd getödtet worden, von Christi Zeit an bis auf das Jahr 1660. Vormals aus unterschiedlichen glaubwürdigen Chronicken, Nachrichten und Zeugnüssen gesammlet und in Holländischer Sprache heraus gegeben von T. J. V. Braght. Nun aber sorgfältigst ins Hochteutsche übersetzt und zum erstenmal ans Licht gebracht* (1748[–49]); [Gerhard Roosen], *Christliches Gemüths-Gesprach Von dem seligmachenden Glauben, Und Erkäntnüss der Warheit, so zu der Gottseligkeit führet in der Hoffnung des ewigen Lebens* (1769). An edition with additional supplements was issued in 1770.

Some essential contemporary literature is necessary to understand the world of religious symbolism on which Beissel and others at Ephrata drew. These are not all of the important works, but they are a good introduction: *Ein Spiegel der Eheleute Nebst schönen Erinnerungen vor ledige Personen, Welche willends sind, sich in den Stand der Ehe zu begeben. Wie auch, Etwas von den Ursachen, warum viele Menschen aus einer Religion in die andere übergehen. Vorgestelt in einem Gespräch zwischen einem Jüngling und Meister* ([Germantown: Christoph Saur], 1758); Thomas Bromley, *The Way to the Sabbath of Rest, or, The Soul's Progress in the Work of the New Birth,* 3d ed. (Germantown: Christopher Saur, 1759); Michael Frantz, *Einfältige Lehr-Betrachtungen, und kurtzgefaßtes Glaubens-Bekäntniß des gottseligen Lehrers, Michael Frantzen; Weyland gewesenen Vorstehers der Täuffer-Gemeine in Canastogoe* (Germantown: Christoph Saur, 1770); [Heinrich Horch], *Mystische und Profetische Bibel Das ist die gantze Heilige Schrifft Altes und Neues Testaments Auffs neue nach dem Grund verbessert Sampt Erklärung Der fürnemsten Sinnbilder und Weissagungen Sonderlich Des Hohen Lieds Salomons und der Offenbarung Jesu Christi wie auch denen fürnemsten Lehren bevoraus die sich in dies letzte Zeiten schicken* (Marburg: Joh. Kürzner, Universitätsbuchdrucks, 1712); Johannes Kelpius, *The Diarium of Magister Johannes Kelpius,* translated by Julius F. Sachse, Proceedings and Addresses of the Pennsylvania German Society, vol. 25 (Lancaster: New Era, 1917).

All of the major printed hymnals and supplements from Ephrata are listed here in chronological order: *Göttliche Liebes und Lobes gethöne Welche in den hertzen der kinder der weiszheit zusammen ein. Und von da wieder auszgeflossen zum lob gottes, Und nun denen schülern der himlischen weiszheit zur erweckung und aufmunterung in ihrem Creutz und leiden aus hertzlicher liebe mitgetheilet. Dann Mit lieb erfüllet sein, bringt Gott den besten Preisz Und giebt zum singen uns, die allerschönste weisz* (Philadelphia: Benjamin Franklin, 1730); *Vorspiel der Neuen-Welt. Welches sich in der letzten Abendroethe als ein paradisischer Lichtes-glantz unter den Kindern Gottes hervor gethan. In* LIEBES, LOBES, LEIDENS, KRAFFT *und Erfahrungs liedern abgebildet, die gedrückte, gebückte und Creutz-tragende Kirche auf Erden. Und wie inzwischen sich Die obere und Triumphirende Kirche als eine Paradiesische vorkost hervor thut und offenbahret. Und daneben, als Ernstliche und zuruffende wächterstimmen an alle annoch zerstreuete Kinder Gottes, das sie sich sammlen und bereit machen auf den baldigen; Ja bald herein brechenden Hochzeit-Tag der braut des Lamms* (Philadelphia: Benjamin Franklin, 1732); *Jacobs Kampff- und Ritter-Platz Allwo Der nach seinem ursprung sich sehnende geist der in Sophiam verliebten seele mit Gott um den neuen namen gerungen, und den Sieg davon getragen. Entworffen* IN UNTERSCHIEDLICHEN GLAUBENS- *u. leidens-liedern, u. erfahrungsvollen austruckungen des gemuths, darinnen sich dar stellet, so wol auff seiten Gottes seine unermuedete arbeit zur reinigung solcher seelen, die sich seiner fuerung anvertraut, als auch Auff seiten des Menschen der ernst des geistes im aus halten unter dem process der läuterung und abschmeltzung des Menschen der Sünden samt dem daraus entspringenden lobesgethön. Zur Gemütlichen erweckung derer die das heil Jerusalems lieb haben* (Philadelphia: B.[enjamin] F.[ranklin], 1736); *Zionitischer WeyrauchsHügel Oder: Myrrhen Berg, Worinnen allerley liebliches und wohl riechendes nach Apotheker-Kunst zu bereitetes Rauch- Werck zu finden. Bestehend In allerley Liebes-Würckungen der in GOTT geheiligten Seelen, welche sich in vielen und mancherley geistlichen und lieblichen Liedern aus gebildet. Als darinnen Der letzte Ruff zu dem Abendmahl des grossen Gottes auf unterschiedliche Weise trefflich aus gedrucket ist; Zum Dienst Der in dem Abend-Ländischen Welt-Theil als bey dem Untergang der Sonnen erweckten Kirche Gottes, und zu ihrer Ermunterung auf die Mitternächtige Zukunfft des Bräutigams ans Licht gegeben* (Germantown: Christoph Sauer, 1739); *Das Gesäng der Einsamen und Verlassenen Turtel-Taube Nemlich der Christlichen Kirche. Oder geistliche und Erfahrungs-volle Leidens u. Liebes-Gethöne, Als darinnen beydes die Vorkost der neuen Welt als auch die darzwischen vorkommende Creutzes- und Leidens-Wege nach ihrer Würde dargestellt, und in geistliche Reimen gebracht, von einem Friedsamen und nach der stillen Ewigkeit wallenden Pilger. Und nun Zum Gebrauch der Einsamen und Verlassenen zu Zion gesammlet und ans Licht gegeben* (Ephrata: Drucks der Brüderschaft, 1747, 1749); *Paradisisches Wunder-Spiel, Welches sich In diesen letzten Zeiten und Tagen In denen Abend-Ländischen Welt-Theilen als ein Vorspiel der neuen Welt hervor gethan. Bestehende In einer gantz neuen und ungemeinen Sing-Art auf Weise der Englischen und himmlischen Chören eingerichtet. Da dann das Lied Mosis und des Lamms, wie auch das hohe Lied Salomonis samt noch mehrern Zeugnüssen aus der Bibel und andern Heiligen in liebliche Melodeyen gebracht. Wobey nicht weniger der Zuruf der Braut des Lamms, sammt der Zubereitung auf den herrlichen Hochzeit-Tag trefflich Praefigurirt wird. Alles nach Englischen Chören Gesangs-Weise mit viel Mühe und grosem Fleiß ausgefertiget von einem Friedsamen, Der sonst in dieser Welt weder Namen noch Titul suchet* (Ephrata: Sumptibus Societatis, 1754); *Nachklang Zum Gesäng der einsamen Turtel-Taube, Enthaltend eine neue Sammlung Geistlicher Lieder (Ephrata: Drucks der Brüderschaft, 1755); Neu-vermehrtes Gesäng der einsamen Turtel-Taube, zur gemeinschafftlichen Erbauung gesammlet und ans Licht gegeben* (Ephrata: Typis Societatis, 1762); *Paradisisches Wunder-Spiel, Welches sich In diesen letzten Zeiten und Tagen In denen Abend-Ländischen Welt-Theilen als ein Vorspiel der neuen Welt hervorgethan. Bestehend in einer neuen Sammlung andächtiger und zum Lob des grosen Gottes eingerichteter geistlicher und ehedessen zum Theil publicirter Lieder* (Ephrata: Typis & Consensu Societatis, 1766). Two interesting lengthy hymns were composed by various members of each celibate order and published separately: by the brothers, *Ein angenehmer Geruch der Rosen und Lilien Die im Thal der Demuth unter den Dornen hervor gewachsen. Alles aus der Brüderlichen Gesellschafft in Bethania* ([Ephrata: Typis Societatis], 1756); by the sisters, *Ein angenehmer Geruch der Rosen und Lilien Die im Thal der Demuth unter den Dornen hervor gewachsen. Alles aus der Schwesterlichen Gesellschafft in Saron.* ([Ephrata: Typis Societatis], 1756). A collection of a few Beissel hymns in English translation can be found in *Ephrata Cloister Chorales: A Collection of Hymns and Anthems Composed by Conrad Beissel,* edited by Russel P. Getz (New York: G. Schirmer, 1971; rpt. Ephrata: Ephrata Cloister Associates, 1990).

Several music manuscripts were used in this work. Currently at the Ephrata Cloister is "Die Blume zu Saron," a music book with illustrations for *Das Gesäng der Einsamen Turtel-Taube* (1746), EC 80.33.2. Several music manuscripts are in the Sachse Collection,

BIBLIOGRAPHICAL ESSAY

Seventh-Day Baptist Historical Society, on loan to Pennsylvania State Archives, Harrisburg. Because the collection was being recatalogued at the time of my research, the old identification numbers are provided here. They are still available for cross-identification in the new system. The manuscripts include a music book for *Das Gesäng der Einsamen Turtel-Taube*, Box 8, no. 3; a music book with illustrations for *Zionitischer WeyrauchsHügel* and *Das Gesäng der Einsamen Turtel-Taube* ("Wm. M. Fahnestock"), Box 7, no. 1000; a music book with illustrations for *Zionitischer WeyrauchsHügel* ("John Deshong"), Box 8, no. 1; a music book with illustrations for *Zionitischer WeyrauchsHügel*, Box 8, no. 4; and a music book with illustrations for *Zionitischer WeyrauchsHügel*, Box 8, no. 5.

The Free Library of Philadelphia holds the following manuscripts, all in the Borneman Collection: a music book with illustrations for *Das Gesäng der Einsamen Turtel-Taube*, B. Ms. 3; a music book with illustrations for *Das Gesäng der Einsamen Turtel-Taube*, B. Ms. 11; a music book with illustrations for *Das Gesäng der Einsamen Turtel-Taube* ("Benja. Zerfuss"), B. Ms. 11.5; a music book with illustrations for *Neuvermehrtes Gesäng der Einsamen Turtel-Taube* ("Schw. Catharina & Veronica"), B. Ms. 11.7; a music book with illustrations for *Zionitischer WeyrauchsHügel*, B. Ms. 2; a music book with illustrations for *Zionitischer WeyrauchsHügel*, B. Ms. 10; and "Reflective and aphoristic verse and hymns," B. Ms. 5.

In the Joseph Downs Collection of Manuscripts and Printed Ephemera in the Winterthur Library in Winterthur, Delaware, is a music book with illustrations for *Zionitischer WeyrauchsHügel*, 65x554. In the Library of Congress are: a music book with illustrations for *Das Gesäng der Einsamen Turtel-Taube*, M 2116.E6 1745; "Die Bittre Süse Oder Das Gesäng der Einsamen Turtel-Taube ("Ephrata Codex"), a music book with illustrations for *Das Gesäng der Einsamen Turtel-Taube* (Ephrata, 1746), M 2116.E6 1746; a music book with illustrations for *Das Gesäng der Einsamen Turtel-Taube*, M 2116.E6 1747(B); a music book with illustrations for *Das Gesäng der Einsamen Turtel-Taube*, M 2116.E6 1749; a music book with illustrations for *Paradisisches Wunder-Spiel* (1751), M 2116.E6 1751; and a music book with illustrations for *Zionitischer WeyrauchsHügel*, M 2116.E6 1745(B).

The following manuscripts from the Historical Society of Pennsylvania were examined, all in the Cassel Collection: a music book with illustrations for *Das Gesäng der Einsamen Turtel-Taube*, Ac. 1901; a music book with illustrations for *Zionitischer WeyrauchsHügel* ("Susanna Gorgas"), Ac. 1891; "Paradisisches Nachts-Tropfen," hymn texts, Ac. 192; "Zionitischer Rosen Garten," a music book with illustrations for *Das Gesäng der Einsamen Turtel-Taube*, Ac. 1922. In the private possession of Guy Oldham, London, is the manuscript I have referred to as Mother Maria's book, a music book with illustrations for *Zionitischer WeyrauchsHügel* ("Schwester Maria," Ephrata, 1751).

BIBLIOGRAPHICAL ESSAY

SECONDARY LITERATURE

General Studies

The best single history of Ephrata is still Oswald Seidensticker's *Ephrata, eine amerikanische Klostergeschichte* (Cincinnati: Mecklenborg & Rosenthal, 1883), despite his jaundiced bias against Ephrata. As noted earlier, Sachse's two-volume history has dominated the secondary literature, most of which depended on it too uncritically. Sachse's influence is clearly visible in Corliss F. Randolph's account of Ephrata, "The German Seventh-Day Baptists," in his *Seventh-Day Baptists in Europe and America*, vol. 2 (Plainfield, N.J.: Seventh-Day Baptist General Conference, 1910; rpt. New York: Arno Press, 1980). Randolph did include some material on Snow Hill that seems less dependent on Sachse. Besides Ernst's and Alderfer's attempts, a less reliable local history is Milton H. Heinicke's *History of Ephrata*, in *Journal of the Historical Society of the Cocalico Valley* 1–11 (1964–75), published in eleven booklets by the Historical Society of the Cocalico Valley. It draws mainly on secondary sources, legends, and personal opinions, although some useful local information is included. John E. Jacoby's *Two Mystic Communities in America* (Paris: Presses Universitaires de France, 1931; rpt. Westport, Conn.: Hyperion Press, 1975) is a very general comparative study. A provocative article on the beginnings of Beissel's Sabbatarian congregation, with some genealogical information, is Jane Evans Best, "Turmoil in Conestoga," *Pennsylvania Mennonite Heritage* 11, no. 1 (January 1993). Not all of the findings in the article are equally supported by source material. The best previous work to attempt to take Ephrata's unique language style seriously was Jobie E. Riley, "An Analysis of the Debate between Johann Conrad Beissel and Various Eighteenth-Century Contemporaries Concerning the Importance of Celibacy" (Ph.D. diss., Temple University, 1973). Helpful information on Ephrata's only daughter cloister, Snow Hill, is available in Charles W. Treher, *Snow Hill Cloister,* Publications of the Pennsylvania German Society, n.s. 2 (Allentown: Pennsylvania German Society, 1968). A listing of the printed and manuscript material formerly housed at Snow Hill and now at Juniata College can be found in Denise Seachrist, "Snow Hill and the German Seventh-Day Baptists: Heirs to the Musical Traditions of Conrad Beissel's Ephrata Cloister" (Ph.D. diss., Kent State University, 1993).

Biographical Studies

The best biographical work on Conrad Beissel, basically on his family background in Eberbach, remains Oskar Kilian, "Konrad Beisel (1691–1768): Gründer des Klosters

Ephrata in Pennsylvanien," *Eberbacher Geschichtsblätter* 56 (1957), and his "Nochmals Konrad Beisel," *Eberbacher Geschichtsblätter* 57 (1958): 54. The only monograph biography of Beissel is Walter C. Klein's *Johann Conrad Beissel, Mystic and Martinet* (Philadelphia: University of Pennsylvania Press, 1942). It is largely derivative with little primary research and proceeds from hostile presuppositions about Beissel. Unfortunately, several biographical articles anticipating the tricentennial of Beissel's birth in 1991 depended too much on Sachse. These include Wendy Everham, "Johann Konrad Beissels Leben und Theologie: Versuch eines Grundverständnisses," *Eberbacher Geschichtsblätter* 90 (1991): 55–67; Leo Schelbert, "Die Ausformung von Konrad Beissels Ephrata Gemeinschaft im Widerstreit geistlicher Traditionen," *Eberbacher Geschichtsblätter* 90 (1991): 41–54; and Ann K. U. Tussing, "The Hungry Orphan, Conrad Beissel," *Communal Studies* 10 (1990). Some information from sources is mingled with speculative interpretation in James D. Beissel's genealogical work, *The Wedge: Beisel/Beissel International Genealogy* (Willow Street, Pa.: Crystal Educational Resources, 1991).

A few biographical articles on other Ephrata members have appeared. Leo Schelbert wrote about Peter Miller in "Die Stimme eines Einsamen in Zion: Ein unbekannter Brief von Bruder Jaebez aus Ephrata, Pennsylvanien, aus dem Jahre 1743," *Zeitschrift für Kirchengeschichte* 85 (1974), which appeared in English as "From Reformed Preacher in the Palatinate to Pietist Monk in Pennsylvania: The Spiritual Path of Johann Peter Müller (1709–1796)," in Hans L. Trefousse, ed., *Germany and America: Essays on Problems of International Relations and Immigration* (New York: Brooklyn College Press, 1980). Schelbert also wrote a well-documented article on the Thommen family from the Basel area, "Von der Macht des Pietismus: Dokumentarbericht zur Auswanderung einer Basler Familie im Jahre 1736," *Basler Zeitschrift für Geschichte und Altertumskunde* 75 (1975), which also appeared in English as "On the Power of Pietism: A Documentary on the Thommens of Schaefferstown," *Historic Schaefferstown Record* 18, no. 4 (October 1984). L. Allen Viehmeyer wrote about Anna Thommen in his "Anna of Ephrata," *Historic Schaefferstown Record* 8, no. 2 (March 1974). An excellent, well-documented study of the movements of the Eckerlin brothers in Virginia, including a good account of Eliseba Böhler's encounters with ghosts, is Klaus Wust, *The Saint-Adventurers of the Virginia Frontier: Southern Outposts of Ephrata* (Edinburg, Va.: Shenandoah History Publishers, 1977).

Background Studies

Reading Ephrata's literature requires some introduction to the world of dissent and reform in the Pietist movement within and outside the established churches of Germany and Switzerland and its spread to the American colonies. The best introduction is the three-volume history edited by Martin Brecht with Klaus Deppermann, *Geschichte des Pietismus* (Göttingen: Vandenhoeck & Ruprecht, 1993–2000). Absolutely essential are the articles in volumes 1 and 2 by Hans Schneider on Radical Pietism and the article in volume 2 by A. Gregg Roeber on Pietism in North America. Johannes Wallmann's *Der Pietismus,* in Bernd Moeller, ed., *Die Kirche in ihrer Geschichte: ein Handbuch,* vol. 4, no. O 1 (Göttingen: Vandenhoeck & Ruprecht, 1990), offers a short introduction to Pietism. Additional articles by Donald F. Durnbaugh are helpful: "Work and Hope: The Spirituality of the Radical Pietist Communitarians," *Church History* 39 (March 1970), and "Radikaler Pietismus als Grundlage deutschamerikanischer kommunaler Siedlungen," *Pietismus und Neuzeit* 16 (1990). Dale W. Brown's *Understanding Pietism* (Grand Rapids, Mich.: Wm. B. Eerdmans, 1978) is generally useful, as is Delburn Carpenter's *The Radical Pietists: Celibate Communal Societies Established in the United States before 1820* (New York: AMS Press, 1975). Ted A. Campbell's *The Religion of the Heart: A Study of European Religious Life in the Seventeenth and Eighteenth Centuries* (Columbia: University of South Carolina Press, 1991) and W. R. Ward's *The Protestant Evangelical Awakening* (Cambridge: Cambridge University Press, 1992) provide helpful introductions, and Jon Butler's *Awash in a Sea of Faith: Christianizing the American People* (Cambridge: Harvard University Press, 1990) helps with the American context.

For the complicated conceptual world of Jacob Boehme, which is the foundation on which Beissel worked, Andrew Weeks provides a lucid introduction in *Boehme: An Intellectual Biography of the Seventeenth-Century Philosopher and Mystic* (Albany: State University of New York Press, 1991). For the network of Boehmist religious dissenters in England, Germany, and Pennsylvania in the seventeenth and eighteenth centuries, see Niels Thune, *The Behmenists and the Phildadelphians: A Contribution to the Study of English Mysticism in the 17th and 18th Centuries* (Uppsala: Almqvist & Wiksells, 1948), and Elizabeth Fisher, "'Prophecies and Revelations': German Cabbalists in Early Pennsylvania," *Pennsylvania Magazine of History and Biography* 109 (1985).

For general introductions to Pietism in Europe and the colonies, see F. Ernest Stoeffler, *German Pietism during the Eighteenth Century,* Studies in the History of Religions, vol. 24 (Leiden: E. J. Brill, 1973), and his *Continental Pietism and Early American Christianity* (Grand Rapids, Mich.: Wm. B. Eerdmans, 1976). His *Mysticism in the German Devotional Literature of Colonial Pennsylvania,* Pennsylvania German Folklore Society, Proceedings and Addresses, vol. 14 (Allentown, Pa.: Schlechter's, 1950), is somewhat dated but useful. David S. Katz, *Sabbath and Sectarianism in Seventeenth-Century England,* Brill's Studies in Intellectual History, vol. 10 (Leiden: E. J. Brill, 1988), and Don A. Sanford, *A Choosing People: The History of the Seventh-Day Baptists*

(Nashville: Broadman Press, 1992), give background on English Sabbatarianism and English Sabbatarian Baptists, respectively. For background on the Dunkers, see Dale R. Stoffer, *Background and Development of Brethren Doctrines, 1650–1987* (Philadelphia: Brethren Encyclopedia, 1989), and Donald F. Durnbaugh, *Brethren Beginnings. The Origin of the Churh of the Brethren in Early Eighteenth-Century Europe* (Philadelphia: Brethren Encyclopedia, 1992).

Volker Press, *Kriege und Krisen: Deutschland, 1600–1715*, vol. 5 of *Neue Deutsche Geschichte*, edited by Peter Moraw, Volker Press, and Wolfgang Schieder (Munich: C. H. Beck, 1991); and Meinrad Schaab, *Geschichte der Kurpfalz*, vol. 2, *Neuzeit* (Stuttgart: W. Kohlhammer, 1992), give the social-historical context of southwest Germany, which was determinative for those who founded Ephrata. For a more succinct account in English, see Rudolf Vierhaus, *Germany in the Age of Absolutism*, translated Jonathan B. Knudsen (Cambridge: Cambridge University Press, 1988). For the early Lancaster area, Jerome H. Wood, Jr., *Conestoga Crossroads: Lancaster, Pennsylvania, 1730–1790* (Harrisburg: Pennsylvania Historical and Museum Commission, 1979), is good.

Ephrata and Gender

Very few published works have dealt explicitly with the unique understandings of gender at Ephrata. Wendy Everham pioneered with an article, "The Recovery of the Feminine in an Early American Pietist Community: The Interpretive Challenge of the Theology of Conrad Beissel," *Pennsylvania Folklife* 39, no. 2 (Winter 1989–90). One later article exploring female imagery in the writings and career of the main prioress at Ephrata is Jeff Bach, "Maria Eicher of Ephrata: A Case Study in Gender and Religion in Radical Pietism," in *From Age to Age: Historians and the Modern Church. A Festschrift for Donald F. Durnbaugh*, in *Brethren Life and Thought* 43, nos. 3–4 (Summer and Fall 1997). The whole study of gender in Pietism is still in its beginnings. Very important background reading for understanding Ephrata's constuction of gender includes the following works: Willi Temme, *Krise der Leiblichkdeit: Die Sozietät der Mutter Eva (Buttlarsche Rotte) und der radikale Pietismus um 1700*, Arbeiten zur Geschichte des Pietismus, vol. 35 (Göttingen: Vandenhoeck & Ruprecht, 1998); Gertraud Zaepernick, "Johann Georg Gichtels und seiner Nachfolger Briefwechsel mit den Hallischen Pietisten, besonders mit A. M. Francke," *Pietismus und Neuzeit* 8 (1989); Richard Critchfield, "Prophetin, Führerin, Organisatorin: Zur Rolle der Frau im Pietismus," in *Die Frau von der Reformation zur Romantik: Die Situation der Frau vor dem Hintergrund der Literatur- und Sozialgeschichte*, edited by Barbara Becker-Cantarino (Bonn: Bouvier Verlag Herbert Grundmann, 1980); and still Fritz Tanner's *Die Ehe im Pietismus* (Zurich: Zwingli Verlag, 1952).

BIBLIOGRAPHICAL ESSAY

Special Works

Some material, mostly articles, has been published on miscellaneous special topics related to Ephrata. These include Michael S. A. Dechert, "The Ephrata Community: An American Utopian Experiment of Anabaptist and Rosicrucian Inspiration," *Spazio e società* 14, no. 54 (April–June 1991); Peter Erb, "Eschatology at Ephrata," in *The Coming Kingdom: Essays in American Millennialism and Eschatology,* edited by M. Darrol Bryant and Donald W. Dayton (Barrytown, N.Y.: International Religious Foundation, 1983); Guy Tilghman Hollyday and Christoph E. Schweitzer, "The Present State of Conrad Beissel/Ephrata Research," *Monatshefte* 68, no. 2 (Summer 1976). For the conflict between Ephrata and the Moravians in 1742, see Peter Vogt, "Zinzendorf und die Pennsylvanischen Synoden, 1742," *Unitas Fratrum* 36 (1994); and a pair of articles focusing on each side of the dispute: Peter Vogt, "The Moravian Theory and Practice of Marriage (*Ehereligion*) as a Point of Contention between Ephrata and Bethlehem," and Jeff Bach, "Ephrata and Moravian Relations: The View from Ephrata," both in *Communal Studies* 21 (2001).

Ephrata Archaeology and Architecture

Archaeological investigations at Ephrata since 1995 have yielded new puzzles as well as abundant new data on the community's life and material culture. The annual reports of Stephen G. Warfel, director of the project, are published as *Historical Archaeology at Ephrata Cloister* by the Pennsylvania Historical and Museum Commission in Harrisburg. This series updates a set of articles from earlier investigations, Dale E. Biever's "A Report of the Archaeological Investigations at the Ephrata Cloister, 1963–1966," in *Four Pennsylvania German Studies,* edited by Frederick S. Weiser, Publications of the Pennsylvania German Society, n.s. 3 (Breinigsville, Pa., 1970).

A flood of unpublished material related to architecture has come from extensive work to preserve the buildings at Ephrata. At one time interpretations of Ephrata's buildings were dominated by G. Edwin Brumbaugh's "Medieval Construction at Ephrata," *Antiques,* July 1944, and his "Continental Influence on Early American Architecture," *American-German Review* 9, no. 5 (February 1943). A series of descriptions and reports was completed in 2000–2001 by Tim Noble and Shelby Weaver Splain on behalf of Marianna Thomas Architects/Perfido Weiskopf Architects JV, titled "Ephrata Cloister Historic Structures Report." The reports include photographs, floor plans, and comparisons with field notes from previous restoration by G. Edwin Brumbaugh and John Heyl. The so-called Craft House (now identified as the Beissel House) is covered in vol. 6 of the reports; vol. 7 concerns the so-called Beissel House and Bake House (now identified as the Physician's House); vol. 9 concerns the so-called Almonry. In addition, dendrochronological testing was conducted in 2000 on Saron, the Saal, the Craft House, the one-and-a-half-story house formerly known as the Beissel House, the "print shop," a cabin once interpreted as a "solitary cabin," the Almonry, and a larger house once interpreted as a "householder's house." Edward R. Cook and others of the Tree-Ring Laboratory of Lamont-Doherty Earth Observatory, Palisades, New York, wrote the report, titled "Tree-Ring Dating of the Ephrata Cloister in Ephrata, Pennsylvania." In 1988 a two-volume study for conservation of Saron and the Saal by Patrick W. O'Bannon and others, on behalf of John Milner Associates, was submitted to the Pennsylvania Historical and Museum Commission, Ephrata Cloister: "Ephrata Cloister: A Historic Structures Report," vol. 1, The History and Archaeology of Ephrata Cloister, and vol. 2, "Architectural Evaluation of Saal and Saron." Stephen G. Warfel also prepared a report in 1990 titled "Historical and Archaeological Investigations Associated with the Ephrata Cloister Fire Detection and Suppression Systems Project." Ann Kirschner wrote a good, detailed description of the construction of the remaining sisters' house, Saron, titled "From Hebron to Saron: The Religious Transformation of an Ephrata Convent" (master's thesis, University of Delaware, 1995). One published article has examined Ephrata's milling legacy: Jack Ward Willson Loose, "A Study of Two Distinct Periods of Ephrata Cloister History," *Historical Papers and Addresses of the Lancaster County Historical Society* 55 (1951). All of these studies and reports raise challenging questions still being interpreted.

Ephrata Manuscript Art

The surviving pieces of Ephrata's manuscript art are scattered to the winds. No single repository holds a majority of pieces, and numerous private collectors also hold pieces. The largest category of surviving pieces comprises the illustrated manuscript music books. The best tool for tracking those works is L. Allen Viehmeyer's index of Ephrata hymn texts and tunes, which includes an excellent bibliography of most of the manuscripts (see below). There is no sure way to track down all of the surviving examples of Ephrata's art. Significant numbers of pieces, most of them music books, are held at the following locations: the Sachse Collection of the Seventh-Day Baptist Historical Society, on loan to the Pennsylvania State Archives in Harrisburg; the Pennsylvania State Library in Harrisburg; the Historical Society of Pennsylvania in Philadelphia and the Borneman Collection of the Free Library of Philadelphia; the Library of Congress; the Joseph Downs Collection of Manuscripts and Printed Ephemera in the Winterthur Library at Winterthur, Delaware. A good description of the Winterthur holdings can be found in Kari M. Main, "Illuminated Hymnals of the Ephrata Cloister," *Winterthur Portfolio* 32, no. 1 (1997). The Ephrata Cloister now holds all of the known surviving wall placards, including the exquisite labyrinth and placard of the Good Shepherd. The Ephrata Cloister also has the singular calligraphy book "Der Christen ABC," along with some music manuscript books. Although these collections are a beginning, many scattered pieces remain to be assembled.

Several works include illustrations of Ephrata's *Fraktur.* Some authors see symbolism in the images; others see whimsy and arbitrary ornamentation. In the former category, John Joseph Stoudt pioneered with his *Consider the Lilies How They Grow: An Interpretation of the Symbolism of Pennsylvania German Art,* Pennsylvania German Folklore Society, vol. 2 (Allentown, Pa.: Schlechter's, 1937); his *Early Pennsylvania Arts and Crafts* (New York: A. S. Barnes, 1964); and his *Pennsylvania German Folk Art: An Interpretation,* Pennsylvania German Folklore Society, vol. 28 (Allentown: Schlechter's, 1966). Continuing Stoudt's approach, Guy Tilghman Hollyday published two critically important articles, "The Ephrata Wall-Charts and Their Inscriptions," *Pennsylvania Folklife* 19 (Spring 1970), and "The Ephrata Codex: Relationship between Text and Illustration," *Pennsylvania Folklife* 20 (Autumn 1970).

Leading the other approach, emphasizing ornamentation for its own sake, Donald A. Shelley wrote *The Fraktur-Writings or Illuminated Manuscripts of the Pennsylvania Germans,* Pennsylvania German Folklore Society, vol. 23 (Allentown: Schlechter's, 1961). Following this approach, Frederick S. Weiser and Howell J. Heaney collaborated to publish a lovely two-volume set, *The Pennsylvania German Fraktur of the Free Library of Philadelphia: An Illustrated Catalogue,* Publications of the Pennsylvania German Society, n.s. 10–11 (Breinigsville, Pa.: Pennsylvania German Society and the Free Library of Philadelphia, 1976). Cynda L Benson's "Early American Illuminated Manuscripts from the Ephrata Cloister" (Ph.D. diss., University of Kansas, 1994) follows this approach, emphasizing patterns common to Ephrata and textile designs, among other sources.

A few samples of Ephrata art were published by the Pennsylvania Farm Museum of Landis Valley in *Pennsylvania German Fraktur and Color Drawings* (Lititz, Pa.: Landis Valley Associates, 1969; rpt. Lancaster, Pa: Acorn Press, 1989). The booklet was based on an exhibit of Pennsylvania Fraktur at the Farm Museum in 1969. For good introductory essays on Pennsylvania German Fraktur, see Don Yoder, "The European Background of Pennsylvania's Fraktur Art" and "The Fraktur Texts and Pennsylvania-German Spirituality," in *Bucks County Fraktur,* edited by Cory M. Amsler, Publications of the Pennsylvania German Society, n.s. 33 (Kutztown: Pennsylvania German Society and Bucks County Historical Society, 1999). This volume offers good samples for comparison with the Fraktur works produced at Ephrata, as does Dennis K. Moyer, *Fraktur Writings and Folk Art Drawings of the Schwenkfelder Library Collection,* Publications of the Pennsylvania German Society, n.s. 31 (Kutztown: Pennsylvania German Society, 1997). Corrine and Russell

BIBLIOGRAPHICAL ESSAY

Earnest's *Fraktur: Folk Art and Family* (Atglen, Pa.: Schiffer, 1999), provides a good introduction to Fraktur.

Music at Ephrata

Space does not allow a discussion of Ephrata music and hymnals in this book, but some references to sources can help interested readers to find more. A crucial beginning point is *An Index to Hymns and Hymn Tunes of the Ephrata Cloister, 1730–1766, Including all Printed and Manuscript Hymnals and Hymnal Fragments and Representative Music Manuscripts,* compiled by L. Allen Viehmeyer (Ephrata: Ephrata Cloister Associates, 1995). This masterful work, a labor of love spanning decades, offers titles of all known hymns in Ephrata hymnals, manuscript and printed. Viehmeyer identified most of the authors of the hymns, an especially difficult task for authors within the Ephrata community. The book includes a system to present the melody of the first line of most of the hymns. And the bibliographic work is invaluable for tracking down hymnals and manuscripts.

Another important early step is to turn to Betty Jean Martin, "The Ephrata Cloister and Its Music, 1732–1785: The Cultural, Religious, and Bibliographical Background" (Ph.D. diss., University of Maryland, 1974). Although more recent research supersedes some of Martin's findings, her work remains important for an introduction. With introductions made, Lucy E. Carroll's work is an important next step. She has prepared several transcriptions of Ephrata music, most unpublished, for presentations at special events at the Ephrata Cloister. Two of her unpublished papers presented in 1995, "Performance Practices in the Music of the Ephrata Cloister" (September 1995) and "The Mystical Singing of Pennsylvania's Ephrata Cloister" (February 1995), offer her theories on performance practice at colonial Ephrata. She prepared an unpublished volume of transcriptions, "Selected Music from the Eighteenth-Century Ephrata Cloister" (November 1999) and is preparing a volume of transcriptions of Ephrata music for publication in the American Research Series: Music in the United States of America. A complete transcription in modern notation of a most remarkable Ephrata composition, a musical setting of Jeremiah 31, has been prepared by Thomas E. Owsinski, "*Jeremia* from the *Paradisisches Wunder-Spiel:* A Critical Edition and Study of a Musical Document of the Eighteenth-Century Ephrata Cloister" (master's thesis, West Chester University of Pennsylvania, 1997). An article by L. Allen Viehmeyer, "The *Bruderlied* and the *Schwesterlied* of the Ephrata Cloister," *Yearbook of German-American Studies* 31 (1996), describes a unique pair of companion compositions by the celibate orders.

In the older literature readers will encounter Julius F. Sachse, *The Music of the Ephrata Cloister; also Conrad Beissel's Treatise on Music as Set Forth in a Preface to the "Turtel Taube"* of 1747, Amplified with Facsimile Reproductions of Parts of the Text and Some Original Ephrata Music of the "Wyrauchs Hügel," 1739; "Rosen und Lilien," 1745; "Turtel Taube," 1747; "Choral Buch," 1745, etc. (Lancaster: New Era, 1903); and Lloyd G. Blakely's corrections to Sachse, "Johann Conrad Beissel and Music of the Ephrata Cloister," *Journal of Research in Music Education* 15, no. 2 (Summer 1967). Betty Martin's dissertation helpfully deals with this material. Helpful information for understanding the background of Ephrata's musical tradition is found in Willard Martin, "Johannes Kelpius and Johann Gottfried Seelig: Mystics and Hymnists on the Wissahickon" (Ph.D. diss., Pennsylvania State University, 1973).

Ephrata and Hidden Knowledge

Essential for understanding Sachse's claims about Rosicrucianism at Ephrata is Johann Frantz Regnier's account in German of his time there in 1734, in Johann Philip Fresenius, *Bewährte Nachrichten von Herrnhutischen Sachen*, vol. 3 (Frankfurt am Main: J. L. Buchner and H. L Brönner, 1748). Good comparative contemporaneous literature includes Sincerus Renatus, *Theo-Philosophia Theoretico-Practica oder Der wahre Grund Göttlicher und Natürlicher Bekanntnüß Dadurch beyde Tincturen Die Himmlische und Irdische können erhalten werden; zugleich Ein Grund aller Particularien und Fundament der wahren Medicin, Dabey gezeigt wird wie in der äußern Natur durch alle Regna zuverfahren damit ein jedes Corpus wieder in seinen reinen Paradiesischen Stand gebracht werden könne durch die Chymie oder Scheidekunst; Nebst einer Erläuterung Des Opera Maximi, und Beyfügung Versprochener Experimenten; Alles zum Lobe Gottes und dem Nutz des Nechsten* (Breslau: Esaia Fellgiebels, 1714); Christoph Schütz, *Die Güldene Rose oder ein Zeugniss der Wahrheit von der uns so nahe bevorstehenden Güldenen Zeit des tausend jährigen und ewigen Reichs Jesu Christi und der damit verbundenen Wiederbringung aller Dinge In drey Theil*, 2d ed. (n.p., 1731); Georg von Welling, *Opus Mago-Cabbalisticum et Theosophicum darinnen der Ursprung, Natur, Eigenschaften und Gebrauch des Salzes, Schwefels und Mercurii in drey theilen beschrieben, und nebst sehr vielen sonderbaren mathematischen, theosophischen, magischen und mystischen Materian, auch die Erzeugung der Metallen und Mineralien, aus dem Grunde der Natur erwiesen wird; samt dem Haupt Schlüßel des ganzen Werks und vielen curieusen mago-cabbalistischen Figuren. Deme noch beygefüget: ein Tractätlein von der Göttlichen Weisheit; und ein besonderer Anhang etlicher sehr rar- und kostbarer chymischer Piecen*, 3d ed. (Frankfurt and Lepizig: in der Fleischerischen Buchhandlung, 1784).

Secondary literature that is helpful for understanding Welling and connections to Richter and Schütz includes Petra Jungmayr, *Georg von Welling (1655–1727): Studien zu Leben und Werk*, Heidelberger Studien zur Naturkunde der frühen Neuzeit, vol. 2 (Stuttgart: Franz Steiner, 1990), and Joachim Telle, "Zum *Opus mago-cabbalisticum et theosophicum* von Georg von Welling," *Euphorion* 77 (1983). For Rosicrucianism, the standard work is Roland Edighoffer, *Rose-Crois et Société Idéale selon Johann Valentin Andreae*, 2 vols. (Neuilly sur Seine: Arma Artis, 1982, 1987). Additional help comes from Carlos Gilly, *Cimella Rhodostaurotica: Die Rosenkreuzer im Spiegel der zwischen 1610 und 1660 entstandenen Handschriften und Drucke* (Amsterdam: Bibliotheca Philosophia Hermetica, 1995). A helpful, understandable introduction to Rosicrucianism is Christopher McIntosh's *The Rosicrucians: The History, Mythology, and Rituals of an Occult Order*, 2d rev. and expanded ed. (Wellingborough: Crucible Press, 1987). For general background on hidden knowledge in eighteenth-century America, see Herbert Leventhal, *In the Shadow of the Enlightenment: Occultism and Renaissance Science in Eighteenth-Century America* (New York: New York University Press, 1976).

Much more material related to Ephrata is available, but these works offer a fair start.

NOTES

PRELUDE

1. *CE*, 52. For artifacts of prehistoric and historic occupation, see Dale E. Biever, "A Report of Archaeological Investigations at the Ephrata Cloister, 1963–1966," in Frederick S. Weiser, ed., *Four Pennsylvania German Studies,* Publications of the Pennsylvania German Society, n.s. 3 (Breinigsville: Pennsylvania German Society, 1970), 22–23. See also Warfel, *Historical Archaeology* (1996), 16–17, and his subsequent reports published in 1997, pp. 14–15, 21–22; in 1998, pp. 20–21; in 1999, p. 23; and in 2000, pp. 27–28.

INTRODUCTION

1. For the church record of Beissel's birth and his parents, see *JHSCV* 10 (1985): 75. This record corrects the long-held but erroneous assumption that his name was Johann Conrad Beissel. Conrad Beissel also wrote under the name of Friedsam Gottrecht and its Hellenized equivalent, Irenici Theodicäi. Friedsam Gottrecht, his spiritual name, means "Peaceable God-righteous."
2. FLP B. Ms. 22, p. 73. The letter, addressed to a "friend in Heidelberg," has an illegible date.
3. *LuW,* 5:71.
4. [Conrad Beissel et al.], *Neuvermehrtes Gesäng der einsamen Turtel Taube, zur gemeinschafftlichen Erbauung gesammlet und ans Licht gegeben* (Ephrata: Typis Societatis, 1762), fol. 3 of the preface.
5. *CE,* 52–53. For the English translation, see Lamech and Agrippa, *Chronicon Ephratense: A History of the Community of Seventh-Day Baptists at Ephrata, Lancaster County, Penn'a,* trans. J. Max Hark (Lancaster: S. H. Zahm, 1889; rpt. New York: Burt Franklin, 1972). For Lamech's identity as Jacob Gaas, see *LuW,* 9:50. Although generally reliable, Hark's translation has some errors. All citations in this book are from the German text, unless otherwise noted. The translations are mine.
6. [Conrad Beissel et al.], *Jacobs Kampff- und Ritter-Platz* (Philadelphia: B[enjamin]. F[ranklin], 1736), 4. The preface is dated "Ephratha in der gegend Canestoges den 27 Aprill, 1736." For Beissel's naming of the community, see *CE,* 90.
7. Michel de Certeau, *The Mystic Fable,* trans. Michael B. Smith, vol. 1 (Chicago: University of Chicago Press, 1992), 23–24. See Weeks, *Boehme,* 3–10; Johannes Wallmann, *Der Pietismus,* in Bernd Moeller, ed., *Die Kirche in ihrer Geschichte,* vol. 4, O 1 (Göttingen: Vandenhoeck & Ruprecht, 1990), 80. Wallmann places Boehme within "mystical spiritualism." See also *GdP,* 1:205–14, 394, where Martin Brecht calls Boehme simply a spiritualist. Hans Schneider, current authority on the history of Radical Pietism, places Boehme in the spiritualist tradition: Hans Schneider, "Der radikale Pietismus im 17. Jahrhundert," in Martin Brecht, ed., *Der Pietismus vom siebzehnten bis zum frühen achtzehnten Jahrhundert,* vol. 1 of Martin Brecht et al., eds., *Geschichte des Pietismus* (Göttingen: Vandenhoeck & Ruprecht, 1993), 393–94. Schneider notes, however, that Johann Georg Gichtel, who published Boehme's complete works, transmitted

NOTES TO INTRODUCTION

Boehme's tradition to a wider German-speaking audience. Gichtel's own writings, primarily letters, were published as *Theosophia Practica,* 3d enl. and exp. ed., 7 vols. (Leyden, 1722). Brecht, Schneider, Wallmann, and many current scholars admit the difficulty of distinguishing spiritualism from mysticism in Boehme. Weeks questions the value of trying. John Joseph Stoudt, *Jacob Boehme* (New York: Seabury, 1968), 299–305, tries to qualify Boehme's thought as a Protestantized mysticism, with less success.

8. *GdP,* 1:234–35. Brecht places Gichtel in the stream of spiritualism, but then credits him as a "mystic with genuine intensity."

9. Bernard McGinn, *The Foundations of Mysticism,* vol. 1 of *The Presence of God: A History of Western Christian Mysticism* (New York: Crossroad, 1992), xv–xvii.

10. Certeau, *Mystic Fable* ,76–77, ix–x.

11. Ibid., 15–16, 21–26, 77–78. See also Steven T. Katz, ed., *Mysticism and Religious Traditions* (New York: Oxford University Press, 1983), 3–60. Katz insisted on the need to study the historical and social context in which mystical literature was produced in order to interpret it well. For a good example applying this model of interpretation, see Andrew Weeks, *Boehme: An Intellectual Biography of the Seventeenth-Century Philosopher and Mystic* (Albany: State University of New York Press, 1991). Weeks's realization of Katz's interpretive model has influenced my work on Ephrata.

12. John E. Jacoby, *Two Mystic Communities in America* (Paris: Presses Universitaires de France, 1931; rpt. Westport, Conn.: Hyperion, 1975).

13. F. Ernest Stoeffler, *Mysticism in the German Devotional Literature of Colonial Pennsylvania,* Pennsylvania German Folklore Society, vol. 14 (Allentown: Schlechter's, 1950), 7–8.

14. *ZS,* 31: "Gott ist ein unbegreiffliches Nichts, und ich bin ein unbegreiffliches Ichts. . . . Wir [haben] zu leiden . . . [bis] alles Seyn in das Nichtseyn und alles Etwas in das Nichts aufgelöst ist"; 39: "So leben wir dann in GOTT und seiner heiligen Wesenheit: sein Leben ist unser Leben, und wir sind in Ihm geworden, daß wir seyn, was wir seyn."

15. "Rose," 312. "Dann kan Erst die Völlige Vereinigung geschehen mit ihrem heiligen Mann Jesum, als ihrem Himmlischen Bräutigam." The passage occurs in a devotion under the name "Sis. Bernice," suggesting that she composed it.

16. Ernst Troeltsch, *The Social Teaching of the Christian Churches,* trans. Olive Wyon, 2 vols. (New York: Macmillan, 1931; rpt. Chicago: University of Chicago Press, 1976, 1981), 729–31. Troeltsch acknowledged some potential limitations.

17. Bryan R. Wilson, *Religious Sects* (New York: McGraw-Hill, 1970), 24–25.

18. *MKZ,* 11. "Es ist ein Unterschied [sic] zwischen der Kirche und einer Secte. Eine Secte erbietet sich aus dem Willen des Mannes, wird auch ins gemein durch denselben unterhalten und mit menschlichem Verstand regieret: die Kirche aber wird verglichen einem Weibe, einem Weibe nun ist das Unterwerffen eigenschafftlich, gleich wie dem Mann das Herrschen." My translation is based on the original text. I favor Hildebrand as the major author of this work because of its similarity to his *Schrifftmässiges Zeuchnüß von dem Himmlischen und Jungfräulichen Gebährungs-Werck* (Germantown: Christoph Saur, 1743), known to be by Hildebrand. The two documents deal with the mystical impregnation, for example, in similar vocabulary and style.

19. *ZS,* 78. Beissel wrote that he saw no difference between the Reformed tradition and the papacy in the moral lives of their members.

20. Ibid., 142. The letter was written about twenty-two years after God had "called him into His vineyard," or about twenty-two years since Beissel's conversion in 1715, so that the letter was written in approximately 1737.

21. Oskar Kilian, "Konrad Beisel (1691–1768), Gründer des Klosters Ephrata in Pennsylvanien," *Eberbacher Geschichtsblätter* 56 (1957): 5. See also Oskar Kilian, "Nochmals Konrad Beisel," *Eberbacher Geschichtsblätter* 57 (1958): 54. Kilian cites *Ratsprotokoll* records of 1683, 1686, and 1689, in which the name Matthias appears also as Matthes and Mattheis.

22. Conrad was baptized March 4, 1691. The godfather was Conrad Dreubel, a citizen and shepherd. Conrad's mother, Anna, was the daughter of Leonhardt Köbler of Untersensbach. See previous notes and

NOTES TO INTRODUCTION

James D. Beissel, *The Wedge: Beisel/Beissel International Genealogy* (Willow Street, Pa.: Crystal Educational Resources, 1991), 65, 71–72. Kilian, "Nochmals," 54, cites the church alms book for the gift to Anna. The spelling, Beissel, was used after Conrad arrived in America.

23. For one very poignant example, see the final "spiritual speech" (*Geistliche Rede*) in *DE, Pars I,* 321, 325–27. The pages cited tell of a youth rejected by his mother and adopted by a second, older mother.

24. Information supplied by a genealogical table and interview with Mrs. Heidi Beissel in Eberbach, March 7, 1996.

25. Kilian, "Nochmals," 54. See also A. Cser, R. Vetter, and H. Joho, *Geschichte der Stadt Eberbach am Neckar vom 16. Jahrhundert bis zur Gegenwart,* vol. 2 (Sigmaringen: Thorbecke, 1992), 51–52.

26. Rudolf Vierhaus, *Germany in the Age of Absolutism,* trans. Jonathan R. Knudsen (Cambridge: Cambridge University Press, 1988), 1–11. See also Volker Press, *Kriege und Krisen: Deutschland, 1600–1715,* vol. 5 of *Neue Deutsche Geschichte,* ed. Peter Moraw, Volker Press, and Wolfgang Schieder (Munich: C. H. Beck, 1991), 161–267.

27. Vierhaus, *Germany,* 12–13, 26–27.

28. Meinrad Schaab, *Geschichte der Kurpfalz,* vol. 2, *Neuzeit* (Stuttgart: W. Kohlhammer, 1992), 145–68.

29. *CE,* 3–4. For the claim to a "godly youth," see *DE, Pars I,* 1. This is perhaps Beissel's most famous single writing from the community's perspective, known in Peter Miller's English translation as the *Dissertation on Man's Fall* (apparently first published in 1765, in English). An English translation appears in *MHT,* 113–52. For the other reference, see *ZS,* 91: "eine abgefallene Beer von dem Weinstock zu Sodom."

30. FLP B. Ms. 22, p. 89. In this letter Beissel mentioned a "certain friend and brother in Mannheim" from his "godly youth." This reference may confirm some time as a journeyman baker in Mannheim.

31. *CE,* 4. Julius Sachse erred in suggesting that Beissel met Michael Eckerlin in Strasbourg. Eckerlin was expelled from Strasbourg for religious separatism in 1705, when Beissel would have been fourteen, ten years before his conversion. See *German Sectarians,* 1:37. See also *Ephrata,* 14, where James Ernst correctly noted that Eckerlin was expelled before Beissel could have come to Strasbourg as journeyman baker but misquoted the date as 1706 rather than 1705. See also Alderfer, *Ephrata Commune,* 20. Alderfer further confused the date, giving 1709. He followed Ernst in claiming that Beissel did not meet Eckerlin in Strasbourg. For documents on Michael Eckerlin, see Donald F. Durnbaugh, ed., *European Origins of the Brethren* (Elgin, Ill.: Brethren Press, 1958), 83–87. See also Klaus Wust, *The Saint-Adventurers of the Virginia Frontier* (Edinburg, Va.: Shenandoah History Publishers, 1977), 107–8. Wust cited church and city records.

32. FLP B. Ms. 22, pp. 90–92. This letter corroborates the *Chronicon*'s account (pp. 5, 7–8) of Prior and his defense of Beissel. See also *German Sectarians,* 1:38–39. Walter C. Klein depended on the *Chronicon,* with no apparent further sources. See his *Johann Conrad Beissel, Mystic and Martinet* (Philadelphia: University of Pennsylvania Press, 1942), 26–27.

33. Vierhaus, *Germany,* 46–47. See also Press, *Kriege und Krisen,* 282–90.

34. Jeremy Black, *Eighteenth-Century Europe, 1700–1789* (New York: St. Martin's Press, 1990). For the role of the putting-out system in German rural areas, see Vierhaus, *Germany,* 23–24, 48–49.

35. Vierhaus, *Germany,* 51. See also Press, *Kriege und Krisen,* 275–82. Press deals with the time in which Beissel entered his trade.

36. *CE,* 3, 5, 64, 109, 247. The third and fourth theosophical epistles indicate about a two-year period between Beissel's conversion and his departure from the Palatinate. The third epistle was addressed to friends who had not seen him in "twenty years," and stated that it had been "eighteen years" since he came to America. Thus he left the Palatinate around 1717 or 1718, about two years before his emigration in 1720. See *ZS,* 81, 83, 86, 95. A death register from Ephrata cited his "spiritual age" since his conversion as fifty-two years in 1768. See HSP Ac. 1926, p. 1 of second section. Beissel's tombstone also gives his "spiritual age" as fifty-two (see *German Sectarians,* 2:392, for text and translation; *CE,* 250, gives the German text). If his "spiritual age" were measured in completed years, it is possible that he died during the fifty-third year after his conversion, thus corroborating 1715 as the year. Sangmeister, *LuW,* 10:34, reported that at the funeral for Beissel, Peter Miller said Beissel was "deeply stirred by God," in 1714. However, this is a

NOTES TO INTRODUCTION

secondhand report, compiled supposedly from several witnesses, and may not be reliable in detail. Wendy Everham's biographical sketch in the *Eberbacher Geschichtsblätter* (1991) contains errors and lacks documentation from published letters and sermons or archives. She mistakenly claimed that Beissel was arrested and expelled in 1715, and offered no evidence that he actually attained the level of *Bäckermeister.* Although she dated his adult baptism correctly in 1724, she wrongly implied that he was a member of the Dunkers in Europe. She also implied that he had contact with Inspirationists during his journeyman years, before his alleged expulsion, which she placed in 1715, which seems unlikely. See Wendy Everham, "Johann Konrad Beissels Leben und Theologie: Versuch eines Grundverständnisses," *Eberbacher Geschichtsblätter* 90 (1991): 55–67, esp. 57–58. She mistakenly gave his name as Johann Konrad rather than Georg Conrad. Leo Schelbert's article accompanying Everham's in the same journal unfortunately relied too much on her and on E. G. Alderfer, *Ephrata Commune,* resulting in several mistakes. Another biographical article by Ann K. U. Tussing relied too much on Sachse and Alderfer and lacks documentation in original sources, making the article unreliable. She psychologized the information taken from secondary sources. See Ann K. U. Tussing, "The Hungry Orphan, Conrad Beissel," *Communal Studies* 10 (1990): 87–101.

37. Johannes Wallmann, *Philipp Jakob Spener und die Anfänge des Pietismus,* 2d rev. ed. (Tübingen: J. C. B. Mohr [Paul Siebeck], 1986), 264–90. See also *GdP,* 1:244–48; Teunis Brienen et al., *De Nadere Reformatie: Beschrijving van haar voornaamste vertegenwoordigers* (The Hague: Boekencentrum, 1986).

38. Wallmann, *Philipp Jakob Spener,* 350–54.

39. See also Wallmann, *Pietismus,* 8–10. For contrasting views, see *GdP,* 1:4; Martin Schmidt, *Pietismus,* 2d, unaltered ed. (Stuttgart: W. Kohlhammer, 1978), 14; F. Ernest Stoeffler, *The Rise of Evangelical Pietism,* Studies in the History of Religion, vol. 9 (Leiden: E. J. Brill, 1965), 3–5; Ted A. Campbell, *The Religion of the Heart: A Study of European Religious Life in the Seventeenth and Eighteenth Centuries* (Columbia: University of South Carolina Press, 1991), 70–90; and W. R. Ward, *The Protestant Evangelical Awakening* (Cambridge: Cambridge University Press, 1992), 54–63.

40. Wallmann, *Philipp Jakob Spener,* 299–324. Some of this group helped to form the Frankfurt Land Company, which aided emigration of some dissenters to Pennsylvania and the founding of Germantown.

41. *GdP,* 1:391.

42. Hans Schneider, "Die unerfüllte Zukunft: Apokalyptische Erwartungen im radikalen Pietismus um 1700," in Manfred Jakubowski-Tiessen et al., eds., *Jahrhundertwenden: Endzeit- und Zukunftsvorstellungen vom 15. bis zum 20. Jahrhundert* (Göttingen: Vandenhoeck & Ruprecht, 1999), 187–212.

43. Campbell, *Religion of the Heart,* 1–17, 159–78.

44. *CE,* 13–14. The *Chronicon* dated Baumann's experience in 1701. See Heinz Renkewitz, *Hochmann von Hochenau (1670–1721),* Berichte des theologischen Seminars der Brüdergemeine in Herrnhut, vol. 12 (Breslau: Maruschke & Berendt, 1935); 2d rev. ed., Arbeiten zur Geschichte des Pietismus, vol. 5 (Witten: Luther-Verlag, 1969), 218–19, esp. for Baumann's tie to Mennonites. See Donald F. Durnbaugh, *Brethren Beginnings: The Origin of the Church of the Brethren in Early Eighteenth-Century Europe* (Philadelphia: Brethren Encyclopedia, 1992), 8.

45. Renkewitz, *Hochmann von Hochenau,* 220. See also Durnbaugh, *Brethren Beginnings,* 9, 66n.

46. Durnbaugh, *European Origins,* 43–51. See also Renkewitz, *Hochmann von Hochenau,* 220–27, and Durnbaugh, *Brethren Beginnings,* 9–10. For a theological analysis, see Dale R. Stoffer, *The Background and Development of Brethren Doctrines, 1650–1987* (Philadelphia: Brethren Encyclopedia, 1989), 65–68. See also William G. Willoughby, *Counting the Cost* (Elgin, Ill.: Brethren Press, 1979), esp. 28–39. Done in popular style, this is the only biography of the organizer of the *Neu-Täufer.*

47. Renkewitz, *Hochmann von Hochenau,* 222.

48. Durnbaugh, *European Origins,* 53–56. Kling had refused to testify against his son-in-law, despite the local pastor's promptings. See also Durnbaugh, *Brethren Beginnings,* 11.

49. HSP Ac. 1926, p. 4.

50. Durnbaugh, *European Origins,* 65–66.

NOTES TO INTRODUCTION

51. Renkewitz, *Hochmann von Hochenau*, 229–32, 415–17. The note locating Schatz in Düdelsheim is on p. 416. See also Durnbaugh, *Brethren Beginnings*, 11.

52. Durnbaugh, *European Origins*, 75. For Pastoir, see Dagmar Drüll, *Heidelberger Gelehrten-lexikon, 1652–1802* (Berlin and New York: Springer-Verlag, 1991), 119. Pastoir taught church history and rhetoric. See also *CE*, 4–5.

53. *German Sectarians*, 1:40.

54. Nils Thune, *The Behmenists and the Philadelphians: A Contribution to the Study of English Mysticism in the 17th and 18th Centuries* (Uppsala: Almqvist & Wiksells, 1948), 33–150.

55. *CE*, 3. The *Chronicon* states that Beissel learned *Kauffmanns-rechnung*, or accounting.

56. Elizabeth W. Fisher, "'Prophesies and Revelations': German Cabbalists in Early Pennsylvania," *PMHB* 109 (1985): 299–300, 310–11. See also *CE*, 11–12. For Horch, see C. W. H. Hochhuth, *Heinrich Horche und die philadelphischen Gemeinden in Hessen* (Gütersloh: C. Bertelsmann, 1876), 20–21, 27–28.

57. *CE*, 6–7. *DE*, Pars 1, 326–27: "Jetzt siehet man einen armen Waysen gehen, von der Mutter der Stadt u. des Landes verwiesen." See also *ZS*, 91; *CE*, 11.

58. *CE*, 8–10.

59. *German Sectarians*, 1:40. Seidensticker implied, without saying explicitly, that Beissel had gone to Schwarzenau. See Seidensticker, *Klostergeschichte*, 32. Ernst, *Ephrata*, 23–28, follows Sachse, *German Sectarians*, with embellishment. Alderfer, *Ephrata Commune*, 23–25, depends on Sachse and Ernst. Everham also made this assumption. She correctly placed Beissel's journeyman years before his time in Heidelberg. See Everham, "Beissels Leben," 57. Walter Klein followed the *Chronicon* more faithfully, placing Beissel in Marienborn, with no mention of a sojourn in Schwarzenau. See Klein, *Johann Conrad Beissel*, 29–33. See *CE*, 5, for a claim that Haller advised Beissel to go to Schwarzenau. The chronicle did not report that Beissel actually went. See also *CE*, 40. According to the chronicle, Mack said, "I am a stranger to him [Beissel]" ("Ich bin ein Fremder an ihm").

60. *CE*, 10–11.

61. Schaab, *Geschichte der Kurpfalz*, 2:122; Ward, *Protestant Evangelical Awakening*, 20–21.

62. *CE*, 10–12, 249. The *Chronicon* noted that Beissel landed in Boston in autumn 1720. See also Beissel, *Wedge*, 252; Durnbaugh, *European Origins*, 283. For dissension among Krefeld Dunkers, see *CE*, 1, 12, 212–13.

63. Aaron S. Fogelman, *Hopeful Journeys: German Immigration, Settlement, and Political Culture in Colonial America, 1717–1775* (Philadelphia: University of Pennsylvania Press, 1996), 4–11.

64. Philip S. Klein and Ari Hoogenboom, *A History of Pennsylvania*, 2d enl. ed. (University Park: Pennsylvania State University Press, 1980), 36–38, 42–43, 45–46.

65. Samuel Whitaker Pennypacker, *The Settlement of Germantown, Pennsylvania, and the Beginning of German Immigration to North America* (Philadelphia: William J. Campbell, 1899); Stephanie Grauman Wolf, *Urban Village: Population, Community, and Family Structure in Germantown, Pennsylvania, 1683–1800* (Princeton: Princeton University Press, 1976). For details on Kelpius, see Ernst Benz, *Die Protestantische Thebais: Zur Nachwirkung Makarios des Ägypters im Protestantismus des 17. und 18. Jahrhunderts in Europa und Amerika* (Wiesbaden: Franz Steiner, 1963), 93–101. See also Julius F. Sachse, *The German Pietists of Provincial Pennsylvania, 1694–1708* (Philadelphia: P. C. Stockhausen, 1895).

66. August Gottlieb Spangenberg, *Leben des Herrn Nicolaus Ludwig Grafen und Herrn von Zinzendorf und Pottendorf* [Barby, 1772–74], 5:1380–82; Fogelman, *Hopeful Journeys*, 104–5.

67. Sally Schwartz, *A Mixed Multitude: The Struggle for Toleration in Colonial Pennsylvania* (New York: New York University Press, 1987), 112, 336, n184. The numbers of effective Reformed and Lutheran clergy may have been slightly smaller.

68. "Ein nichts-bessessender auf dieser Erde" and "Ein nach der stillen Ewigkeit wallender Pilger." These appellations appear frequently throughout Beissel's letters. See Tussing, "Hungry Orphan," 87–101.

NOTES TO INTRODUCTION

I agree with part of Tussing's premise, that social conditions strongly influenced Beissel. I am less confident that one can psychologize about Beissel's personality from those conditions.

69. Jerome H. Wood, Jr., *Conestoga Crossroads: Lancaster, Pennsylvania, 1730–1790* (Harrisburg: Pennsylvania Historical and Museum Commission, 1979), 7–8.

70. *CE*, 13–15. See also *German Sectarians*, 1:56, 71–73. There is virtually no documentation for Beissel's activities between 1722 and his baptism in 1724. All writers after Sachse have depended on his account.

71. *CE*, 13. See also *German Sectarians*, 1:59–70. Sachse made much of the contact with the Labadists. They disbanded in 1722. Observance of Labadie's teachings could hardly have been lively. See Trevor J. Saxby, *The Quest for the New Jerusalem: Jean de Labadie and the Labadists, 1610–1744* (Dordrecht and Boston: Martinus Nijhoff, 1987), 308. Saxby stated that Beissel took home a few Labadist books but cited no documentation. See also Ernest Green, "The Labadists of Colonial Maryland (1683–1722)," *Communal Studies* 8 (1988): 119. Green believes that the Labadists influenced Beissel's design for community. However, Green also depends partly on Alderfer, *Ephrata Commune* (pp. 33–34). I am grateful to Don Durnbaugh for calling Green's article to my attention.

72. *CE*, 15–20. The letter is in FLP B. Ms. 22, pp. 251–52, and is partly quoted in *CE*, 17: "Nun gedachte ich gewonnen zu haben und gedachte meinem Gott in der Stille des Geistes ohne Unterlaß (als von allen Menschen geschieden) Tag und Nacht zu dienen in seinem H.[eiligen] Tempel."

73. FLP B. Ms. 22, 252–53. The *Chronicon* (17–18) quoted part of this letter, claiming that in it Beissel took credit for starting the awakening.

74. *CE*, 20–21.

75. *LuW*, 4:18.

76. *CE*, 22–28, 48. In 1728 Meyle rebaptized Beissel, who then rebaptized the other six. For Meyle's baptism at Germantown, see Martin Grove Brumbaugh, *A History of the German Baptist Brethren in Europe and America* (Elgin, Ill.: Brethren Publishing House, 1899), 155. Jane Evans Best has attempted to trace Jan Meyle to Hans Millan, an early Germantown settler, and on back to a Mayle/Meili family who were originally Swiss Anabaptists and made their way to Alsace and the Palatinate. See Jane Evans Best, "Turmoil in Conestoga," *Pennsylvania Mennonite Heritage* 11, no. 1 (January 1993): 3, 12–13.

77. *LuW*, 4:28.

78. *CE*, 61, 64, 88–90, 100–101, 107–8, 133–34, 166–67.

79. Ibid., 57–58, 84–85. See also *Contemporaries*, 12. See also August Spangenberg's report to David Nitschman in Donald F. Durnbaugh, ed., *The Brethren in Colonial America* (Elgin, Ill.: Brethren Press, 1967), 274–75.

80. *CE*, 112, 171; Jack Ward Willson Loose, "A Study of Two Distinct Periods of Ephrata Cloister History," *Papers of the Lancaster County Historical Society* 55, no. 6 (1951): 145–75, esp.163–75. Loose relied at times on Sachse. Loose mistakenly claimed that Ephrata had the first press to use gothic and roman type and to print in English and German.

81. *CE*, 94–100.

82. HSP Ac. 1926, pp. 3–5 of first section.

83. *CE*, 144. Tussing, "Hungry Orphan," 100, summarizes conjectures about Beissel's final illness. Various descriptions allow for several possible diseases, although some kind of intestinal or stomach disorder seems plausible. Sangmeister added the possibility of venereal disease. See *LuW*, 10:14.

84. *CE*, 242–46. These are not the only conflicts of Beissel's later years, but they are perhaps most important for Ephrata as a community.

85. I am indebted to Clarence Spohn, who has helped me to understand the complex legal documents and to interpret Sangmeister's group as a faction within the community.

86. *LuW*, 10:10–34.

87. *CE*, 111.

88. Ibid., 247–49.

NOTES TO CHAPTER 1

CHAPTER 1. THE RELIGIOUS THOUGHT OF EPHRATA: CONRAD BEISSEL

1. *Contemporaries*, 139, 195.
2. [Conrad Beissel], *A Dissertation on Man's Fall* [trans. Peter Miller] (Ephrata: [Typis Societatis], 1765). This is the earliest known published version. An untitled German version was published at the beginning of the printed sermons (*Geistliche Reden*) in *DE, Pars I* (1773), 1–48. It was published separately in 1789, with a few minor changes in wording and without Peter Miller's explanatory notes of the 1773 version. See [Conrad Beissel], *Göttliche Wunderschrift* (Ephrata: [Typis Societatis], 1789). The preface of the 1789 edition stated that the *Wunderschrift* first appeared in 1760. The *Chronicon* reported that Beissel received the inspiration to write a "*Wunderschrift*" when he was ill, probably in 1741 (*CE*, 114). It is unclear, however, when Beissel actually wrote the *Wunderschrift*. Peter Erb published in *MHT* (113–31) an English translation by Klaus M. Lindner based on the text in *DE, Pars I* and Miller's translation. Lindner's translation was mistakenly titled "First Sermon," since it is the first piece in *Pars I*. However, the speech directly following it was numbered the first *Geistliche Rede*. Unfortunately, Lindner's translation is inaccurate in some places and must be used with caution. Even Peter Miller's translation has some problems because English words have shifted in nuance in the intervening years. Therefore all quotations are my own translations from the German text of 1773.
3. Durnbaugh, *Brethren in Colonial America*, 272, 274.
4. *LuW*, 9:7.
5. Hans-Jürgen Schrader, *Literaturproduktion und Büchermarkt des radikalen Pietismus: Johann Henrich Reitz' "Historie der Wiedergebohrnen" und ihr geschichtlicher Kontext* (Göttingen: Vandenhoeck & Ruprecht, 1989), 108–30.
6. *CE*, 286. Although the *Chronicon* said as much and Seidensticker reiterated it, Sachse's Rosicrucian theory has led many readers astray. Chauncey David Ensign, "Radical German Pietism (c. 1675–c. 1760)" (Ph.D. diss., Boston University, 1955); Durnbaugh, *Brethren in Colonial America*; and Erb, *MHT*, have eventually pointed out the centrality of Jacob Boehme's thought at Ephrata.
7. *DE, Pars I*, 4–6.
8. [Heinrich Horch], *Mystische und Profetische Bibel, Das ist Die gantze Heil. Schrift Altes und Neues Testament, Auffs neue nach dem Grund verbessert Sampt Erklärung Der fürnemsten Sinnbilder und Weissagungen, Sonderlich Des H. Lieds Salomons und der Offenbarung J. C. Wie auch Denen fürnemsten Lehren, bevoraus die sich in diese letzte Zeiten schicken* (Marburg, 1712), prefatory comments to the Song of Solomon. The work is unpaginated. For a biography of Horch, see Hochhuth, *Heinrich Horche*. See also *GdP*, 2:120–21, 176n116–19.
9. [Horch], *Mystische und Profetische Bibel*, commentary on Rev. 2–3: "die erste liebe sol [sic] wiederkommen daß die glaubigen abermal ein hertz u.[nd] eine seele werden"; "die Filadelfische liebe leider wiederum verkülen wird."
10. *Contemporaries*, 64–65.
11. Quoted in Max Goebel, "Geschichte der wahren Inspirations-Gemeinden, von 1688 bis 1850, I," *Zeitschrift für die Historische Theologie* 19 (1854): 389.
12. *Contemporaries*, 74.
13. Durnbaugh, *Brethren in Colonial America*, 272.
14. Jürgen Büchsel, *Gottfried Arnold, Sein Verständnis von Kirche und Wiedergeburt* (Witten: Luther-Verlag, 1970), 31–39.
15. Peter C. Erb, *Pietists, Protestants, and Mysticism: The Use of Late Medieval Spiritual Texts in the Work of Gottfried Arnold (1666–1714)* (Metuchen, N.J.: Scarecrow Press, 1989), 124–28.
16. Ensign, "Radical German Pietism," 16, 282.
17. Robert Friedmann, *Mennonite Piety through the Centuries: Its Genius and Its Literature* (Goshen, Ind.: Mennonite Historical Society, 1949; rpt. Sugarcreek, Ohio: Timely Publications, 1980, 1995).
18. Alexander Mack, Sr., *Kurze und einfältige Vorstellung der äussern, aber doch heiligen Rechte und Ordnungen des Hauses Gottes* (Baltimore: Samuel Sower, 1799), in *The Complete Writings of Alexander Mack*, ed. William R. Eberly (Winona Lake, Ind.: BMH Books, 1991), 64, 88–89.

NOTES TO CHAPTER 1

19. Ensign, "Radical German Pietism," 285, 278–79. Concerning the use of avoidance, Ensign correctly noted that the practice is more characteristic of "the less liberal Mennonites" than of the Radical Pietists (278). His assumption that the "corresponding *cultus* and discipline" (279) of a New Testament church was important to Radical Pietism is overstated.

20. Wallmann, *Philipp Jakob Spener,* 299–324, 337–38, 340–41, 346–47.

21. Lydie Hege and Christoph Wiebe, eds., *The Amish: Origin and Characteristics,* Actes du colloque international de Sainte-Marie-aux-Mines, Aug. 19–21, 1993 (Ingersheim: Association Française d'Histoire Anabaptiste-Mennonite, 1996), 19–71.

22. Friedmann, *Mennonite Piety,* 11–13.

23. Gottfried Arnold, *Unparteyische Kirchen- und Ketzer-Historie,* 2 vols. (Franfurt am Main: Thomas Fritsch, 1699–1700). It was later expanded to 3 vols.

24. More recent writers have questioned Friedmann. See Carl F. Bowman, *Brethren Society: The Cultural Transformation of a "Peculiar People"* (Baltimore: Johns Hopkins University Press, 1995), 46–50, although on 5–6 Bowman seems to accept the older interpretation. See also Theron F. Schlabach, *Peace, Faith, Nation: Mennonites and Amish in Nineteenth-Century America* (Scottdale, Pa.: Herald Press, 1988), 21, 88, 90, 94.

25. Best, "Turmoil in Conestoga," 2–27.

26. Friedmann, *Mennonite Piety,* 62–64, 233–34.

27. *Contemporaries,* 60, 76.

28. *ZS,* 33. J. J. Stoudt corrected Ernst's belief that these men were followers of Beissel. See Ernst, *Ephrata,* 59. Ernst named them as Georg Adam Weidner and David Kaufmann (Caufmann). They were followers of Matthias Baumann, not Beissel.

29. *German Sectarians,* 1:118.

30. "Snow Hill Letterbook," untitled, paginated manuscript in the Sachse Collection of the Seventh-Day Baptist Historical Society, Box 4, no. 15, on loan to PSA, 106–21. The quotation is on 119. The excerpt is from pp. 22–38 of Thomas Bromley, *Das Gesetz der Beschneidung* (no publication information provided in manuscript). The German translation was published in 1712. See also Thune, *Behmenists,* 219.

31. Jacob Boehme, *Sämtliche Schriften,* ed. Will-Erich Peuckert and August Faust, 11 vols. (Stuttgart: Frommanns, 1955–61), facs. rpt. of *Theosophia Revelata. Das ist: Alle Göttliche Schriften des Gottseligen und Hocherleuchteten Deutschen Theosophi Jacob Böhmens,* ed. Johann Georg Gichtel and Johann Wilhelm Ueberfeld (Amsterdam, 1730). The passage is from vol. 7 (*Magnum Mysterium,* vol. 1), 411: "die viehische Vermischung Mannes und Weibes vor Gottes Heiligkeit ein Eckel sey." Citations hereafter are keyed to volume numbers of the facsimile reprint of the 1730 edition.

32. *TP,* 1:302: "das eben am Hinderthiel des Thiers die Schaam und Venae spermaticae ligen, und Gott uns lehren wollen, daß Er an unseren thierischen Gliedern kein Gefallen habe."

33. *ZS,* 194: "Darum . . . mußte alles, was männlich war, an diesem Glied beschnitten werden, anzuzeigen daß es vor Gottes heiligen Augen ein Eckel sey. Dahero auch die Vermischung zwischen beyderley Geschlecht vor Gott und Menschen ein Eckel ist."

34. Ibid., 125–26: "wann wir mit Christo . . . in das Inwendige und Allerheiligste eindringet. . . . Da findet sich das güldene Rauch-Faß . . . in welchem die Gebäte der Heiligen ohne Unterlaß als ein heiliges Rauchwerck zu Gott aufsteigen." Cf. *TP,* 3:2185: "Denn ein Priester Gottes der stets im Allerheiligsten dienen, und Rauch-Opfer vor den Herrn bringen sol, muß kein Vernunft-Feuer ins Allerheiligste bringen."

35. *ZS,* 125: "Alsdann lernen wir reden mit neuen Zungen und können Gott ohne Unterlaß dinen [*sic*] in seinem heiligen Tempel."

36. Cunrad Beyssel, *Mystyrion Anomias, the Mystery of Lawlesness: Or, Lawless antichrist Discover'd and Disclos'd,* trans. M.[ichael] W.[ohlfahrt] ([Philadelphia: William Bradford?], 1729).

37. Seidensticker, *Klostergeschichte,* 39–40; *German Sectarians,* 1:116; Ernst, *Ephrata,* 59; Alderfer, *Ephrata Commune,* 35.

38. *CE,* 35–36. Beissel observed the Sabbath earlier (16, 26). The *Chronicon* wished to present Beissel's Sabbatarianism as independent of other influences.

NOTES TO CHAPTER 1

39. See Don A. Sanford, *A Choosing People: The History of Seventh-Day Baptists* (Nashville: Broadman Press, 1992), 102–9, for a concise summary. Other congregations were founded later. Sanford's work depends primarily on Morgan Edwards's *Materials toward a History of the American Baptists, Both British and German* (Philadelphia: Cruikshank & Collins, 1770–92). See also *German Sectarians*, 1:27–28. Ernst, *Ephrata*, 44, depended on Sachse. Alderfer, *Ephrata Commune*, 34, probably depended on Sachse and Ernst without citing them. See Brumbaugh, *History of the German Baptist Brethren*, 443–44. Brumbaugh agreed with Sachse. Durnbaugh concurs. See his article "Baptists, Keithian," in his *Brethren Encyclopedia*, 3 vols. (Philadelphia: Brethren Encyclopedia, 1983).

40. Fisher, "'Prophesies and Revelations,'" 311–13. It is interesting that Fisher made no mention of Gichtel, even though he profoundly influenced many of the Pennsylvania Germans she described.

41. Sanford, *Choosing People*, 95–101.

42. David S. Katz, *Sabbath and Sectarianism in Seventeenth-Century England*, Brill's Studies in Intellectual History, vol. 10 (Leiden: E. J. Brill, 1988), 134–212.

43. *SS*, 1:82–143. Boehme derives seven spirits of sin in the fall of Lucifer by inverting the seven divine source spirits in chaps. 14–16.

44. Ibid., 177–79.

45. *SS*, 6 (*De signatura rerum*): 97: "Darum hieß ihn Gott den Sabbath oder den Ruhe-Tag. . . . Er ist der Göttliche Hall in der Kraft oder die [*sic*] Freudenreich."

46. Thomas Bromley, *The Way to the Sabbath of Rest, or, The Soul's Progress in the Work of the New Birth*, 3d ed. (Germantown: Christopher Saur, 1759), 53–54. The first edition was published in 1691. See also Thune, *Behmenists*, 53–54. Seidensticker, *Klostergeschichte*, 42, fabricated a link between Ephrata and Jan van Leiden's militant Anabaptist Kingdom at Münster in the sixteenth century.

47. *GdP*, 1:394–97, 400–404.

48. Johannes Kelpius, "Letter to Steven Momfort in Rhode Island," in Kelpius, *The Diarium of Magister Johannes Kelpius*, trans. Julius F. Sachse, Pennsylvania German Society Proceedings and Addresses, vol. 25 (Lancaster: New Era, 1917), 48.

49. See, e.g., Max Goebel, *Geschichte des christlichen Lebens in der rheinisch- westphälischen evangelischen Kirche*, vol. 3 (Coblenz: Karl Bädeker, 1860), 66–68. See also *GdP*, 1:32–33 (Puritans), 70–71, 81 (Voetius), 94, 268 (Nethenus), and 290–91 for Spener's own esteem of Sunday as a day of worship, devotion, and rest.

50. Beysell, *Mystyrion Anomias*, 4, 7, 11. For the derivation of the beast's number, 666, see 22–23, 31–32.

51. Ibid., 14, 28.

52. Mack, Sr., *Writings*, 51.

53. Beysell, *Mystyrion Anomias*, 20–21.

54. Ibid., 31.

55. *CE*, 36–37. See also J. William Frost, *A Perfect Freedom: Religious Liberty in Pennsylvania* (University Park: Pennsylvania State University Press, 1993), 69–73, 144–46; Schwartz, *Mixed Multitude*, 115.

56. *TP*, 4:2494: "Die fleischliche Hurerey, auch im Ehestand, ist Gott ein Greuel, Gott verwirfts." For the Dunkers' attitude, see Mack, Sr., *Writings*, 88. For the Inspirationists, see Jonathan G. Andelson, "The Gift to Be Single: Celibacy and Religious Enthusiasm in the Community of True Inspiration," *Communal Societies* 5 (1985): 1–32, esp. 1–13.

57. *MKZ*, 15–17. "Eine Zucht-Ordnung über den abgefallenen Menschen" (15); "Dieser Stand wieder muss aufgelöset werden" (16).

58. [Conrad Beissel], *Mystische und sehr geheyme Spruechwe welche in der Himlischen schule des heiligen geistes erlernet* (Philadelphia: B. Franklin, 1730), 9–10; translation mine. See also *MHT*, 68–69. For another English translation, see Georg Conrad Beissel, *Some Theosophical Maxims or Rules of the Solitary Life*, trans. Michelle Long, ed. Nadine A. Steinmetz (Ephrata, Pa.: Ephrata Cloister Associates, 1991), 31–40. The mystical sayings were embedded in a later collection of maxims appended to the *Theosophische Lectionen*, published in 1752. Long translated the entire set.

NOTES TO CHAPTER 1

59. *German Sectarians*, 1:164; Klein, *Johann Conrad Beissel*, 72–74. Curiously, Seidensticker thought that the *Mystische und sehr geheyme Sprueche* were lost. See Seidensticker, *Klostergeschichte*, 43.

60. [Conrad Beissel et al.], *Vorspiel der Neuen Welt* (Philadelphia: B. Franklin, 1732), 189.

61. Ibid., 190, letter *N:* "Nichtes wollen, nichtes wissen, Darauf sey mit ernst beflissen, So wird Gott dir alles seyn, Dass du kanst in ruhe sein." Cf. Johannes Tauler, *Predigten,* ed. Georg Hofmann and Alois Haas, vol. 2 (Einsiedeln: Johannes Verlag, 1987), 420: "Tauche ein in dein Nichtwissen und Nichtwissen-Wollen. Halte dich von allem entblößt, an deinen verborgenen und unbekannten Gott . . . bleibe vielmehr in Stille und Ruhe."

62. [Beissel et al.], *Vorspiel der Neuen Welt,* 190, letters *R* and *S.*

63. Mack, Sr., *Writings,* 79. See also 33–35, 70–74.

64. Getreuen Aufrichtigen Mitbruder [Georg Adam Martin], *Christliche Bibliothek* (Ephrata: [Typis Societatis], 1792), 87–111. The booklet is a latter-day confession of faith for the Sabbatarian group. The initials of the pseudonym indicate Martin's authorship. This work's late date places it outside the scope of this project.

65. Certeau, *Mystic Fable,* 94–101, 108–12.

66. Michael Wohlfahrt's *Die Weisheit Gottes* (1737), now lost, is the only doctrinal or devotional work known to be published in that period that was not a hymnal.

67. HSP Ac. 1926, 3 (in second section). The obituary of Benedict Jüchlie indicated that he was trying to help get a press when he died in Philadelphia in 1741 en route to Europe.

68. The copy containing both prefaces is at the Ephrata Cloister: EC 2000.2.2.

69. [Conrad Beissel et al.], *Erster Theil der Theosophischen Lectionen, Betreffende die Schulen des einsamen Lebens* (Ephrata: [Typis Societatis], 1752), 351–95. More poems appear on 396–432.

70. ZS, 20. The *Chronicon* quoted at least one meditation about the origins of Ephrata, without citing its published source. See *CE,* 108. *Gemütsbewegung* cannot be readily translated. I have chosen "meditation" as an approximation.

71. ZS, 98. Only one letter in this section, to a sister in Basel, 1733, names a destination and date. He may have written this one to Margaretha Thoma of Niederdorf, near Basel. See Leo Schelbert, "On the Power of Pietism: A Documentary on the Thommens of Schaefferstown," *Historic Schaefferstown Record* 18, no. 4 (October 1984): 49. For examples of conflict, see 248–50, 246–48; for examples of prophecy, see 85, 98.

72. McGinn, *Foundations of Mysticism,* 1:xviii–xix, 31–33, 37–38, 40–43, passim. See McGinn's index entry for "Apophatic language and theology."

73. ZS, 31: "Gott ist ein unbegreiffliches Nichts, und ich bin ein unbegreiffliches Ichts . . . und werden wir zu leiden haben . . . bis alles Ichts in Nichts und alles Seyn in das Nichtseyn und alles Etwas in das Nichts aufgelöst ist . . . wo alle Ichheit, wo alle Zweyheit, wo alle Selbheit aufhöret."

74. Ibid., 39: "Sein Leben ist unser Leben, und wir sind in Ihm geworden, dass wir seyn, was wir seyn. Sein Leben ist in uns verwandelt, und hat unsere Nichtigkeiten verwandelt, und aufgelöset die Bände der Eitelkeiten. . . . Er is Wir worden, und wir sind in unserm Wir zu nichte worden. O ein herrlicher Wechsel! wer mit Nichts Alles erkauffet, was ehmals gewesen, und auch in Ewigkeit seyn wird."

75. SS, 6 (*De Signatura Rerum*): 156–69. The quotation is on 169: "So ist mein inwendiger Mensche in Christi Tod mit Ihme gestorben und lebet nicht mehr der Ichheit. . . . In mir selber wird das Paradeis [*sic*] seyn: alles was Gott der Vater hat und ist, das soll in mir erscheinen."

76. *TP,* 3:2318: "Als das Göttliche Licht im Gemüt aber durchgebrochen, zeigete es mir Jesum und lehrete mich an Jesum halten, da muste meine Ichheit und Wissen in den Tod."

77. Jacoby, *Two Mystic Communities,* 24, 26, 29–32; Stoeffler, *Mysticism in the German Devotional Literature,* 55–58, 49, 60. Stoeffler mistakenly called Beissel's *Dissertation* the *Urständliche und Erfahrungs-volle Hohe Zeugnüsse,* which is really the title of the second variant of the book of theosophical epistles.

78. McGinn, *Foundations of Mysticism,* 1:xviii, 161–65, 173–74, passim. See also McGinn's index entry for "Cataphatic language and theology."

79. Fritz Tanner, *Die Ehe im Pietismus* (Zürich: Zwingli-Verlag, 1952), 40–41.

NOTES TO CHAPTER 1

80. Stoeffler, *Mysticism in the German Devotional Literature*, 52–53, 56, 61; Jacoby, *Two Mystic Communities*, 33–34.

81. *German Sectarians*, 1:419–22, 2:236. Eugene Doll and Anneliese Funke noted that the page of the supposed 1745 edition that Sachse reproduced was typographically consistent with the version in the 1773 *Deliciae Ephratenses*. They doubted that a version was printed in 1745 and suggested that Sachse may have collected a copy of the *Dissertation* that was separated from the rest of the 1773 volume. See *Ephrata Cloisters*, 107, 112, 120. See also Karl John Richard Arndt and Reimer C. Eck, eds., *The First Century of German Language Printing in the United States of America*, vol. 1, Publications of the Pennsylvania German Society, vol. 21 (Göttingen: Niedersächsiches Staats- und Universitätsbibliothek Göttingen, 1989), 187, 301.

82. Wallmann, *Pietismus*, 7.

83. *DE, Pars I*, 1–11. Peter Erb's sorcebook, *MHT*, has an English translation prepared by Klaus M. Lindner based on the German text.

84. Ibid. The seven topics could be outlined as follows: (1) sin and God, 12–13; (2) creation and the two falls, 13–21; (3) ministry, 21–25; (4) soteriology, 26–28; (5) Christology/Sophiology, 28–30; (6) ecclesiology, 30–31; (7) restoration, 31–35. The second topic, creation and the two falls, could be further categorized to cover the creation of Adam (13), first fall of desire (14), second fall of deception (16–18), and exhortation to men to maintain the traditional gender hierarchy yet seek virginity (19–21). Interestingly, Beissel does not deal with the Sabbath at all in this important work. Because Jesus and Sophia are male and female aspects of the same Christ for Beissel, the heading of "Sophiology" is added to "Christology" in this analysis.

85. Ibid., 2: "woher doch das Böse seine Kraft hätte . . . weil selbst mein Gutes-wollen alles dieses verursachte, daß das Böse so rege gemacht wurde."

86. Weeks, *Boehme*, 113–14, 43–48, 55–59.

87. *DE, Pars I*, 10: "Also geschahe durch die Lust im Anschauen der Thiere schnell ein Ehbruch."

88. *SS*, 1:30–36; 2 (*De tribus principia*): 84–150; 4 (*De incarnatione verbi*): 47–52. See *DE, Pars I*, 11–15; *ZS*, 194: "die unreinen Glider der Fortpflantzung welche der Mensch mit allen Thieren gemein hat, sie waren nicht vor dem Schlaf, dann sie gehören nicht zu dem Bilde Gottes" (the impure members of propagation which the human has in common with all animals were not there before [Adam's sleep], because they do not belong to the image of God).

89. *SS*, 4 (*Der Weg zu Christo*): 119–20.

90. Ibid. (*De incarnatione verbi*): 37–40; 6 (*De signatura rerum*): 58–61. In this last passage, Boehme blamed Lucifer's poison for Adam's erring will.

91. *TP*, 5:3640–41: "Also ist Sophia in ihr Aether gangen [*sic*] und Eva offenbar worden."

92. *DE, Pars I*, 10: "Also geschahe durch die Lust im Anschauen der Thiere schnell ein Ehbruch, dass seine himmlische Weiblichkeit von ihm wich, eben zur Zeit, da er hätte sollen sein Brautbett besteigen, fiel er nieder und starb." See also *ZS*, 194.

93. Mark A. Noll, ed., *Confessions and Catechisms of the Reformation* (Grand Rapids, Mich.: Baker Book House, 1991), 137. According to the Heidelberg Catechism, the Law teaches humans of their sin and its "wretched consequences." It is unclear whether Beissel knew the fuller discussion in Calvin's *Institutes*, but he probably knew the Heidelberg Catechism.

94. *DE, Pars I*, 17: "sie sich mit der Schlange einließ . . . mehr durch der Schlangen Magia, als durch ihre Worte vergifftet worden."

95. For the Heidelberg Catechism's teaching of the bondage of the will, see Noll, *Confessions*, 138, 148–49, 155. For Boehme see *SS*, 6 (*Von der Gnadenwahl*). Wallmann, *Pietismus*, 80, noted a tendency in Reformed Pietism for predestination to be transformed into a kind of election for the reborn.

96. *ZS*, 119.

97. *MHT*, 13. For a Reformed perspective, see Noll, *Confessions*, 138.

98. The Schwarzenau Brethren (Dunker) position closely followed earlier Mennonite statements. See Mack, Sr., *Writings*, 50, 30–32. For the Mennonite position, see, e.g., Dirk Philips, *Enchiridion*, in *The Complete Writings of Dirk Philips*, trans. and ed. Cornelius J. Dyck, William E. Keeney, and Alvin J. Beachy (Scottdale, Pa.: Herald Press, 1992), 88–91. See also Stoffer, *Background and Development*, 79.

99. *Güldene Aepffel in Silbern Schalen* (Efrata, 1745), 106–22. This volume, published with the help of local Mennonites, was a reprint of the original 1702 edition printed for Swiss Anabaptists. It includes the confession of faith of Thomas Imbroich, martyred in Cologne in 1558. J. ten Doornkaat Koolman has shown that Imbroich's confession relied on Philips's treatise on baptism. See J. ten Doornkaat Koolman, *Dirk Philips, 1504–1568* (Haarlem: H. D. Tjeenk Wilink en Zoon, 1964), 74. Through the *Güldene Aepffel*, which also influenced Mack, some Dutch Mennonite views came to Swiss Anabaptists. For an English translation, see *Golden Apples in Silver Bowls: The Rediscovery of Redeeming Love*, trans. Elizabeth Bender and Leonard Gross (Lancaster, Pa.: Lancaster Mennonite Historical Society, 1999).

100. *CE*, 28. Concerning infants, Beissel reportedly said: "Sie haben zwar noch nicht gesündiget; aber um deswillen sind sie nicht unschuldig, dann es ist in ihnen die böse Art." When asked if he believed they were damned, Beissel reportedly answered, "Wir halten daß sie durch ein gewisses Fegfeuer von dem Erb-übel wieder müssen geschieden werden."

101. *DE, Pars I*, 25–28. "Daß die Gottbetrübte Weiblichkeit wieder zu ihrem rechten Mann komme, als der nicht im Grimm über sie herrsche" (25).

102. Ibid., 28: "So ist nun Christus die Versöhnung zwischen Feuer u.{nd} Licht, und hat aus beyden wieder eins gemacht." Cf. *SS*, 1:22–24, 39–44.

103. *Contemporaries*, 73.

104. *CE*, 124; *ZS*, 72: "Unschuld und Reinigkeit des Leibes."

105. *ZS*, 62: "zum Tode als ein Übelthäter verurtheilet"; 70: "Der Wille anfängt zu versencken in sein eigen Nichts, und wird zweiffelhafftig an seinen guten Wercken."

106. Ibid., 73: "so wird das Leben und die Seligkeit in seiner allerinnersten Wurtzel mit Kraft darinnen offenbar"; 139–40: "Unsere beste Wercke zur Sünde gemacht werden. . . . [Gnade] erweiset sich erst, wann der Mensch durch das Gesetz getödet ist . . . zum neuen Leben in Gott durch seinen Geist."

107. Ibid., 70; 116–17: "Nun ruhen alle Verheissungen des neuen Bundes auf dem Tode Jesu Christi . . . durch die Taufe Jesus Christi zur Gleichförmigkeit seines Todes gebracht ist."

108. Stoeffler, *Mysticism in the German Devotional Literature*, 53–54.

109. *DE, Pars I*, 30. "Alles nun, was durch den Creutzes-Todt ins Ersterben gebracht wird: das wird dem ewigen Geist, oder der himmlischen Mutterschafft, zum herrlichen Ausgrünen in den Schooß geliefert."

110. *ZS*, 134: "So ist Gott unser Vater, Christus unser Bruder, und der H[eilige] Geist unsere Mutter."

111. *DE, Pars I*, 22: "Die ewige Mutter, als die himmlische Weiblichkeit."

112. Ibid., 25.

113. Ibid., 30: "die, der ewigen Mutter in den Schooß geliefert werden."

114. *ZS*, 125: "reden mit neuen Zungen." Cf. Beysell, *Mystyrion Anomias*, 21–24.

115. Kelpius, *Diarium*, 30, 32. Kelpius thought that the wilderness would be like a "rose garden," but instead it was an "oven of tribulation." See 65 and 82 for Kelpius on "brotherly love," alternating with criticism of the organized church groups he encountered. Beissel shared this attitude. See also Fisher, "'Prophesies and Revelations,'" 332–33. See also Renkewitz, *Hochmann von Hochenau*, 183–90, and Benz, *Protestantische Thebais*, 81–85, 93–101.

116. *DE, Pars I*, 195–96. The *Chronicon* (*CE*, 50–51) cites this passage. See also *ZS*, 20, 89–90.

117. [Conrad Beissel et al.], *Zionitischer WeyrauchsHügel, Oder: Myrrhen Berg* (Germantown: Christoph Saur, 1739). The "Vorrede" (preface) is unpaginated, but the paragraphs are numbered. The cited material is in paragraphs 9–10.

118. FLP B. Ms. 22, 75: "Die Babel-Kirche hat den dritten Zeugen vom Himmel, den Heiligen Geist, der alle Sprache einet, verloren."

119. Ibid., 170: "wo man die einige Mutter Sprache redet."

120. *ZS*, 20: "In diesem Sinn hat sich hernach Ephrata erbauet, als in lauter Noth und Leiden." See also *CE*, 90.

121. *TP*, 5:3383: "Wir müssen auch mit Christo leiden, sterben und durch viel Leiden zu seiner Herrlichkeit eingehen." Cf. *ZS*, 96, 198: "daß wir durch vil Trübsal müssen in das Reich der Himmeln eingehen."

122. *ZS*, 115: "der Natur Bitter schmäckt." Gichtel had claimed that Sophia overcomes all bitterness of wrath like sugar to gall (*TP*, 2:1039). See Stoeffler, *Mysticism in the German Devotional Literature*, 63. Beissel's theosophical maxims appended to the *Theosophische Lectionen* included reflections on his sufferings as a leader. Although this attitude was present in his earlier period, a much stronger sense of joy counterbalanced the complaints.

123. Stoeffler, *Mysticism in the German Devotional Literature*, 63.

124. See Gichtel's discussion of the Melchizedek priesthood in *TP*, 5:3851. See *Contemporaries*, 79, 100, for accusations that Beissel and others thought their prayers could atone for sin. See 193 and 195 for rebuttals by Peter Miller, who claimed that Ephrata believed in the merits of Christ alone.

125. *ZS*, 111. For Saur, see *Contemporaries*, 13–27. Saur called Beissel the Antichrist.

126. [Conrad Beissel], *Geistliche Briefe eines Fridesamen Pilgers, Welche er von 1721 bis an seine 1768 darauf erfolget Entbindung geschrieben* ([Ephrata:] gedruckt [bey Salomon Mayer?], 1794), 16. The letter is addressed to "Timotheo," but headings on pp. 7–20 indicate "to Br. GAM," or Georg Adam Martin, the leader at Antietam (later Snow Hill). An internal reference to forty-eight years since Beissel entered his "pilgrimage," presumably his conversion (17), indicates that the letter was written about 1763. Peter Miller, the likely author of the preface, may have withheld publication of these two letters until Georg Adam Martin's death in 1794. In the letters, Beissel blesses Martin and the Antietam congregation as the heirs to his work at Ephrata. However, Miller succeeded Beissel at Ephrata.

127. *LuW*, 10:23–24.

128. *GdP*, 1:404–5; Wallmann, *Philipp Jakob Spener*, 338–39; Thune, *Behmenists*, 73–78.

129. Mack, Sr., *Writings*, 98–99. Mack preferred teaching "how to escape the wrath of God" over teaching that "eternal punishment has an end." See also Stoffer, *Background and Development*, 82, 95–96, and Michael L. Hodson, "A Historical Relationship: Brethren and Universalists, 1770–1790," *BLT* 22, no. 1 (Winter 1977): 33–41.

130. Christoph Schütz, *Güldene Rose oder ein Zeugnis der Wahrheit von der uns so nahe bevorstehenden Güldenen Zeit des tausend jährigen und ewigen Reichs Jesu Christi und der damit verbundenen Wiederbringung aller Dinge*, 2d ed. (n.p., 1731), 118–26.

131. *DE, Pars I*, 30–35.

132. *ZS*, 109: "werden gequälet werden von Ewigkeit zu Ewigkeit, in einem unauflößlichen Band der Schmerzen."

133. *DE, Pars I*, 320–40: "Sehr geheime u.[nd] von der Welt her verborgene Rätzel von der ewigen Mutter Kirchenzeit und Staat: und was es seyn wird, wann derselbe, nach ihrem langen Witwenstand wird offenbar werden."

134. Ibid., 321–22.

135. Ibid., 323: "wie der Thau aus der Morgenröthe."

136. Ibid., 326–27: "Dieses Kindes Landes-verweisung hat einen grosen Ruf gegeben in alle Lande."

137. Cf. *SS*, 4 (*Weg zu Christo*): 79–82, 103–4.

138. *DE, Pars I*, 326–28: "Dann deine Mutter, die dich verstosen, ist nicht des Manns rechtes Eheweib, sondern eine Feindselige, die den Mann mit List hat an sich gebracht" (327).

139. Ibid., 329: "noch nicht alt genug war, um Hochzeit zu halten."

140. Ibid., 330–33.

141. FLP B. Ms. 22, 167, 170: "Die Ausgiesung des Geistes geschiehet, als welcher Geist-Wein uns so truncken und sinnenlos machet, daß wir wohl dürffen in der Braut kammer geführet werden" (167).

142. *DE, Pars I*, 333–35: "Ein jungfräuliches Heer, gleich als im Vorspiel, sich gesammlet, einen Tantz an zu fangen, sich einander die Kräntze aufgebunden" (335).

143. Ibid., 335–37.

144. Ibid., 338: "welches eigentlich kein Feuer des Zorns und Gerichts ist, sonst hätte es wieder dergleichen erweckt; es ist vielmehr das jungfräuliche Feuer, das durchs Blut-schwitzen und hernach am Creutz erworben."

NOTES TO CHAPTER 2

145. Ibid., 339: "Ich solte mich nur fleisig im Verwerden meiner selbst üben, damit ich möchte das H.[eilige] unter sich sincken lernen, und also folglich selbst jungfräulich würde." The phrase "verwerden meiner selbst" is unusual in Ephrata literature, although the concept it expresses is familiar.

146. Ibid., 339-40: "und als mit einem paradisischen Licht-Flämmlein umgeben, gantz in sich verwandeln, u.[nd] weiblich machen, und zugleich mit einverleiben in ihren obern Jungfrauen-Chor, als welche allzusammen die Braut des Lamms ausmachen. Und so bald diese Zahl wird voll seyn, so wird freylich noch eine Hochzeit gehalten werden."

147. Ibid., 340: "wird der Herr unser Gott nur Einer seyn. . . . Jetzt ist auch meine Hochzeit gehalten, Amen Hallelujah."

148. *Chymische Hochzeit Christiani Rosencreutz. Anno 1459* (Strasbourg, 1616). Ezechiel Foxcroft's 1690 English translation was reprinted in Paul M. Allen, ed., *A Christian Rosencreutz Anthology* (New York: Rudolph Steiner, 1968), 68f. For a concise summary of the tale, see Frances A. Yates, *The Rosicrucian Enlightenment* (Chicago: University of Chicago Press, 1972; rpt. New York and London: Routledge & Kegan Paul, 1986), 59-64.

CHAPTER 2. THE RELIGIOUS THOUGHT OF EPHRATA: OTHER WRITERS

1. *CE*, 113. Beissel expelled Israel Eckerlin in 1745. Only two lengthy manuscripts of allegedly many writings by Eckerlin are extant. They show that despite his conflict with Beissel, the two agreed on many significant religious matters. Eckerlin later held a quietist critique of the ritual life of the community, which Ezechiel Sangmeister also adopted. Because most of Israel Eckerlin's writings were lost or destroyed, the two manuscripts do not figure greatly in this book.

2. *LuW*, 9:63-64. Sachse stated without documentation that Hildebrand attended the first Brethren love feast in America in 1723: *German Sectarians*, 1:91. Brumbaugh accepted this also (*German Baptist Brethren*, 147, 159), as did John S. Flory, who claimed that Hildebrand was among the first Brethren to immigrate to America. See his *Literary Activity of the German Baptist Brethren in the Eighteenth Century* (Elgin, Ill.: Brethren Publishing House, 1908), 222. Neither Brumbaugh nor Flory provided documentation for his claims. George N. Falkenstein's history of the Germantown congregation, *The German Baptist Brethren or Dunkers* (Lancaster: Pennsylvania-German Society, 1900), 34, merely quoted Sachse on the matter.

3. *CE*, 100: "einer der ersten Erweckten dieses Jahrhunderts."

4. *LuW*, 4:22, 21. Jane Evans Best noted that in 1733 Hildebrand patented 166 acres on Mill Creek at present-day South Groffdale Road. He purchased the land from Simon König (King), who also sold land to Christopher Sauer, Sr., that year. See Best, "Turmoil in Conestoga," 8. See also *German Sectarians*, 2:126-27. Sachse claimed Hildebrand bought 168.5 acres. This is probably a misreading of the map of König's land sales, which Sachse included on p. 125. The map itself seems to indicate 166 acres.

5. *German Sectarians*, 1:133-34. See also *CE*, 100. Sachse claimed that the disagreement was over the Sabbath, but offered no support. S. R. Zug et al., *History of the Church of the Brethren of the Eastern District of Pennsylvania* (Lancaster: New Era, 1915), 324, 327, claimed that Hildebrand was the first deacon, not pastor. The 250th anniversary booklet prepared by the Conestoga Church of the Brethren provides no helpful information on Hildebrand's life. See Anniversary Committee, *Conestoga Church of the Brethren: Two Hundred Fiftieth Anniversary, 1724-1974* (Lancaster: Forry & Hacker, 1974).

6. *LuW*, 4:23-24, 32. The published version of the *Chronicon* omitted any mention of Hildebrand's association with Beissel's congregation before Hildebrand, as an "apostate," returned to the Conestoga congregation of Dunkers. Hildebrand was obviously troublesome to Ephrata.

7. "Brother Kenan's Notebook," 17. See also HSP Ac. 1926, p. 7 (in first section). These two notices of Margaretha Hildebrand Mack's death confirm that Margaretha was the wife of Valentin Mack. The *Chronicon* conflates her with Hildebrand's daughter Maria. Sangmeister's excerpt of the *Chronicon* manuscript names a daughter, Eusebia, who left to marry. See *LuW*, 4:29. The *Chronicon* mentions a Sister Abigail, supposedly a daughter of Hildebrand, as one of the first four female virgins to live in Kedar in 1735, who left

NOTES TO CHAPTER 2

and married. It is impossible that this Sister Abigail was the later wife of Valentin Mack, as the *Chronicon* claims, because Valentin and Margaretha Mack had a three-year-old daughter in 1735, when Kedar was opened. All the scholarship, significantly Sachse, Brumbaugh, and Flory, has conflated these names and persons, and should be disregarded in this respect. At this point, the identity of Sister Abigail awaits further research. "Brother Kenan's Notebook," 39, and HSP Ac. 1926, pp. 13 (of section 1) and 22 (of section 2), all list Constantia's death in 1782. Both documents give her age as 50, putting her birth in 1732.

8. *LuW*, 4:38. Sachse claimed both 1738 and 1739 as the date for Hildebrand's return to Ephrata. See *German Sectarians*, 1:353 (for 1738) and 281 and 377 (for 1739).

9. *LuW*, 9:64. See also *CE*, 100: "tiefe Einsichten in Jacob Boehms Schrifften." John S. Flory, an early twentieth-century Brethren scholar, claimed that Hildebrand, like others who followed Beissel, believed that Christianity was "merely a matter of the spirit," and had difficulty holding to "a rational, consistent basis of Christian faith and practice." See Flory, *Literary Activity*, 220–21. Flory sought to recast the Brethren as progressive rationalists.

10. *CE*, 129. Hildebrand wrote *Schrifftmässiges Zeuchnüß* as "still another supplement" (noch einen Zusatz) to his anti-Moravian works. In this one he argued that "the married state originated in the fall of mankind" (dass der Ehestand seinen Urstand vom Fall des Menschen hätte). For the second printing of *Eine Ruffende Wächterstimme* in Württemberg, see *Das Heutige Signal, Oder Posaunen-Schall!* (Ephrata: John Ruth, 1812), 27. I am grateful to Don Durnbaugh for reminding me of the importance of this source for Hildebrand. The critique of congregations appeared in Johannes Hildebrand, *Ein Gespräch zwischen einem Jüngling und einem Alten von dem Nutzen in Gottseeligen Gemeinschafften* (Germantown: Christopher Saur, 1754). The book on comets is discussed in Chapter 7.

11. *German Sectarians*, 1:354. In the same place he argued that Beissel taught "Rosicrucian doctrine pure and undefiled," without documenting the claim. Ernst depended on and embellished Sachse; see *Ephrata*, 129–30. Alderfer depended on Sachse and Ernst; see *Ephrata Commune*, 69–71. Peter Erb believed it possible that the Zionitic Brotherhood based its views and rites on Masonic and Rosicrucian literature; see *MHT*, 31–32, 52. Leo Schelbert repeated Sachse's view, alleging that the Zionitic Brotherhood represented an unspecified hermetic tradition differing from Beissel's Sophiological piety. See Leo Schelbert, "Die Ausformung von Konrad Beissels Ephrata Gemeinschaft im Widerstreit geistlicher Traditionen 1735–1745," *Eberbacher Geschichtsblätter* 90 (1991): 41–54, esp. 42–44. Klein seems not to have followed Sachse on this point; see Klein, *Johann Conrad Beissel*, 138–39, 151–64. Seidensticker knew nothing of Masonic rites practiced by the Eckerlins or the Zionitic Brotherhood; see *Klostergeschichte*, 115–23.

12. Johannes Hildebrand, *Wohlgegründetes Bedencken der Christlichen Gemeine in und bey Ephrata Von dem Weg Der Heiligung, Wie derselbe nicht allein in der Versöhnung Christi, sondern Hauptsächlich in seiner Nachfolge zu suchen. Ingleichem. Von der Verführung, da Fleisch und Blut sich zur Ungebühr des Versöhn-Opfers Jesu Christi anmaßt. Auf begehren etlicher Freunde ans Licht gebracht durch Johannes Hildebrand. Bey veranlassung Eines von der so genannten Herrenhutischen Gemeine erhaltenen Briefs* (Germantown: Christoph Saur, 1743), 9–10.

13. *CE*, 129: "Zuchtlosen Leben und fleischlichen Bekehrsucht."

14. See *German Sectarians*, 2:70. Flory, however, attributed the authorship to Hildebrand, but without stating his reasons: *Literary Activity*, 223. Cf. Seidensticker, *Klostergeschichte*, 84–85, 111–12. Seidensticker reiterated Hildebrand's authorship of the *Schrifftmässiges Zeuchnüß*, but he stated that the authorship of the *Mistisches und Kirchliches Zeuchnüß* was unknown. Doll and Funke claimed that Seidensticker positively identified Hildebrand as the author; see *Ephrata Cloisters*, 44.

15. *CE*, 129: "Einen Anhang, der nicht wehniger beissend war."

16. *MKZ*. I have translated from the original. The translation in *MHT* by Elizabeth Sauer is faulty at several points. The headings are as follows: (1) "Von Gott und dem Fall des Menschen" (3–5); (2) "Von der Ausbreitung des Menschen-Baums und der Kirche des alten Bundes" (5–8); (3) "Von Christo Jesu/dem Mittler. des neuen Bundes" (8–10); (4) "Von der Christlichen Kirche" (11–13); (5) "Von den zweyerley Ständen in der Kirche" (13–17); (6) "Von dem Kirchen-Regiment" (17–19); (7) "Von der Unterwerffung und Schul-Zucht" (19–22); and the final heading, "Von der ersten Erweckung von Buße und Glauben [etc.] und dem Rathschluss Gottes über den abgefallenen Menschen" (23–24).

NOTES TO CHAPTER 2

17. Ibid., 3. I have cited the German to make clearer the association with Tauler. I would translate as follows: "God is a unified One, an incomprehensible No-thing, an inapprehensible, invisible being." The passage continues, "God cannot be known, understood or comprehended" (das weder erkant noch verstanden noch begriffen mag werden). For one possible source in Tauler, see his *Predigten,* 395. Cf. *ZS,* 31.

18. *MKZ,* 3–4: "Ihm die Weissheit als sein Fräulein zugesellet wurde. . . . So ist sein Aug durch allzu starcke Imagination verunreiniget worden. Da verliess ihn Jungfrau Sophia dann Ihr keusches Ehebett ward besudelt"; "Der Abfall muste in seiner innersten Essentz u.[nd] Wurtzel offenbart werden. . . . Darum liess Gott den Versuchungs-Baum in einer zerbrechlichen Frucht Gut und Böß aufwachsen." Cf. Beissel's *Dissertation* in *DE, Pars I,* 9–10, 15–17.

19. *MKZ,* 5: "Ringe-Rad der sechs Tage . . . denselben auf eine besondere Weise gesegnet." The other quotation reads: "Bis daß die ängstliche Geburt der sechs Tagwerck der Kinder Gottes wird aufgelöset und in denselben Sabbath verwandelt seyn." The reference to "the same Sabbath" (*denselben Sabbath*) refers to the seventh day as a precious gift of grace, as mentioned above. The double meaning of labor at birth and the six working days reinforces Ephrata's view of the sinfulness of reproduction as well as of working on the seventh day. The translation of this passage in Erb's sourcebook (*MHT*) is completely wrong.

20. *SS,* 7:104.

21. *MKZ,* 7: "In dem Fall des Menschen der grimmige Feuer-Qual war entzündet worden." See also *TP,* 5:3433. "Das Melchisedechische Priestertum ist ewig . . . es ist gestiftet und mit dem Liebes-Feuer, nicht wie die Aaronische mit dem Zorn-Feuer angezündet wird."

22. *MKZ,* 7. Unfortunately, Sauer's translation in *MHT* inserts a phrase that is not present in the original, blaming the serpent for Adam's fall. The *Mistisches und Kirchliches Zeuchnüß* blames Adam's fall on his speculation on the animals' genders. The error creates a mistaken impression that the *Mistisches und Kirchliches Zeuchnüß* differs from Beissel's *Dissertation* on this point, which is not the case.

23. *Contemporaries,* 73. Johann Adam Gruber's 1730 comment (p. 3) that the celibates rejected "unnecessary goods and animals" may corroborate the tradition that no animal labor was used for a period. Further support comes from a 1739 letter by Stephan Koch, summarized by Max Goebel, which claimed that the community lived by farming, which "they carried out only with the hoe and without draft animals." See Goebel, *Geschichte des christlichen Lebens,* 3:265.

24. Michael S. Showalter, "'And We, the Fathers of Families . . . ': A Study of the Householders of the Ephrata Cloister," *JHSCV* 13 (1988): 20. Showalter showed that Jacob Gorgas, his son of the same name, and some other householders fought in the American Revolution.

25. Anthony Benezet, *Eine kurtze vorstellung des theils von Africa, Welches bewohnt wird von Negroes* (Ephrata: Drucks der Societät, 1763). For information on Kimmel, see the supplement to "Ephrata Cloister Interpretation Manual: A Guide to the Interpretation of the Ephrata Cloister," unpublished manual of site interpretation (Ephrata: Pennsylvania Historical and Museum Commission, Ephrata Cloister, 1993). I am grateful to Clarence Spohn for pointing this work out to me.

26. *MKZ,* 8: "Soll aber Christus nach dem inwendigen Verständnus des Geistes in uns auferstehen, so muß er erst nach dem buchstäblichen Erkäntnuß an uns gecreutzigt werden."

27. Hildebrand, *Wohlgegründetes Bedencken,* 6: "Ich sterbe täglich, also büsset man auch täglich und wird mit Christo vollkommen gemacht."

28. *MKZ,* 9–10: "Der Sohn des lebendigen Gottes . . . das ausgedrückte Bild seines Wesens . . . hat seine Himmlishce Menschheit mit unserer Menschheit überkleidet. Sein heiliges Opfer am Creutz vollendet, ist darauf mit seiner erworbenen Versöhnungs-Krafft hinunter gefahren, denen Geistern im Gefängnuß zu predigen, und endlich von den Todten wieder aufgestanden, gen Himmel gefahren, und hat die Kirche des alten Bundes aufgelöset."

29. Ibid., 10: "Dann nun war Adams Riß wieder geheilet, und die Weißheit gieng in die offene Seite ihres Jungfräulichen Manns Jesu wieder ein." Unfortunately, in *MHT* Sauer mistranslated *Weißheit* as "knowledge," when it is obviously a technical term as it is used repeatedly in Ephrata literature. Sauer omitted the phrase "open side" and mistranslated "virginal husband" (*jungfräulicher Mann*) as "Jesus, born

NOTES TO CHAPTER 2

of a virgin." The full sentence should read thus: "The outpouring of the Holy Spirit followed, and in this outpouring, the divine birthing work was done in a quite special manner, which could now happen for the first time: Adam's cleft [or tear] was healed, and Wisdom entered again into the open side of her virginal husband, Jesus." I am grateful for Don Yoder's suggestion to translate *Riß* as "cleft." Literally it means a rip or a tear, but in reference to the wound in Jesus' side, "cleft" is more poetic.

30. Ibid., 11.

31. *ZS*, 126. See also Beysell, *Mystyrion Anomias*, 20–21. Cf. *DE, Pars I*, 336, 340.

32. *MKZ*, 11: "Sonst bleibet die Kirche ein Jungfräuliches Weib und ihr Man ist Christus Jesus, derselbe hat sie bey seiner Creutzigung in seine offne Seite eingenommen, und in Ihm wird Sie fruchtbar, daß Sie kan ihr Kinder ausgebären."

33. Ibid., 12: "In so weit wir nun in derselben heilige [*sic*] Zucht und Schrancken gebracht, in so weit erkennen wir uns auch zu seyn Glieder derselben." The translation in *MHT* is obscured by errors.

34. Ibid., 13: "Auch braucht sie unsers treibenden Manns-willens nicht zu ihrer Besamung, sintemal sie schon ihr männliches Feuer und Samen in sich hat . . . wir werden der mystischen Schwängerung theilhafftig, in welcher unser unter sich gesunckener Manns-Wille weiblich wird."

35. FLP B. Ms. 22, Free Library of Philadelphia, fol. 153: "müssen wir unsren selbst-würckenden und feuer mannlichen Manns-willen bringen in ein sencken, und gewißer maaßen weiblich werden." The letter was dated 20th of the 3d month, 1756.

36. *MKZ*, 13: "man hat genug an seinem eigenen Land zur Frucht und Ackerbau." Cf. [Beissel], *Mystische und sehr geheyme Sprueche*, 5, 7 (nos. 14 and 32, respectively).

37. *MKZ*, 13–15: "weil er noch nicht durch das Joch der Welt verstrickt ist" (14). *Stände* are not "positions," as Sauer mistranslated.

38. Ibid., 15–16: "eine Zucht-Ordnung über den abgefallenen Menschen" (15); "daß es bey Gottseeligen Ehleuten, wann sie anderst in ihrem Beruff treulich fortfahren, nothwendig vorkomme, daß dieser Stand wieder muß aufgelöset werden" (16).

39. *CE*, 65, 108, 133–34.

40. *Contemporaries*, 6.

41. *MKZ*, 17–18: "Melchisedechische Priester-Ordnung in der Kirche des neuen Bundes unter der Führung des Ober Hohen Priesters Jesu Christi" (17).

42. *TP*, 2:899: "von Gottes Geist selbst erlernet und empfangen haben"; 5:3851: "Ein Melchisedechischer Priester muß der Gleichheit Christi in seinem niedrigen Stand gleichförmig werden und der Welt Sünden tragen, und ohn Unterlaß mit Aufopferung seiner Seelen für alle Menschen den Zorn Gottes in der Creatur versöhnen und transmutiren"; 2:1091: "Diese Priester haben Jesum angezogen und wandeln in Mysterio."

43. *MKZ*, 19–20: "samt allem, was wir sind und haben, wieder in Unterwerffung an Gott bringen. Dann in der Kirche wird dieselbe aufs höchst tractirt. Hier ist eine gantze Monarchia zu zerbrechen, samt so viel Machten und Obrigkeiten" (19); "Aber sein Reich, weil es in der tiefesten Erniedrigung stehet, vermag nicht zu fallen" (20).

44. *ZS*, 61–62. Since the epistles were printed in 1745, one could wonder if Beissel borrowed from the confession of faith. While not impossible, this seems unlikely.

45. Hildebrand, *Schrifftmässiges Zeuchnüß*, 6–7. See the letter by Anna Thoma to Hieronimus d'Annoni reporting the death of her mother in 1742, "in the twelfth month," in Leo Schelbert, "On the Power of Pietism: A Documentary on the Thommens of Schaefferstown," in *Historic Schaefferstown Record* 18, no. 4 (October 1984): 59. Schelbert forgot to adjust for the calendar change. Hildebrand gives the exact date as "the first day of the twelfth month called February of this year." That dates the composition of the treatise to 1743.

46. Ibid., 7: "Die sich als reine geduldige Lämmer zum täglichen Schlachtopfer freywillig hingeben bis zum völligen mortificiren ihres alten thierischen Menschen." See *SS*, 4 (*De incarnatione verbi*): 120–76.

47. Hildebrand, *Schrifftmässiges Zeuchnüß*, 5, 7. See *SS*, 4 (*De incarnatione verbi*): 26–29. Boehme rehearsed this account in other works as well.

NOTES TO CHAPTER 2

48. Hildebrand, *Schrifftmässiges Zeuchnüß*, 3: "Ferner, wie er durch Betrachtung der in den Thieren in zweyerley Geschlechte zertheilten Eigenschafften in ihren Vermehrungs-Tincturen einen so grossen Unterscheid [*sic*] gesehen: So entstund in ihm durch Verwunderung im Anschauen derselben eine Magische Subtile Lust, eine solche Gehüllffin zur Vermehrung um sich zu haben."

49. Ibid., 9, 8: "Diese Rippe war die starcke Magische weibliche Kraft in Adam, oder seine ihm eingepflantzte und angeschaffene Jungfräuliche Matrix. . . . Es war die Helffte [*sic*] der Adamischen Menschheit, Adams Rosen-Garten und seine Weiblichkeit, dadurch er hätte können ausgebähren ohne auswendige Beyhülfe" (9).

50. Ibid., 19: "Dann sie beyde hatten noch die Himmlische Jungfrau in ihnen; aber getheilet in zwey Bildnisse." See *SS*, 4 (*De incarnatione verbi*): 46–49.

51. For Boehme, see *SS*, 4 (*De incarnatione verbi*): 30–31, 37, 50; and 4 (*Der Weg zu Christo*): 121–22: "bestial organs for reproduction and the stinking stomach" (thierischen Glieder zur Fortpflanzung und den stinkenden Madensack [*sic*]). Cf. Hildebrand, *Schrifftmässiges Zeuchnüß*, 10–11, 19: "so seynd ihre starcke magische geistliche Leibes-Kräfte durch die Impression in harte Knochen verwandelt worden"(11); "Da sie einen nacketen [*sic*] thierischen Leib, und stinckenden Speise-Sack und Vermehrungs-Glieder bekommen hatten" (19).

52. Hildebrand, *Schrifftmässiges Zeuchnüß*, 10–11: "Gottes Gebähren ist . . . nicht aus dem unterstern irrdischen stinckenden und verwesenlichen Bauch wie die Thiere" (10); "weil es nach Art der Thiere war, gleich wie es auch vor Gottes Heiligkeit ein Eckel ist" (11). Cf. *TP*, 1:302: "am Hindertheil der Thiere die Schaam und Venae spermaticae ligen, und Gott uns lehren wollen, daß Er an unseren thierischen Gliedern kein Gefallen habe." Cf. Beissel, *ZS*, 194: "daß es vor Gottes heiligen Augen ein Eckel sey."

53. Hildebrand, *Schrifftmässiges Zeuchnüß*, 11: "ist Ihm also im Schlaf seine himmlische jungfräuliche Matrix wieder erbauet."

54. Ibid., 8: "So ward die Empfängnuß und Gebährung im Geist in Jungfräulicher Krafft wieder ersetztet und ward Weg gemacht, daß eine geistliche Jungfräuliche Menschheit wieder konte ausgebohren werden aus dem in Liebe brennenden Hertzen Jesu Christi." For Boehme's emphasis on the wound in Christ's side as a sign of appeasing God's wrath, see *SS*, 4 (*De incarnatione verbi*): 49, and all of Part II. Cf. Hildebrand's emphasis on gender balance in *Schrifftmässiges Zeuchnüß*, 11, and *MKZ*, 12–13.

55. Hildebrand, *Schrifftmässiges Zeuchnüß*, 15–17. A pagination error occurs here, with two pages numbered 15. The second p. 15 has the account of the kidneys: "Dann die Nieren sind das zweyte Hertz, woraus die Kraft zur Leibwerdung herkommt, dahero sind es zwey Nieren eine in einer Männlichen, die ander [*sic*] in einer Weiblichen Eigenschafft."

56. Ibid., 12: "Nun stehet sein Hertz der Liebe in seiner eröffneten Seite weit offen, und ziehet Er mit vollem Liebes-Zug in voller Kraft in unserm Hertzen an uns: Dann Er will uns in sich einnehmen und uns nach Gottes Bilde in Ihm wieder neugebähren."

57. Ibid., 15 (the second p. 15): "Dann die Milch-Brüste stehen am Ober-Leib fornen vor dem Hertzen, anzuzeigen, daß des Menschen wahre Nahrung müsse aus der Brust Jesu, und aus seiner hertzlichen Liebe gesogen werden."

58. Ibid., 13: "Ihr braucht keine solche harte Sprünge und selbst-erwählte Leidens-Processe zu unternehmen, das Lamm hat solches alles für euch gethan." Here Hildebrand paraphrased the Moravian position, which he rejected in his argument for identifying experientially with Christ's death. *Process* can also refer to a chemical reaction, alluding to alchemical metaphors for rebirth.

59. See a concise and accurate analysis in Peter Vogt, "Zinzendorf und die Pennsylvanihcen Synoden 1742," *Unitas Fratrum* 36 (December 1994): 23, 31–32, 54–55. For a detailed analysis of the disagreements and polemics, see Peter Vogt, "The Moravian Theory and Practice of Marriage (*Ehereligion*) as Point of Contention in the Conflict between Ephrata and Bethlehem," and Jeff Bach, "Ephrata and Moravian Relations: The View from Ephrata," both in *Communal Studies* 21 (2001).

60. FLP B. Ms. 22, p.161. See also *ZS*, 195–96.

61. Johannes Hildebrand, Ephrata, to Christoff Saur and Alexander Mack, Dec. 20, 1759, Cassel Collection, MS 48, Juniata College Library, Huntingdon, Pa.

NOTES TO CHAPTER 2

62. Johannes Hildebrand, *Ein Gespräch zwischen einem Jüngling und einem Alten von dem Nutzen in Gottseeligen Gemeinschafften* ([Germantown: Christoph Saur], 1754), 7: "Und wird durch sein gnädiges Wort das neue Samen-Körnlein zu einem neuen göttlichen Leben ... [die Seele] von diesem göttlichen Samen schwanger ist worden.... Darum wird Gott und Christi Geist sich nun und dan in dir in deiner Seele in dieser neuen Menschheit offenbahren."

63. Ibid., 5: "Dan die andern Mitglieder der Gemeine, ob sie schon dasselbe in Ihnen haben, so können sie ihr nichts davon mittheilen."

64. Ibid., 4: "Dan die Gemeinschafft bestehet in äusserlichen sichtbahren leiblichen Mitgliedern, als Menschen, die man sehen kan; Aber Gottes und Christi Geist ist unsern leiblichen Augen unsichtbar: Er wohnet zwar in jedem wahren Mitgliede der Gemeine geheim im verborgenen Grund der Seelen."

65. Ibid., 9: "Dan die reine Liebe Gottes, wo sie ist, da ist sie ein solches Band, das die Seelen unzertrennlich verbindet mit der gantzen Kirche, die von Abel an gewesen bisher ... ja noch in den Ewigkeiten die wahre seyn wird, daß keine äussere Form, Ceremonie oder Handschrifft so fest verbinden kan."

66. Sangmeister's baptismal record and name, taken from the "Kirchenbuch der evangelischen-lutherischen Kirchengemeinde Beddingen, Jahrgang 1723," 79, are cited in Wust, *Saint-Adventurers*, 112, where Sangmeister's naturalization record is also cited.

67. *LuW*, 5:65–70, 8:147–48. See also Wust, *Saint-Adventurers*, 40–54.

68. Felix Reichmann, "Ezechiel Sangmeister's Diary," *PMHB* 68 (1944): 292–313.

69. Wust, *Saint-Adventurers*, 66–75. See also Clarence E. Spohn, "The Historical Significance of the Writings of Ezechiel Sangmeister," *JHSCV* 13 (1988): 41–54.

70. *Heutige Signal*, 30. The *Signal* indicated that Sangmeister's writings were extant, still in manuscript.

71. *LuW*, 5:77, 6:25, 45.

72. Ezechiel Sangmeister, *Mystische Theologie, oder Wahrer Wegweiser nach unserem Ursprung und Vaterland* (Ephrata: Joseph Bauman, 1819–1820), 155–56. He described mystical experiences of the soul leaving the body during prayer.

73. *GdP*, 1:415–16, 434n189 (see also Erb, *Pietists, Protestants, and Mysticism*, 37, 98); T. A. Birrell, "English Catholic Mystics in Non-Catholic Circles, II," *Downside Review* 315 (April 1976): 99–105. Birrell helpfully shows the connections between continental and English Catholic mystical literature, circulating in part through networks of the Philadelphian movement in England and Germany.

74. Koch and Rissmann corresponded with Tersteegen. See Gerhard Tersteegen, letter to unknown addressee [at Ephrata?], May 14, 1752, in "Copies of Letters, etc.," Miscellaneous Manuscripts, Cassel Collection, Ac. 188, Historical Society of Pennsylvania, Philadelphia. Tersteegen greeted Koch and Rissmann by name, indicating that he had received letters from them. For Philemon's identity being Rissmann, see Durnbaugh, *Brethren in Colonial America*, 605.

75. *LuW*, 5:104, 73, 80; 6:10; 7:67, 84; 8:126–27.

76. Brother Philemon [Johann Conrad Rissmann], untitled, paginated copybook of excerpts, Muddy Creek Farm Library, Denver, Pa. I am especially grateful to Clarence Spohn for calling this manuscript to my attention during the time it was deaccessioned from the Dauphin County Library in Harrisburg, and to Amos Hoover, proprietor of the Muddy Creek Farm Library, for generous permission to work with the volume. "Bro. Philemon" appears on the inside cover, and the subsequent writing appears to be in the same hand. A brief note on p. 2 explains that the excerpts were taken from a "book of pure letters" printed in Leipzig, Saxony, in 1730. The copybook is divided into two parts, the first of 176 numbered pages, the second of 200 numbered pages. Pages 114–16 are typical of many copied passages counseling a silent, interior life in order to find God's presence.

77. *LuW*, 5:95–96; 8:144; 5:83, 104.

78. Ibid., 5:67.

79. Sangmeister, *Mystische Theologie*, 8, 37.

80. Ibid., 9–11: "Sie finden den Herrn im Grunde des Hertzen." Sangmeister may have been inspired by Gottfried Arnold's *Die Abwege oder Irrungen und Versuchungen gutwilliger und frommer Menschen, aus Beystimmung des gottseeligen Alterthums* (Frankfurt am Main: Thomas Fritschen, 1708). Arnold cited authors

from Christian antiquity to defend the moderation of his earlier leanings toward asceticism. Sangmeister apparently drew on little, if any, of Arnold's material.

81. Sangmeister, *Mystische Theologie,* 14: "inwendigen, züchtenden Gnade"; 15: "Babel stürmen."

82. Ibid., 16–17: "die Schrifften der Heiligen als eine grosse Gabe von Gott" and "den Menschen inwendig treiben" (17).

83. Ibid., 18–20, 23: "Und weilen sie selbsten keine Bestrafung in Liebe auf sich kommen lassen, zu ihrer Besserung, so bestrafen sie auch niemanden in Liebe."

84. Ibid., 24: "Diese Seelen welche einmahl von Gott in der dürren Wüsten und Einde gefunden worden, sind durch viel Jammer und Elend gegangen.... Solche Seelen halten sich zu denen Stillen im Lande ... und sind gerne verborgen und unbekannt." For Brother Ezechiel's use of mystics as models, see also *LuW,* 7:67.

85. Sangmeister, *Mystische Theologie,* 35–52.

86. Ibid., 100–101, 103–4.

87. Ibid., 105–7: "beyden Tincturen, männlich und weiblich."

88. Ibid., 115: "O mein Jesu, Gebäre du dich neu in uns." For the fifth epoch, see 117–19.

89. Ibid., 121: "die Menschen dem thierischen Leben abfallen wurden."

90. Ibid., 121–22: "sie nach seinem Bilde gebähren" (121); "in ihren leiblichen Leben wird die Natur gecreutziget durch tägliches sterben" (121); "die von Gott geboren" (122); "sie haben männlein und fräulein in einer Person" (122).

91. Ibid., 123: "ein Tausendjährigen Sabbath, zum Vorbilde der Ewigen Ruhe seyn möge ... daß alles was in Adam verloren war, nun wiederum neugeboren worden."

92. Ibid., 126–30: "um in einer magischen Weise zu gebären" (128); "Die Liebe Jesu besänfftiget das Manns-Feuer tausendmal und macht es sinkend, vielmehr als alle Weiblichkeit von aussen" (128).

93. Ibid., 131–40.

94. *LuW,* 5:71–73.

95. Ibid., 10:15.

96. Ibid., 5:74, 76; 7:55; 10:61. For his moderation, see Sangmeister, *Mystische Theologie,* 144: "I eat, drink, and sleep, etc. like others" (ich esse, trincke und schlafe, etc. wie anderen), he wrote, but claimed that grace had subordinated his nature. This last quotation comes actually from a brief autobiography that he attached to *Mystische Theologie.*

97. The two Kelp brothers were both named Johann Adam; the younger was sometimes known as Jonathan and the older as Adam. For the deaths of the Kelps, see Clarence E. Spohn, "The Kelp/Kölb Family of the Cocalico Valley," *JHSCV* 18 (1993): 37–39. For the death of Sister Melania, see "Rose," 386.

98. *Contemporaries,* 103–4. Brother Ezechiel noted in his autobiography both his desire to maintain a house fellowship and the brothers' agitation to abandon the special habit.

99. Spohn, "Kelp/Kölb Family," 38. Spohn cited the will of Johann Adam Kölb the elder, which mentioned that his house was located on Mount Zion at Ephrata.

CHAPTER 3. "HOLY CHURCH PRACTICES": RITUAL AT EPHRATA

1. *MKZ,* 18.

2. Seidensticker, *Klostergeschichte,* 67–72. Seidensticker tried to fit Ephrata's ritual life into a Protestant model of sacraments consisting of baptism, Lord's Supper, and sermon. His model ignores the rich meanings of Ephrata's ritual life.

3. Miri Rubin, *Corpus Christi: The Eucharist in Late Medieval Culture* (Cambridge: Cambridge University Press, 1991), 6–7. See also Clifford Geertz, *The Interpretation of Cultures* (New York: Basic Books, 1973), 90–94.

4. See Edwards, *Materials toward a History of the American Baptists,* vol. 1, cited in Durnbaugh, *Brethren in Colonial America,* 174. Edwards listed these as the ritual practices of the Brethren.

5. Durnbaugh, *European Origins*, 128–29, 133, 142, 149, 150. Dompelaars were also an immersionist sect in northern Germany and the United Provinces at the time. See Dennis L. Slabaugh, "Dunkers and Dompelaars," in *From Age to Age: Historians and the Modern Church. A Festschrift for Donald F. Durnbaugh*, ed. David B. Eller, *BLT* 42, nos. 2–3 (Summer and Fall 1997): 68–116. See also "Dompelaars," in Harold S. Bender et al., eds., *The Mennonite Encyclopedia: A Comprehensive Reference Work on the Anabaptist-Mennonite Movement*, 5 vols. (Scottdale, Pa.: Herald Press, 1955–90).

6. Durnbaugh, *Brethren in Colonial America*, 173.

7. See Durnbaugh, *European Origins*, 111–13, 125–26, 127. In his 1702 confession of faith, Hochmann rejected only infant baptism. Had he gone further in questioning all outward baptism in favor of spirit baptism only, he would have jeopardized his release from prison. See Hochmann's *Glaubens-Bekänntniß*, reprinted in Renkewitz, *Hochmann von Hochenau*, 403–4.

8. Mack, Sr., *Writings*, 9–10. See also Durnbaugh, *Brethren Beginnings*, 21–23. For source documents, see Durnbaugh, *European Origins*, 110–50.

9. Mack, Sr., *Writings*, 10. See also Durnbaugh, *Brethren Beginnings*, 21–22, 55–57, for the argument that the foreigners were Dutch Collegiants and a list of Collegiants who later joined the Brethren.

10. Andrew C. Fix, *Prophecy and Reason: The Dutch Collegiants in the Early Enlightenment* (Princeton: Princeton University Press, 1991), 117, 145. In this excellent monograph Fix noted the possible influence of Polish Socinians on Collegiant immersion baptism. Alexander Mack, Sr., quoted from Jeremias Felbinger's *Christliches Hand-Büchlein*, a document associated with Polish Brethren literature and endorsing immersion baptism. For a discussion of this link, see Stoffer, *Background and Development*, 58–63. See also Durnbaugh, *Brethren Beginnings*, 28.

11. Mack, Sr., *Writings*, 10–13.

12. Ibid., 22–32.

13. Ibid., 47–48, 51–53.

14. Peter C. Erb, "The Brethren in the Early Eighteenth Century: An Unpublished Contemporary Account," *BLT* 22, no. 2 (Spring 1977): 107. Erb's translation is based on a typescript (the original is now lost) in the Schwenkfelder Library at Pennsburg, Pa. The account and the diary were published in Peter C. Erb, ed., *The Spiritual Diary of Christopher Wiegner* (Pennsburg, Pa.: Schwenkfelder Library, 1978), 96.

15. Durnbaugh, *European Origins*, 160.

16. *Contemporaries*, 70–71.

17. *CE*, 21.

18. Seidensticker, *Klostergeschichte*, 38; *German Sectarians* 1:98–100; Klein, *Johann Conrad Beissel*, 53, 56–57. See also Ernst, *Ephrata*, 51–52; Alderfer, *Ephrata Commune*, 40. The earlier Brethren historians Martin G. Brumbaugh and George Falkenstein simply quoted Sachse uncritically.

19. *CE*, 16–17.

20. *ZS*, 125: "sondern must [sic] dein Heil suchen in dem unschuldigen vergossenen Lämmleins-Blut, welche Seligkeit uns in dem Bunde der Gnaden durch das Wasser der Taufe vorgestellet wird."

21. John T. McNeill, *The History and Character of Calvinism* (Oxford: Oxford University Press, 1954, 1967), 226; *GdP*, 1:246, 409. Some of Neander's hymns also conveyed aspects of federal theology.

22. *SS*, 6 (*De Testamenta Christe*): 2:57: "ein Siegel des festen, ewigen Bundes Gottes."

23. *ZS*, 124: "Verächtern der äuseren [sic] Tauf."

24. *TP*, 1:302–3; *SS*, 6 (*De Testamenta Christi*): 22, 62–63, 36.

25. *ZS*, 116–17: "Nun ruhen alle Verheissungen des neuen Bundes auf dem Tode Jesu Christ. . . . So sind wir dann durch die Taufe mit Ihm zu gleichem Tod gepflantzet . . . in welchem die Verheissung zur neuen Auferstehung mit einem neuen Kraft-Leibe . . . geschiehet" (116); "durch die Taufe Jesu Christi zur Gleichförmigkeit seines Todes gebracht" (117). The date derives from a reference to Beissel's visit among the addressees "about fifteen years ago." Since the letter is addressed to acquaintances in Europe, the latest possible date of composition would be 1735, fifteen years after his emigration.

26. Ibid., 80: "Weil es dann demnach gantz wider die Ordnung des neuen Bundes ist, jemand zu taufen, der selbst sein Wort nicht darzu geben kann. . . . Und so taufet man alles hinweg ohne Ausnahm,

wenn auch Vater und Mutter samt dem Tauf-Paten mit einander in ihren Häusern in Neid und Zanck, in Zorn und Haß, in Feindschaft und Unzucht, in Hurerey u.[nd] Betrug und in Lügen leben." The letter's date comes from a reference to his conversion twenty-three years earlier (76) and his arrival in Pennsylvania "eighteen years ago" (81). Boehme had emphasized the importance of faith at baptism, but believed spiritually reborn parents could impart faith to infants. See *SS, 6 (De Testamenta Christi)*: 41–47. Beissel did not accept this view.

27. *SS, 6 (De Testamenta Christi)*: 38–39, 46: "Diese alle beydes die Eltern und Beysteher, als gläubiger Tauffer und Paten, wircken mit ihrem Glauben in des Kindes Eigenschaft, und reichen es mit ihrem Glauben dem Bunde Christi dar" (39). Boehme conceded that a child born of godly parents should eventually "put on such covenant" in its own right ("so soll es doch auch solchen Bund in eigener selbständiger Person, in seinem eignen Lebens-Willen, anziehen") (40). However, Boehme did not describe a ritual to mark this passage.

28. *ZS*, 70: "Und ist also kein ander Mittel, davon gereinigt zu werden, als durch den Glauben in Jesum Christum, und durch den neuen Gnaden-Bund in dem Wasser der Taufe bestätigt, allwo wir durch den Glauben in Jesum die Vergebung der Sünden erlangen."

29. Ibid., 70–71: "Allwo sich der Wille anfängt zu versencken in sein eigen Nichts und wird zweiffelhafftig an seinen guten Wercken. . . . In solchem Fall muß dem Menschen ein anderes Licht aufgehen . . . und bringet uns zur Taufe im Wasser, in welcher uns der Bund der Gnaden geöffnet wird durch das Wort des Vaters" (70). "Deswegen sagen wir auch ab in dem Wasser der Taufe, welches gleichsam den Bund der Gnaden in der neuen Auferstehungs-Kraft in sich hält, allem Leben und Lust des Lebens" (71).

30. Ibid., 73.

31. Ibid., 134, 165: "So werden wir . . . dreymal ins Wasser getaucht, als im Namen des Vaters und des Sohns und des H.[eiligen] Geistes, anzuzeigen, daß dieser auswendige Mensch nach allen drey Theilen müsse untergehen und gerichtet werden" (134).

32. Ibid., 181: "welches Wort magisch ist, u[nd] ein wesentliches Einsprechen in die gantze Menschheit, nach Geist, Seel und Leib." Beissel also referred to the word spoken by God consecrating the water of baptism and the covenant of God's grace in a manuscript letter to Wilhelm[us] Jung. See FLP B. Ms. 22, p. 221.

33. *SS, 6 (De Testamenta Christi)*: 28.

34. *ZS*, 134: "wir zeigen nur den Bund an, wie nemlich derselbe mit so gewaltigen und wichtigen Zeugen bestättiget wird."

35. *CE*, 130.

36. *DE, Pars I*, 20–23, 29–30, 33–34.

37. *ZS*, 175: "Der Ritter Christus Jesus als der andere Adam, wird uns schon noch zu unserer Braut helfen, welcher wir verlobet sind in dem Wasser der H.[eiligen] Taufe durch den Tod Adams am Creutz."

38. Peter Miller, undated manuscript letter in the Mühlenberg Papers, AFSt/M 4C3:49, Archives of the Franckesche Stiftungen, Halle, Germany, 244. I am indebted to Erika Passantino for calling this letter to my attention. The German text reads: "Die Taufe . . . beydes der Scheidbrief ist, den wir dem Geist dieser Welt geben, und auch das Ehe-Verlöbnuß, das wir mit Christo, unserm himmlischen Bräutigam, aufrichten."

39. *CE*, 41–42. See also *LuW* 4:42–43. Sangmeister criticized the repeated baptisms.

40. *CE*, 148, 163–64. Beissel himself was baptized more than once.

41. Ibid., 103. See also Seidensticker, *Klostergeschichte*, 71. Seidensticker merely quoted the *Chronicon*.

42. D. Michael Quinn, *Early Mormonism and the Magic World View* (Salt Lake City: Signature Books, 1987), 14, 80–81, 130–32. See also John L. Brooke, *The Refiner's Fire: The Making of Mormon Cosmology, 1644–1844* (Cambridge: Cambridge University Press, 1994), 64, 242–44. An earlier, confusing article is William L. Knecht, "Mysteries of the Kingdom: More or Less," *Brigham Young University Studies* 5 (Spring/Summer 1964): 231–40. First mention of this connection appeared in 1921 in the article by I. Woodbridge Riley, "Saints, Latter-Day," in James Hastings et al., eds., *Encyclopaedia of Religion and Ethics*, vol. 11 (New York: Scribner, 1921), 82–90. I am indebted to Donald F. Durnbaugh for calling my attention to the Riley and Knecht articles.

43. Arnold, *Unparteyische Kirchen- und Ketzer-Historie*, 1:61, 34.
44. Goebel, "Geschichte der wahren Inspirations-Gemeinden," *Zeitschrift für die Historische Theologie* 19 (1854): 399–406. See also Ulf-Michael Schneider, *Propheten der Goethezeit: Sprache, Literatur und Wirkung der Inspirierten* (Göttingen: Vandenhoeck & Ruprecht, 1995), 81–95. Schneider focuses particularly on the Inspirationist love feast of Oct. 20, 1715, in Büdingen as a special occasion and audience for ecstatic speech. The Inspirationists held the first and last of their five love feasts in Schwarzenau, the rest in Isenburg.
45. See a concise discussion of Ritschl in Wallmann, *Pietismus*, 8–9.
46. Gottfried Arnold, *Die Erste Liebe Der Gemeinen Jesu Christi, Das ist, Wahre Abbildung Der Ersten Christen* (Frankfurt am Main: G. Friedeburg, 1696), 519–23. See also Arnold, *Unparteyische Kirchen- und Ketzer-Historie*, 1:34, 61. "Das Abendmahl hielten sie täglich bey der Mahlzeit und sonderlich by ihren gemeinen Liebes-Mahlen. Dabey ihr Hauptzweck bloß auff die Gedachtnüß des Herrn und Verkündigung seines Todes gieng" (They held the Lord's Supper daily with their meals, especially with their common love feasts. Thereby their main purpose was the memorial of the Lord and the proclamation of his death) (34).
47. Mack, Sr., *Writings*, 61–62.
48. Ibid., 61–63.
49. *GdP*, 1:250, 268–69.
50. Menno Simons, *The Complete Writings of Menno Simons, c. 1496–1561*, trans. Leonard Verduyn, ed. J. C. Wenger (Scottdale, Pa.: Herald Press, 1956; rpt. 1984), 417, 1061.
51. Dirk Philipps was one of the first Anabaptists to present this twofold intepretation for the practice of foot washing. See Philipps, *Complete Writings*, 367–68.
52. The best historical summary of foot-washing practices and interpretations among Anabaptists remains Harold S. Bender's article "Footwashing" in *Mennonite Encyclopedia*. See also "Feetwashing" in *Brethren Encyclopedia*. Unfortunately this distinctive ritual has barely been treated in the body of Anabaptist studies, and has been similarly neglected in treatments of Brethren and Brethren in Christ groups.
53. John Roth, trans. and ed., *Letters of the Amish Division* (Goshen, Ind.: Mennonite Historical Society, 1991), 21, 98. Uli Ammann claimed that foot washing became an issue only after the division was under way. Neither Jacob Ammann nor the transplanted Swiss Anabaptists in the Palatinate who answered him mentioned the issue of foot washing in the division.
54. Ibid., 145–46.
55. *MKZ*, 18.
56. Ibid., 20; *CE*, 215, 254. On at least one occasion, Beissel and Rudolf Nägele, the former Mennonite minister, offered foot washing as an act of hospitality.
57. Charles Mifflin to his father, Dec. 23, 1769 (with letter of Oct. 2, 1769), Mifflin Family Papers, William L. Clements Library, University of Michigan, unpaginated manuscript. I am indebted to Michael Showalter for calling these letters to my attention.
58. Charles Mifflin to his father, Nov. 29, 1769, Mifflin Family Papers.
59. Some form of the double mode of foot washing was practiced by many Brethren congregations in the eighteenth and nineteenth centuries. A Brethren minister, D. P. Sayler, discovered during oral interviews in 1872 that virtually all Dunker congregations except the first one at Germantown used the double mode. Germantown and a group in western Illinois who had migrated from early Dunker settlements in the Carolinas used the single mode. In the single mode, one person washes and dries the feet of the member seated adjacent; that person then performs the ritual on the next seated member, and so on. In a three-way division of the Brethren tradition in 1880–82, the most conservative party, known as the Old German Baptist Brethren, retained the double mode, which they still observe. The other factions all adopted the single mode.
60. *Contemporaries*, 100, 136.
61. Ibid., 55–57.
62. *CE*, 224.
63. By the nineteenth century it was customary for each member, in passing the elements, to repeat a phrase based on 1 Cor. 10:16. For the bread, each member would say, "The bread which we break is the

communion of the body of Christ." For the cup, each would repeat, "The cup which we bless is the communion of the blood of Christ." When this practice began is not documented. Apparently Ephrata never observed it.

64. *CE*, 225: "weil sie davor hielten es müsse alles gleich seyn, und also keinen Vorzug oder gemajestätete Person wolten unter sich haben." Hark's English translation is faulty here.

65. *CE*, 168, 149. P. 149 recounts a brief time just before Israel Eckerlin's expulsion when Beissel allowed Israel to administer the elements, even to Beissel.

66. Miller, undated letter, in the Mühlenberg Papers, AFSt/M 4C3:49, Archives of the Franckesche Stiftungen, Halle, Germany, 245. The text reads: "Dann wer ist so unerfahren, daß er nicht wisse, was das Geheimnuß des Brodbrechens in sich habe; nemlich daß man durch dasselbe unter einander ein Leib wird." The translation is difficult because Miller assumes a group, but writes about the act in the third person singular. In this letter Miller referred to the Eucharist as the "Sacrament . . . of the holy body and blood of Christ" (Sacrament . . . des H.[eiligen] Leibs und Bluts Christi). I am indebted to Erika Passantino for calling this letter to my attention.

67. *MKZ*, 18. The sentence reads, "Auf dieselbe [i.e., Brotbrechung] muß gewiß Gott seine Gegenwart auf eine besondere Weise niedergelegt haben." Calling these practices a "seal on God's covenant" echoed some Reformed language, yet also drew on Boehme. See *SS*, 6 (*De Testamenta Christi*): 57.

68. *Contemporaries*, 3; *CE*, 50.

69. Schneider, *Propheten der Goethezeit*, 94.

70. *LuW*, 5:84, 4:14, 5:83–84. Sangmeister noted that had he counted all of the love feasts, there would have been "three times as much to report."

71. Ibid., 5:87, for love feasts by special invitation; 4:40; 10:39 for memorials after the deaths of important people. See *CE*, 62, 133, for love feasts to consecrate buildings.

72. *CE*, 75. The German reads: "alle Aemter verwalteten."

73. Victor Turner, *The Ritual Process: Structure and Anti-structure* (Ithaca, N.Y.: Cornell University Press, 1969), 96–97, 127–29, 131–33.

74. *CE*, 120–21; *LuW*, 4:39. According to Sangmeister, the *Chronicon* extolled the powers of prophecy that came on Wohlfahrt after he was anointed. Sangmeister reported that Samuel Eckerlin had confided that the anointing had no effect.

75. Arnold, *Unparteyische Kirchen- und Ketzer-Historie*, 1:61: "Eben dahin zielte auch der Kuß der Liebe und des Friedens damit sie vornemlich als denn und sonst zum öftern ihre Vereinigung bezeugten."

76. Rüdiger Mack, *Pietismus und Frühaufklärung an der Universität Gießen und in Hessen-Darmstadt* (Gießen: Justus-Liebig Universität Gießen, 1984), 218–19. Mack quoted from a deposition in the Solms-Laubach archives.

77. *CE*, 32. This reference to withholding the handshake and kiss from persons who had been banned appears in the context of the alienation between Germantown and Conestoga in 1728, just before the official division. The passage illustrates the practices of both Beissel's group and the Germantown group. See *LuW*, 4:25, where Sangmeister recounted the same story in his annotations to the now lost *Chronicon* manuscript.

78. Peter Nead, *Theological Writings on Various Subjects* (Dayton, Ohio: B. F. Ells, 1850), 135. Nead described the nineteenth-century Brethren practice of the holy kiss as "simply to touch with the lips."

79. *Contemporaries*, 72. Acrelius observed in 1753 that the Sabbatarians always addressed one another as "brother" and "sister" and that they "kiss each other when they meet."

80. *CE*, 101, 225. The second occasion was when Beissel consecrated Georg Adam Martin to minister at Antietam. The German phrase is *Auflegung der Hände* (laying on of hands).

81. Renkewitz, *Hochmann von Hochenau*, 117–25. References to the Priesthood of Melchizedek pervade Gichtel's correspondence. See, e.g., *TP*, 1:373, 417–19, 483; 2:899.

82. Goebel, "Geschichte der wahren Inspirations-Gemeinden," *Zeitschrift für die Historische Theologie* 20 (1855): 137.

83. *CE*, 94–100; *LuW*, 4:36–37.

NOTES TO CHAPTER 3

84. Klein, *Johann Conrad Beissel*, 98–99; Ernst, *Ephrata*, 147; Alderfer, *Ephrata Commune*, 75.

85. *TP*, 5:3690–91, 3:1879–89, 4:2624–25.

86. Michael Müller, untitled, undated manuscript leaf containing spiritual testimony, in Muddy Creek Farm Library, Denver, Pa. An English translation by Alan G. Keyser is available in "Michael Müller/Miller of Cocalico Township, Lancaster County, and His 'Debt Book' (1748–1786)," *JHSCV* 20 (1995): 1–2.

87. *CE*, 91, 101. The candidates included Brother Nehemia (a son of Ulrich Hagemann), Peter Miller (Brother Jaebez), and Israel Eckerlin's younger brother, Gabriel (Brother Jotham). Sangmeister reported that Israel came into the office of prior only after the death of Wohlfahrt. According to Sangmeister, Israel was elected and moved into Wohlfahrt's old room in Zion (*LuW*, 4:40).

88. *CE*, 207. Sangmeister recorded an "intense struggle" to succeed Beissel after his death. Jaebez reportedly won the struggle for the office. See *LuW*, 10:39.

89. Ibid., 59–61, 104–5, 222–23. Beissel instructed the Bermudian congregation to receive Martin as they would himself. See also *Contemporaries*, 183.

90. *ZS*, 197–98. Maria Eicher was the only woman who could have been considered an abbess when the letter was published, about 1745.

91. "Rose," 136–37. Portions of "Die Rose" appear in English translation in *German Sectarians*, 1:300–304 and 2:181–201, and also in *MHT*, 267–90. The latter translation depends partly on Sachse.

92. "Rose," 11, 79.

93. *CE*, 45. Sangmeister claimed that at Ephrata Maria Christina Saur had a "second husband," Jacob Weiss, whom she did not marry. She left Ephrata in 1744. See *LuW*, 4:30, 45. See also "Rose," 31, 79. For Sister Jael's succession, see *LuW*, 9:42.

94. Ann Kirschner arrived at this conclusion also, although she suggested that perhaps the sixth class, consisting of Sisters Athanasia and Paulina, may have organized the singing. See Ann Kirschner, "From Hebron to Saron: The Religious Transformation of an Ephrata Convent" (M.A. thesis, University of Delaware, 1995), 98. The organization of the brothers' orders before and after Eckerlin is unknown, because the alleged counterparts to "Die Rose" for the brothers, the so-called church books, are lost.

95. *LuW*, 4:39, 45–46. Cf. *CE*, 107. Hark's translation (126) erred by changing the singular "brother" who received tonsure along with Beissel and Israel Eckerlin to the plural "Brethren." This change creates the wrong impression of two occasions when the brothers received tonsures in the beginning. The original German states that their hair was cut (*die Haare abgeschnitten*) and the tonsure was cut (*eine Platte geschoren wurde*) and then the tonsure was made by shaving off a portion of the hair to create a smooth disk of scalp on top of the head. The translation of the *Chronicon* by Hark claims that Israel Eckerlin and Alexander Mack, Jr., were the two brothers whose complaints occasioned the first tonsure. Hark had no evidence, however, other than Israel Eckerlin's being the first to receive tonsure. See Lamech and Agrippa, *Chronicon Ephratense*, trans. Hark, 125–26. Sangmeister provides the names of the two as Brothers Eleasar and Timotheus. Until further evidence suggests differently, Sangmeister is probably more reliable. For the ritual renewing tonsure, see *LuW*, 4:46.

96. Seidensticker, *Klostergeschichte*, 63. Seidensticker accurately recounted the *Chronicon*'s narrative.

97. *German Sectarians*, 1:373–74; Ernst, *Ephrata*, 170–72. Ernst repeated the implication that the entire brotherhood was shorn twice. Ernst created a distasteful interpolation that Beissel brought the cut hair of the sisters to Zion and gently stroked it (171). There is no evidence in any of the sources for this allegation. Sangmeister claimed that in 1745 Beissel put the shorn hair of the sisters in a box; but Sangmeister had not yet arrived at the community. Ernst also repeated several condemnations of the tonsure without documentation (172). See *CE*, 163, for the account of rebaptisms and haircuts without tonsure in autumn 1745. Alderfer gives his version of the practice of tonsure in *Ephrata Commune*, 75.

98. *CE*, 107: "Eine im Pabstthum entstandene Sache wieder aufwärmete."

99. Arnold, *Erste Liebe*, 530–31. Later Arnold criticized all fasting that was done for recognition or for a show of piety, insisting that humility and inward fasting were needed as well. See Arnold, *Abwege oder Irrungen*, 470–85.

100. *Contemporaries*, 47, 54, 82. Cf. *LuW*, 9:47.

101. "Rose," 146, 152–53.

102. *Contemporaries*, 59.

103. Walter A. Knittel, *Early Eighteenth-Century Palatinate Emigration* (Philadelphia: Dorrance, 1937; rpt. Baltimore: Genealogical Publishing Co., 1979), 30–31. See Tussing, "Hungry Orphan," 97–100. Although Tussing made errors, she related the scarcity of food during Beissel's life in Europe to his later asceticism.

104. *LuW*, 10:32, 8:123. Sachse raised the possibility that Johannes Kelpius taught such a view, on the strength of Henry Melchior Muhlenberg's report about a "Herr G" who believed he would not die but be transfigured. Sachse identified "Herr G," whom Muhlenberg only heard about secondhand, as Kelpius. See Sachse, *German Pietists*, 246–48. Willard Martin has shown from Kelpius's own writings that he probably expected to die eventually. See Willard Martin, "Johannes Kelpius and Johann Gottfried Seelig: Mystics and Hymnists on the Wissahickon" (Ph.D. diss., Pennsylvania State University, 1973), 75–77.

105. FLP B. Ms. 22, 278–79. The phrase reads: "vielleicht wird die göttliche Jugend das Alter übernehmen." The addressee is Brother Grieß in Mannheim. In the copy of the letterbook in the Cassel Collection of the Historical Society of Pennsylvania, Ac. 1923 (p. 114), the name is spelled Greiß.

106. *Chronicon*, 114: "daß es noch möglich wäre ohne thierische Speiße und Auswurf derselben zu leben."

107. *SS*, 4 (*De incarnatione verbi*): 29–33: "Und der äussere Leib aß Paradeis-Frucht im Munde, und nicht in Leib" (29); "Es war die Möglichkeit in ihme: Er konte magisch gebären" (33). See also *SS*, 4 (*Der Weg zu Christo*): 116–18.

108. *CE*, 55–56.

109. *German Sectarians*, 1:192–95. Ernst simply followed Sachse. See *Ephrata*, 98. Alderfer followed them both. See *Ephrata Commune*, 59–60. All these sources lack documentation.

110. Herbert C. Kraft, *The Lenape or Delaware Indians* (South Orange, N.J.: Seton Hall University Museum, 1990), 35.

111. *Historical Archaeology*, 1996, 17–18. I am indebted to Stephen Warfel and his students for discussions with me in the summer of 1995 about the archaeological evidence for dietary animal bones.

112. *Contemporaries*, 59.

113. *LuW*, 8:127.

114. [Conrad Beissel et al.], *Das Gesäng der einsamen und verlassenen Turtel-Taube Nemlich der Christlichen Kirche* (Ephrata: Drucks der Brüderschaft, 1747), fols. 12–13 in the unpaginated preface.

115. "Diaetetica Sacra: Die Zucht des Leibes, Zur Heiligung der Seelen beförderlich Aus richtigen Natur Gründen, Jedoch Aller Göttlichen Ordnung gantz gemäß vorgeßeset, Mir und allen meinen Mit-Streitern zur täglichen Erinnerung und nöthigen Ubung: Ja Zum wahren Wachsthum des Neuen Lebens und auch durch solche Zucht zu werden und zu bleiben die zu denen Füßen Jesu Sitzende Kinder; und zu dießer Weißheit können immer näher und inniger geführet und geleitet zu werden," Photocopy of unpaginated manuscript, Pennsylvania Historical and Museum Commission, Ephrata Cloister. I am indebted to Hans Schneider for calling to my attention the printed version of *Dietaetica Sacra* (copy in Universitätsbibliothek, Philipps Universität, Marburg) and for help in deciphering Carl's name from the title page anagram, "Iesu Sitzende Kinder" (Iohann Samuel Karl). This book corrects my earlier theory that the manuscript originated at Ephrata because of a reference to a person named Armella (fol. 26r of the manuscript). Two women were called Sister Armella at Ephrata. Because Carl's printed book contains the same passage, it must refer to someone else.

116. Ibid., fols. 48–49. For advice on fasting, see fols. 42v and 50.

117. *ZS*, 37: "Mein Brod daß ich esse ist dises [*sic*], daß ich ohne Ablaß Gott und seinem reinen Wesen zu gekehrt bleibe: mein Wasser, das ich trincke ist, daß ich mich nimmermehr weder von Gott noch seiner Liebe scheide."

118. *CE*, 45. I disagree with Esther Fern Rupel's description of the Ephrata pilgrim dress that preceded the monastic habit. Her information comes from Julius Sachse with no other documentation. See

NOTES TO CHAPTER 4

Esther Fern Rupel, *Brethren Dress: A Testimony to Faith* (Philadelphia: Brethren Encyclopedia, 1994), 31, 33. Cf. *German Sectarians*, 1:83.

119. *LuW*, 4:31, 35.

120. *CE*, 72–73: "den Leibe des Todtes um seiner Schande willen . . . zu hüllen . . . die gemeine Tracht des männlichen Geschlechts also eingerichtet ist, daß man dem weiblichen gefalle."

121. Ibid., 73: "Dabey war ein Ueberwurf, welcher vornen einen Schurtz hatte, hinten aber eine Schleyer, der den Rücken bedeckte. . . . Im Gottesdienst aber trugen sie noch Mäntel, die bis an den Gürtel reichten, daran gleichfalß [*sic*] eine Kappe befestigt war."

122. Ibid.: "daß wehnig [*sic*] zu sehen war von dem verdrießlichen Bild, das durch die Sünd ist offenbar worden . . . ein groser Schleyer, der vornen gantz und hinten bis an den Gürtel bedeckte."

123. "Rose," 10: "Ich habe einen hefftigen Trieb in mir um mir ein Nonnen-Kleid machen zu lassen." Cf. Sachse, *German Sectarians*, 2:182; Erb, *MHT*, 291.

124. "Rose," 137–40, 145–46. The quotation is on 144. See Erb, *MHT*, 275–79, for an excerpt that follows Sachse's partial translation of "Die Rose." See also Ernst, *Ephrata*, 255–57, and Sachse, *German Sectarians*, 2:191–93.

125. A photograph of the book plate for Brother Amos's *Martyrs' Mirror* is in the possession of the Ephrata Cloister. The location of the book is unknown at present. The smaller image is in a manuscript music book for *Zionitischer WeyrauchsHügel*, Ephrata, 1751, created for Maria Eicher and now in the possession of Guy Oldham, London, 23, 41.

126. *CE*, 63.

127. *Contemporaries*, 47; "Rose," 152; *German Sectarians*, 1:252–53. See also Ernst, *Ephrata*, 109, and Alderfer, *Ephrata Commune*, 57. Ernst and Alderfer followed Sachse.

128. *TP*, 1:287–88. The letter was written in 1697, when he was fifty-nine.

129. *CE*, 63.

130. *LuW*, 5:71, 73, 80, 83. The passages also mention kneeling for prayer. For the hours of prayer and perpetual prayer, see 4:48–49.

131. *Contemporaries*, 67, 83, 142.

132. *ZS*, 38–39: "Das Gebät ist ein unablässiges magisches Essen unsers Geistes aus Gottes heiligem Wesen durch den Feuer-Willen der anziehenden und magischen Begirden unserer Seelen . . . und wir sind in Ihm verkläret mit der Klarheit, die allezeit bey Ihm selber gewesen."

133. *LuW*, 10:39, 12; 6:25.

134. *CE*, 148. John Brooke sees this as one of the forerunners of the Mormon breastplate of the Priesthood of Melchizedek. See Brooke, *Refiner's Fire*, 44.

135. *Contemporaries*, 176.

136. Seidensticker, *Klostergeschichte*, 85. Seidensticker believed that Ephrata's mysticism faded primarily after Beissel's death. However, his death probably only accelerated a process that had begun by the early 1760s, as Antietam (Snow Hill) emerged as a new center for Beissel's piety.

CHAPTER 4. MANLY VIRGINS AND VIRGINAL MEN: GENDER AT EPHRATA

1. *ZS*, 193: "So ist dann das Weib ein Mangel des Manns und der Mann ein Mangel des Weibes."

2. In using the term "gender" I acknowledge that gender and gender roles are socially constructed. See Gerda Lerner, *The Creation of Patriarchy*, vol. 1 of *Women and History* (New York and Oxford: Oxford University Press, 1986), 238. While Lerner's point that "sex" defines a group by its biological distinctiveness is helpful, I am less confident that the significance of biological distinctiveness is self-evident apart from interpretation by social systems. Hence I prefer "gender" here, despite the liabilities of the word that Lerner points out.

3. Wendy Everham, "The Recovery of the Feminine in an Early American Pietist Community: The Interpretive Challenge of the Theology of Conrad Beissel," *Pennsylvania Folklife* 39, no. 2 (Winter

NOTES TO CHAPTER 4

1989–90): 50–57. Everham pioneered the study of gender concepts at Ephrata, a topic that needs much more analysis. I differ somewhat from Everham in that I believe Ephrata sought a kind of recovery of the female for men and of the male for women.

4. See Steven Ozment, *When Fathers Ruled: Family Life in Reformation Europe* (Cambridge: Harvard University Press, 1983), 1–72, 80–99, for the interpretation of Protestantism's "liberation" of women. See Lyndal Roper, *Holy Household* (Cambridge: Cambridge University Press, 1990), for an argument that Protestants offered nothing new, and actually reduced options for women available under Catholicism.

5. Markus Matthias, *Johann Wilhelm und Johanna Eleanora Petersen: Eine Biographie bis zur Amtsenthebung Petersens im Jahre 1692* (Göttingen: Vandenhoeck & Ruprecht, 1993), 81–95.

6. Ibid., 254–300.

7. *GdP*, 1:401.

8. Richard Critchfield, "Prophetin, Führerin, Organisatorin: Zur Rolle der Frau im Pietismus," in Barbara Becker-Cantarino, ed., *Die Frau von der Reformation zur Romantik: Die Situation der Frau vor dem Hintergrund der Literatur- und Sozialgeschichte* (Bonn: Bouvier Verlag Herbert Grundmann, 1980), 112–37. Gerda Lerner also treats Pietism with a little confusion, focusing on Radical Pietism and largely passing over Pietism within the established churches. See Gerda Lerner, *The Creation of Feminist Consciousness: From the Middle Ages to 1870*, vol. 2 of *Women and History* (New York and Oxford: Oxford University Press, 1993), 94–100.

9. Gertraud Zaepernick, "Johann Georg Gichtels und seiner Nachfolger Briefwechsel mit den Hallischen Pietisten, besonders mit A. M. Francke," *PuN* 8 (1982): 74–118, esp. 94–110.

10. Weeks, *Boehme*, 114, 237n. See also Everham, "Recovery of the Feminine," 53–55. Everham suggests that Beissel may have labored to recover an ancient, suppressed Sophia religion derived from gnostic thought. I am less confident that he did so intentionally.

11. *SS*, 2 (*De tribus principiis*): 100–150.

12. For literature exploring the suppression of earlier goddess worship by male-dominated religions, including Christianity, see, e.g., Elisabeth Schüssler Fiorenza, *In Memory of Her: A Feminist Theological Reconstruction of Christian Origins* (New York: Crossroad, 1983); idem, *Jesus: Miriam's Child, Sophia's Prophet* (New York: Crossroad, 1995); and Anne Baring and Jules Cashford, *The Myth of the Goddess: Evolution of an Image* (London: Penguin, 1991). For an alternative view, see, e.g., Cynthia Eller, "The Feminist Spirituality Movement," in Catherine Wessinger, ed., *Women's Leadership in Marginal Religions: Explorations outside the Mainstream* (Urbana: University of Illinois Press, 1993), 182–84.

13. Tanner, *Ehe im Pietismus*, 10–19.

14. *SS*, 2 (*De tribus principiis*): 130–50. See also the comments in Weeks, *Boehme*, 115–16.

15. Weeks, *Boehme*, 116. Cf. Lerner, *Creation of Patriarchy*, 184, 195–97.

16. For Boehme, Sophia is a part of the Godhead and of Christ. To the extent that Boehme's Christ is androgynous, my term "Christology" is intended to include Sophia in the Boehmist Christ. However, because Boehme tended increasingly to personify Sophia in later works, it can also be useful to speak of Christ/Sophia as a unity.

17. *SS*, 4 (*De incarnatione verbi*): 33–49, 66–67, 88–100, 73–78. The quotation there reads: "So kriegte der Held im Streit männliche Zeichen . . . [soll] des Vaters brennende Essentien im Feuer wieder gelöschet werden" (74). See also 88–96 for believers attaining an androgynous balance of characteristics. See also Weeks, *Boehme*, 150–51.

18. *SS*, 6 (*De signatura rerum*): 136–70. See also Weeks, *Boehme*, 192, 194–95.

19. *TP*, 1:395: "Sie ist nicht Gott, sondern sein Spiegel; Sie ist nicht Jesus, sondern sein himmlisch [*sic*] Fleisch und Blut, und wenn wir Jesum anziehen, so ziehen wir auch Sophiam an." Tanner noted that Gichtel was less precise in his use of Sophia. See Tanner, *Ehe im Pietismus*, 19–36.

20. Thune, *Behmenists*, 46–49. Pordage's book appeared in German translation the next year.

21. Erb, *Pietists, Protestants, and Mysticism*, 94–98.

22. Gottfried Arnold, *Das Geheimnis der Göttlichen Sophia oder Weisheit* (Leipzig: 1700; facs. rpt. Stuttgart: Friedrich Frommann, 1963), 24–29, 44–45. See Tanner, *Ehe im Pietismus*, 36–46.

NOTES TO CHAPTER 4

23. Arnold, *Geheimnis der Göttlichen Sophia*, 52–53, 82–83, 90, 112–13, 118, 136–38.
24. *TP*, 1:572. Gichtel condemned Arnold's marriage in several passages.
25. Kelpius, *Diarium*, 44–45, 71–77, 84, 89.
26. Beysell, *Mystyrion Anomias*, 20–21.
27. *DE, Pars I*, 11: "So ward Gott genöthiget, aus seiner Vestung zu weichen, seine Einheit verlassen, und wider seine Natur die in ihm verborgene Mannheit erwecken." Beissel compares the unified Godhead to a fortress (*Vestung*), drawing on Boehme. The passages quoted from Beissel's *Dissertation* (*Wunderschrift*) are the same in the 1773 and 1789 editions, with minor variations in spelling.
28. *DE, Pars I*, 11–12: "Jetzt ist Gott genöthiget, die gantze Schöpfung in Männlich und Weiblich zu theilen, und das Weibliche, als dem sanfte Theil, dem Männlichen, als seiner Obrigkeit, unter zu ordnen."
29. Ibid., 25: "Dieses dienet nicht wehnig, die Würde des Mittleramts J.[esu] C.[hristi] zu vergrösern, weil er in den Riß getreten, und die Temperatur in der Gottheit wieder hat hergestellt." Miller's annotations do not appear in the 1789 ed. or in the English ed. of 1765.
30. Ibid., 4–7: "Der feurige Manns-Wille hatte ein unveränderliches Rebelliren gegen die himmlische Weiblichkeit (7)."
31. Ibid., 8–9: "Adams Mannheit . . . müsse ans Creutz gebracht werden."
32. Ibid., 25–26: "Und daß auch die Göttliche Mannheit wieder entladen werde von dem Amt der Gerechtigkeit, und also wieder eingekleidet werde in den weiblichen Habit, als wodurch all Getheiltheiten wiederum aufgelößt . . . so muß sich die himmlische Weiblichkeit selbst einen Mann aus der ewigen Mutterschafft ausgebähren: als der da habe die Gott-mann-weibliche Eigenschafft."
33. Ibid., 30–31: "Alles durch die himmlische Weiblichkeit müsse wiedergebracht werden. . . . Alles nun, was durch den Creutzes-Tod ins Ersterben gebracht wird: das wird dem ewigen Geist, oder der himmlischen Mutterschafft, zum herrlichen Ausgrünen in den Schooß geliefert . . . daß selbst das königliche Amt J.[esu] C.[hristi] wird aufhören, und er wird sich selbsten in seiner gewesenen Mannheit aufgeben, sich der ewigen Gutheit überlassen."
34. Ibid., 23, 26: "unbefleckt aus der himmlischen Weiblichket ausgebohren" (23); "Jetzt ist eine Jungfrau schwanger von dem Saamen des himmlishcen Weibes" (26).
35. Ibid., 26: "Dieser Mann Jesus hat sein Amt zwar in der Gestalt des Manns geführet; die Beschaffenheit seiner selbst aber war nicht männlich sondern weiblich: weil er in der Unterthänigkeit und Gehorsam einher gieng bis zum Todt am Creutz."
36. Ibid., 320–40.
37. FLP B. Ms. 22, p. 156. The letter is dated "20tn des 3tn Mands 1756."
38. Ibid., 150: "Als dann begegnet sie uns im Duncklen, wo man sie nicht kennt, uns [probably copyist's error; should be "und"] gibt uns einen Kuß, verwundet daneben unser Hertz mit einem Pfeil Sophianischer Liebe; gar bald werden wir darauf, als wie in einer Paradisischen Entzückung gebracht, also daß wir meinen, wir ruheten bereits der Weisheit in dem Schooß, oder schliefen in ihren Armen."
39. Arnold, *Geheimnis der Göttlichen Sophia*, 120: "feuriges Liebes-Pfeil."
40. FLP B. Ms. 22, pp. 152, 154: "Allhier tritt Sophia selbst mit in den Streit, und hilffet den männlichen feuer-willen [*sic*] besänfftigen"; 156: "Dann in diesem Handel hat die Jungfrau die heilige Tinctur in sich, als wordurch [*sic*] Jacobs irdisch Venus spermatica [*sic*] ausgeheilet."
41. Ibid., 156, 155: "Dieses ist die geistliche Verschneidung ums Himmelsreichs willen . . . durch das verrücken der Hiffte Jacobs" (155).
42. *TP*, 1:302. "Daß aber Gott an diesem Naschen und irdischen Beyschlaf oder Fleisch-Essen einen Eckel gehabt . . . daß eben am Hindertheil der Thiere die Schamm und Venae spermaticae ligen, und Gott uns lehren wollen, daß Er an unseren thierischen Gliedern kein Gefallen habe." The scribe of Beissel's letter wrote "venus spermatica" according to the sound of the words, unaware of the spelling in Gichtel's passage.
43. Ibid.: "mich um des Himmelreichs willen beschnitten, auch die Frau gäntzlich verläugnet habe." Gichtel used *beschnitten* (circumcise) in this letter to refer to what he has done for the sake of the Kingdom of Heaven. Beissel used *verschneiden* (castrate), which follows Matt. 19:12. It is unclear why Gichtel chose this word here.

44. Lerner, *Creation of Feminist Consciousness*, 275–76.

45. Ibid., 274.

46. "Rose," 25–26: "die alle frühzeitig mit als urständerinnen, der obern Mutter dieses gebährungs werck sind in den Schooß gesetzt worden." For translated excerpts from "Rose," see *German Sectarians*, 1:300–304, 2:181–201. Much of these portions appear in *MHT*, 267–90. Erb's passages rely in part on Sachse, checked against a Snow Hill copy of the original. The Snow Hill copy is in the Cassel Collection, Historical Society of Pennsylvania, Philadelphia, Ac. 1924. The Snow Hill copy contains some errors. Both Sachse and Erb omitted basically all of the devotions by and about the sisters. The quotations here are from the original (Ac. 1925); the translations are mine.

47. "Rose," 305: "Die Gottliche [*sic*] Weisheit wolle sich je länger je mehr herunter lassen auf uns, und wolle ihre Tieffe und geheime wege mehr offenbahren . . . dann die Weisheit hat ihr spiel in der Nidrigkeit [*sic*]. Darum sind so wenige die sie finden." The devotion identifies Sister Jael by name. Whether Sister Jael wrote it or someone else composed it about her is not clear. Several of the devotions use the first person, which suggests that various sisters composed them.

48. Ibid., 339: "anfängerin, Mutter und Königen des Himmels aus welcher sie gebohren sind. . . . Aus dieser hohen Wunder-geburt des sohnes Gottes und Jungfrauen Maria, hat sich auch das werck dieser gesellschafft so gleich mit im geheimnis als ein wunder ohne zutuhn eines Mannes ausgeboren . . . das wir unserm geschlecht als die wir uns aus der Mutter der Himmlischen Jungfrau rühmen zu seÿn."

49. Ibid., 51, 59, 68.

50. Ibid., 312: "wan dan dieselbige wohl durch leutert und bewähret ist. Dann kan Erst die Völlige Vereinigung geschehen mit ihrem heiligen Mann Jesum, als ihrem Himmlischen Bräutigam, dan wird sie durch überschattung des heiligen Geistes besamet und fruchtbar werden." For the date of Bernice's death, see ibid., 367, and "Brother Kenan's Notebook," 56, where she is named as one of the first four celibate women in communal housing. Obviously "Die Rose" compiled some material written before the reorganization of 1745.

51. "Rose," 196: "ihres allerliebsten Bräutigams mit deme sie sich täglich und stündlich auf nimmt vermählet und verbindet um einig und allein sein eigenthum zu seÿn."

52. Ibid., 194: "So bestehet also unser gantzes Leben in einer beständigen ertödtung so wohl in geistes- als leiblichen dingen."

53. Ibid., 300–301: "Ich habe mich ja vor [*sic*] dich lassen ans X [Creutz] nagelln."

54. Julia Stanley, "Sexist Grammar," unpublished paper presented to South Eastern Conference of Linguistics, Atlanta, Nov. 7, 1975, cited in Dale Spender, *Man Made Language* (Boston: Routledge & Kegan Paul, Ltd., 1980), 19–21.

55. See Lerner, *Creation of Patriarchy*, 205–10, for a summary from a feminist perspective.

56. *TP*, 4:2704–5: "Die Weiber besänftigen leider den feurigen Limbum des Mannes wol, aber die Kraft des Willens brechen sie . . . und über seinen Willen zu Herren ein [probably misprint for "sein"], und herrschen, wie offenbar ist." Gichtel explicitly claims that women "soften" men by "softening" the male "limbum," or sex organ.

57. Ibid., 5:3748: "Was die Jungfrauen betrifft, so sie Jesum anziehen, werden sie männliche Jungfrauen mit beyden Tincturen . . . und können so wol das Melchisedechische Priester-Amt geistlich bedienen als wir, es ist aber was rares."

58. Cf. *MHT*, 118. The English translation in *MHT* omits some phrases, transposes several, and contains some translation mistakes for the *Dissertation* text as it appears in *DE, Pars I*, 16–19.

59. *DE, Pars I*, 16. The text reads: "so kam der Geist der Arglistigkeit und Verschlagenheit, als welcher eine Tochter in dem magischen Willen Lucifers war, und suchte die wenige übrig gebliebene Weiblichkeit vollends gar zu verderben." The critical phrase is "als welcher eine Tochter." The "welcher" is a demonstrative pronoun referring to a masculine antecedent, which in the passage can only be "der Geist." Hence it is "der Geist der Arglistigkeit" (the spirit of deceit) that is a "daughter in the magic will of Lucifer." Obviously this critical error completely distorts Beissel's view of Eve. Although Beissel considered Eve inferior to Adam, nowhere in the *Dissertation* did he call her a daughter of Lucifer. Peter Miller's

NOTES TO CHAPTER 4

1765 English translation, which was supposedly the basis for the translation in Erb's sourcebook, makes clear my point.

60. Ibid., 19–20; *ZS*, 195: "Und der Eva Töchter haben ihr Bild an der reinen Jungfrau Maria, daß sie auch ihren rechten Mann Jesum wieder in sich ausgebähren."

61. *DE, Pars I,* 29: "daß die Auferstehung Christi von den Todten ein H.[eiliges] Weib zum ersten Apostel machte, um diese Gesandschafft an die Apostel zu bringen."

62. "Michael Müller . . . and His 'Debt Book.'" Entries for the sisterhood are too numerous to cite.

63. *CE,* 244–45. Cf. *LuW,* 9:60. See "Rose," 377. The entry dates her death as Dec. 24, 1784, at age 74. I am indebted to Clarence Spohn for calling my attention to Maria's purchase from her brother of land across the creek in 1763. Maria also gave away her splendidly ornamented music book in 1764. See also Jeff Bach, "Maria Eicher of Ephrata: A Case Study of Religion and Gender in Radical Pietism," in Eller, *From Age to Age,* 117–57.

64. *ZS,* 194–96: "[Ist also Jesus] . . . nach seinem weiblichen Theil dem männlichen [Geschlecht] eine mänliche Jungfrau."

65. FLP B. Ms. 22, p. 153: "Wir müssen unsern selbst-würckenden und feuer mannlichen [*sic*] Manns-willen bringen in ein einsinken und gewisser maassen weiblich werden."

66. Ibid., 153, 156: "Wir müssen einfach der edlen Jungfrau eine reine Matrix darbringen, weilen sie schon in sich das Feuer des heiligen Samen für die himmlische Fruchtbarkeit hat" (153); "weilen sie also mit ihrem Jungfräulichen Mann-feuer gar leicht an unsere in Gott geheiligte Matrix kommen kan [*sic*]" (156).

67. *ZS,* 195–96: "O wie wirbet Sophia oder Jesus an der Seele des Menschen, um sie wiederum in das keusche Ehebett ein zu führen" (195). See 196: "Da fehlet bey dem Weiblichen nichts Männliches, und bey dem Männlichen nichts Weibliches."

68. *LuW,* 109; Sangmeister, *Mystische Theologie,* 107: "Gott wollte diese Fortpflanzung nie . . . den Erweckten Seelen, insbesondere dem männlichen Geschlecht, der Samenfluß ist eine fast unerträgliche Last."

69. Willi Temme, *Krise der Leiblichkeit: Die Sozietät der Mutter Eva (Buttlarsche Rotte) und der Radikale Pietismus um 1700* (Göttingen: Vandenhoeck & Ruprecht, 1998), 311–23, 331–32, 348–50, 353–56; idem, "Die Buttlarsche Rotte. Ein Forschungsbericht," *PuN* 16 (1990): 53–75.

70. *TP,* 6:1604 ("eine publique Hure"), 1664; Renkewitz, *Hochmann von Hochenau,* 191–93. See also E. Bauer, "Die Buttlarsche Rotte in Sassmannshausen," *Wittgenstein* 38, no. 4 (1974): 148–61. For two brief summaries in English, see Donald F. Durnbaugh, "Buttlar, Eva von," in *Brethren Encyclopedia,* and Ward, *Protestant Evangelical Awakening,* 202. See also Tanner, *Ehe im Pietismus,* 46–57. Hochmann believed that the highest of five degrees of marriage was spiritual marriage to Christ through celibacy.

71. Hildebrand, *Schrifftmässiges Zeuchnüß,* 14–15: "So hat ernandter Graff uns also geantwortet: . . . Wann Ich just zu der Zeit als Ich im Beyschlaf mit meiner Frauen bin, stürbe, so könte Ich sagen zum Heyland: Ich komme eben von dieser Arbeit (so viel zu sagen, die Ich in deinem Namen verrichtete)."

72. [Israel Eckerlin], *Ein kurtzer Bericht von den Ursachen, warum die Gemeinschaft in Ephrata sich mit dem Grafen Zinzendorf und seinen Leuten eingelassen. Und wie sich eine so grosse Ungleichheit im Ausgang der Sachen auf beyden Seiten befunden* (Germantown: Christoph Saur, 1743), 42: "Wir kein einziges Exempel . . . hätten . . . daß eine so fleischliche Vermehrung der Kirche Gott gefällig wäre . . . Christus aber, der reine Jungfrauen-Sohn, hat ein gantz ander Gebährungs-Werck im Geist eröffnet, wodurch die Kirche mit lauter Jungfräulichen Geistern soll angefüllet werden." See also [Hildebrand], *Unpartheyisches Bedencken,* 27–32.

73. *CE,* 28, 36–37. Later Daniel Eicher joined the Ephrata community. See also "Rose," 9. This passage was translated into English in *MHT,* 269–70. See "Rose," 377, for Maria's age, and see *LuW* 4:22.

74. *CE,* 48–49. Anna Landis's husband reportedly told her that "your will should be subordinate to your husband" (dein Wille soll deinem Mann unterworfen seyn) (48). For an alternative account, see Sangmeister, *LuW,* 4:31.

75. *CE,* 29, 43–46, 56–57.

NOTES TO CHAPTER 5

76. The name is also spelled Sauer. See Donald F. Durnbaugh, "Christopher Sauer, Pennsylvania-German Printer: His Youth in Germany and Later Relationships with Europe," *PMBH* 82 (1958): 316–40, esp. 322–36. See also Donald F. Durnbaugh, "Christopher Sauer and His Germantown Press," *Der Reggeboge* 4, no. 2 (June 1970): 3–16, esp. 8–13; Stephen L. Longenecker, *The Christopher Sauers* (Elgin, Ill.: Brethren Press, 1981), 12–13, 21–22, 27–33; and Schrader, *Literaturproduktion,* 224–25, 476n. Schrader claimed that Maria was the daughter of the Inspirationist Eberhard Ludwig Gruber. Durnbaugh (1970) noted that no records indicate that Gruber had any daughters.

77. *LuW,* 4:30.

78. *Ein Spiegel der Eheleute Nebst schönen Erinnerungen vor Ledige Personen Welche willens sind, sich in den Stand der Ehe zu begeben. Wie auch, Etwas von den Ursachen, warum viele Menschen aus einer Religion in die andere übergehen. Vorgestellt in einem Gespräch zwischen einem Jüngling und Meister* ([Germantown]: Gedruckt unter der Presse [bey Christoph Saur], 1758), 9–10, 15, 16–17: "als wann sie dem Mann fast alles was er thut und anordnet, mit halßstarrigen [*sic*] stürmischen Affecten widerspricht, um dem Mann und sich selbst dadurch das Leben bitter und sauer zu machen" (17). The book is attributed to the Saur Press on the basis of typographical evidence. See Arndt and Eck, *First Century,* 1:111. See also Durnbaugh, "Christopher Sauer, Pennsylvania-German Printer," 325.

79. *Spiegel der Eheleute,* 24–25: "Ein unersetzlicher Schade ist, wann das Weib über den Mann herrschet, wegen der Kinder-Zucht" (24); "die Ruthe ist zu hart widergangen, daß es roth worden, oder wohl gar ein paar tropffen Blut hat gegeben" (25). *Loses Maul* (loose mouth) is especially derogatory, because *Maul* is the word used for an animal's mouth, not a human's.

80. See the letter by Saur in Durnbaugh, *Brethren in Colonial America,* 38. See Durnbaugh, "Christopher Sauer and His Germantown Press," 10–11, and Longenecker, *Christopher Sauers,* 30–31.

81. *CE,* 45. See also *LuW,* 4:45. Maria returned to her son's home in autumn 1744 and was reconciled with her husband the following summer. She died in 1752. The *Chronicon* credited her son with persuading her, but Sangmeister credited Georges de Benneville, a separatist.

82. Joseph J. Kelley, Jr., *Pennsylvania: The Colonial Years, 1681–1776* (Garden City, N.Y.: Doubleday, 1980), 150.

83. *CE,* 4.

84. *LuW,* 10:12, 14, 39; 4:51–52.

85. *CE,* 46, 68–69.

86. *LuW,* 4:29; 10:12, 14, 30. Sangmeister claimed that Christina Höhn, who had been close to Beissel, told Ezechiel that Beissel told her he was "not free" in the matter of Daniel Eicher's daughter, presumably Anna. This is a secondhand report and deserves some caution, coming from Sangmeister. See *CE,* 68–69. The *Chronicon* reported the story also, but collapsed nearly all of the information about Anna Eicher over several years into one passage.

87. *LuW,* 9:47.

88. *CE,* 66.

89. Onesimuß, "Ein Evangelisches Zeugnüß und geistliger Bericht," 1755, unpaginated manuscript, Pennsylvania Historical and Museum Commission, Ephrata Cloister, 14.66.119, fol. 180r-v: "Und wie dich die verstorbene N.N. hatte von ausen zu fall zu bringen, also bist du von ihrer schwester gantz geschwechet und dem geistlichen nach zu [V]all gebracht worden, daß sie dich da zu mal schon unter den füssen hate, und sie war der Priester nicht nur in ihrem werck sondern in der gantzen gemeinde, sie alles unter sich hatte."

90. *CE,* 60. Accusations flew that Ephrata was another "Eva's gang," a reference to Eva Buttlar.

CHAPTER 5. "GOD'S HOLY POINT OF REST": EPHRATA'S MYSTICAL LANGUAGE IN SPACE AND TIME

1. G. Edwin Brumbaugh, "Pennsylvania German Colonial Architecture," in *Proceedings and Papers of the Pennsylvania German Society, October 17, 1930,* vol. 41 (Norristown: Pennsylvania German Society, 1933),

NOTES TO CHAPTER 5

1–60. Brumbaugh publicized Ephrata as having "in many ways the most authentic medieval German structures erected in Pennsylvania" (48). Others' interpretations of Ephrata's art as "illuminated manuscripts" reinforced an impression of Ephrata as a conscious attempt to reproduce medieval monasticism. While Beissel created a cloister, he did so with Radical Pietist spirituality, not a self-conscious imitation of the Middle Ages.

2. CE, 25, 33, 24, 62–63.

3. *German Sectarians*, 1:120–21, 170–71. See also "Brother Kenan's Notebook," 108 (for dimensions) and 14 (for his joining Ephrata in 1744). The house was 25' long, 20' wide, and 8' 6" in height under the joists. Sachse omitted the 6' "borch" (porch) drawn in the plans. Cf. Patrick W. O'Bannon et al., "Ephrata Cloister: A Historic Structures Report" (unpublished report of examinations of historical structures at Ephrata Cloister submitted to the Pennsylvania Historical and Museum Commission by John Milner Associates, West Chester, 1988), 1:11–12.

4. *CE*, 53–54, 63–64. Unlike the English word "magazine," the German *Magazin* implies merely a storehouse, not a place to store ammunition. In his translation, Hark simply used the cognate English word. The potential for unnecessary confusion over this term was introduced in Tim Noble and Shelby Weaver Splain, "Ephrata Cloister Historic Structures Report, Ephrata, Pennsylvania," vol. 9, "Building I: Almonry," unpublished manuscript (Zionsville, Pa.: Noble Preservation Services, Dec.19, 2000), 4. See also *Contemporaries*, 198.

5. In an oral interview at the Almonry with the author and Clarence Spohn on July 12, 1995, Alan G. Keyser pointed out several features that make a date in the 1760s more probable. The floor beams are sawn rather than hand-hewn and are much lighter than those in buildings on the site from the 1740s. Strips of wood were nailed to the beams to support the floor. The rafters in the attic are much lighter than the Germanic timbers and braces that would have been used on a stone building in the 1730s and lighter than the roof rafters of Saron, built in 1743. The style of the Almonry's roof appears more English than German, according to Mr. Keyser. These details suggest construction later than the 1730s, perhaps in the 1760s. The so-called Almonry could not be the *magazin* built in 1734. See also Noble and Weaver Splain, "Building I: Almonry," 76.

6. Edward R. Cook and William J. Callahan, "Tree-Ring Dating of the Ephrata Cloister in Ephrata, Pennsylvania," unpublished manuscript (Palisades, N.Y.: Lamont-Doherty Earth Observatory, Sept.10, 2000), 5, 11. Cook and Callahan conclude that this building can reasonably be dated to the early 1750s.

7. *CE*, 88. For construction of stone and wood, see *LuW*, 4:50. It is unclear whether the stone was the foundation or part of the structure. Sangmeister reported that in 1747 (probably Sept. 18–19) the brothers "demolished the Berghaus and carried away stone and wood," then leveled the site with pickaxes. See also Stephen G. Warfel, "Historical and Archaeological Investigations Associated with the Ephrata Cloister Fire Detection and Suppression Systems Project," unpublished manuscript reporting archaeological test explorations (Harrisburg: State Museum of Pennsylvania, 1990), 7–8. The house is mentioned in Seidensticker, *Klostergeschichte*, 54. Sachse mentioned the Berghaus without further comment in *German Sectarians*, 1:249; repeated in Ernst, *Ephrata*, 95, and Alderfer, *Ephrata Commune*, 53–54, 57.

8. *CE*, 88–89.

9. *German Sectarians*, 1:256–57. Neither Ernst nor Alderfer repeated this mistake. Tieleman Jansz van Braght, *Het Bloedig Tooneel-Plaats der doopsgezinden en weerlozen Christen*, 2d ed. (Amsterdam, 1685), title page. The ornament appeared in another Ephrata imprint with a different inscription in Albaro Alonso Barba, *Gründlicher Unterricht von den Metallen* (Ephrata: J. Georg Zeissiger, 1763), 118. Zeissiger was a member of Ephrata. His name on the title page suggests that he helped to support the publication of this book.

10. Warfel, "Historical and Archaeological Investigations," 9, 53–54, 71–74. Warfel identifies three periods of the community's architecture: 1732–34, solitary period; 1735–45, communal growth; 1746–1813, reform, consolidation, and decline (7–10). The three major segments are helpful categories for analysis, although I differ somewhat about details.

11. *CE*, 62: "nebst einen Raum vor Versammlung, grose Säle mit aller Zurüstung vor die *Agapas* oder Liebes-mähler, dabey waren noch Cellen angebaut vor Einsame, nach der Gewohnheit der alten Griechischen Kirche."

NOTES TO CHAPTER 5

12. Erb, *Pietists, Protestants, and Mysticism*, 29, 31. Arnold's portrayals of ancient Christianity influenced Ephrata. See also Benz, *Protestantische Thebais*, 11–25, 103–4. Peter Miller may have added the specific references to Egyptian Christian asceticism to the printed *Chronicon*. Conrad Beissel mentioned the desert ascetics only occasionally.

13. Kelpius, *Diarium*, 56.

14. *CE*, 62. In his translation (76) Hark has two sisters housed with Sister Abigail in Kedar, when the original *Chronicon* clearly states three.

15. *German Sectarians*, 1:252 (Sachse cited no documentation for this statement). Ernst, *Ephrata* (107), and Alderfer, *Ephrata Commune* (58), simply repeated Sachse without question.

16. Warfel, *Historical Archaeology* (1999), 27–29. See also the reports from the years 1996 and 1997.

17. Ibid. (1999), 29. Warfel believes there is evidence for possibly one hearth. Interestingly, the five seasons of excavations at the entire site identified as Kedar produced only half as many artifacts as two seasons' work on a limited portion of Zion's convent. See ibid. (2000), 30.

18. Ernst, *Ephrata*, 107. See also *German Sectarians*, 1:401–2.

19. *SS*, 6 (*De signatura rerum*): 38–39.

20. *LuW*, 4:43; Biever, "Report of Archaeological Investigations," 21, 30–32.

21. *CE*, 64: "So wollte er von seinem Vermögen noch ein Bäthaus an Kedar anbauen nebst einem Wohnhaus vor den Vorsteher, so könte hernach Kedar in ein Schwestern-Convent verwandelt werden." On p. 65 (misnumbered 64) the *Chronicon* referred to Beissel's dwelling as attached to the *Bäthaus*: "Als ihm nun an dieses Haus eine Wohnung ist angebauet worden." The German clearly indicates that the *Bäthaus* was attached to Kedar (64) and Beissel's dwelling was attached to the *Bäthaus* (65). The German refers to Beissel's dwelling as both *Wohnhaus* (64) and *Wohnung* (65, misnumbered 64). When the *Bäthaus* was destroyed, Beissel "had" to move into the sisters' house, Kedar (65).

22. "Brother Kenan's Notebook," 54. See "Rose," 375, for the death of Sister Rahel (Rachel) in 1773, at age 49. P. 39 gives her age at death as 49 years and 9 months, stating that she was the daughter of Brother Sealthiel. Thus she would have been born in February 1724 and would have been about 12 years old when she was accepted into Kedar, which became the sisters' house upon completion of the *Bäthaus*. Maria's sister was younger, and left the cloister around 1744, perhaps close to the age of 20. See HSP Ac. 1926, p. 5 (of second section). For Brother Sealthiel's death, see "Brother Kenan's Notebook," 61.

23. *CE*, 64 (a printing error in the *Chronicon* resulted in two pages numbered 64; this passage is on the second): "Dieses Haus war ein ansehnlich Gebäu, mit einem Sahl [*sic*] vor Liebesmähler und einem Raum vor Versammlungen versehen, welcher zwo Port-Kirchen zum Gebrauch der Einsamen hatte, nebst einem Altan, der mit grauen Vätern besetzt war." In his English translation Hark took "Port-Kirchen" into the text without translating it. *Altan* can be translated as balcony or gallery, implying a higher location in the room.

24. Seidensticker, *Klostergeschichte*, 55.

25. See Harold Wickliffe Rose, *The Colonial Houses of Worship in America* (New York: Hastings House, 1963), 350–51, for pictures and brief accounts of the Mennonite and Dunker meetinghouses in Germantown. See Durnbaugh, *Brethren in Colonial America*, 173–86, and cf. James H. Lehman, *The Old Brethren* (Elgin, Ill.: Brethren Press, 1976), 343–47. For the Moravians, see Joseph Mortimer Levering, *A History of Bethlehem, Pennsylvania, 1741–1892, with Some Account of Its Founders and Their Early Activity* (Bethlehem, Pa.: Times Publishing Co., 1903).

26. *CE*, 64.

27. Warfel, "Historical and Archaeological Investigations," 7: "Structure and evolution of Cloister community plan throughout the 18th century directly reflect Beissel's will to maintain segmented social order."

28. *Contemporaries*, 47.

29. *CE*, 90–91. See also *LuW*, 4:35. For Koch's letter, see Durnbaugh, *Brethren in Colonial America*, 98.

30. *German Sectarians*, 1:357–58.

31. Ernst, *Ephrata*, 131–33. J. J. Stoudt corrected Ernst and Sachse by stating that "there is no evidence that the Ephrata Brethren practiced the extreme rites" that Sachse attributed to secret Rosicrucian precepts. See Alderfer, *Ephrata Commune*, 69–70. Alderfer offers the qualification that Sachse may have

overestimated the influence of Freemasonry on the Zionitic Brotherhood (227n). See Seidensticker, *Klostergeschichte*, 55–56.

32. *German Sectarians* 1:380. For the original vignette, see "Der Christen ABC ist Leiden, Dulden Hofen Wer dieses hat gelernt der hat sein Ziel Getroffen" (Ephrata, 1750), unpaginated illustrated manuscript of calligraphy patterns, ink on paper, Pennsylvania Historical and Museum Commission, Ephrata Cloister, EC 75.04.01, title page.

33. *CE*, 100–101, 108. Rudolf Nägele and Martin Funk, former Mennonites, financed it. See *German Sectarians*, 1:378, for scandals about the brothers worshiping with the sisters at night. Ernst, *Ephrata*, 141, repeats Sachse, without citation. Sachse drew on the *Chronicon*'s report (p. 62) of rumors over brothers and sisters living in Kedar.

34. *CE*, 101: "an Zion ein Bät- und Schulhaus zu bauen.... Dieses Bäthaus war ein groses [*sic*] ansehnliches Gebäu, unten war ein mit Stülen versehener groser [*sic*] Raum, mit Fractur-Schrifften ausgezieret vor die Gemeinde, darinnen hatte der Vorsteher seinen Sitz, hinter ihm war ein Chor angebauet, darin saßen unten die einsame [*sic*] Brüder und oben die Schwestern. Im zweyten Stock war abermal ein groser [*sic*] Saal, mit aller Zurüstung versehen die Agapas zu halten; aber im dritten Stock waren Wohnungen vor acht Einsamen." Stephen Warfel interprets the description according to the American convention of naming the ground floor as the first floor.

35. *CE*, 100–101. See also *LuW*, 4:38–39. Alderfer seems to conflate and confuse the building of the two structures, wrongly suggesting that "Zion Saal was completed in October" 1738 (*Ephrata Commune*, 69). Zion's Saal, or *Bäthaus*, was not begun until October 1739. This error is probably due to Alderfer's dependence on Ernst, who erroneously referred to the Zion convent as "Zion Saal" (*Ephrata*, 131), although Alderfer did not cite Ernst here. The dormitory was named Zion; its Saal or *Bäthaus* did not have a specific name. See also *Contemporaries*, 63–64.

36. Biever, "Report of Archaeological Investigations," 20–23. Biever believed he found evidence for a central hearth within the Saal and drains originating inside. Biever acknowledged the inconclusiveness of some of his work on Zion. See O'Bannon et al., "Ephrata Cloister," 1:19.

37. Warfel, *Historical Archaeology* (2000), 13–16, 19–22, 29–31. Warfel suggests that the 40′ by 40′ foundation Biever discovered was for the planned expansion of Zion that was never carried out. In light of this new evidence, I withhold my earlier theory about the dimensions of Zion's Saal.

38. *CE*, 101: "Dieses andächtige Bäthauß ... hat länger nicht gestanden als 38 Jahr, und ist in dem Krieg von den Americanern in ein Spital verwandelt und auch hernach nicht mehr aufgebauet worden." In the English translation, Hark translated "nicht mehr aufgebauet worden" as "it was never restored again." The German seems clear that the structure was not rebuilt.

39. Seidensticker, *Klostergeschichte*, 56 and 5. Seidensticker implied with this note that a meetinghouse known as Zion still stood. However, he may have meant that worship was held in a building known as Zion, which could have been the convent, not the Saal.

40. Christoph Daniel Ebeling, *Erdbeschreibung und Geschichte von Amerika*, vol. 4 (Hamburg: Carl Bohn, 1797), in *Contemporaries*, 155–56. Seidensticker, *Klostergeschichte*, 5, quoted Ebeling's description of the buildings, which *Contemporaries* omitted. Apparently Seidensticker was confused about which names belonged to which buildings. Seidensticker wrote, "Some of the older cloister and worship buildings, Kedar, Zion and Peniel, were torn down long ago before 1790, with the exception of Zion. Ebeling remarks in his geography of Pennsylvania that in that year [1790], three cloister buildings were to be found in Ephrata: Bethania for the brothers, Saron for the sisters and Zion for devotional meetings [*Andachtsübungen*]." Obviously Seidensticker was confused, because Peniel is still standing, although by his time it was probably already known simply as the Saal. Seidensticker, not Ebeling, provided the names of the buildings that he presumed had been razed.

41. Jedidiah Morse, *The American Geography* (Elizabeth Town, N.J.: Shepard Kolluck, 1789), quoted in *Contemporaries*, 142.

42. For comparison with Morgan Edwards, *Materials towards a History of the American Baptists*, see Durnbaugh, *Brethren in Colonial America*, 112–13, 173–75.

43. "Indenture between Barbara Bremin, Catharina Henry and Catherina Fulls to Jacob Kimmel, Sr., and others," EC92.1.6, Pennsylvania Historical and Museum Commission, Ephrata Cloister. I am indebted to Clarence Spohn for calling this detail to my attention.

44. *German Sectarians,* 2:425, 1:386. Cf. Ernst, *Ephrata,* 349, and Alderfer, *Ephrata Commune,* 165.

45. Michael Showalter, "The Good Samaritan Reconsidered: The Revolutionary War Hospital at Ephrata Cloister," *Der Reggeboge* 36, no. 1 (2002): 28–40. See also Clarence E. Spohn, "The Myths Surrounding the Ephrata Cloister and the Revolutionary War Era," *JHSCV* 27 (2002), 22–48. C. H. Martin, "The Military Hospital at the Cloister," *Papers Read Before the Lancaster County Historical Society* 51, no. 5 (1947): 130–33. Biever quoted this in his "Report on Archaeological Investigations," 15. O'Bannon's unpublished report also stated that Zion and its Saal (along with Kedar) were burned. However, the report cited only Ernst and Alderfer, who say nothing of burning the buildings. See O'Bannon et al., "Ephrata Cloister," 1:43. See Warfel, "Archaeological Investigations," 10, for support of this tradition, which he has since modified. The *Chronicon* and Seidensticker say nothing about the buildings' being burned.

46. Warfel, *Historical Archaeology* (2000), 29–30; (2002), 2–3, 19–24, 26–27. Warfel suggests the possibility of an additional house of worship on Mount Zion (3).

47. Warfel's research challenges the tradition that part of the Zion buildings were burned. Cf. Biever, "Report of Archaeological Investigations," 19, 23.

48. *LuW,* 4:38. See also Stephan Koch to Johann Lobach in Crefeld, Germany, Oct. 20, 1739, quoted in Goebel, *Geschichte des christlichen Lebens,* 3:264. Goebel cited as his source a collection of correspondence, *Sammlung erbaulicher Briefe,* 2:6–12, 108–13, without further information. Lobach was a Dunker, as had been Koch.

49. Anna Thommen, "Brief an den lib werten Freund Hironymüs Annony," in Nachlaß d'Annoni F II, Nr. 921, Universitätsbibliothek Basel. The text is given in full with a copy of part of the manuscript in Leo Schelbert, "Von der Macht des Pietismus: Dokumentarbericht zur Auswanderung einer Basler Familie im Jahre 1736," *Basler Zeitschrift für Geschichte und Altertumskunde* 75 (1975): 110–14. See also Schelbert, "On the Power of Pietism," for the same article in English. I am grateful to Dorothy Duck for calling this letter to my attention.

50. *CE,* 75: "ein besonderer Aufzug von H.[eiligen] Matronen und Jungfrauen, welche kein Oberhaupt erkenneten als Christum."

51. Ibid., 65 (misnumbered 64), 108: "Die Gemeinde muß sich noch ein eigen Bäthaus bauen." Alderfer mistakenly said that Kedar's *Bäthaus* "had been erected only six years before." The *Chronicon* stated "about four." See Alderfer, *Ephrata Commune,* 88.

52. Goebel, *Geschichte des christlichen Lebens,* 3:264–65.

53. *CE,* 101, 103.

54. Peter Gay, *The Science of Freedom,* vol. 2 of *The Enlightenment: An Interpretation* (New York: Knopf, 1969; rpt. New York: Norton, 1977), 241–43. See also Rudolf Vierhaus, *Germany in the Age of Absolutism,* trans. Jonathan B. Knudsen (Cambridge: Cambridge University Press, 1988), 37.

55. Ernst, *Ephrata,* 191.

56. Cook and Callahan, "Tree-Ring Dating," 4, 12.

57. *CE,* 128, 157. See also *LuW,* 4:40, 44–45. By transposing the occasion for building Zion's Saal to the building of Peniel, Alderfer has thoroughly confused the story, rendering his account of Peniel useless (*Ephrata Commune,* 87). Alderfer erred on the name of one of the donors. Martin Funk was the father of Samuel Funk. Alderfer also set his account of Peniel in the context of events in 1743, but gave no date of construction.

58. *ZS,* 250. The letter can be dated by a reference (p. 249) to Beissel's retreat to the Cocalico "nine years ago." Thus the letter was written nine years after 1732, or in 1741.

59. Beissel to Becker, 1756, in FLP B. Ms. 22, p. 155: "Nichts war die männliche Willens-macht als die der Engel des Bundes nicht übermöchte, bis er das Gelenck seiner Hüffte verruckte. Dieses ist die geistliche Verschneidung ums Himmelsreichs willen"; "ihn durch das heilig unter sich sinken überwunden."

60. *TP,* 1:302.

61. O'Bannon et al., "Ephrata Cloister," 1:23–24.

62. *SS*, 4 (*De incarnatione verbi*): 35. Cf. *SS*, 6 (*De signatura rerum*): 119. Boehme's symbolism contrasts with Sachse's theory that 40 represented perfection. See *German Sectarians*, 1:389.

63. *SS*, 4 (*De incarnatione verbi*): 48. See also 47–54.

64. Joachim Telle, "Zum *Opus mago-cabbalisticum et theosophicum* von Georg von Welling," *Euphorion* 77 (1983): 359–79, esp. 363–66. See also Petra Jungmayr, *Georg von Welling (1655–1727): Studien zu Leben und Werk*, vol. 2 in Heidelberger Studien zur Naturkunde der frühen Neuzeit, ed. Wolf-Dieter Müller-Jahncke and Joachim Telle (Stuttgart: Franz Steiner, 1990), 15–29. I am indebted to Konstanze Grutschnig-Kieser for calling these works to my attention.

65. Telle, "Zum *Opus mago-cabbalisticum*," 366–69; Jungmayr, *Georg von Welling*, 32–40. Jungmayr and Telle are uncertain whether Richter and Welling actually met. See Christopher McIntosh, *The Rosicrucians: The History, Mythology and Rituals of an Occult Order*, 2d rev. and expanded ed. (Wellingborough: Crucible Press, 1987), 86–88. McIntosh believes that the Gold and Rose Cross Rosicrucianism in the second half of the eighteenth century derives from a loose network of a few scattered individuals in the first half of the century, nurtured in part by cabbalistic, numerological, and alchemical traditions from Knorr von Rosenroth and aided by the arrival of Freemasonry in Germany. This fellowship of the Gold and Rose Cross was "the first identifiable Rosicrucian organization" (82). It began in Germany around the time of Beissel's death.

66. Georg von Welling, *Opus Mago-Cabbalisticum et Theosophicum*, 3d ed. (Frankfurt am Main: Fleischer, 1784), 72–75. "Die wahre jungfräuliche Erden-figur ist cubisch" (72). See also Jungmayr, *Georg von Welling*, 50.

67. Welling, *Opus Mago-Cabbalisticum*, 75: "Diese 12 corporibus sind die 12 Grund-Säulen der wahren, unsichtbaren Kirche." For the mystic number: "Das heilig Nummer, das mystische Nummer, welches auch ist die 24 Ältesten der ersten Kirche dreymal."

68. Ibid., 76–77.

69. O'Bannon et al., "Ephrata Cloister," 1:24–25. O'Bannon suggested that this unusual architectural feature represents the four rivers in Eden and that the central chamfered pillar symbolized the tree of life (Gen. 2). I propose different symbolism based on Boehme.

70. Untitled calligraphy placard, ink on paper, Pennsylvania Historical and Museum Commission, Ephrata Cloister, 14.65.0740: "In der Mitte dieser vier Welt Theilen ist Gottes heiliger Ruhe Punct, auf denselbigen Punct ist erbauet die Stadt des Friedens oder das heilige Jer[usalem]." See Guy Tilghman Hollyday, "The Ephrata Wall-Charts and Their Inscriptions," *Pennsylvania Folklife* 19 (Spring 1970): 40–41. My translation varies from Hollyday's more poetic one.

71. O'Bannon et al., "Ephrata Cloister," 1:25–26.

72. Ibid., 23. Beissel left Germany before Freemasonry arrived there. See McIntosh, *Rosicrucians*, 84.

73. *Contemporaries*, 55, 57.

74. Hollyday, "Ephrata Wall-Charts," 40: "In der Mitten des innwendigen Heiligtums gehen die Priester und Leviten. . . . In dem allerheiligsten wird das ewiggrünende Priestertum verwalten . . . der Hohe Priester . . . welcher ein gülden Rauchfass in Handen hat." Cf. *ZS*, 125–26.

75. Welling, *Opus Mago-Cabbalisticum*, 81. For the alchemical background, see Allison Coudert, *Alchemy: The Philsopher's Stone* (Boulder, Colo.: Shambhala, 1980), 59–60.

76. O'Bannon et al., "Ephrata Cloister," 1:24. Although plausible, O'Bannon's suggested interpretation of the central post as the tree of life and the four rivers of Eden and the meanings of circles and squares (23) does not take account of the Radical Pietist hermeneutics through which Ephrata interpreted Scripture. See also 26.

77. Certainly Jacob Martin knew and quoted Welling's work. However, Martin's earliest confirmed presence in Ephrata can be dated only in 1761. See Chapter 7.

78. Lauren R. Stevens, *Old Barns in the New World: Reconstructing a History* (Lee, Mass.: Berkshire House, 1996); Karl H. West, Jr., "Is This a Barn Pattern?" *Chronicle of the Early American Industries Association* 51, no. 1 (March 1998):17–18; Eugene George, "Letter on Barn Patterns," *Chronicle of the Early American Industries*

Association 51, no. 2 (June 1998): 98. I am indebted to Michael Showalter for calling these articles to my attention.

79. *CE*, 158. The chroniclers reported that it was conjectured that the Eckerlins, not just Israel, instigated the plan. Sachse and Ernst typically embellished the *Chronicon*. See *German Sectarians*, 1:468–69, and Ernst, *Ephrata*, 215–16. Ernst particularly expanded Israel's alleged role. Alderfer calls the plan "a thinly disguised plot of the Eckerlings" (*Ephrata Commune*, 95).

80. Cook and Callahan, "Tree-Ring Dating," 4, 12–13; O'Bannon et al., "Ephrata Cloister," 2:43.

81. *German Sectarians*, 1:469; Alderfer, *Ephrata Commune*, 95. Sachse speculated about "mystical theosophy," suggesting without documentation that Hebron signified the "common tomb of the patriarchs." Unfortunately, Alderfer embellished Sachse by claiming that Hebron was designed with "Rosicrucian symbolism." Ernst, however (*Ephrata*, 221), corrupted Sachse's account by stating that Hebron "means 'the common tomb of the Pharaohs'" rather than "patriarchs." Of course Hebron has nothing to do with pharaohs.

82. O'Bannon et al., "Ephrata Cloister," 2:37. Ann Kirschner has given the precise dimensions as 71' 6" long by 29' 6" wide and 68' to the roof peak, on the basis of drawings and photographs from G. Edwin Brumbaugh's restoration work. See Kirschner, "Hebron to Saron," 16. Sachse gave the dimensions of 70' by 30' in his text, but the floor plan illustrating the text erroneously shows 72' for the length. See *German Sectarians*, 1:470–71. Ernst cited the dimensions in Sachse's text. See Ernst, *Ephrata*, 222.

83. *DE, Pars I*, 84: "Hier wird erst der 7ten Zahl durch 1 und 0 geholfen, da das ende seinen Anfang findet." The context relates Enoch to the seventh age or epoch, when the millennium arrives.

84. Beysell, *Mystyrion Anomias*, 32. Ernst cited 3, 7, and 10 as "mystical numbers" without recourse to Ephrata writings or explaining the mystical significance. See Ernst, *Ephrata*, 222. Alderfer claimed that the dimensions were "in accord with theosophic and Rosicrucian symbolism," without citing any sources. See *Ephrata Commune*, 95.

85. *DE, Pars I*, 84. Beissel also derived 30 as the sum of multiplying 6 by 5, from the 65 years of Enoch's minority under the law.

86. *CE*, 133. Ernst repeated his earlier error that no metal was used in Hebron or Peniel, immediately after a sentence stating that the common rooms were heated with small iron stoves (*Ephrata*, 222).

87. O'Bannon et al., "Ephrata Cloister," 1:29–30.

88. [Beissel], *Mystische und sehr geheyme Sprueche*, 19: "Die Himmels thür ist klein, wilt du dardurch eingehen/Must du ein kindlein sein, sonst bleibst du draussen stehen."

89. *Klostergeschichte*, 4. Seidensticker noted that Bethania's cells were about 7' high, 5' wide, and 10' long. These architectural features in Bethania and Saron raise the question whether Zion and Kedar also had them. It seems unlikely that the earlier houses would have been more spacious.

90. HSP Ac. 1926, 2 (in second section). This document credits Jüchly with purchasing the mill for the brothers. Cf. *CE*, 89. The *Chronicon* says that Jüchly planned to return to Switzerland to claim an inheritance to purchase the mill. His sudden death allowed the brothers to inherit the mill or buy it. Sangmeister only noted the date of purchase: *LuW*, 4:40. See John A. Parmer, "Notes on the Geography of the Cloister Lower Mill Tract," *JHSCV* 27 (2002): 14–21.

91. *CE*, 146, 179–80. See *LuW* 9:46.

92. *CE*, 133–35, 144–59.

93. Ibid., 134–35, 164–65.

94. O'Bannon et al., "Ephrata Cloister," 1:32–34; Kirschner, "Hebron to Saron," 35–36, 91, 104–6. Kirschner confused Sister Athanasia with Sister Anastasia (98). The latter, not the former, helped promote singing at Ephrata. Still, Kirschner offers a valuable, detailed description of Saron's architecture.

95. O'Bannon et al., "Ephrata Cloister," 1:35–36.

96. *CE*, 165–66. The Ephrata brethren did not realize in 1746 that these buildings would be their last dormitory and meetinghouse.

97. *Klostergeschichte*, 4–5.

98. Lawrence Kocher, "The Early Architecture of Pennsylvania, Part II," *Architectural Record* 49 (January 1921): 34. Alderfer noted the buttressing without interpretation. See O'Bannon et al., "Ephrata

NOTES TO CHAPTER 5

Cloister," 1:36, for a persuasive interpretation. Additionally, both O'Bannon ("Ephrata Cloister," 22) and Kirschner ("Hebron to Saron," 24) point to steep, kicked roofs and shed-roof dormers as medieval details. It is unclear why these details should be considered specifically medieval; they are common in early modern buildings in Germany.

99. Biever, "Report of Archaeological Investigations," 24–29, 37–42. See *German Sectarians*, 2:486–87.

100. Biever, "Report of Archaeological Investigations," 41.

101. *CE*, 166: "Dieses war ein stattliches Gebäu, hatte einen Versammlungsraum für die Gemeinde, mit Fractur-schriften besonders ausgezieret, dabey waren noch Gallerien und Säle für Liebesmähler." See *Contemporaries*, 52, for Acrelius's description of three chambers in Bethania's Saal. Biever, "Report of Archaeological Investigations," 41, found archaeological evidence to verify the three chambers on the north end of the building that Acrelius had reported.

102. *German Sectarians*, 1:481–84. Sachse also drew the compass orientation wrong on the floor plan. Saron and Bethania with their meetinghouses have virtually the same orientation. Sachse cited no sources for the account from Cammerhoff. Ernst repeated Sachse's error, although with less of the original story (*Ephrata*, 286). Alderfer avoided the erroneous dimensions but repeated the mistaken notion that no iron was used (*Ephrata Commune*, 118).

103. *DE, Pars I*, 83: "In den Zahlen 300 finden wir das Geheimnuß der H.[eiligen] Dreyheit, dann der 3ter als eine Gestalt stellet uns dar die erniedrigte Menschheit des Sohns Gottes als vereinet mit dem Vater und H.[eiligen] Geist. Die zwo Nullen bedeuten noch zwey besondere Ewigkeiten als die letzte Haushaltung u.[nd] Herrlichkeit des Sohns Gottes, und dann hernach die Haushaltung des H.[eiligen] Geists."

104. In 1746 the community did not know it had completed its last large structures. However, the triangular outline of Zion, Saron, and Bethania was the most prominent pattern. Stephen Warfel's point that the post-built structure he identified as Kedar lies in the center of the triangle assumes that Beissel intended in 1735 to build two more large structures at the locations of Saron and Bethania. See *Historical Archaeology* (1999), 29. When Kedar was built in 1735, the center of the community was still alongside Cocalico Creek. At that time the post-built structure would have stood off by itself.

105. [Beissel], *Mystische und sehr geheyme Sprueche*, 4–5, 11: "Zur nacht wanns trüb und finster ist, so wende dein aug allezeit gegen aufgang" (4); "wende dein angesicht gegen Auffgang; so wird dich ihr helles liecht wiederum umgehen" (11). The word "ihr" probably refers to "die Sonne" (sun), which appears at the beginning of this maxim on 11.

106. *LuW*, 4:49–51. Ernst created an outlandish story that Sister Blandina and other sisters had made the Berghaus their brothel (*Ephrata*, 290, repeated in Alderfer, *Ephrata Commune*, 119). There is no evidence for this charge. Sangmeister reported that Emmanuel Eckerlin and others alternated living in the Berghaus until its destruction. Sister Blandina died at age 62 in 1799 ("Rose," 382; HSP Ac. 1926, p. 25 of first section); thus she would have been 10 when the Berghaus was destroyed.

107. *CE*, 179–81. See also *LuW*, 4:51. Sangmeister quoted the amount of loss from an earlier manuscript of the *Chronicon*. He also indicated that the fire occurred in the tenth month. The printed *Chronicon* followed the new-style calendar, whereas the community kept to the old style. The tenth month old style (December) explains how the fire could have happened on "one of the coldest nights of the winter," as the *Chronicon* stated, despite the date of Sept. 5 in the same passage. I am grateful to Clarence Spohn for calling this detail to my attention. Sangmeister noted that the fire began in the fifth hour, which in Ephrata's system would be between 11 P.M. and midnight.

108. *CE*, 185.

109. *Contemporaries*, 75. Acrelius noted in 1753 that "at some distance from the convent several hermits live in houses by themselves." The community had helped to build these houses, according to Acrelius.

110. Ibid., 74.

111. HSP Ac. 1926, p. 1 (in second section).

112. Onesimuß, "Evangelisches Zeugnüß," fol. 134r–v: "Sein aufsteigen ist die zwölf nummer gestiegen . . . aus dem abend und dem morgen wird der gantze Tag Gottes offenbahrt."

NOTES TO CHAPTER 6

CHAPTER 6. ROSES IN THE WILDERNESS: EPHRATA'S MANUSCRIPT ART

1. *Contemporaries*, 168.
2. Ibid., 39.
3. *CE*, 64. The description of the *Bäthaus* reads: "daneben waren hin und wieder Fractur-schrifften aufgehänget." The description is on the second of two pages numbered 64. Hark translated *Fractur-schrifften* as "texts in black-letter" (80 in his translation).
4. *CE*, 144, 168: "ihnen auf dem Heiligungs-weg zur Creutzigung der Natur gedient hat: die Schriften sind in den Capellen zur Zierde aufgehänget oder an Liebhaber ausgetheilt worden" (144). My translation varies somewhat from Hark's (169). See also *LuW*, 5:71.
5. *CE*, 144. Calligraphy served those who had no gift for singing. "Wollen wir noch der Schreibschule gedencken, darinnen das Fractur-schreiben behandelt wurde, und welche hauptsächlich zum Dienst derer aufgerichtet wurde, welche keine Gaben zum Singen hatten."
6. See Jeffrey A. Bach, "Voices of the Turtledoves: The Mystical Language of the Ephrata Cloister" (Ph.D. diss., Duke University, 1997), chap. 9, for a discussion of some of the symbolism in the manuscript ABC book. Space limitations prevent the inclusion of that material here.
7. Donald A. Shelley, *The Fraktur-Writings or Illuminated Manuscripts of the Pennsylvania Germans*, Pennsylvania German Folklore Society, vol. 23 (Allentown: Schlechter's, 1961), 22, 101.
8. For two fine introductory essays, see Don Yoder, "The European Background of Pennsylvania's Fraktur Art" and "The Fraktur Texts and Pennsylvania-German Spirituality," both in Cory M. Amsler, ed., *Bucks County Fraktur*. Publications of the Pennsylvania German Society, n.s. 33 (Kutztown: Pennsylvania German Society and Bucks County Historical Society, 1999), 15–61. For a good illustrated introduction to *Fraktur*, see Corrine and Russell Earnest, *Fraktur: Folk Art and Family* (Atglen, Pa.: Schiffer, 1999). See also John Joseph Stoudt, *Consider the Lilies How They Grow: An Interpretation of the Symbolism of Pennsylvania German Art*, Pennsylvania German Folklore Society, vol. 2 (Allentown: Schlechter's, 1937), 25, 148–49; idem, *Pennsylvania German Folk Art: An Interpretation*, Pennsylvania German Folklore Society, vol. 28 (Allentown: Schlechter's, 1966), 78–79; idem, *Early Pennsylvania Arts and Crafts* (New York: Nobles, 1964); Frederick S. Weiser and Howell J. Heaney, comps., *The Pennsylvania German Fraktur of the Free Library of Philadelphia: An Illustrated Catalogue*, vol. 1, Publications of the Pennsylvania German Society, n.s. 10 (Breinigsville: Pennsylvania German Society and Free Library of Philadelphia, 1976), xxvi.
9. *German Sectarians*, 2:296–97, 1:56.
10. *ZS*, 121.
11. Shelley, *Fraktur-Writings*, 22–23. Even though Shelley's best examples of European patterns for Pennsylvania German *Fraktur* came from the calligraphy books of the early modern period, he still made the association with medieval illumination. A comparison with lettering of the Middle Ages shows that the sharp points and breaks of gothic type and *Fraktur* calligraphy are more characteristic of the early modern period. See, e.g., Marc Drogin, *Medieval Calligraphy: Its History and Technique* (New York: Dover, 1980). While this is a practitioner's book, it illustrates characteristics of medieval script. See also Stoudt, *Pennsylvania German Folk Art*, 10–11, and Alderfer, *Ephrata Commune*, 125. These writers are only a few of many who have seen Ephrata *Fraktur* as a continuation of medieval illumination. See *Contemporaries*, 49, for a comment written in 1752 linking Ephrata *Fraktur* to medieval manuscript art.
12. Stoudt, *Consider the Lilies*, 31.
13. Hollyday, "Ephrata Wall-Charts," 34–46; idem, "The Ephrata Codex: Relationships between Text and Illustration," *Pennsylvania Folklife* 20, no. 1 (Autumn 1970): 28–43. The so-called Ephrata Codex is an illustrated book of musical notation accompanied by the first stanzas of hymns in an Ephrata hymnal, *Das Gesäng der einsamen und verlassenen Turtel-Taube* and Zionitischer WeyrauchsHugel.
14. Shelley, *Fraktur Writings*, 175–78.
15. Weiser and Heaney, *Pennsylvania German Fraktur*, 1: xvi, xxvii.
16. *CE*, 144. Hark's translation overlooks the importance of this technical term. He translated the phrase: "the power to produce rests within everybody," rendering *Gebährungswerck* as "to produce."

NOTES TO CHAPTER 6

Obviously *Gebährungswerck* refers to Beissel's and Hildebrand's concept of the fruit of a spiritual "womb," restored through rebirth and celibacy, from which "spiritual fruit" is born.

17. *DE, Pars I*, 10.

18. Cynda L. Benson, "Early American Illuminated Manuscripts from the Ephrata Cloister" (Ph.D. diss., University of Kansas, 1994), 66–70, 99–100, 125–29. Cf. Shelley, *Fraktur-Writings*, 23–28.

19. Peter C. Erb, "Emblems in Some German Protestant Books of Meditation: Implications for the *Index Emblematicus*," in Peter M. Daly, ed., *The European Emblem: Towards an Index Emblematicus* (Waterloo, Ont.: Wilfrid Laurier University Press, 1980), 121–34, esp. 121–23, 126–28. I agree with Erb's thesis that the emblematic illustration in some ways heightens the possibility of devotion apart from the text. I also agree with his cautions about the emblems used in Boehme's works.

20. Menno Simons, *Complete Writings*, 171.

21. [Horch], *Mystische und Profetische Bibel*, commentary on Song of Solomon 2:1. As noted earlier, this work is unpaginated. See also *GdP*, 2:120–21.

22. Schütz, *Güldene Rose*, 10, 11: "darinnen nicht nur ein klares Zeugnis von der zukünfftigen güldenen und lieblich blühenden Zeit welche auch der Prophet Micah mit ausdrücklichen Worten eine güldene Rose nennt, Micah 4:8"; "Die schöne Sarons-Blum und liebliche Thal-Rose Jesu Christi . . . alle Gottes-Bienlein welche sich mit einer reinen Honigbegierd [*sic*] dabey einfinden und erquicken wird."

23. FLP B. Ms. 22, pp. 76–77. Horch, in the preface to Song of Solomon in *Mystische und Profetische Bibel*, described the Church as the "bride of Christ," a "lily among thorns" (eine lilie unter den dornen). In the comments on Song of Solomon 2:2, Horch warned that the "daughters of the fleshly Jerusalem are pointed thorns" who wound the innocent (Die Töchter des fleischlichen Jerusalem, . . . sind sie nicht anders als spitzige dornen). Beissel's dependence on Horch is obvious. See also *DE, Pars I*, 128: "Die Rosen hie und da aus den Knotten hervor brechen . . . die Biene des Paradieses den Honig aus den Blumen hohlen [*sic*] ohne Stachel."

24. Peter Miller et al., "Die Bittre Suse Oder Das Gesäng der einsamen Turtel Taube, der Christlichen Kirchen hier auf Erden," variously paginated manuscript of illustrated text and music, Ephrata, 1746, LC M2116.E6 1746, dedication page.

25. [Horch], *Mystische und Profetische Bibel*, commentary on Isa. 35:1: "blühen wie die Rosen."

26. *SS*, 4 (*De incarnatione verbi*): 170–72: "Also auch zeucht Gottes Sonne des Menschen Lilie als den neuen Menschen immer in seine Kraft von der bösen Essentz aus" (172).

27. *SS*, 6 (*De signatura rerum*): 65: "der Lilien-Zeit zu einer Rosen welche wird blühen im Mayen, wann der Winter vergehet."

28. See Don Yoder, ed., *Pennsylvania German Fraktur and Color Drawings*, Exhibition at Landis Valley Museum (1969) (Lititz, Pa.: Wagaman Bros., 1969; rpt. Lancaster, Pa.: Acorn Press, 1989), plate 14.

29. Johannes Kelpius, "Von der Wüsteneÿ der Jungfraulichen Heimlichen Creutzes Liebe," in Willard Martin, "Johannes Kelpius and Johann Gottfried Seelig: Mystics and Hymnists on the Wissahickon" (Ph.D. diss., Pennsylvania State University, 1973), 133–34, 138: "Denck an die Sonnen Wend die auch in dunckelheiten/Mit treuem angesicht den liebsten kan begleiten"; "Dan steh ich still in dir, Ich deine Sonnen Wendt." Kelpius used the older German term for sunflower, *Sonnen Wendt*.

30. One source is John Ruusbroec, *The Spiritual Espousals and Other Works*, trans. James A. Wiseman (New York: Paulist Press, 1985), 64, where Ruusbroec compares the soul's purity of heart to "the whiteness of the lily," to the "redness of the rose" as a symbol of the martyrs' faithfulness, and finally to the sunflower, "one of the highest adornments of nature." Souls with a pure heart are most receptive to love for Christ, the bridegroom of the soul. Gottfried Arnold published a German translation of Ruusbroec's works in 1701 and quoted liberally from them in his own works; yet Erb suggested that Ruusbroec did not profoundly shape Arnold's thinking: *Pietists, Protestants, and Mysticism*, 185–91.

31. On the title pages of the Ephrata hymnals, *Zionitischer WeyrauchsHügel* and *Das Gesäng Der einsamen und verlassenen Turtel-Taube*.

32. *SS*, 6 (*De signatura rerum*): 111, 168. "Ich bin derselbe Christus, als ein Zweig am selben Baume." The same imagery occurs in chap. 8 of *De incarnatione verbi*.

NOTES TO CHAPTER 6

33. See, e.g., *SS*, 1:99–100. See also *SS*, 6 (*De signatura rerum*): 29–40.

34. *SS*, 1:150–51: "[den kleinen Kindern] . . . die im Mayen, wenn die schönen Röselein blühen, miteinander in die schönen Blümlein gehen und pflücken derselben ab, und machen seine [*sic*] Cräntzlein daraus . . . und machen ihnen schöne Cränzlein und freuen sich in dem schönen Mayen Gottes."

35. Shelley, *Fraktur-Writings*, 57.

36. *Contemporaries*, 49.

37. Ibid., 168.

38. Hollyday, "Ephrata Wall-Charts," 34–36. Hollyday apparently believed that Fahnestock really had seen walls covered with a plethora of *Fraktur* placards. Hollyday identified one of the thirteen surviving placards, then at Snow Hill, as coming from Ephrata. Generous donors returned this thirteenth placard to Ephrata in 2000, after it had been sold to another party at the 1997 Snow Hill auction. The other twelve were carefully restored as much as possible by Marilyn Kemp Weidner. Hollyday quoted the work of William Fahnestock, I. Daniel Rupp, Julius F. Sachse, and Oswald Seidensticker, recording the texts of three placards now supposedly lost. One is a euology of Sister Zenobia. The text of the placard that Seidensticker quoted appears in the first half of the large *Fraktur* frontispiece of the ABC Book. Sachse, *German Sectarians*, 1:478, quoted a placard whose text eulogized Sister Bernice. The text he quoted appears in "Rose," 367. Whether this was actually a placard is undocumented.

39. Hollyday, "Ephrata Wall-Charts," 38.

40. Weiser and Heaney, *Pennsylvania German Fraktur*, 1:xxviii.

41. *Fraktur* wall placard, ink on paper, Pennsylvania Historical and Museum Commission, Ephrata Cloister, 14.65.0741: "Gott und das Keusche Lamm muss stetig in uns walten: Und uns in Ewigkeit nicht lassen mehr erkalten." See Hollyday, "Ephrata Wall-Charts," 38. My translations of the placards are somewhat less poetic than Hollyday's. This text appears in [Beissel et al.], *Erster Theil der Theosophischen Lectionen*, 405 (no. 36). The other placard text found in this work appears on 428 (no. 128).

42. *Fraktur* wall placard, ink on paper, Pennsylvania Historical and Museum Commission, Ephrata Cloister, 14.65.0747: "So steht der Tempel da erfüllt mit reinen Seelen/Die sich das keusche Lamm zu eigen tut vermählen." See Hollyday, "Ephrata Wall-Charts," 44.

43. *Fraktur* wall placard, ink on paper, Pennsylvania Historical and Museum Commission, Ephrata Cloister, 14.65.0743: "Die Tür zum Eingang in das Haus/Wo die vereinte Seelen wohnen/Läst keines mehr von da hinaus/Weil Gott tut selber unter ihnen trohnen." See Hollyday, "Ephrata Wall-Charts," 43.

44. *Fraktur* labyrinth, ink on paper, Pennsylvania Historical and Museum Commission, Ephrata Cloister, 14.65.0740. See Hollyday, "Ephrata Wall-Charts," 40–42.

45. Ibid: "der Hohe Priester, als welcher ein gülden Rauchfass in Handen hat . . . u[nd] machet die heilige Gebäte als ein liebliches Rauchwerck aufsteigen"; "Dieses Priestertum versöhnet alle Lande und alle Volcker um Jerusalem her."

46. *Fraktur* wall placard, ink on paper, 1755, Pennsylvania Historical and Museum Commission, Ephrata Cloister, 14.65.0738. See Hollyday, "Ephrata Wall-Charts," 39–40: "der gute Hirte [?] Sie leitet und führt zu der reinen Tränck an dem Strom oder Brunnen des Lebens . . . singen wie ein neu Lied . . . der Jungfrauen die dem Lamm nachfolgen wo es hingehet." Hollyday transcribed one phrase: "singen wie ein neu Lied." The phrase might be: "singen wir ein neu Lied."

47. Ibid.: "Ist es dann nicht ein Paradisisches Blumen-Feld, das [?] die Kinder der neuen Welt in Freuden einander hertzen, und mit Frolocken sich über die Schönheit der Blumen erfreuen."

48. *TP*, 5:3254: "Sie öffnet im Gemüte das Paradis, und gibt aus derselben Harmonie schöne, liebliche wolriechende Blümlein."

49. *Contemporaries*, 169. For Athanasia's illustration, see illustrated, paginated manuscript music book for *Zionitischer WeyrauchsHügel*, Joseph Downs Collection of Manuscripts and Printed Ephemera, Winterthur Library, Winterthur, Del., 65 × 554, p. 121. See also Dorothy Duck, "Artist's Signature Identified in Ephrata Hymnal at Winterthur," *Journal of the Lancaster County Historical Society* 97, no. 4 (Winter 1995): 134–51. Duck has suggested that Athanasia and Anastasia may have been the same person. I believe there is insufficient evidence for such an identification. For a good introduction to the Ephrata hymnals at

NOTES TO CHAPTER 6

Winterthur, see Kari M. Main, "Illuminated Hymnals of the Ephrata Cloister," *Winterthur Portfolio* 32, no. 1 (Winter 1997): 65–78.

50. Illustrated, paginated manuscript music book for *Zionitischer WeyrauchsHügel*, Borneman Collection, B. Ms. 10, FLP, 42. This manuscript has been severely defaced by cutting out of illustrations. Ink stains suggest that several of these illustrations were created with a similar pattern imitating cross-stitch embroidery. If they were the work of one artist, Naema Eicher would be the likely artist.

51. Miller et al., "Die Bittre Suse," LC M2116.E6 1746, dedication page.

52. Several manuscripts remain for *Das Gesäng der einsamen und Verlassenen Turtel-Taube*, a hymnal with two major variants (1747, 1749).

53. The six manuscripts used in this study, all for the *Zionitischer WeyrauchsHügel*, are: B. Ms. 2, Borneman Collection, FLP; Ac. 1891, Cassel Collection, HSP; LC M2116.E6 1745(B); nos. 4 and 5 in the Julius Sachse Collection of the Seventh-Day Baptist Historical Society, Box 8, on loan to PSA (the Sachse Collection was being recatalogued at the time of my research, so the older identification numbers are used here); and a photocopy and photographic slides of the songbook prepared for Mother Maria Eicher, now in the possession of Guy Oldham, which I refer to as Mother Maria's book.

54. The "pages" in the music manuscripts are numbered as the book is held open, so the two facing pages are numbered as one. Mistakes occur in numbering in some of the books. In these six samples, however, the numbers are consistently accurate.

55. LC M2116.E6 1745(B).

56. FLP B. Ms. 2.

57. LC M2116.E6 1745(B).

58. Mother Maria's book, 121, is illustrated with a large vertical border characteristic of pp. 104–24 in that manuscript. This vertical border is the only one to be ornamented with a garland of six roses.

59. Conrad Beissel, "O Jesu meiner Seelen Lust," in *Zionitischer WeyrauchsHügel*, 721, stanza 3.

60. PSA, Sachse Collection, Box 8, no. 4, p. 3.

61. The single exception for p. 22 is ibid.

62. The two are HSP Ac. 1891 and Mother Maria's book.

63. "Ich will mit Liebesfurcht anbeten," in *Zionitischer WeyrauchsHügel*, 187, stanza 4. Stanza 6 continues, "I see, taste and feel, enjoy, kiss and suckle."

64. PSA, Sachse Collection, Box 8, no. 5.

65. FLP B. Ms. 2.

66. Angelus Silesius, "Ihr Töchter Zions die ihr," in *Zionitischer WeyrauchsHügel*, 194, stanzas 2–3.

67. Johann Feuchter, "Ihr Töchter Zions kommt," ibid., 195, stanzas 2, 8. Stanzas 6–8 follow the Christological *triplex munus* of priest, prophet, and king.

68. Gottfried Arnold, "Laß mich dich mein Heiland," ibid., 197, stanza 3. This is the third hymn on p. 23.

69. HSP Ac. 1891.

70. The manuscripts are HSP Ac. 1891 and PSA, Sachse Collection, Box 8, no. 5. No Ephrata manuscript explicitly designates a name for any of the floral designs.

71. The manuscripts are HSP Ac. 1891 and FLP B. Ms. 2.

72. "Der das Wort hat ausgebohren," in *Zionitischer WeyrauchsHügel*, 289, stanzas 3–4. This hymn resembles Tauler's writings on the birth of the Christ child in the soul of the seeker.

73. Michael Müller, "Der Herr hat selbst" and "Der Herr ist König," ibid., 655 and 663. The hymns are poetic settings of Psalms 110 and 93, respectively.

74. The manuscripts are FLP B. Ms. 2 and PSA, Sachse Collection, Box 8, no. 4.

75. Angelus Silesius, "Reinste Jungfrau," in *Zionitischer WeyrauchsHügel*, 172, stanza 4. Another hymn from *Zionitischer WeyrauchsHügel* on this manuscript page, Johann Joseph Winckler's "Ringe recht" (p. 537), exhorts believers to struggle until they have "won the pearl" and to "hold your crown firmly" (stanzas 6, 8). Winckler lived in Europe and was not a member of Ephrata.

76. The large tree in LC M2116.E6 1745(B) may portray Boehme's imagery of being grafted to Christ as a branch to a tree.

NOTES TO CHAPTER 7

77. PSA, Sachse Collection, Box 8, no. 5; LC M2116.E6 1745(B); Mother Maria's book.
78. PSA, Sachse Collection, Box 8, no. 4; FLP B. Ms. 2; HSP, Ac. 1891; Mother Maria's book.
79. A spreading tree in leaf appears on p. 88 in PSA, Sachse Collection, Box 8, no. 5. Small blue tulips appear in the capitals of the second two hymn titles in LC M2116.E6 1745(B), a rare motif in this manuscript.
80. In Mother Maria's book, p. 89 is a full-page floral creation. P. 88 displays a pelican plucking its breast and feeding its chicks with its blood. The pelican appears occasionally in Ephrata music manuscripts, contrary to Betty Martin's assertion that only doves appear. See Betty Martin, "The Ephrata Cloister and Its Music, 1732–1785: The Cultural, Religious, and Bibliographical Background" (Ph.D. diss., University of Maryland, 1974), 111. In European lore, the pelican was thought to feed its young with its own blood, and thus was a religious motif for Christ. See *Physiologus*, trans. Michael J. Curley (Austin and London: University of Texas Press, 1979), 9–10, 71–72. The pelican also appeared in some emblem books of the early modern period; e.g., Gabriel Rollenhagen, *Selectorum emblematum centuria secunda* (Arnhem, 1613), no. 12. This emblem shows a crucifixion in the background, reinforcing the Christological symbolism. It is cited in Daly, *European Emblem*, 10–11. Whether Ephrata artists knew these emblem books is unknown.
81. Ernst Lange, "Seyd froh ihr unbesteckte," in *Zionitischer WeyrauchsHügel*, 248, stanzas 1–2. Lange was a European author and not a member of Ephrata.
82. HSP Ac. 1891.
83. PSA, Sachse Collection, Box 8, no. 5.
84. Ibid., no. 4; FLP B. Ms. 2; HSP Ac. 1891. The manuscript in the Sachse Collection differs most from the other two.
85. Manuscript music book for *Zionitischer WeyrauchsHügel*, in the Joseph Downs Collection of Manuscripts and Printed Ephemera, Winterthur Library, 65x554, Winterthur, Del., 121.
86. See n. 49 above.
87. Johann Daniel Herrnschmidt, "Liebster aller lieben," in *Zionitischer WeyrauchsHügel*, 266–68, stanzas 1, 2, 8.
88. Mother Maria's book, 55. Crucifixion scenes are rare in surviving Ephrata music books. In this scene, a sister wearing the habit kneels at the right of the cross, while a brother in habit stands at the left, pointing to the dying Christ.
89. Ibid., 99. The grape arbor is very rare in Ephrata manuscripts.
90. John L. Kraft, "Ephrata Cloister, an Eighteenth-Century Religious Commune," *Antiques*, October 1980, 724–37.

CHAPTER 7. "HEAVENLY MAGIC": HIDDEN KNOWLEDGE AT EPHRATA

1. Keith Thomas, *Religion and the Decline of Magic* (New York: Scribner, 1971), 41.
2. Stanley Jeyaraha Tambiah, *Magic, Science, Religion and the Scope of Rationality*, Lewis Henry Morgan Lectures 1984 (Cambridge: Cambridge University Press, 1990), 31.
3. Jon Butler, "Magic, Astrology, and the Early American Religious Heritage, 1600–1760," *American Historical Review* 84 (April 1979): 317–46. See also Jon Butler, *Awash in a Sea of Faith: Christianizing the American People* (Cambridge: Harvard University Press, 1990), 67–97.
4. Tambiah, *Magic*, 28–30.
5. William Monter, *Ritual, Myth, and Magic in Early Modern Europe* (Athens: Ohio University Press, 1984), 115–16. See also Herbert Leventhal, *In the Shadow of the Enlightenment: Occultism and Renaissance Science in Eighteenth-Century America* (New York: New York University Press, 1976), 1–10. Two writers have tried to evaluate some of the legacy of hidden knowledge at Ephrata. Eugene Taylor, *Shadow Culture: Psychology and Spirituality in America* (Washington, D.C.: Counterpoint, 1999), includes Ephrata in a survey of spiritual traditions in America that he considers to be precursors of New Age spirituality. Willis Shirk, "The European Roots of the Ephrata Commune," *Journal of the Lancaster County Historical Society* 98, no. 3

NOTES TO CHAPTER 7

(Autumn 1996): 130–60, offers a somewhat confusing view of European sources for hidden knowledge at Ephrata.

6. *ZS*, 181–82: "Dieses ist die Stimme des Worts, ... welches Wort Magisch ist, u.[nd] ein wesentliches Einsprechen in die ganze Menschheit nach Geist, Seel und Leib, durch welches Wort der Mensch zum neuen Schöpfungs-Werck von Gott innen die Hand genommen wird."

7. *DE, Pars I*, 33–34, 38: "O eine heilige und himmlische Magia! Als die wiederum durch Jesum und Mariam in die zertheilte Tincturen menschlichen Geschlechts eingeführet";"Dann seine Magia ziehet starck an uns, damit das Kind der Ewigkeit werde zur Welt gebracht."

8. *SS*, 4 (*Sex puncta mystica*): 94–95: "In der Magia liegen alle Gestalten des Wesens aller Wesen" (94); "Sie [Magia] ist von Ewigkeit ein Grund und Halter aller Dinge. ... Magia ist die Mutter zur Natur, und der Verstand ist die Mutter aus der Natur" (95); "Sie [Magia] ist nicht der Verstand, sondern sie ist eine Macherin nach dem Verstande" (94).

9. Ibid., 95: "Durch Magiam wird alles vollbracht, Gutes und Böses; Ihre eigene Wirckung ist Nigromantia.... Sie dienet den Kindern zu Gottes Reich, und den Zauberern zu des Teufels Reich."

10. Weeks, *Boehme*, 151, 192–95.

11. *SS*, 4 (*Sex puncta mystica*): 95–96: "Magia ist die beste Theologia; denn in ihr wird der wahre Glaube gegründet und gefunden.... Sie ist ein Meister der Philosophiae, und auch eine Mutter derselben"; "Mysterium ist anders nichts als der magische Wille der noch in der Begierde stecket.... Denn Mysterium Magnum ist anders nichts als die Verborgenheit der Gottheit, mit dem Wesen aller Wesen."

12. *TP*, 5:3153–55.

13. Ibid., 4:2609: "Wir verstehen den Grund der heiligen Magie oder Glaubens gar wohl; welcher aber im Licht der Drey-Zahl bilder [*sic*], da die Magie der Nigromantie in der Schärfe der Finsterniß." See also 5:3840: "Also wird auch die Magia des Glaubens mit der Vernunft nicht verstanden. Wie die Magia der Finsternis durch einen giftigen Zauberer mit seiner giftigen Imagination einem irdischen unwiedergebornen Menschen Böses in Leib und Seel kan einführen; Also die gute Glaubens-Magie kan in einem heiligen Menschen ebenfalls mit der Lichts-Imagination die Tinctur rege und empfindlich machen."

14. *ZS*, 34–35: "der lebet im Ungehorsam und ist noch kein Gottes-Kind weil er noch in der Zauberey-Sünde lebt ... dann es ist auch kein ander Gutes als das jenige, so aus unserm Nicht-seyn oder Ent-seyn von Gott selber aus uns gemacht wird."

15. Weeks, *Boehme*, 151, 194.

16. *ZS*, 38–39: "Das Gebät ist ein unablässiges magisches Essen unsers Geistes aus Gottes heiligem Wesen durch den Feuer-Willen der anziehenden und magischen Begirden unserer Seelen. So leben wir dann in Gott und seiner heiligen Wesenheit: sein Leben ist unser Leben, und wir sind in Ihm geworden, daß wir seyn, was wir seyn. Sein Leben ist in uns verwandelt und hat unsere Nidrigkeiten verwandelt."

17. [Conrad Beissel et al.], *Erster Theil der Theosophischen Lectionen*, 358: "Wilt du aber recht bäten, so dringe mit deinem Willen auser Welt und Zeit, so erreichest du die Göttliche Magie, alwo alles gefunden, was unser Gebät will."

18. *LuW*, 10:30.

19. *SS*, 1: 43–45, 355–403.

20. *SS*, 6 (*De signatura rerum*): 29–40, 114–38.

21. Weeks, *Boehme*, 54–58, 89–90, 188–90. See also Leventhal, *In the Shadow*, 15–16.

22. *TP*, 5:3154: "Ich weiß aber wie wir arme Würmer uns im Astro beängstigen, Gottes Mysteria zu ergreifen, und ist doch nicht möglich." See also 4:2610.

23. Ernest Lashlee, "Johannes Kelpius and His Woman in the Wilderness: A Chapter in the History of Colonial Pennsylvania Religious Thought," in Gerhard Müller and Winfried Zeller, eds., *Glaube, Geist, Geschichte: Festschrift Ernst Benz zum 60. Geburtstag am 17. November 1967* (Leiden: E. J. Brill, 1967), 329–31. Lashlee's report that the Wissahickon hermits built an observatory depends largely on Sachse's undocumented work. See Sachse, *German Pietists*, 221–23. See also Oswald Seidensticker, *Bilder aus der deutsch-pennsylvanischen Geschichte*, vol. 2 of *Geschichtsblätter: Bilder und Mittheilungen aus dem Leben der Deutschen in Amerika*, ed. Carl Schurtz (New York: E. Steiger, 1885), 97.

24. Fisher, "'Prophesies and Revelations,'" 299–333, esp. 318–20.

25. Kelpius, *Diarium*, 20, 26, 43–44, 48. The travel diary also records phases of the moon and some positions of planets.

26. Monter, *Ritual, Myth, and Magic*, 118–19. See also Leventhal, *In the Shadow*, 13–65.

27. *DE, Pars I*, 10, 35.

28. *CE*, 105: "Elimelech, einer von den Eckerlins, welchen daß Gestirn zum Priester und Versöhner des fleischlichen Lebens formirt hatte."

29. *Ernstliche Erweckungs-Stimm, in ein Lied verfasset ueber den so lang gestandenen und grosen Cometen, welcher sich im X Monat des Jahrs 1743 das erste mal sehen liess, und 10 Wochen lang gestanden* (Ephrata, 1745); hereafter cited as *Cometenlied*. The only known copy is in the Cassel-Brumbaugh-Swigart Collection of Juniata College Library, Huntingdon, Pa. Alderfer assumed that Beissel wrote it. See *Ephrata Commune*, 108. The preface of the tract says that the author is "unknown" and it was sent by a "friend" with the request to print it. A facsimile reproduction has a rather free translation by Will Parsons, *Cometen* (Huntingdon, Pa.: Chestnut Books, 1986). The translations here are my own. The text was appropriately designated for the melody "Es ist gewisslich an die Zeit."

30. Johannes Hildebrand, *Gründliche und Natur-gemässe Verhandelung von den Cometen und deren Erscheinung; Darinnen die Frage umständlich erörtert wird: Ob sie nur bloß Phaenomena der Natur sind oder ob sie Gerichts-Botten der zukünfftigen Straff seyen, Ausgeführt nach den Principien beydes der natürlichen Astronomie und Theosophia durch Johannes Hildebrand. Bey Veranlassung einer aus Teutschland übersandten Schrifft betreffend den letzt erschienenen grossen Cometen* (Germantown: Christoph Saur, 1746), 1–3. A photocopy was made available from the Niedersächsisches Staats- und Universitätsbibliothek in Göttingen for this study. In September 1993 a second copy of this work surfaced among the deaccessioned holdings of the Dauphin County Historical Museum and was sold at auction.

31. *German Sectarians*, 1:417–18. Ernst and Alderfer followed Sachse. See *Ephrata*, 193–94, and *Ephrata Commune*, 86.

32. *Cometenlied*, 6: "Dann, seine, in der Lust dieses Lebens entzündete Begierden, urständen nicht aus Gott . . . sondern sie entstehen aus dem strengen Feuer-Quaal des entzündeten Zorns Gottes in ihm."

33. Ibid., 12–14: "Ihr Armen, Reichen, Groß, und Klein, Den Stern laßt euch ein Warnung seyn, sonst folgt ein böses Ende" (14).

34. Hildebrand, *Gründliche und Natur-gemässe Verhandelung*, 3: "von einem hochgelehrten Mann in Augspurg."

35. Ibid., 6: "Sie nahmen ihre Leiber an durch eine Magische Magnetische Krafft aus dem Caos aus der Prima Materia aller sichtbaren Leib-Wesenheit."

36. Ibid., 9, 13. "Gegen diesen Satz will man erweisen, dass die Erde der Mittel-Punct der gantzen Schöpfung seye, und nicht die Sonne."

37. Martha R. Baldwin, "Magnetism and the Anti-Copernican Polemic," *Journal for the History of Astronomy* 16, pt. 3 (October 1985): 155–74. Schott lived from 1608 to 1666.

38. Ibid., 169.

39. Hildebrand, *Gründliche und Natur-gemässe Verhandelung*, 8: "Unser Hauptzweck hierin besteht, daß dieser falsche GrundSatz gemelter Cometen zum Dienst des Satans ist erdacht worden." See also 13: "Wie aber das Volck durch den Unglauben sich verführen liese, und in den Gerichten umkam, also kamen auch solche falsche Propheten mit ihnen um, eben also wird es auch solchen Ateistischen Astronomen ergehen in den zukünfftigen durch den Cometen angedroheten Zorn-Gerichten."

40. Some horoscope charts appear in the papers of Jacob Martin. They are copies of example horoscopes in Georg von Welling's *Opus Mago-Cabbalisticum* and not all are accurately copied. It seems unlikely that the copier was creating a horoscope.

41. This date depends on a record of debts with Georg Dechert dated Mar. 10, 1761, included in manuscript papers apparently in Martin's hand. See Jacob Martin, untitled manuscript of alchemical notes, second document in Pennypacker Collection, Pennsylvania Historical and Museum Commission, Ephrata Cloister, no. 52, Mss. 46, fol. 4r. These manuscripts are cited hereafter as Pennypacker Collection.

NOTES TO CHAPTER 7

42. The tombstone at Ephrata reads: "Hir ruhen des hohen Philosopher Jacob Martin Er ist im Europa geboren 10 Juni 1725 und ist gestorben als guter Christ d. 19 Juli 1790 im 66sten Jahr seines Alters." Information about the Martin family comes from the will of Jacob Martin, copy on file at Pennsylvania Historical and Museum Commission, Ephrata Cloister.

43. [Jacob Martin?], undated, untitled manuscript for calculating longitude, in Pennypacker Collection. Unfortunately, the several manuscripts in the Pennypacker Collection have never been formally organized and catalogued. The authorship of this particular manuscript is somewhat uncertain. However, the Beissel hymn links it to Ephrata. Another fragment in the collection containing a table for solar positions as observed from 40° east latitude bears the signature of "John Martin, Cocalico Township, Lancaster Co." John was a son of Jacob Martin. This fragment suggests that the one with the hymn fragments does belong with Jacob Martin's papers. Two other untitled fragments in the collection, one on dating Easter and one measuring planetary movements, appear to be written by different hands.

44. [Jacob Martin], ["Göttlichen ver Einigung"], undated manuscript on astrology and spiritual union, in Pennypacker Collection. I have assigned the title from a heading that appears on the third folio, which reads "Tridens Blatt von Solcher Madere oder Göttlichen ver Einigung." The handwriting appears to be consistent with that of treatises in the collection that Jacob Martin signed.

45. Onesimuß, "Evangelisches Zeugnüß," fol. 68v: "Du bist ein geistlicher alchemist, lösest die worter und gebirst das geistliche leib, das Gold des glaubens."

46. *SS*, 4 (*De incarnatione verbi*): 111–17. See also *SS*, 6 (*De signatura rerum*): 41–46.

47. Weeks, *Boehme*, 82–83, 193.

48. *TP*, 5:3336: "Sag ich nicht, daß in den Metallen zu arbeiten sündig sey, sondern daß man müsse von Gott ersehen, und mit Weisheit von Gott begabt seyn, sonsten irre man in diesem Labyrinth vielfältig." See also 3221–22.

49. Ibid., 3117: "[Ich] achte die geistliche Chymie und Magie viel höher als die äußere, welche ich keines weges verwerfe; aber sie kan mich mit Gott nicht, wie die himmlische, vereinigen."

50. I am helped by Hugh Ormsby-Lennon's article on language in the sciences and esoteric arts of the seventeenth century. Ormsby-Lennon focuses on Rosicrucians and the Royal Society, yet his "Rosicrucian linguistics" applies in part to alchemy. See Hugh Ormsby-Lennon, "Rosicrucian Linguistics: Twilight of a Renaissance Tradition," in Ingrid Merkel and Alan Debus, eds., *Hermeticism and the Renaissance* (Cranbury, N.J.: Universities Press, 1988), 311–41, esp. 328–33.

51. Jacob Martin, "Philosophische Schrift-stellen, & Processe, auf daß Jahr Anno 1762 & hernach," unpaginated manuscript in Pennypacker Collection, fol. 5r: "Nim demnach ein Glaß, so ein Fiol genant wird darrin thu die helffte deines gereinigten ☿, und behalt die Andere helffte in verwaarung, biß du deren wirst benötigt sein, und bey Ein geschließenes gläßlein auf den (gleichfals eben geschlißen, mund des Glaßes, setz daß Glaß auf einen offen in eine Capele mit gesiebten Asche, oder stelle es in Tripode Arcanorum (im 3. theil operis mineralis pag. 29 beschrieben) oder in den offen, worin du die Geister Calcinirist, und gieb Ihr feüer, so heiß als die sonne miten im sommer scheinet, und nicht heißer, oder beÿnahe etwas heißer, oder auch ein wehnig kälter, nach dem du es Am besten treffen kanst, Gäbest du ab er größere hitze, nemlich sothanne daß man damit bley im fluß erhalten könte, so wurde deine materi geschmoltzen." The text continues for one more paragraph of the same length. I have retained Martin's idiosyncratic spelling.

52. Ibid., fol. 6r.

53. [Jacob Martin], untitled, unpaginated manuscript of alchemical notations, in Pennypacker Collection, fol. 3v.

54. Ibid., fol. 1r, for one example.

55. Jacob Martin to Jacob Sennsnig, n.d., and Martin to unnamed correspondent, Dec. 11, 1766, both in Pennypacker Collection.

56. Martin to Sennsnig. The relevant passage from Welling can be found in his *Opus Mago-Cabbalisticum*, 373–74. Martin quoted only paragraph 9, but paragraph 8 also gives directions about working with mercury. Although this research was done with Welling's 3d ed., the page and paragraph numbers correspond accurately to Martin's citations.

NOTES TO CHAPTER 7

57. *German Sectarians*, 2:173. Ernst and Alderfer simply followed Sachse. See *Ephrata*, 325, and *Ephrata Commune*, 148. Seidensticker wrote nothing about an attempt to produce gold. See *Klostergeschichte*, 84.

58. Biever, "Report of Archaeological Investigations," 33.

59. Martin, ["Göttlichen ver Einigung"], fol. 1. Cf. *SS*, 6 (*De signatura rerum*): 29–40, which reworks the seven qualities named in Boehme's *De Tribus Principiis, oder, Von der Beschreibung der Drey Principien Göttliches Wesens* and replaces the seven qualities in the first work, *Aurora*. See Weeks, *Boehme*, 71, 73, 108–9. Martin's first six qualities are (1) desire (*Begirlichkeit*), (2) movement (*Beweglichkeit*), (3) sensitivity (*Empfindlichkeit*), (4) fire or life (*Feuer, Leben*), (5) light or love (*Licht, Liebe*), and (6) understanding or knowledge (*Verstentnis, Erkantniß*). The seventh quality is rest (*Rue* [sic]), or Sabbath, which subsumes all other six. Although different in name from Boehme's seventh quality (*Corpus*), Martin's seventh quality functions like *Corpus*, in that Boehme's seventh quality included and engendered all other six. Martin's third quality, *Empfindlichkeit*, may be analagous to Boehme's sense of "impression" that comes with *Angst*. Martin's surviving writings are too few to obtain a fuller sense of his terminology. Boehme's seven qualities in *De signatura rerum* are (1) herb, contraction (*einziehen*), (2) sting, moving (*bewegen*), (3) dread, impression (*Angst*), (4) fire, life (*Feuer, Leben*), (5) pleasure (*Lust*), in a secondary form leading to light and love (*Licht, Liebe*), (6) multiplicity (*Vielheit*), creating different understanding (*Verständnis*), and (7) body (*Corpus*).

60. Martin, ["Göttlichen ver Einigung,"], fol. 1. See also Weeks, *Boehme*, 193.

61. Martin, ["Göttlichen ver Einigung,"], fols. 2–3: "Alß daß das verblichne bilt in Adam durch Christo oder in Christum wieder funden alß dann thun sich die krefften des Paradises wieder herfür, und durch daß durch tringen der 6 tag werk der unruh und beweglichkeit komt der mensch wieder in die Ruh und sabath alß in die vereinigung mit und in Gott, weil alle beweglichkeit der sinnen und des gemüts durch den über Gebenen willen an Gott, Gantz stille und Gelassen durch tegliches [sic] sterben"; "Wer nun diesen Process ist durch Gegangen, und durch Christum mit Gott vereinigt ist, der hat Christum alß den schatz im Acker, und daß Perlein Gefunden . . . in daß Centerum der Ruhe alß in den Mittelpunct und jnnersten [sic] Grunde alwo Jesus Gefunden wird."

62. *DE, Pars I*, 1, 34–35, 39–40.

63. [Jacob Martin], "Christliche Erklärung von der Schöpfung der Engel und dem fall Lucefer und Adam," undated, unpaginated manuscript in Pennypacker Collection, fol. 1. The handwriting of this treatise appears consistent with that of the documents signed by Martin in this collection.

64. Ibid., fols. 1–2: "Dann nach seiner Gottheit ist er daß hertze-Gottes, als die Gottliche Sonne; nach seiner Englischen Creaturlichkeit, ist er daß hertz des Engels und Englische Sonne . . . mit und durch dieselben außfliesete (thut er alles) alles erfüllen [lacuna] und ob er schon nach seinem reinen fixen Tinctural-Leib, nach seiner Englischen Creatürlichen Langte. höchte und breiten . . . das Gantze Systema erfühl[t] alles lauter Sollarische weßenheit." The treatise opens by identifying Christ as the "first and highest angel of all angels" (der erste und höchste Engel aller Engeln).

65. [Jacob Martin], "Geistlicher brief von der Wiedergeburt," unpaginated manuscript in Pennypacker Collection, fol. 1r-v: "Dann der alte Adam, wurde in Seiner Mixtur, Auff einmahl zerstreuet und auffgelöst (durch die Englische Liecht-waßer Aesch-maiim) . . . alhier führt die jungfrau Sophia, die Seele in den Paradisischen Roßen-Garten und zeigt der Seelen, die vielerley Roßen und blumen, die all von dem Liecht Scha-maiim sind außgebohren worden."

66. *LuW*, 10:23.

67. Ibid., 7:90, 8:129. Keller later joined the Freemasons. See 7:60 for the story of gold tincture.

68. Ibid., 10:37–41, 44, 50.

69. [Eliseba Böhler (Henrietta Wilhelmine von Höning)], *Abgeforderte Relation der Erscheinung eines entleibten Geists Dem Publico zur Nachricht getreulich aus dem Mund derer, die von Anfang bis ans Ende mit interessirt, aufgeschrieben* (Ephrata: Typis & Consensu Societatis, 1761), 1–2. One manuscript letter remains in Beissel's letterbook, addressed to a Georg von Höning in Guntersblum, who may be a relative of Eliseba. A fine, accessible English translation of the account is available in Wust, *Saint-Adventurers*, 82–101. See also *CE*, 226–31. Ernst and Alderfer merely summarized the *Chronicon* account. See *Ephrata*, 316–19, and *Ephrata Commune*, 148–49.

NOTES TO CHAPTER 7

70. *LuW,* 4:33–34. Hans Schule died in 1737.
71. [Böhler], *Abgeforderte Relation,* 35–39.
72. See Thomas, *Magic,* 587–606. See *Verschiedene alte und neuere Geschichten von Erscheinungen der Geister, Und etwas von dem Zustand der Selen Nach dem Tode nebst verschiedenen Gesichtern,* 3d and expanded ed. (Germantown: Christoph Saur, 1755), 24–32, esp. 27–28. Koch wrote of the vision in a letter to Johann Lobach in Germany, and it was published in the Radical Pietist periodical *Geistliche Fama* in 1736.
73. Zaepernick, "Gichtels und seiner Nachfolger Briefwechsel," 99–100.
74. *Klostergeschichte,* 83–84. Seidensticker ridiculed Beissel's thought, comparing him with the Pied Piper of Hamelin.
75. *German Sectarians* 1:362: "Little authentic information has come down to us from the Zionitic Brotherhood itself.... A little insight, however, is gleaned from the MSS. of Johann Franz Regnier, who was one of the first to attempt to gain physical and spiritual regeneration at Ephrata according to the mystic ritual of the *Zionitische Brüderschaft.*"
76. *Ephrata,* 132–34; *Ephrata Commune,* 70–71: "Beissel had already tried to dissuade Regnier from undergoing the full Zionitic regeneration process." Alderfer conceded that it was "unlikely that the Brotherhood applied the extreme rites as a general rule." See *MHT,* 2 31–32, 52n., 87–89. Erb wrote, "There is no doubt that such a practice was carried out but the doctrinal significance of the various stages is not known (32)."
77. Johann Franz Regnier, "Das Geheimniss der Zinzendorfischen Sekte, oder eine Lebens-Beschreibung Johann Franz Regnier," in Johann Philip Fresenius, *Bewährte Nachrichten von Herrnhutischen Sachen,* vol.1 (Frankfurt am Main and Leipzig: J. L. Buchner and H. L. Brönner, 1748), 327–479. The episode with Beissel's Sabbatarians appears on 357–61. For completion of the Berghaus in the summer of 1734, see *LuW,* 4:34.
78. *German Sectarians,* 1:362. All subsequent quotations from Sachse come from his altered translation of Regnier, found in 1:362–64. Unfortunately, Reichmann and Doll simply copied Sachse's altered translation without checking the original. See *Contemporaries,* 9–12.
79. Fresenius, *Bewährte Nachrichten,* 350. Neither Fresenius nor Sachse looked closely at Regnier's own words to find this passage. Fresenius inserted an editorial comment that he did not know what "sign" Regnier meant. He conjectured that the "sign" was Regnier's willingness to do whatever the Eckerlins said, since such willingness is "a general sign of sects."
80. Ibid., 359.
81. Ibid., 360.
82. Ibid., 361.
83. *German Sectarians,* 1:354.
84. A good introduction and synopsis in English is still Frances A. Yates, *The Rosicrucian Enlightenment* (Chicago: University of Chicago Press, 1972; rpt. London and New York: Ark Paperbacks, 1986), 41–69, 238–60. She provides reliable English translations of the *Fama* and *Confessio.* A briefer synopsis but broader, sympathetic overview in English of the whole Rosicrucian phenomenon is available in McIntosh, *Rosicrucians,* 42–59. An earlier comprehensive history in English is Arthur E. Waite, *The Brotherhood of the Rosy Cross, Being Records of the House of the Holy Spirit in Its Inward and Outward History* (1924; New Hyde Park, N.Y.: University Books, 1961). Yates and McIntosh surpass Waite. A more scholarly history of the Rosicrucian phenomenon, primarily in the context of German esoterica, is Will-Erich Peuckert, *Das Rosenkreutz,* pt. 3 of *Pansophie,* 2d rev. ed. (Berlin: Erich Schmidt, 1973). The standard scholarly work now, concentrated overwhelmingly on the seventeenth century, is Roland Edighoffer, *Rose-Croix et société idéale selon Johann Valentin Andreae* (Neuilly sur Seine: Arma Artis, 1982–87). Histories of Rosicrucianism by Rosicrucian lodges serve the claims of their respective groups to be legitimate bearers of the tradition; e.g., R. Swinburne Clymer, *The Rosicrucian Fraternity in America* (Quakertown, Pa.: Philosophical Publishing Co., 1941), representing the Fraternitatis Rosae Crucis. Another large, widespread Rosicrucian group in America is the Ancient and Mystical Order Rosae Crucis (AMORC), founded by H. Spencer Lewis, with headquarters now in San Jose, Calif.

85. Edighoffer, *Rose-Croix*, 1:370–85; Yates, *Rosicrucian Enlightenment*, 50. Yates proposed the singular theory that the driving inspiration for the German Rosicrucian literature was the influence of the British alchemist John Dee.

86. McIntosh, *Rosicrucians*, 70–75.

87. Arnold, *Unparteyische Kirchen- und Ketzer-Historie*, 2:624–25, 774–75. Arnold stated that forty brothers and sisters accompanied Kelpius to Pennsylvania. See also Edighoffer, *Rose-Croix*, 1:211.

88. Kelpius, *Diarium*, 80–83.

89. Martin, "Johannes Kelpius and Johann Gottfried Seelig," 16–17, 46–47, 53–54. Donald F. Durnbaugh has also discounted a Rosicrucian identity for the Kelpius community; see his "Work and Hope: The Spirituality of the Radical Pietist Communitarians," *Church History* 39 (March 1970): 74–76.

90. Waite, *Brotherhood of the Rosy Cross*, 601–10.

91. Sachse, *German Pietists*, 62. For a favorable identification of Kelpius and the Wissahickon hermits with the Rosicrucians, see Lucy E. Carroll, "The Rosicrucian Legacy of the Wissahickon Hermits," *Rosicrucian Digest*, January 1986, 8–11.

92. Benz, *Protestantische Thebais*, 94, 96.

93. Fisher, "'Prophesies and Revelations,'" 320, 307–10, 325–28.

94. Martin, "Johannes Kelpius and Johann Gottfried Seelig," 53–54.

95. McIntosh, *Rosicrucians*, 72–75.

96. Jungmayr, *Georg von Welling*, 34–35; Telle, "Zum *Opus mago-cabbalisticum*," 367–68. Telle quoted from Christian Gottlieb Jöcher's *Allgemeines Gelehrten-Lexicon* (Leipzig, 1751), giving Richter's home as Reichau. Richter claimed to be only editor, not author. Later historians consider him the author.

97. Sincerus Renatus, *Die Wahrhafte und vollkommene Bereitung des philosophischen Steines aus dem Orden der Brüderschaft des Gulden und Rosen Kreutz* (Breslau, 1710). The rules are reprinted in Peuckert, *Rosenkreutz*, 342f. Rule 11 (343) prescribes the greeting as follows: A: "Ave, Frater"; B: "Rosae et Aureae"; A: "Crucis." Then the two brothers recite together, "Benedictus Dominus Deus noster qui dedit nobis signum." See also McIntosh, *Rosicrucians*, 73. Both Peuckert and McIntosh (74) see Richter's publication and any who used it as the connecting link between seventeenth- and eighteenth-century Rosicrucianism in Germany.

98. Peuckert, *Rosenkreutz*, 342 (rule 1).

99. Ibid., McIntosh, *Rosicrucians*, 73, notes that Richter's Rosicrucian order had lost the anti-Catholic polemic typical of the seventeenth-century writings.

100. While Ezechiel Sangmeister's quietist faction coexisted with Beissel's supporters, Sangmeister agreed with Beissel on the Sabbath and celibacy and on a certain amount of ascetic discipline. Sangmeister was indifferent to any church order, but would have been equally indifferent to an order like that of the Gold and Rose Cross.

101. Peuckert, *Rosenkreutz*, 344–45.

102. *CE*, 139–40.

103. Peuckert, *Rosenkreutz*, 344. Yet the same rule implies it is no dishonor to have a child, since a brother who is a father should protect the child's honor as his own. Rule 34 discourages the traveling brothers from associating or conversing much with women.

104. Sincerus Renatus, *Theo-Philosophia Theoretico-Practica Oder der wahre Grund Göttlicher und Natürlicher Bekanntnüß* (Breslau, 1714), 224, 205–6, 209. The original Rosicrucian treatises of 1614–18 lack a detailed account of the androgynous Adam espoused to Sophia.

105. Ibid., 207, 211, 215. "The human did not withstand, rather allowed earthly desire, which Lucifer introduced into the Salniter, to take him [Adam] captive. [Hier aber bestunde der Mensch nicht, sondern ließ die irrdische Sucht welche Lucifer in den Salniter geführet sich fangen]" (207). On 215 Richter stated that at the fall, humans received the "spirit of the world, which proceeds from all magic constellations [Spiritus Mundi, so aus allen magischen Gestirnen ausgeht]," which have "power and force over people [Macht und Gewalt über den Menschen]."

106. Ibid., 222. Richter expressed some sense of union with Christ: "The person who is united with the divine love-tincture with Christ Jesus is bodily united with Christ [Der mit göttlichen Liebes-Tinctur

NOTES TO CHAPTER 7

mit Christo Jesu vereinigte Mensch wird leibhafftig mit Christo vereiniget]." There is no mention of a mystic death.

107. Ibid., 201, 210, 217–23, 332–66.

108. McIntosh, *Rosicrucians,* 80–81. McIntosh relies more on Oriental alchemy for this point. "It seems unlikely that the tradition of sexual alchemy was completely unknown in the West" (81). But he offers no documentation.

109. Ibid., 86–88.

110. *Geschichten von Erscheinungen,* 3d ed., 30: "Er sagte: Ob ich ehemahlen hätte gehöret oder gelesen von Leuten die in Alt-Engeland gewesen, welche man Rosen-Creutzer gennenet hätte? Ich antwortete: Ich hätte niemalen nichts davon gelesen; aber Ich hätte hören sagen, daß solche Leute da gewesen wären, wovon man gesagt, daß sie könten Gold machen. Darauf sagte er gantz freundlich zu mir: Er wäre einer von solchen Leuten; und ich sollte mit ihm gehen, um zu sehen sein Hauß, welches inwendig voll Gold und Edelgestein war."

111. *CE,* 78–84. See also Durnbaugh, *Brethren in Colonial America,* 96–99, for a letter by Koch to Johann Lobach in Germany describing Ephrata in 1738. Koch says nothing about Rosicrucians.

112. McIntosh, *Rosicrucians,* 85–86, 88.

113. Welling, *Opus Mago-Cabbalisticum,* 101–63.

114. Ibid., 165–339, 503–31, 556–77; McIntosh, *Rosicrucians,* 88. The young Goethe read Welling, but found the language too esoteric to comprehend.

115. Allen G. Debus, *The Chemical Philosophy: Paracelsian Science and Medicine in the Sixteenth and Seventeenth Centuries,* vol. 2 (New York: Science History Publications, 1977), 447–92, 531–53.

116. Leventhal, *In the Shadow,* 13–17, 38–40. See Brooke, *Refiner's Fire,* 42–44, 125–27, 192, 194; Quinn, *Early Mormonism,* 80–81, 130–32, 193. I question Quinn's identification of a drawing in Jacob Martin's papers as a "salamander man."

INDEX

Aaron, priesthood of, 52, 53, 56
Abraham the Jew (alchemist), 178
Acrelius, Israel, 27, 40, 72, 80
  on architecture, 127
  on dietary habits of Ephrata, 88
  on prayer at Ephrata, 92
  on Sabbatarian concept of time, 138
  on Zion meetinghouse, 120
Adam (biblical), 33, 34, 87
  "adultery" against Sophia, 52
  alchemy and, 179–80
  androgyny of, 28, 35, 58, 99
  baptismal practices of Ephrata and, 75
  fall of, 38–39, 58, 187
  gendered rebellion of, 40
  loss of Sophia, 99
  sin of, 63, 92, 107, 179
adultery, 34, 38, 52
Agabus, Brother. *See* Koch, Stephan (Brother Agabus)
Agonius, Brother. *See* Wohlfahrt, Michael
agriculture, 55
Agrippa, Brother. *See* Miller, Peter (Brother Agrippa)
alchemy, 124, 147, 171, 173, 177–80, 191
  hexagram symbol and, 128–29
  as resistance to Enlightenment, 189–90
  spiritual, 168
  waning of, 190
Alderfer, 86, 119, 121, 130, 182
allegory, 43, 46
Almonry building, 116, 251 n. 5
American Geography (Morse), 121
American Revolutionary War, 53, 63, 121
Amish Anabaptists, 29, 78
Ammann, Jacob, 78
Amos, Brother, 90
Anabaptists, 28–29, 54, 70–71, 78

Anastasia, Sister (Anna Thomen), 122, 161, 187
Andreae, Johann Valentin, 46, 146, 181–82, 185
androgyny, 28, 33, 35, 38, 97
  baptism and, 75
  calligraphy and, 168
  fall of first couple and, 39, 58
  Lucifer's rebellion and, 66
  magic and, 173
  monastic dress and, 90
  restoration of, 129
  vegetarianism and, 64
  virgin Sophia and, 99
Angel Brothers, 84
animals, 58, 64, 104, 187
Annoni, Hieronymus d', 122
anointing, 82
Antichrist, 32, 33, 60
Antietam/Snow Hill congregation, 80, 85, 193, 194–95, 202
apocalyptic language, 45, 94
apophatic language, 36, 37
architecture, 8, 115–39
Aristotle, 107
Arnold, Gottfried, 26, 29, 71, 98, 117, 149
  bridal imagery and, 37
  on early Christians, 27–28
  on Eucharist, 77
  on fasting, 87
  on holy kiss ritual, 82–83
  hymns by, 163, 164
  Quietism and, 62
  on Sophia, 100–101
  on virginity, 34
asceticism, 65, 76, 77, 184. *See also* celibacy
  divorce and, 56
  monastic practices and, 93–94
  women's autonomy and, 113

271

INDEX

Asseburg, Rosamunde Juliane von der, 09
astrology, 171, 173, 174–77, 190, 191
Athanasia, Sister, 166
Augsburg Confession, 185
Augustine, Saint, 101
Aurora (Boehme), 174

ban (judging practice), 35, 83
baptism, 4, 14, 18, 70–76
   on behalf of the dead, 94, 93
   immersion, 32, 40, 70, 71, 72, 75
   infant, 39, 71, 74
   as Protestant sacrament, 69
Baptists, 31, 121
Barba, Alonso Alvaro, 116, 177, 180, 203
Bauman, Joseph, 61, 62
Baumann, Matthias, 12
Bayle, Pierre, 175
Bebern, Hennrich von, 16, 18
Bebern, Isaac von, 18
Bechtold, Hans, 12
Becker, Peter, 16, 18, 104, 109, 123
Beissel, Anna Köbler, 8
Beissel, Georg Conrad, 3, 7, 12, 122
   architecture and, 118
   astrology and, 176–77
   attitudes toward men, women, and sexuality, 107–13
   baptized into Neu-Täufer, 18–19, 71, 72
   biography of, 8, 9–10
   critics/detractors of, 19, 23, 49, 60, 61, 194
   death of, 23, 138, 194
   Eckerlins and, 133, 135
   emigration to America, 15–18
   esoteric knowledge and, 191
   evangelizing of, 20
   flight from Palatinate, 44, 221–22 n. 36
   on Fraktur manuscript art, 144–45
   friends of, 13
   on gender, 97, 103, 104–5
   ghosts and, 181
   as hermit, 18, 19
   hymns by, 162–63
   illnesses of, 21
   legal troubles in Germany, 14
   letters of, 200–201
   love feast ritual and, 80, 81
   magic and, 172–74
   monastic practices and, 85–86, 87–89, 92, 93–94
   mystical language of, 66, 94, 106, 138
   on nature of God, 6
   numerology and, 13–14
   Pietism and, 4
   power and authority of, 84–85, 107
   religious vision of, 23
   sources of thought, 26–29
   successor of, 193
   theology of, 46–47
   titles of, 21
   view of circumcision, 73
   women in life of, 103–4
   writings of, 5, 19, 25, 30–47
Beissel, Matthias, 8
Bender, Esbert, 12
Benedict, Brother (Benedict Jüchly), 131
Benezet, Anthony, 53
Benneville, Georges de, 180
Benson, Cynda, 146
Benz, Ernst, 185
Berghaus (Hill House), 116, 117, 135
Berniece, Sister (Maria Heidt), 106, 111
Bethania building, 131, 133–35, 134
Bethany church, 121
Beussel, Johannes, 8
Bevan, Catherine, 112
Bewährte Nachrichten (Fresenius), 182
Bible, 11, 14, 26. *See also* Revelation (biblical book); Song of Solomon
Biever, Dale, 118, 120, 134, 178
Blum, Ludwig, 21
Boehme, Jacob, 5, 13, 26, 33, 143
   on Adam's fall, 38, 99, 100
   alchemy and, 177–78, 179
   androgynous Christ and, 246 n. 16
   astrology and, 174
   on baptism, 73, 74–75
   on circumcision, 30
   Fraktur manuscript art and, 160
   on loss of self, 37
   magic/sorcery and, 173
   numerology and, 124
   Priesthood of Melchizedek and, 57
   rose symbol and, 146
   Rosicrucianism and, 181–82, 186, 190
   on Sabbath, 53
   students of, 50
   symbolism of, 149, 163
   theosophy of, 31–32, 171
   on virginity, 34

INDEX

writings of, 57, 58
Böhler (Beeler), Eliseba, 181
Bowman, Carl, 28
Boyle, Robert, 190
Braght, Thieleman van, 29
Bremer, Martin, 89
Brethren, 4, 19
British monarchy, 16
Bromley, Thomas, 13, 30, 32, 63
Brooke, John, 190
Brotherhood of Bethania, 21
Brown, Dale, 28
Büchsel, Jürgen, 27
Butler, Jon, 172
Buttlar, Eva von, 110, 188

cabbala, 29, 31, 124, 128–29, 135, 173
  alchemy and, 180
  astrology and, 175
  as element of Radical Pietism, 171
calligraphy, 141, 142, 157, 168
Calvin, John, 7, 39
Calvinism, 32–33, 41, 73
Campbell, Ted, 11
Camp of the Solitaries, 4
Carl, Johann Samuel, 14, 16, 88
cataphatic language, 37
celibacy, 4, 19–20, 21, 28, 46. *See also* asceticism
  Beissel's attitude toward, 109–13
  circumcision and, 30
  end of, 65
  estates of the Church and, 56
  laying on of hands and, 84
  marriage and, 33, 34
  monastic practices and, 94
  as spiritual castration, 104, 124
  vegetarianism and, 53, 64, 87–88
  waning of, 94
Certeau, Michel de, 5–6
charity, 19, 37, 84
Chemical Wedding of Christian Rosenkreutz, The (allegory), 184–85
chiliasm, 29, 32
Christ, return of, 11, 12, 27. *See also* Jesus Christ
  astrology and, 174
  numerology and, 14
  pure love and, 27
  virginal choir and, 45
"Christen ABC, Der" manuscript, 119, 119, 142, 145, 148, 161

Christianity, 5, 8, 138. *See also* Protestantism; Radical Pietism; Roman Catholicism
  allegorical chronology of, 26–27
  ancient, 77, 81, 83
  cabbalism and, 14, 31, 124, 171
  Church as community, 41
  early Church, 27–28
  esoteric knowledge and, 191
  estates within the Church, 55–56
Christliche Bibliothek (Martin), 35
Christology, 38, 41, 53–54, 54, 99, 187
Chronicon Ephratense, 4, 31, 61, 106, 130, 197–98
  on architecture, 116–19, 121, 122, 134
  on baptism, 73, 76
  on Beissel's life, 9, 10, 15–16
  on Beissel's writings, 30, 37–38
  on foot washing ritual, 78
  on Heidelberg Pietists, 13
  on Hildebrand, 50
  on laying-on-of-hands ritual, 83–84
  on love feast ritual, 80
  on manuscript art, 141, 144–45
  on monastic practices, 87, 89, 90, 93
  on name "Ephrata," 42
  on Neu-Täufer fellowship, 18
  on Rosicrucianism, 188
church, sect and, 6–7
Chymische Hochzeit Chiristiani Rosenkreutz (Andreae), 46
circumcision, 30, 64, 73
Clymer, R. Swinburne, 185
Cocceius, Johannes, 73
comets, 60, 175–76
community, 60, 62, 65, 82, 138
Community of True Inspiration, 14
Conestoga region, Penn., 17–18, 19, 20, 50
Confessio fraternitatis, 184, 185
Counter-Reformation, 11
covenants, new and old, 30, 52, 54, 56, 73

Darius, Brother, 118
death
  baptism on behalf of the dead, 76, 93, 94
  mystic, 40–41, 46, 57, 74, 94, 187
  universal restoration and, 43
"Debt Book" (Mueller), 204
De incarnatione verbi (Boehme), 57, 58, 177
Deliciae Ephratenses (Beissel), 26, 36, 37, 200
Denmark, 11

INDEX

Descartes, René, 185
De signatura rerum (Boehme), 36, 100, 174, 177, 179
Diaetetica Sacra (Carl), 88
Diehl, Nicholaus, 13
Dissertation on Man's Fall (Beissel), 25, 37–47, 52, 179, 200, 225 n. 2
    Adam's fall in, 107
    on magic, 173
    Sophia (divine female) in, 102
    soteriology of, 54
Divine Other, 6
divorce, 56
Doll, Eugene E., 199
Dordrecht Confession, 78
Duché, Jacob, 65
Duck, Dorothy, 161, 166
Dunkers, 4, 14, 50
    arrival in Pennsylvania, 17
    attitude toward Scriptures, 27
    baptism among, 70, 73, 76
    distribution in American colonies, 22
    ecclesiology of, 35
    Ephrata ritual practices and, 69, 77, 94. *See also* Neu-Täufer
    opposition to slavery, 53
    original sin doctrine and, 39
    origins of, 28
    as source of Beissel's thought, 26
    views on marriage, 33
Durnbaugh, 28
Dutch Collegiants, 71
Dutch Reformed Church, 10, 11, 32

East Nantmeal (French Creek) congregation, 31
ecclesiology, 38, 54–57
Eckerlin, Anna, 50
Eckerlin, Emmanuel, 19, 76
Eckerlin, Israel (Brother Onesimus), 20, 21, 36, 51–52, 119, 191
    on alchemy, 177
    in Almonry building, 116
    architecture and, 118
    on Beissel's celibacy, 112
    building of Peniel and, 130
    economic plans of, 131, 133
    expulsion from Ephrata, 133, 232 n. 1
    as leader of Zionitic Brotherhood, 84
    tonsure and, 86
Eckerlin, Michael, 50

Eckerlin, Samuel, 21, 23, 61
    anointing ritual and, 82
    legal claim to Ephrata land, 65–66
    return from Virginia, 135, 193
Eckstein, Christian (Brother Gideon), 82, 108, 193
Edwards, Morgan, 121
Efigenia, Sister, 106
egalitarianism, 80, 85, 98
Ehe, das Zuchthaus fleischlicher Menschen, Die (Beissel), 33
Eicher, Anna, 112–13
Eicher, Christian (Brother Eleasar), 86, 87
Eicher, Maria, 23, 87, 90, 93, 106, 161
    music manuscripts and, 142
    power of, 112
    succession of leadership at Ephrata and, 193
Eicher, Naema, 161
Eleasar, Brother (Christian Eicher), 86, 87
Eller, Vernard, 28
England, 11, 26
Enlightenment, 6, 172, 189–90
Ensign, C. David, 28
Ephrata, ein amerikanische Klostergeschichte (Seidensticker), 208
Ephrata Cloisters (Doll & Funke), 199
Ephrata Codex, 143, 147, 161, 162
Ephrata community, 3–5, 93–95. *See also* Sabbatarianism
    anointing ritual at, 82
    architecture of, 115–39
    baptism at, 70–76
    Cloister, 36, 88, 161
    confession of faith, 50
    conflicts in, 21
    emigration motives and, 17
    esoteric knowledge and, 190–91, 216–17
    holy kiss ritual at, 82–83
    laying on of hands at, 83–85
    legacy of, 193–95
    literature about, 197–217
    love feasts at, 76–82
    manuscript art of, 141–69, 213–15
    maps of, 20, 122, 136–37
    as milling center, 21
    monastic practices at, 85–93
    nuns of, 65, 105–7, 194
    origin of name, 42
    printing press of, 21, 29, 35
    religious thought of, 25–26, 49, 52–60

INDEX

ritual at, 69–70
Rosicrucianism and, 182, 185, 186–87
sectarianism and, 6–7
size of, 4
Sophia (divine female) concept at, 102–7
time at, 138
epistles, 35–36, 57
Erb, Peter, 28, 39, 107, 146, 182
Ernst, 86, 119, 121, 130, 182
Ernsthafte Christenpflicht, 29
eroticism, 3
Erster Theil der Theosophischen Lectionen (Beissel, ed.), 201
eschatology, 26, 27, 32, 43, 46, 60
   Radical Pietist origins and, 11
   as restoration, 38
   Sabbath and, 53
Eucharist, 69, 70, 73, 76, 80, 81
Eunice, Sister, 110–11
Evangelical Awakening, 11
evangelism, 18
Eve (biblical), 30, 39
   creation of, 99
   femaleness of men and, 55
   second fall and, 39, 52, 107
evil, 7, 38, 42, 58, 64–65, 104

Fahnestock, William, 94, 141, 157, 159
Fama fraternitatis, 184
fasting, 87–89, 94
Feuchter, Johann, 164
Fisher, Elizabeth, 185
flagellation, 93
Fogelman, Aaron, 16
folk art, 8
foot washing ritual, 57, 69, 70, 76, 241 n. 59
Fox, George, 31
Fraktur script, art of, 5, 119, 141, 142, 168–69. *See also* manuscript art
   definition of, 142
   metaphor and, 144, 144–46, 145
   in Peniel, 127, 128
Francke, Anna Magdalena von Wurm, 98–99
Francke, August Hermann, 11, 98
Frankenberg, Adam von, 167
Franklin, Benjamin, 25, 33
Freemasonry, 184, 189, 255 n. 65
free will, 39
French Prophets, 14, 98
Fresenius, Johann Philipp, 182

Freylinghausen, Johann Anastasius, 99
Friedmann, Robert, 28, 29
Funk, Jacob, 199
Funke, Anneliese M., 199
Furley, Benjamin, 31

Gaas, Jacob (Brother Lamech), 4, 197
Geheimnis der Göttlisches Sophia (Arnold), 100, 101
Geistliche Reden, 14
gender, 8, 24, 31, 36, 47, 113–14. *See also* sexuality
   Adam and, 38–39
   animals and, 53, 58
   architecture and, 117–18
   Christ's wound and, 58–59, 99
   soteriology and, 39–40
   third gender, 90
   virgin birth of Jesus and, 100
geocentric astronomy, 176
Georg, Johann, 13
George, Eugene, 129
Gerhardt, Paul, 166
German language, 4, 78
German Sectarians of Pennsylvania, The (Sachse), 197
Germantown, Penn., 17, 49
Germany, 8–16, 15, 26
Gesäng der Einsamen und Verlassenen Turtel-Taube, Das (hymnal), 161, 162
ghosts, 180–81
Gichtel, Johann Georg, 5, 26, 33, 75, 84, 98
   on Adam's fall, 100
   on alchemy, 177–78
   on astrology, 174
   on circumcision, 64
   on loss of self, 37
   magic and, 173
   on male willpower, 123
   as popularizer of Boehme, 13
   on Priesthood of Melchizedek, 57
   on sexual desire, 39
   on virginity, 34
Gideon, Brother (Christian Eckstein), 82, 108, 193
God
   creation of Eve, 39
   creation of gender, 102
   female aspect of, 33
   immediate presence of, 4, 5, 8, 36, 57, 157, 172

275

INDEX

God (cont'd)
  as incomprehensible Nothing, 6, 36, 52
  individual quest for, 62
  restoration of sinners and, 43
Godhead, 31, 99, 100, 102
Gold and Rose Cross fraternity, 125, 186, 187, 188, 190, 255 n. 65. *See also* Rosicrucianism
Good Shepherd, placard of the, 159–60
Göttliche Liebes- und Lobes-Gethöne (Beissel), 33
Gottrecht, Friedsam. *See* Beissel, Georg Conrad
grace, 30, 32, 39, 46–47, 63
  baptism and, 73, 74
  foot washing ritual and, 78
Great Britain, 11, 26
Gruber, Eberhard Ludwig, 27
Gruber, Johann Adam, 81
Gründlicher Unerricht von den Metallen (Barba), 116, 177, 203
Güldene Aepffel in Silbern Schalen, 29
Güldene Rose, Die (Schüz), 145, 146
Guyon, Madame, 61

Haller, Johann Adam, 12–13
hands, laying on of, 83–85
Hark, Max J., 4, 84, 86, 197–98
Heaney, Howell, 143, 157
Hebron. *See* Saron (Hebron) building
Heidelberg Catechism, 16
Heidt, Maria (Sister Bernice), 6, 111
Hellenthal (Höllenthal), Anton, 61, 65
Helmont, Francis van, 31
hermits, 16, 62, 116, 118, 138, 174
Herrnschmidt, Johann Daniel, 166
Hibshman, Jacob, 121
Hildebrand, Johannes, 26, 49–60, 66, 191, 201–2
  on androgynous creation, 57–59
  on church community, 60
  comet booklet of, 175–76
  love feasts and, 232 n. 2
  on sexuality, 110
Hochenau, Hochmann von, 12, 42, 71, 84
Höcker, Ludwig (Brother Obed), 204
Höhn, Christina, 93, 110
Holland, Isaac, 178
Hollyday, Guy Tilghman, 143, 146, 157, 159
holy kiss ritual, 70, 82–83
Holy Spirit, 71, 72, 149
homoeroticism, 83
Horch, Heinrich, 14, 26, 37, 63, 73, 146
householders (house estate), 4, 19, 21, 55–56, 57, 123

hymnals, 4, 34, 35, 205–7
  Fraktur manuscript art and, 161–64, 165, 166–68, 168
  mystical, 33

Ifigenia, Sister, 161
individualism, 35
Inspirationists, 14, 17
  love feast ritual and, 77, 81
  physical gyrations of, 27
  revelation and, 26
  views on marriage, 33

Jacob (biblical), 104, 123–24
Jacobs, Anna Eva, 98
Jacoby, John, 6, 37
Jael, Sister, 105, 248 n. 47
Jansenism, 11
Jephune, Brother. *See* Eckerlin, Samuel
Jesus Christ, 30, 37, 45. *See also* Christ, return of
  androgyny of, 66
  baptism of, 71, 73–74
  betrothal to women, 83, 93, 106, 108
  celibacy and, 104
  crucifixion of, 58, 74, 99–100, 100, 113, 129
  foot washing commandment of, 77
  gender division in the Godhead and, 102
  as high priest, 56–57
  magic/sorcery and, 172
  private fellowship with, 60
  public ministry of, 130
  spiritual offspring of, 84
  symbolism and, 148, 149, 152, 163, 167
  union with Sophia, 75
  as virginal man, 39–40, 103
  virgin birth of, 64, 65, 100, 105–6
  womb of, 58–59, 100
Jews, 30
Johann Conrad Beissel and the Ephrata Community (Erb), 199
Jojada, Brother (Rudolf Nägele), 19, 29, 115, 139
Jüchly, Benedict (Brother Benedict), 131
Junkerroth (nobleman), 14
Justin Martyr, 101

Kant, Immanuel, 172
Kaufmann, David, 30
Kedar building, 91, 117–18, 121, 122, 133
  Bäthaus of, 86
  Chronicon description of, 116–17

INDEX

Fraktur manuscript art in, 141, 153, 157
Keith, George, 31
Keller, Sebastian, 180
Kelpius, Johannes, 14, 15, 17, 31
  astrology and, 174–75
  community and, 41–42
  followers of, 18
  on Kedar building, 117
  Rosicrucianism and, 185–86
  on sleep restriction, 92
  on Sophia, 101
  on sunflower symbolism, 149
Kelp (Kölb) brothers, 65
Kenan, Brother, 116
Key of Solomon, The (magic handbook), 180
Keyser, Alan G., 116
Kimmel, Jacob, 53
Kirschner, Ann, 133
Klein, Walter, 34, 73, 84
Kling, Johann Valentin, 12–13
Knorr von Rosenroth, Christian, 14, 31, 175, 186, 188
Koch, Stephan (Brother Agabus), 62, 118, 122, 123, 181, 188
Kocher, Lawrence, 134
König, Simon, 16
Köster, Bernard, 31
Kurtzer Brief, Ein (I. Eckerlin), 52

Labadie, Jean de, 18
Lancaster County, Penn., 20
Landert, Sigmund (Brother Sealthiel), 118
Landis, Anna, 110
Lange, Ernst, 166
language, 5, 30–31, 36, 42
Last Supper, 77
Lavoisier, Antoine-Laurent, 190
Law, the, 39, 40, 65
Law of Circumcision, The (Bromley), 30
Leade, Jane, 13, 43
Leben und Wandel (Sangmeister), 61
Lenne Lenape (Delaware) tribe, 88
Lerner, Gerda, 105, 114
Lewis, Ralph M., 186
Locke, John, 172
Lord's Supper. *See* Eucharist
Louis XIV (king of France), 9
love feast ritual, 18, 57, 62, 76–82, 88
  foot washing in, 70
  in Kedar building, 116, 118

Lucifer (Satan), 38, 46, 52, 66, 99
  alchemy and, 179, 180
  devil's wedding, 173
  rebellion of, 102, 189
  women and, 108
Luther, Christian and Christina, 181
Luther, Martin, 7
Lutheranism, 11, 17, 146, 185
  Beissel's numerology and, 32
  Rosicrucianism and, 187, 188

Mack, Alexander, Jr. (Brother Timotheus), 76, 85–86
Mack, Alexander, Sr., 12, 14, 20, 43, 77
Mack, Johann Valentin, 50, 60
McGinn, Bernard, 4, 5, 6
McIntosh, Christopher, 185, 186, 188, 189
Magdalene, Mary, 108
magic, 171, 172–74, 190
Magnum Mysterium (Boehme), 53
Mallott, Floyd, 28
manuscript art, 141–46, 168–69, 213–15. *See also* Fraktur script, art of
  music books, 160–64, 161, 165, 166–68, 168
  mystical language and, 146
  symbol vocabulary of, 146–50, 147–48, 150–52, 153, 154–56
  wall placards, 153, 157–60, 158
Marcella, Sister (Saur, Maria Christina), 85, 111
marriage, 28, 33–34, 45–46, 56, 109–13
Martin, C. H., 121
Martin, Georg Adam, 23, 35, 85, 108, 193, 194
Martin, Jacob, 176–77, 181, 191
  as alchemist, 178–80
  Rosicrucianism and, 188–89
  writings of, 202–3
Martin, Willard, 185
Martyrer-Spiegel (Martyrs' Mirror) (van Braght), 29, 90, 116
Matthäi, Conrad, 16, 32
Melania, Sister, 65
Melchizedek, Priesthood of, 30, 42–43, 53, 56–57
  criticism of, 60
  laying on of hands and, 84
  New Jerusalem and, 159
  numerology and, 130
  Rosicrucianism and, 188
  virginal women in, 107
men, 4, 97
  Beissel's attitude toward, 109

INDEX

men *(cont'd)*
  male domination, 103, 108
  male dress, 89
  mystic impregnation and, 55
  virgin birth and, 100
Mennonites, 12, 17, 18, 28
  Anabaptist diversity and, 29
  architecture of, 118
  baptismal practices of, 71, 76
  foot washing ritual and, 77–78
  opposition to slavery, 53
  original sin doctrine and, 39
messianism, 42
Meyer, Barbara, 85
Meyle, Jan, 19
Mifflin, Charles, 78–79, 80
Miller, Peter (Brother Agrippa), 20, 25, 26, 191, 193–94
  in Almonry building, 116
  on baptism, 73, 75
  as Beissel's assistant, 85
  in Berghaus, 184
  on Christ's mediation, 102
  on decline of Ephrata community, 193
  as editor of Chronicon Ephratense, 4, 197
  English translations by, 37
  Ephrata rituals and, 69
  Hildebrand writings and, 51
  on love feast ritual, 80, 81
  on mystical language of Ephrata, 3
milling centers, 20–21
ministry (authority), 38, 41, 43, 57
Mistisches und Kirchliches Zeuchnüß (Beissel), 25, 50–51, 52, 53, 54–57, 59
  foot washing ritual in, 78
  on marriage, 33
  rituals named in, 69
Molinos, Miguel, 61
Momfort, Stephen, 31, 32
monastic dress, 89–90, 91
Moravians, 17, 26, 50, 51–52
  Rosicrucianism and, 182, 183–84
  view of marriage, 49, 57, 110
Mormons, 76, 190
Morse, Jedidiah, 121
Mother Maria's book, 161, 162, 164, 165, 166, 168
Mount Zion, 116, 118, 120, 121, 135
Müller, Maria Catherine, 84, 108
Müller, Michael, 84, 108, 164, 204
Murphy, Peter, 112

mysticism, 5–6, 37
  apophatic, 37
  architecture and, 117
  biblical books and, 26–27
  mystic death, 40–41, 46, 57, 74, 94, 187
Mysticism in the German Devotional Literature of Colonial Pennsylvania (Stoeffler), 6
Mystische Theologie (Sangmeister), 5, 61, 62–65
Mystische und Profetische Bibel (Horch), 26, 146
Mystische und sehr geheyme Sprueche (Beissel), 33, 55
Mystyrion Anomias (Beissel), 31, 33, 53, 55, 63
  chiliasm and, 32
  numerology in, 14
  Sophia (divine female) in, 102

nadere reformatie, 10–11, 32
Nägele, Rudolf (Brother Jojada), 19, 29, 115, 139
Neander, Joachim, 163, 167
Nethenus, Samuel, 35
Netherlands, 11
Neu-geboren (the Newborn), 12
Neu-Täufer, 12, 14–15. *See also* Dunkers
  baptism among, 70–71
  confession of faith, 25
  emigration to America, 16
  fellowship of, 18
  ritual practice of, 28
New Born of Oley, 17
New Jerusalem, 133, 158, 158–59, 160, 169
New-Mooners, 17
New Testament, 71, 77, 84, 133, 138, 160
Newton, Isaac, 190
Newtown congregation, 31
New York colony, 17
Nied, Rudolf, 178
Nine Years' War (War of the Grand Alliance), 9
Noble, Able, 31
numerology, 13–14, 171
  architecture and, 124, 126–27, 130, 133, 134–35
  chiliasm and, 32

O'Bannon, Patrick W., 127, 129, 130, 134
Ohnenheim Attestation, 78
Old German Baptist Brethren, 83
Old Testament, 31, 56, 93, 138
Oneida community, 6
Onesimus, Brother. *See* Eckerlin, Israel (Brother Onesimus)

INDEX

Opus Mago-Cabbalisticum et Theosophicum (Welling), 125, 125, 178, 189
Order of Spiritual Virgins, 19
original sin, doctrine of, 39

pacifism, 53
Palatinate (region in Germany), 8, 9, 29, 87
    Beissel's flight from, 14, 44, 221–22 n. 36
    emigration from, 16
    Pietism in, 12, 13
    werewolves in, 173
Paradisisches Wunder-Spiel, 153, 161, 162
Pastoir, Mrs., 13
Peniel meetinghouse, 56, 120, 123–30, 124, 126, 128
Penn, William, 23, 194
Pennepek congregation, 31
Pennsylvania, colonial, 6, 121
    Fraktur manuscript art in, 142
    German immigration into, 12, 16, 17, 61
    German printing in, 21
    tolerance in, 33
    women's autonomy in, 111
perfection, 12, 135
Permersdorffs (dissenting couple), 19
Petersen, Eleanora von Merlau, 13, 32, 43, 98
Petersen, Johann Wilhelm, 13, 32, 43, 98
Philadelphian Society, 13, 18, 26, 35, 46
    apocalypticism of, 32
    Boehmist thought and, 29
    holy kiss ritual and, 83
    restoration doctrine and, 43
    Rosicrucianism and, 186
    Sophia (divine female) concept and, 100–101
Philemon, Brother (Johann Rissmann), 62, 88, 202
Philip, Prince Elector Carl, 16
Pietism, 10, 28–29, 77. *See also* Radical Pietism; Reformed Pietism
pilgrimage, 17
Poiret, Pierre, 62
Pordage, John, 13, 100
prayer, 91–92
predestination, doctrine of, 39
printing presses, 21, 29, 35
Profetische und Mistische Bibel (Horch), 63
prophecy/prophets, 26, 45, 46, 84, 98
Protestantism, 4, 7, 16. *See also* Christianity; Radical Pietism
    bridal imagery and, 37

Fraktur manuscript art and, 157
justification (non imputata) in, 40, 66
Pietism and, 10
sacraments of, 69

Quakers, 17, 31, 53, 89, 111
Quietism, 11, 61, 62

Radical Pietism, 4, 10–14, 195. *See also* Christianity; Reformed Pietism
    Anabaptism and, 28–29
    astrology and, 174–75
    baptism in, 70, 71, 75
    egalitarianism in, 85
    eschatology of, 27
    Fraktur manuscript art and, 146, 148, 149, 153, 160
    holy kiss ritual and, 82–83
    individualism of, 35
    ingredients of, 171–72
    invisible church and, 60
    numerology and, 14
    Quietist influences in, 62
    Rosicrucianism and, 182, 186, 188, 190
    Sabbatarianism and, 31
    Sophia (divine female) concept and, 98–99
    spiritual love and, 18
    "true Church" and, 41
    women in, 107
rebirth, spiritual, 40–41, 46–47, 50, 55, 101
    androgyny and, 64
    baptism and, 72
    cabbalism and, 180
    Christ's wound and, 59
    divine womb of Christ and, 100
    esoteric knowledge and, 191
    magic and, 173
    manuscript art symbolism and, 148
    mystic impregnation and, 57, 109
    reborn soul, 60
    Sophia (divine wisdom) and, 66, 103
Rechte und Ordnungen (Mack), 43
redemption, 36, 46, 66
Reformation, 11, 77, 98
Reformed churches, 16, 17, 32
Reformed Pietism, 28, 32, 73, 75, 77. *See also* Radical Pietism
Regnier, Johann Franz, 87, 112, 131, 182–84
Reichmann, Felix, 61
"religion of the heart," 11

INDEX

Remonstrants, 71
repentance, 11, 57, 59, 71–72, 81, 177
restoration, 38, 43, 64, 98
resurrection, 54
revelation, 26
Revelation (biblical book), 32, 41, 138, 157, 159, 189
Richter, Samuel (Sigmund), 125, 186–87, 190
righteousness (justification), 40
Rights and Ordinances (A. Mack, Sr.), 72, 77
Rissmann (Reissmann), Johann (Brother Philemon), 62, 88, 202
Ritschl, Albrecht, 77
Rittenhouse, David, 177
Roman Catholicism, 7, 11, 16, 26, 90. *See also* Christianity
   Beissel's numerology and, 32
   laying on of hands and, 84
   monasticism of, 77, 86, 93
   sacraments of, 69
"Rose, Die," 87, 89, 90, 105, 106
Rosenbach, Johann Georg, 12
Rosenkreutz, Christian, 46, 184
Roses of Saron, 21, 105, 133, 187
Rosicrucianism, 13, 46, 87, 117, 146, 181–90. *See also* Gold and Rose Cross fraternity
Rubin, Miri, 70
Ruffende Wächterstimme, Eine (Hildebrand), 50
Rutter, Thomas, 31
Ruusbroec, Jan, 149

Saalhof circle, 11, 13, 98
Sabbatarianism, 4, 20, 31. *See also* Ephrata community
   attitude toward Scriptures, 27
   baptismal practices of, 62, 70, 73, 76
   distribution in American colonies, 22
Sabbath, seventh-day, 19, 31, 32–33, 46, 52–53
Sachse, Julius, 13, 14, 30, 31, 34, 134
   on alchemy, 178
   on architecture, 119
   ology and, 175
   'igraphy, 142
   cabins, 116
   Ephrata, 92
   m, 181, 182, 183, 184
   hood, 50–51

Sangmeister, Henry (Brother Ezechiel), 3, 19, 21, 42, 93, 194
   on architecture, 118, 121
   autobiography of, 23, 26, 61, 180, 198
   on Beissel's alleged magic, 174
   career of, 62
   on celibacy, 109–10
   death of, 194
   esoteric knowledge and, 191
   on ghosts, 180–81
   on Gichtel, 26
   on Hildebrand, 49–50
   life of, 65–66
   love feast ritual and, 81
   on monastic dress, 89
   return from Virginia, 135
   tonsure and, 85–86
   writings of, 62–65, 202
Sarah (biblical), 130
Saron (Hebron) building, 124, 130–31, 131, 132, 133, 157
Saur, Christoph (Christopher), 21, 42
Saur, Christoph (Christopher), Sr., 92, 111, 118
Saur, Maria Christina (Sister Marcella), 85, 111
Schatz, Jacob, 13, 14
Schott, Gaspar, 176
Schrifftmässiges Zeuchnüß (Hildebrand), 50, 54, 57–60
Schuchart, Anna Maria, 98
Schule, Hans, 181
Schütz, Christoph, 43, 125, 129, 190
Schütz, Johann Jakob, 11, 28–29
Schwarzenau Brethren, 70, 76, 83
Schwenkfelders, 17, 72
Sealthiel, Brother (Sigmund Landert), 118
sectarianism, 5, 6–7, 17, 54
Seelig, Johann Gottfried, 175
Seidensticker, Oswald, 31, 121, 133, 181, 208
self-denial, 59, 73, 87, 175
   alchemy and, 177
   gender division and, 194
   immediate presence of God and, 36–37
Sendivogius, Michael, 178
Sensenig, Jacob, 178
sevens, system of, 31, 35
Seventh-Day Baptists, 31, 116, 121, 194, 195
Seven Years' War, 21
sexuality, 23, 28. *See also* gender
   Adam's paradisal body and, 87
   alchemy and, 188

INDEX

baptism contrasted with, 75
  Beissel's attitude toward, 109–13
  at Ephrata, 61, 112
  fall of first couple and, 58
  holy kiss ritual and, 83
  loathing of sexual intercourse, 33
  Pietistic attitudes toward, 110
  self-denial and, 37
  sin and, 39, 46
Sharon church, 121
Shelley, Donald, 142, 143, 146
Silesius, Angelus, 163, 166
Simons, Menno, 78, 146
sin, 28, 36, 38, 39, 46
  baptism and, 74, 94
  foot washing ritual and, 78
  forgiveness of, 56
slavery/slaves, 17, 53
sleep, restriction of, 92, 94
Smith, Joseph, 76, 190
Snow Hill. *See* Antietam/Snow Hill congregation
social classes, 10
sociology, 6–7
solitary estate, 55–56
Song of Solomon, 27, 146, 147, 153, 163, 167
Sophia (divine female), 33, 34, 35, 44, 47
  Adam's loss of, 92
  "adultery" with, 38, 39, 52
  architecture and, 129
  baptism and, 75
  betrothal to men, 83, 93, 101
  Christ's wound and, 54–55
  at Ephrata, 102–7
  in Godhead, 246 n. 16
  Jesus as "husband" of, 40, 42, 46, 58, 100, 106
  Radical Pietism and, 98–99
  soul's marriage to, 37
  spiritual offspring of, 84
  as virgin, 99–101
soteriology, 38, 39–40, 54, 99
South Carolina colony, 21, 22
Spangenberg, August Gottlieb, 26, 27
Spener, Philipp Jakob, 10, 11, 84, 98
Spiritual Guide (Guyon & Molinos), 61
Spohn, Clarence, 65, 203
Stanley, Julia, 107
Stevens, Lauren, 129
Stieffel, Georg, 14, 16, 18
Stoeffler, F. Ernest, 6, 37, 41
Stoffer, Dale, 28

Stoudt, John Joseph, 142–43, 182
Stuntz, Jacob, 16, 18
Succoth house, 116, 135
suffering, 42, 55, 65
Sweden, 11
Switzerland, 16, 29, 182

Tambiah, Stanley, 172
Tauler, Johannes, 35, 52, 64
theodicy, 38, 59
Theo-Philosophia Theoretico-Practica (Richter), 187
Theosophischen Lectionen, 157
theosophy, 31, 101, 117, 171
Thirty Years' War, 8
Thoma, Margareta, 57
Thomas, Keith, 172
Thomen (Thoma), Anna (Sister Tabea, Sister Anastasia), 122, 161, 187
Timotheus, Brother (Alexander Mack, Jr.), 76, 85–86
toleration, 23–24, 71
tonsure, 70, 85–86, 93
Trinity, 41, 72, 101, 110, 134, 135
Troeltsch, Ernst, 6, 7
Turner, Victor, 82
turtledoves, symbolism of, 4
Two Mystic Communities in America (Jacoby), 6

Undereyck, Theodor, 11, 35, 73
Unparteyische Kirchen- und Ketzer-Historie (Arnold), 29
Unpartheyisches Bedencken (Hildebrand), 51–52

Valentine, Basil, 178
Valentinianism, 101
vegetarianism, 53, 63–64, 80
Virginia colony, 61, 62, 135
virginity, 58–59, 99–101, 129
Virgin Mary, 100, 166
Vorspiel der Neuen Welt (Beissel), 34

Wahre Abbildung der Ersten Christen (Arnold), 27
Wahrhafte und volkommene Bereitung, Die (Richter), 186
Waite, A. E., 185
Wallmann, Johannes, 11, 28
Ward, Reginald, 16
Warfel, Stephen, 117, 118, 120–21
War of the Spanish Succession, 9

INDEX

Way to the Sabbath of Rest, The (Bromley), 32, 63
Weeks, Andrew, 174, 177
Weg zu Christo, Der (Boehme), 38
Weidner, Georg Adam, 30
Weiser, Conrad, 20, 112
Weiser, Frederick, 143, 157
Weiss, Jacob, 111
Welling, Georg von, 124–27, 133, 135, 178, 189
Wesley, John and Charles, 11
Wetzel, Catharina Elisabeth, 83
Whitefield, George, 11
Wiegner, Christoph, 72
Willoughby, William, 28
Wilson, Bryan, 7
Wohlfahrt, Michael, 18, 20, 25, 81
   hymns by, 163, 164
   laying on of hands and, 84
Wohlgegründetes Bedencken (Hildebrand), 50, 54
women, 4, 97–98
   Beissel's attitude toward, 107–8
   Church compared to woman, 54
   love feast ritual and, 82
   as prophets, 98
   Rosicrucianism and, 187
   subordination of, 98, 99, 103, 113
Wust, Klaus, 61

Zeissiger, Georg, 116, 177, 204
Zimmerman, Johann Jacob, 14, 174–75, 185, 186
Zinzendorf, Count Nicholas Ludwig von, 21, 35, 52, 110
Zionitic Brotherhood, 19, 50–51, 118
   cabbalism and, 175
   laying on of hands and, 84
   purchase of mill, 131
   Rosicrucianism and, 181, 184
Zionitischen Stiffts, I Theil (Beissel), 36
Zionitischer WeyrauchsHügel (hymnal), 35, 142, 161, 162, 167
Zion meetinghouse, 118–21, 133
Zoar (Reamstown, Penn.), 20, 20